D1712901

# Bloom's Modern Critical Views

*Bloom's Modern Critical Views*

# WILLIAM SHAKESPEARE:
## COMEDIES
### *New Edition*

*Edited and with an introduction by*
## Harold Bloom
Sterling Professor of the Humanities
Yale University

BLOOM'S
LITERARY CRITICISM
*An imprint of Infobase Publishing*

Bloom's Modern Critical Views:
William Shakespeare: Comedies—New Edition

Copyright © 2009 by Infobase Publishing
Introduction © 2009 by Harold Bloom

Bloom's Literary Criticism
An imprint of Infobase Publishing
132 West 31st Street
New York NY 10001

**Library of Congress Cataloging-in-Publication Data**
William Shakespeare: Comedies / edited and with an introduction by Harold Bloom.
—New ed.
    p. cm.—(Bloom's modern critical views)
Includes bibliographical references and index.
ISBN 978-1-60413-631-9 (acid-free paper)
1. Shakespeare, William, 1564–1616—Comedies. I. Bloom, Harold.

PR2981.W494 2009
822.3'3—dc22                    2009018266

Bloom's Literary Criticism books are available at special discounts when purchased in bulk quantities for businesses, associations, institutions, or sales promotions. Please call our Special Sales Department in New York at (212) 967-8800 or (800) 322-8755.

You can find Bloom's Literary Criticism on the World Wide Web at
http://www.chelseahouse.com.

Cover design by Takeshi Takahashi

Printed in the United States of America
MP BCL 10  9  8  7  6  5  4  3  2  1

This book is printed on acid-free paper.

All links and Web addresses were checked and verified to be correct at the time of publication. Because of the dynamic nature of the Web, some addresses and links may have changed since publication and may no longer be valid.

# Contents

# *Editor's Note*

My introduction surveys Shakespeare's comedy, finding it his natural mode while indicating also its superb range, from knockabout farce to visionary romance.

Lisa Marciano studies the dark comedy of *Twelfth Night,* where Viola and Feste serve as the most charming of moral teachers.

*As You Like It,* most original and refreshing of pastorals, finds enlightened defense of its genre from Linda Woodbridge, while cuckoldry, Shakespeare's knowingly obsessive jest, is illuminated in *The Merchant of Venice* and *As You Like It* by Emily Detmer-Goebel.

The servant-master relationship in *The Two Gentlemen of Verona* is studied by Elizabeth Rivlin, after which Roy Eriksen examines originating process in *The Taming of the Shrew.*

Castiglione's influence in *Much Ado About Nothing* is set forth by Philip D. Collington, while Kent Cartwright chronicles magical aspects of *The Comedy of Errors.*

*The Merry Wives of Windsor,* a dreadful travesty of the sublime Falstaff, receives more than it deserves from Michael Steppat.

Cynthia Lewis catches the precise tonalities of mortal accountings in the magnificent *Love's Labor's Lost,* after which Aaron Kitch somberly addresses himself to the paradox of Shylock, whose legal case founds itself upon the mercantile rationale for Venice's potency.

In this volume's final essay, Hugh Grady labors to restore an aesthetic dimension to current criticism of Shakespeare. Admirably informed as Grady is, I am moved to appeal to the common reader and the common playgoer. Except for "socially guilty" academics, does the aesthetic, pure or impure, truly need to be returned to *A Midsummer Night's Dream?*

HAROLD BLOOM

*Introduction*

I

The greatness of Shakespeare's high comedies—*A Midsummer Night's Dream, As You Like It, The Merchant of Venice,* and *Twelfth Night, or What You Will*—fully matches the magnificence of his four High Tragedies: *Hamlet, Othello, King Lear,* and *Macbeth*. Shakespeare's natural gift was for comedy; he is already fully himself in the early farces, *The Comedy of Errors* and *The Taming of the Shrew*. The shadow of Christopher Marlowe darkens *Titus Andronicus* and *Richard III,* but Marlowe had no interest and little talent for comedy. *The Tempest* is still essentially comedy, little as we tend to apprehend this.

II

*A Midsummer Night's Dream* is unique in Shakespeare, because it is the most visionary of his dramas, beyond even *The Tempest* as a transcendental enterprise. Ariel and the spirits are of another order of representation than are Puck, Titania, Oberon and Bottom's good friends: Cobweb, Mustardseed, Peaseblossom, and Moth, all elves of the greatest charm and amiability, worthy of the sublime Bottom himself. Of Bottom, no praise can be excessive. Ancestor of Joyce's Poldy Bloom, Bottom radiates good will and good sense; he is sound at the core, and is the skein upon which the play's elaborate designs is wound. One of Shakespeare's great originals, Bottom is not always well served by modern criticism, which tends to underestimate his innate dignity. Natural man, so much maligned by moralists, whether Christian or Marxist, achieves an apotheosis in Bottom.

1

And yet there is much more to Bottom than even that grand dignity. He alone, of the play's humans, is open to the realm of the fairies, and he alone enjoys the bottomless dream that in some sense is the ethos of Shakespeare's visionary play. Weavers are in touch with uncanny forces, and Bottom is the prince of weavers. He holds God's secrets, even if he is unaware of them. There is a link between Bottom's sweet good nature and the high, good spirits of Shakespeare's true genius Sir John Falstaff.

### III

If Falstaff (and Hamlet) have a rival for audacious intelligence, and slyly agile wit in all Shakespeare, then she must be the superb Rosalind, heroine of *As You Like It,* the most joyous of the comedies. The Forest of Arden may not be an earthly paradise, but in Shakespeare it is the best place to be, and Rosalind is the best person to be with in all of literature. William Hazlitt wonderfully said of Rosalind: "She talks herself out of breath, only to get deeper in love." I myself tend to emphasize her originality, in which she fully rivals Falstaff and Hamlet. In one crucial way, she transcends even them. As the audience, we can achieve perspectives upon Falstaff and Hamlet that are not available to them, but we enjoy no such privilege in regard to Rosalind. Dramatic irony can and does victimize Falstaff and Hamlet, but never Rosalind. She sees herself and her play all around, as it were; she arranges her own surprises. You cannot close the doors upon Rosalind's wit; it will out at the casement. Neither passive nor aggressive, Rosalind's wit is the subtlest I have encountered in literature.

### IV

*The Merchant of Venice,* insofar as it is Portia's play, is high comedy, but history has made it Shylock's play also, which has rendered this great work highly problematic. Shylock's play can be done as farce, as tragicomedy, or as something for which we lack a name. One doesn't have to be Jewish to be horrified by forced conversion, on threat of death, to Christianity, but of course there is a particular shudder involved for Jewish playgoers and readers, like myself. What are we to do with *The Merchant of Venice*? Portia, though she squanders herself, is almost of Rosalind's splendor. Shylock's energy of being, the heroism of his malevolent will, and most of all his shattering eloquence: these combine to render him as memorable as he is frightening, a permanent slander against the Jewish people and its traditions of trusting to Yahwistic righteousness. I yield to no one in Bardolatry, but still must affirm that the role of Shylock has done grievous harm.

Yet *The Merchant of Venice* remains a masterwork of Shakespearean comedy, even if we do not laugh with it as Shakespeare's own audiences did. The ravishing Act V, set in Portia's Belmont, is a lyrical triumph, juxtaposing fulfilled Romantic love with ironic overtones of love's betrayal. Shylock's absence in the final act is both a tribute to the sophisticated power of Portia's world, and a critique of its limitations.

## V

Of Shakespeare's early farces, *The Taming of the Shrew* maintains a perpetual popularity. The loving struggle for supremacy between Kate and Petruchio is an epitome of a crucial element in nearly every marriage, and the war between men and women is of universal relevance. It is too easy to get this play quite wrong; there are feminist visions of the "brutal" Petruchio pursuing Kate with a whip! In mere fact, she slaps him, and he confines his assaults to language. What Shakespeare actually gives us is the subtle self-education of Kate, who achieves dominion over the swaggering Petruchio through a parody of submission. What is profoundly moving is the representation of two ferocious beings who fall in love at first sight (though Kate conceals it) and who eventually make a strong alliance against the rest of the world. Beneath the surface of this knockabout farce, Shakespeare pursues one of his most illuminating contentions: the natural superiority of women over men.

## VI

*Twelfth Night* is Shakespeare's farewell to high comedy, and may be his greatest achievement in that mode. Whose play is it; does it center upon Viola, Olivia, Malvolio, or Feste? That is rather like asking whether *King Lear* centers upon Edmund, the Fool, Edgar, or Lear himself? A beautifully complex comedy, *Twelfth Night* refuses the perspective that would make it poor, victimized Malvolio's tragicomedy. Like Shylock, Malvolio is one of Shakespeare's displaced spirits; he is not at home in the comic world of the play. And yet the play *needs* Malvolio; his undeserved downfall is essential to Shakespeare's vision. There is no poetic justice (or Christian consolation) in Shakespeare: the whirligig of time accomplishes its revenges. A delight and a madness, *Twelfth Night*'s only sane character is the remarkable Feste, the most admirable of Shakespeare's clowns. Viola is benign and lovable, yet she is as much a zany as Orsino, whom she will marry or Olivia, who rarely gets anything straight. *Twelfth Night*, a sublime Feast of Fools, is as crowning an achievement as are *King Lear* and *The Tempest,* all summits of their mode.

LISA MARCIANO

# The Serious Comedy of Twelfth Night:
## Dark Didacticism in Illyria

In "Or What You Will," Barbara Everett notes that Shakespeare's *Twelfth Night* "poses in a nicely acute form a problem inherent in all the earlier comedies: why do we take them seriously? Or how, rather, best to explain the ways in which it is hard not to take them seriously—the sense that at their best they achieve a lightness as far as possible from triviality" (294). Everett has discovered a question that surely concerns any scholar of Shakespearean drama, for the bard's comedies are undoubtedly serious. But what, precisely, accounts for the dark dimension that pervades so many of the plays? My response is this: close scrutiny of the dramas indicates that, beginning as early as *Love's Labour's Lost* and continuing on into the romances, Shakespeare's comic characters repeatedly come face to face with mortality, learn that one must, therefore, live well, and teach others wisdom accordingly. Oddly enough, then, having a brush with death and urging others to live wisely are staples of Shakespeare's comedies. *Twelfth Night* is a good test case, for this drama, perhaps more than any other, abounds with jests and merriment, yet it also brims over with situations in which characters who are aware of mortality try to bring others to reform by means of this knowledge. Examining Shakespearean drama through the lens of *Twelfth Night*, then, we can respond to Everett's question as follows: a dark didacticism, an urgent sense that life must be lived well because it is short, often underlies

*Renascence: Essays on Values in Literature*, Volume 56, Number 1 (Fall 2003): pp. 3–19.

Shakespeare's plays, and this principle, at least in part, accounts for the seriousness with which we regard Shakespeare's comedies.

As a brief survey of the canon indicates, several plays have distinct moments in which characters become wiser after encountering death. For instance, in *Love's Labour's Lost,* Marcade's abrupt announcement that the King of France has died impels the Princess to diagnose the defects plaguing the court of Navarre; Shakespeare declines to make clear, however, whether the young gentlemen will indeed change their ways. In *Much Ado about Nothing* and *All's Well that Ends Well,* either the wronged lovers or their advisers circulate false news of the women's deaths to provoke Claudio and Bertram to repentance. In *Cymbeline* and *The Winter's Tale,* Posthumus and Leontes instantly feel the weight of their guilt upon hearing of the "death" of their wives. And in *The Tempest* Prospero deliberately makes the shipwrecked parties on his island think that he is dead or that others have perished, all to make the castaways repent and reform.[1]

Yet few critics systematically examine how the awareness of death is a didactic tool in Shakespearean comedy, and in *Twelfth Night* in particular. One critic who does speak of didacticism in his work is John Hollander, author of "*Twelfth Night* and the Morality of Indulgence." In this essay Hollander asserts that there is a "moral process" at work in this play: characters indulge themselves to their hearts' content, eventually purging themselves of at least some undesirable elements (221–222). In Hollander's own words,

> The Action of *Twelfth Night* is indeed that of a Revels, a suspension of mundane affairs during a brief epoch in a temporary world of indulgence, a land full of food, drink, love, play, disguise and music. But parties end, and the reveler eventually becomes satiated and drops heavily into his worldly self again. . . . The essential action of a revels is: To so surfeit the Appetite upon excess that it "may sicken and so die". It is the Appetite, not the whole Self, however, which is surfeited: the Self will emerge at the conclusion of the action from where it has been hidden. The movement of the play is toward this emergence of humanity from behind a mask of comic type. (222)

There is, of course, merit to Hollander's argument, for the characters in this drama do indulge themselves and do show signs of reform before the final curtain. But Hollander's analysis seems to discount somewhat the actions of Viola and Feste in achieving these reforms. R. Chris Hassel, Jr., author of *Faith and Folly in Shakespeare's Romantic Comedies,* also examines the didacticism of *Twelfth Night,* stressing many of the passages I do. However, he posits that the means of instruction in Illyria is humiliation (rather than the practice of reminding characters about death's presence). He writes, "The attempt to edify the prideful characters of Illyria without losing their good will is a central challenge of the comedy . . . " (150). He does not place any emphasis on the awareness of death as an instructional tool in Illyria.

With regard to such an awareness, Theodore Spencer lays some of the groundwork for an assessment along these lines in his 1936 study *Death and Elizabethan Tragedy*. He states that "more than any other period in history, the late Middle Ages were preoccupied with the thought of death," adding that "in more ways than one, consciously and unconsciously, it [this period and its emphasis on mortality] influenced Elizabethan thought, and without it the Elizabethan mind, and its product Elizabethan literature, would have been a very different thing from what it was" (3–4). Spencer goes on to discuss how this emphasis on mortality pervades numerous literary works, including a handful of Shakespeare's comedies (most notably *Measure for Measure* and *Much Ado about Nothing*). As his title implies, however, he does not restrict his comments to Shakespeare or devote much time to works outside of the tragedies. Among more recent scholars, Marjorie Garber has done some interesting work in this area. In her article "'Remember Me': Memento Mori Figures in Shakespeare's Plays," Garber remarks, "In the dramatic architecture of Shakespeare's plays . . . the literal appearance of a memento mori, a physical figure or image of death, often intrudes itself upon the developing dramatic action, and alters the understanding of the onstage spectator—and his offstage counterpart as well" (3–4). She then briefly assesses how these memento mori figures affect a number of dramas, including *Twelfth Night*. Her analysis of this play, however, focuses primarily upon Olivia's mourning and marriage, Malvolio's captivity, and Feste's songs. Her treatment of the drama thus differs from mine in two respects. First, it is somewhat selective, ignoring numerous passages where characters consciously remind others of the presence of death. Second, her article does not emphasize that these memento mori figures almost always provoke repentance and reform in Shakespeare's comic communities.

To be sure, Anne Barton's introductions in the Riverside edition come closest to undertaking the systematic study called for in this paper. She does, for instance, acknowledge the dark undercurrents that run throughout many of the dramas in her introduction to *Much Ado about Nothing*. There she states that "virtually all of Shakespeare's comedies involve some kind of confrontation with death before the characters are allowed to win through to the happiness of the final scene" (330). And her introduction to *Twelfth Night* perceptively examines the excessiveness of Olivia's mourning, notes the bitterness of Viola's statement that women, like flowers, "die, even when they to perfection grow," and observes that references to death escalate as the play continues (406). But, although better than most, even Barton's remarks do not go far enough in bringing up the didacticism that is a key dimension of

*Twelfth Night.* This play clearly demonstrates how the awareness of death provokes wisdom in Shakespearean comedy, and it merits further consideration along these lines.

Undoubtedly death's powerful presence in this and other plays should be acknowledged more widely by the criticism. In *"Twelfth Night:* The Limits of Festivity," critic Thad Jenkins Logan notes that "there are thirty seven [references] to destruction and death" in this drama (236). A key moment, for example, occurs in the second scene when Viola washes ashore, thinking her twin brother has drowned:

Viola:    What country, friends, is this?

Captain:  This is Illyria, lady.

Viola:    And what should I do in Illyria?

          My brother he is in Elysium.

          Perchance he is not drown'd—what think you, sailors? (1.2.1–5)[2]

Again in this pivotal scene, Viola hears the dark genealogy of Countess Olivia,

> a virtuous maid, the daughter of a count
> That died some twelvemonth since, then leaving her
> In the protection of his son, her brother,
> Who shortly also died, for whose dear love,
> They say, she hath abjur'd the [company]
> And [sight] of men. (1.2.36–41)

The inevitability of death and the passage of time are almost always the subjects of the music in this drama. Threats of death multiply as the play progresses, as Barton has pointed out: Sir Andrew and Cesario nearly duel; Sebastian gives Sir Andrew a bloody head; and Antonio notes that, if he is caught in Illyria, he shall "pay dear" for warring against Orsino's nephew, who lost a leg in the battle (406). And, oddly enough, characters often identify places, people and events by their relationships to the dead. Antonio, thinking that Sebastian has abandoned him in his hour of need, exclaims, "This youth that you see here / I snatch'd one half out of the jaws of death" (3.4.359–360). The priest, confirming that Olivia and Sebastian have married, pinpoints the time of the nuptials by saying, "Since [the marriage], . . . my watch hath told me, toward my grave / I have travell'd but two hours" (5.1.162–163). Even in the recognition scene between the twins, Sebastian calls his sister "drowned Viola" (5.1.241). Our last glimpse of Illyria is that of the solitary Feste narrating the stages of a man's life. He makes us aware of mortality by singing of childhood, early youth, mature adulthood, and old age, ending the song there; we know death is the final stage in the progression. Mortality is, then, always in the background of *Twelfth Night*—yet it fails to move the Illyrians to wisdom until Viola and Feste call attention to its presence.

Olivia is the first character who will reform after being schooled by Viola and Feste. Though the reality of death is especially vivid for the Countess, instead of prompting her to get on with the business of life—marrying and raising children, who are, after all, one means of prolonging life and preserving a family's name—the death of her brother moves her to withdraw from life. As Valentine explains, she plans to mourn for seven years:

> [L]ike a cloistress she will veiled walk,
> And water once a day her chamber round
> With eye-offending brine; all this to season
> A brother's dead love, which she would keep fresh
> And lasting in her sad remembrance. (1.1.27–31)

This passage reveals the excessiveness of the endeavor. Though the servant may mean that the saltiness of Olivia's tears will sting her eyes, he also implies that Olivia weeps so such over the loss that her tears "offend" the very eyes that produced them. Anne Barton notes that "the underlying image here is homely, even a little grotesque. Like a housewife who carefully turns a piece of pickled meat once a day in its brine bath, Olivia intends through salt tears to preserve the memory of her dead brother beyond the normal span of grief. There is something forced and abnormal about such mourning . . ." (405). The attempt to keep the memory fresh, too, rather than grieving and then moving on, as is the normal course of things, indicates a strange effort to protract her sorrow. Fred Turner notes, "Death should be mourned, as ritual demands, and having been mourned, it should be forgotten; certainly it should not be allowed to interfere with the living of one's life in the present. Olivia is living in the past . . ." (59). Even the time span she has chosen to mourn—seven years—is excessive, as no one can keep a memory fresh for such an extended period. Again Barton observes, "Olivia is engaged in a war against Time and human forgetfulness. In her case, the struggle takes the form . . . of resistance to that natural psychological process by which, gradually, we cease to grieve for the dead. . . . Seven years is a long time, and youth is very short" (405). Olivia's mourning means she will not go forward with her life: she will neither marry nor reproduce, and she will partake of none of the functions in which a woman of marriageable age usually engages, none of the functions that give humankind consolation in times of sorrow.

Into this situation comes Viola, who teaches Olivia that the inevitability of death obliges one to live wisely. After pointedly observing that Olivia is wrong to withhold herself from marriage, Viola then requests to see the Countess's face, employing language that will remind Olivia of the certainty of death:

Olivia: Have you any commission from your lord to negotiate with my face?

    You are now out of your text; but we will draw the curtain, and show you the picture.

    Look you, sir, such a one I was this present. [Unveiling.]

    Is't not well done?

Viola: Excellently done, if God did all.

Olivia: 'Tis in grain, sir, 'twill endure wind and weather.

Viola: 'Tis beauty truly blent, whose red and white

    Nature's own sweet and cunning hand laid on.

    Lady, you are the cruell'st she alive

    If you will lead these graces to the grave

    And leave the world no copy. (1.5.231–243)

Interestingly, when Viola makes this impassioned plea to Olivia, the Countess purposely interprets "copy" not as progeny, Viola's intended meaning, but as an itemized list. But providing an inventory of one's features as Olivia does—"item, two lips, indifferent red; item, two grey eyes, with lids to them" (1.5.247–248)—is far different from bearing a child who will resemble her and live on after her. Olivia deliberately misinterprets, as Ronald R. Macdonald notes, because she does not want to hear the message Viola is trying to tell her (110).

If the Countess responds incorrectly to death, as many in her household note, then Viola responds rightly to it, appreciating life more intensely because of its very brevity. It is significant, therefore, that Shakespeare tells the story of Olivia twice in Act 1, folding the story around Viola's arrival in Illyria like a pair of bookends. The two women are foils for each other, as Olivia's life of mourning is a very real alternative for Viola, but one that Viola refuses to accept. Though the two share much in common (similar names and the loss of a brother and father), Viola refuses to luxuriate in her sorrow and waste the remainder of her life; she recognizes that the inevitability of death means one should make the most of life, not halt one's life in protracted grief. As a result, she exhibits an acute awareness of the passage of time throughout the drama. Upon first arriving in Illyria, she says, "What else may hap, to time I will commit" (1.2.60). And later on, as she accidentally causes Olivia to fall in love with her, Viola again says, "O time, thou must untangle this, not I, / It is too hard a knot for me t' untie" (2.2.40–41). Viola thus allows her recognition of the inevitability of death to move her to action, for she serves as a kind of teacher who schools her pupils to use time wisely and to live well.

A second character who needs Viola's wisdom is the Duke, whose passivity is as obvious as Olivia's but more difficult to explain. Although we could call the Duke's weakness self-indulgence (and, indeed, he does preoccupy himself with his own desires throughout the play), we might better call his condition a sort of defective romantic imagination. There is a discrepancy between what he imagines will satisfy him and what actually does so—a discrepancy between theory and practice, we might say. In Act 2, the Duke's own words indicate that his imagination is, indeed, the cause of his melancholy. Giving love advice to Cesario, he says,

> If ever thou shalt love,
> In the sweet pangs of it remember me;
> For such as I am, all true lovers are,
> Unstaid and skittish in all motions else,
> Save in the constant image of the creature
> That is belov'd. (2.4.15–20)

His advice, we realize, is faulty. He is "skittish" and unsteady in all other things because he has managed to obtain them, but his love is only constant because it is unrequited. We suspect that, if he were to obtain Olivia's hand, he might be dissatisfied with her as well. Barton perhaps puts it best in her essay on *Twelfth Night:* "Orsino's love-melancholy is essentially sterile and self-induced, a state of mind dependent upon that very absence and lack of response from Olivia which it affects to lament" (405).

Because of this defective romantic imagination, Orsino is unwilling to accept the reality of Olivia's rejection. In Act 1, when Valentine returns with news of the Countess's mourning, Orsino responds by saying:

> O, she that hath a heart of that fine frame
> To pay this debt of love but to a brother,
> How will she love when the rich golden shaft
> Hath kill'd the flock of all affections else
> That live in her; when liver, brain, and heart,
> These sovereign thrones, are all supplied and fill'd
> Her sweet perfections with one self king! (1.1.32–38)

His response can be paraphrased thus: "If she has such ardor in mourning her brother, imagine how she will love when Cupid's arrow strikes!" Once again we can see a discrepancy between what the Duke imagines and what is actually the case. Orsino is so caught up in imagining his future bliss that he fails to grasp a key part of the message: Olivia is not interested in having a suitor. And, too, the emotion that Orsino imagines to be love is not love at all. Love entails desiring what is best for the other, but Orsino never seriously considers Olivia's sorrow. In *The Breath of Clowns and Kings: Shakespeare's Early Comedies and Histories,* Theodore Weiss is right to ask, "With such a supine hero, and such a complex opening, one might well wonder how either the hero or the play will ever stand erect, let alone act. What can possibly stir them? . . . [Orsino] is in love with his own figures, not the world's: a mental Narcissus, an egotist sublime. Unheard music may not be sweetest to him, but beyond doubt an unseen or at least unavailable love is" (303).

Viola and Feste, however, come to the rescue, moving Orsino to reform by the same techniques used on Olivia; they warn him that death is inevitable and that he must, accordingly, stop wasting time. Orsino, in turn, gives them more to work with than Olivia did, for he clearly realizes that death will come for others, though he seems to overlook the fact that it will come quickly for himself as well. The task of Viola and Feste, then, is to get the Duke to see that he is not immune to death, either. Act 2 contains numerous examples of the Duke's blindness and of Viola's and Feste's actions on his behalf. When asking Feste for a song, for instance, Orsino requests one that he heard the night before, one that is "old and plain. / The spinsters and the knitters in the sun, / And the free maids that weave their thread with bones, / Do use to chaunt it" (2.4.43–46). His very words, as Leah Scragg explains in *Discovering Shakespeare's Meaning,* are replete with suggestions of death:

> His [the Duke's] reference to the "spinsters" (i.e., spinners) and "knitters" by whom the song is traditionally sung, together with his mention of "their thread" evokes an image of the Fates, spinning the thread of human life, and this suggestion is heightened by the use of the word "chant," with its ritual connotations, and by the allusion to the lacemakers' bobbins as "bones".
> Ideas of fate, transience and mortality thus underlie the surface meaning of the words, generating a wistfulness. . . . (215–216)

Feste then sings the song Orsino requested:

> Come away, come away, death
> And in sad cypress let me be laid.
> [Fly] away, [fly] away, breath,

I am slain by a fair cruel maid.
My shroud of white, stuck all with yew,
O prepare it!
My part of death, no one so true
Did share it. (2.4.51–58)

The Duke no doubt enjoys this song because it suits the melancholy nature of a man who is love-stricken. But could the Duke reflect upon this song, he would learn quite a bit. The lesson of the song is that the unrewarded lover who continues to pursue his suit risks a lonely demise, a dark death that, as Scragg again notes, is "seen, not in terms of renewal, but of physical decay" (216). The song thus portrays the ugly, sterile dimension of unrequited love. Although the message should jar the Duke to look for a more suitable object of his love, it does not.

Viola likewise tries to move Orsino to action by alluding to death's claim upon all. In the following exchange, the Duke only admits that women must act with urgency because of death's inevitability; thus, he neatly excepts himself from those who must be aware of death's approach:

Duke:   *[W]omen* are as roses, whose fair flow'r

      Being once display'd, doth fall that very hour.

Viola:   And so they are; alas, that they are so!

      To die, even when they to perfection grow! (2.4.38–41, emphasis added)

Both comments are ironic. Viola's remark clearly is self-reflective, but Orsino's remark shows a lack of recognition. Do not men also have a limited lifespan in which to love? Throughout this play the Duke pursues Olivia at his leisure; he does not have the awareness of death and time that Viola has come by through hard experience.

So Viola makes yet another effort to educate the Duke, using a variant of this same approach. She falsifies her ancestry, explaining that she had a sister who died for love:

Viola:   [S]he never told her love,

      But let concealment like a worm i' th' bud

      Feed on her damask cheek; she pin'd in thought,

      And with a green and yellow melancholy

      She sate like Patience on a monument,

      Smiling at grief. . . .

Duke:   But died thy sister of her love, my boy?

Viola:  I am all the daughters of my father's house (2.4.110–115, 119–120)

Once more we see a double meaning in this speech. Viola is coming to a growing realization that her own situation is not satisfactory, that she may soon have to reveal her love or risk the same fate as Cesario's "sister." But she also gives a warning that serves the same purpose as Feste's song. Unlike the young girl in the story, the Duke has declared his love. But like the young girl in the story, the Duke also risks dying of "green and yellow melancholy." In other words, unrequited love in any form can be decidedly injurious to the one who suffers from it. In speaking with Olivia, Viola has already said that Orsino, because his love goes unfulfilled, lives a "deadly life" (1.5.265), and such an existence is equivalent to sitting "like Patience on a monument / Smiling at grief." But we do have reason to hope; the Duke's questions to his page, his interest in the young girl's demise, intimate that with time he will learn his lesson.

And learn he does, as he reveals in Act 5, scene one—an act that again makes reference to death. Realizing that Olivia loves his page, Orsino jealously tells the Countess he will kill Cesario; Viola's response to the threat, however, is merely to profess her continued devotion.

Duke:   But this your minion, whom I know you love,

And whom, by heaven I swear, I tender dearly,

Him will I tear out of that cruel eye,

Where he sits crowned in his master's spite.

Come, boy, with me, my thoughts are ripe in mischief.

I'll sacrifice the lamb that I do love,

To spite a raven's heart within a dove.

Viola:  And I most jocund, apt, and willingly,

To do you rest, a thousand deaths would die. (5.1.117–119, 125–131)

In "Mistakes in *Twelfth Night* and Their Resolution: A Study in Some Relations" Porter Williams Jr. analyzes these very lines by saying, "Shortly after this when Viola is unmasked, of course, the Duke is fully prepared to call Viola 'Orsino's mistress and his fancy's queen' (5.1.387). At last he finds his right love, but surely not through the kind of constancy of which he had bragged. Such constancy was Viola's alone, and there is no more moving proof of this than the moment at which Viola turns to follow the angry Duke to her own sacrifice. . . . Comedy here touches for a fleeting moment the pathos of tragedy. Viola's love would have endured a test as final as Desdemona's" (198). The passage is certainly revealing, for Orsino intimates that he might do violence to the very page he adores. Yet even in the face of such threats, Viola professes a steadfast love for him. Under such dire circumstances, Viola appears all the more noble because she offers the Duke a selfless love and counts as little the possibility of her own demise. In finally uniting these two, Shakespeare merely unravels the rest of the plot. With lightning rapidity, he reveals that Olivia is married, and thus not a suitable object for the Duke's adoration. Sebastian, not Cesario, is Olivia's spouse, so the page is still unattached. And Cesario is actually a woman, not a man. The Duke, therefore, is confronted with the fact that the only eligible candidate for marriage is the page he has loved all along—and that she loves him even unto death. There are no more obstacles to surmount, save the retrieval of her clothes and the performance of the nuptial ceremony.

With regard to the lesser members of the play—Sir Toby and company and Malvolio—the task of effecting reform falls primarily to Feste. In depicting Olivia's estate, though, Shakespeare has shown an interesting contrast. Olivia errs by turning away from life, while those around her err by self-indulgently immersing themselves in life, filling each day with nothing more substantive than singing, dancing, drinking and jesting. Both responses are unhealthy, but both can be remedied by Feste and Viola's didactic strategy. During the scene of night revels, for instance, the clown comes upon Sir Toby and Sir Andrew, who ask for a song. When Feste asks whether they would have a love song or a song telling how to live a good life, the two naturally select a love song, which Feste duly gives them. But as he continues, Feste also gives them exactly what they did not want, a "song of good life":

> What is love? 'Tis not hereafter;
> Present mirth hath present laughter;
> What's to come is still unsure.
> In delay there lies no plenty,
> Then come and kiss me sweet and twenty;
> Youth's a stuff will not endure. (2.3.47–52)

This song has the same object as nearly all of Feste's words. It attempts to move these Illyrians out of their self-absorption to consider more worthwhile pursuits by reminding them of the inevitability of death. As John Hollander explains, the song could be paraphrased thus: "This feast will have to end, and so will all of our lives. You are not getting any younger . . ." (233).

But Feste is forced to repeat his correction yet again as the scene continues. Sir Toby's exuberant singing provokes an angry response from Malvolio, who, hearing the music outside, exclaims: "Have you no wit, manners, nor honesty, but to gabble like tinkers at this time of the night? . . . Is there no respect of place, persons nor time in you?" Sir Toby lamely responds, "We did keep time, sir, in our catches [songs]" (2.3.87–93). Sir Toby then, again in song, affirms his own immortality—an illusion that Feste quickly corrects:

Sir Toby:  Farewell, dear heart, since I must needs be gone.

Maria:     Nay, good Sir Toby.

Malvolio:  Is't even so?

Clown:     His eyes do show his days are almost done.

Sir Toby:  But I will never die.

Clown:     Sir Toby, there you lie. (2.3.102–107)


Once again, Feste points out that death will come for Sir Toby, whether he likes it or not.

In addition to singing to avoid thoughts of serious issues, the characters in the subplot also partake of excessive festivity by filling each day with play, jests and pranks. They drink, brag about their skill in "cutting a caper," deceive Malvolio, and even play tricks upon each other. In sport, for example, Sir Toby sets Cesario and Sir Andrew against each other, unwittingly pulling Sebastian into the fray. Now, such conduct was right in line with the Epiphany, the occasion to which the title of the play, *Twelfth Night,* refers, the last day of the Christmas season and the day upon which the Magi came to adore the infant Christ. The occasion of Twelfth Night, as Barton explains in her introduction to this play, was an occasion of merriment, a time when the normal order of things was overturned (as it is with carnival), a period in which the usual rules and customs did not apply (404). The members of the household clearly live up to the occasion. In *The First Night of Twelfth Night,* Leslie Hotson notes, "In the freedom of Twelfth Night, you do what you will, say what you will," and that is exactly what the members of Olivia's household do—what they will (148). There is just one problem with such an arrangement, as we can see from C. L. Barber's comments. He says, "Holiday, for the Elizabethan sensibility, implied a contrast with 'everyday'. . . . Occasions like May day and the Winter Revels . . . were maintained within a civilization whose daily view of life focused on the mortality implicit in the vitality . . ." (10). But in this society, every day is a holiday, for the Illyrians focus on vitality, but neglect to acknowledge mortality—an acknowledgement which could provoke widespread reform.

Feste, in contrast, displays the ideal attitude toward festivity; he is a clown, and thus is closely associated with festivity, but like Viola, he realizes that there are, or should be, limits to such festivity. Though he clearly enjoys merriment (his name reminds us of festivals and lightheartedness), he also sees the defects in his society and attempts to correct them by wisely pointing out the inevitability of death and the importance, therefore, of a life well-lived. It is he, we must recall, who reminds the revelers that "youth's a stuff will not endure" (2.3.52), who corrects Sir Toby's false assertion about immortality, and who schools Olivia about grief. It is he who sings about the stages of man in Act 5, a song that, as Barbara Everett notes, teaches us about "simply growing up, accepting the principle that nights before have mornings after; that life consists in passing time, and in knowing it" (308).

A final citizen who needs correction is Malvolio, whose self-love causes him to disdain the other members of his household; to understand how Feste tries to reform Malvolio by means of references to death, however, we must first understand the flaw that mars this complex character. In *Shakespeare's Comic Commonwealths,* Camille Wells Slights provides a skillful study of why Malvolio is so distasteful: "The measure of Malvolio's self-love is not his miserliness or covetousness but his presumptuous belief that he lives in a sphere above and beyond ordinary human relationships" (225–226). Indeed, in Act 1, Olivia herself establishes that Malvolio's high opinion of himself is a weakness. After the fool has "catechized" Olivia not to mourn so incessantly for her brother, Malvolio (whose name does, after all, mean "ill will") shows his immense disrespect for Feste by heaping insults upon the fool's head. Olivia responds by saying, "O, you are sick of self-love, Malvolio, and taste with a distemper'd appetite. To be generous, guiltless, and of free disposition, is to take those things for bird-bolts that you deem cannon-bullets" (1.5.90–93). Mafia, likewise, finds that Malvolio's defect is that "it is his grounds of faith that all that look on him love him" (2.3.151–152) and vows that her revenge on him will make use of this very defect of character.

Although Mafia's plan does just that, employing Malvolio's high self-regard to make him look foolish—it is not this aspect of the jest that is important to my analysis. Granted, many commentators focus upon the intricacies of the box-tree scene with good reason, for this scene is, arguably, one of the funniest of the entire play. But another dimension of the prank—the imprisonment—deserves further scrutiny, for here Feste again tries to correct the steward by referring to death. To remedy Malvolio's habit of holding himself in high regard above others, Feste reminds the steward of his relationship to others—a relationship he may have forgotten:

Clown:     What is the opinion of Pythagoras concerning wild-fowl?

Malvolio: That the soul of our grandam might happily inhabit a bird.

Clown:     What think'st thou of his opinion?

Malvolio: I think nobly of the soul, and no way approve his opinion.

Clown:  Fare thee well.

> Remain thou still in darkness. Thou shalt hold th' opinion of Pythagoras ere I will allow of thy wits, and fear to kill a woodcock lest thou dispossess the soul of thy grandam. Fare thee well. (4.2.50–60.)

At first glance this conversation merely appears part of an overall strategy to make Malvolio think he is mad, but upon further consideration Feste seems to have an instructional purpose and method that again make reference to mortality. By turning to Pythagoras's ideas, articulated by Ovid (a writer with whom Shakespeare obviously was familiar, as we can see by the Pyramus and Thisby episode in *A Midsummer Night's Dream*), we can see more clearly Feste's project. In Book 15 of the *Metamorphoses,* Ovid presents Pythagoras's view concerning reincarnation by saying,

> [O]ver souls—be sure—death has no sway: each soul, once it has left one body, takes another body as its home, the place where it lives on. . . . For all things change, but no thing dies. The spirit wanders: here and there, at will, the soul can journey from an animal into a human body, and from us to beasts: it occupies a body, but it never perishes. As pliant wax is still the selfsame wax, so do I say that soul, however much it may migrate, is still the same. And thus, lest piety suffer defeat when faced with the belly's greed, do not expel—so I, a prophet teach—the souls of others by your butchery: those souls are kin to your own souls; don't feed your blood upon another's blood. (519, emphasis added)

According to Pythagoras's theory of reincarnation, souls take new forms after death, and these forms may be human or animal; thus, a kinship arises among all things. In light of this kinship, one should not eat of another creature, because in doing so, one may be committing an offense against another's soul.

But how does the passage relate to Malvolio and to the warnings about death found throughout the play? Ovid's warning is relevant because the insolent steward needs to recognize the common bonds he has with all things, whether they be clowns, wildfowl, or serving women. And, because of this kinship, he should not elevate himself at others' expense. In trying to teach Malvolio, Feste again uses the language of death employed elsewhere in the play; at this point, however, Malvolio refuses to learn his lesson. Unlike Olivia and the Duke, he does not become wiser even after being schooled using the dire language of death.

It is little wonder that Viola and Feste expend such great effort trying to reform Illyria's citizens, going from one character to another to point out the brevity of human life and the importance, therefore, of a life well-lived. For, as critics have noted, there is a lack of community exhibited in this play. Camille Wells Slights notes that "Illyria is plagued with stagnation" and claims that "the native Illyrians present a spectacle of isolation rather than confrontation, not so much a society in disorder as a series of discrete individuals without the interconnections that constitute a society" (217). Similarly, Alexander Leggatt explains that here, "[W]e are aware of each character as an individual, out on his own, the lovers trying to make contact but with limited success, and the comic figures either openly hostile or forming relationships based on temporary expediency. . . . Certainly individual characters come more clearly into focus than in any previous comedy of Shakespeare's, and the sense that they can be bound together in a common experience is weaker" (222–223).

But this sense of fragmentation begins to turn with the entrance of Viola, who after her shipwreck advises her new society that death will come for all and that, therefore, one must live wisely while there is time to do so. Then, a whole series of interlocking reversals occurs—all spurred on by Viola's and Feste's admonishments. Olivia begins to see that time is, indeed, valuable and that she has erred in not conducting her life accordingly. As Fred Turner observes, "Olivia realizes that she has been misusing her time, that the present moment is something valuable, and to mourn the past is a sin. . . . She has caught something of Viola's sense of urgency, the . . . feeling of the preciousness of life . . . " (63). A secondary result of Olivia's new wisdom is that she reveals her distaste for Sir Toby's actions with such forcefulness that the household becomes better managed as a result—a strength that partly accounts for Sebastian's esteem of her. The marriage of Olivia then leads to the end of Orsino's pining for her. With the revelation of the marriage and of Sebastian's presence, Viola can disclose her true identity (thus, she is released from the bondage of her disguise), and Orsino can acknowledge the love he has felt for Viola all along. Sir Toby and Malvolio can reform if they choose to do so; they have certainly been equipped by Viola and Feste with the tools they need to see the error of their ways. But on this point Shakespeare gives ambiguous signals.

Returning to our initial deliberations, then, a detailed look at *Twelfth Night* provides one answer to the issue that Barbara Everett raises in her critique—that of the serious undertone that pervades many of the comedies—and gives us a window into the dramas; yet, we need to look more deeply at the plays to trace how encounters with death and their resultant warnings to live wisely consistently prompt reform in Shakespearean comedy. For Viola,

Feste, and their fellow Illyrians, the outcome is a society which is generally wiser, albeit with a few exceptions. And the same holds true for many more Shakespearean communities, where characters come to realize the inevitability of death and make this knowledge the impetus for a life well-lived. The words of Susanne Langer are quite helpful, then, in pointing out how natural this learning process is and how integral it is to Shakespeare's comic form. Langer says that the "pure sense of life is the underlying feeling of comedy" (120) and explains that, "no matter how people contrive to become reconciled to their mortality, it puts a stamp on their conception of life: since the instinctive struggle to go on living is bound to meet with defeat in the end, they look for as much life as possible between birth and death" (125). Certainly such is the case with Shakespeare's Illyrians. In this society, the awareness of death often provokes characters to live more wisely—a point that is generally overlooked by the critics. To acknowledge the prevalence of this pattern here and in other Shakespearean dramas is to uncover a new depth and richness to the plays—a new profundity and poignancy in Shakespeare's comic form.

## Notes

1. I include *The Tempest* and *The Winter's Tale* in this discussion of comedy since they were listed as comedies in the First Folio and since these later works, like the comedies, tend to emphasize that the awareness of death should lead one to wisdom.

2. All quotations of Shakespeare are taken from *The Riverside Shakespeare*, ed. G. Blakemore Evans (Boston: Houghton Mifflin, 1974).

## Works Cited

Barber, C. L. *Shakespeare's Festive Comedy: A Study of Dramatic Form and Its Relation to Social Custom.* Princeton: Princeton University Press, 1959.

Barton, Anne. Introduction to *Much Ado about Nothing.* The Riverside Shakespeare. Ed. G. Blakemore Evans. Boston: Houghton Mifflin, 1974. 327–331.

———. Introduction to *Twelfth Night.* The Riverside Shakespeare. Ed. G. Blakemore Evans. Boston: Houghton Mifflin, 1974. 403–407.

Carlin, Patricia. *Shakespeare's Mortal Men: Overcoming Death in History, Comedy and Tragedy.* Studies in Shakespeare 1. Ed. Robert F. Wilson Jr. New York: Peter Lang, 1993.

Everett, Barbara. "Or What You Will." *Essays in Criticism* 35 (October 1985): 294–314.

Garber, Marjorie. "'Remember Me': Memento Mori Figures in Shakespeare's Plays." *Renaissance Drama* 12 (1981): 3–25.

Hassel, R. Chris, Jr. *Faith and Folly in Shakespeare's Romantic Comedies.* Athens: University of Georgia Press, 1980.

Hollander, John. "*Twelfth Night* and the Morality of Indulgence." *Sewanee Review* 67 (1959): 220–238.

Hotson, Leslie. *The First Night of Twelfth Night.* New York: Macmillan, 1954.

Langer, Susanne. "The Comic Rhythm." *The Form of Comedy.* Ed. Robert Corrigan. San Francisco: Chandler, 1965. 119–140.

Leggatt, Alexander. *Shakespeare's Comedy of Love*. London: Methuen, 1974.

Logan, Thad Jenkins. "'*Twelfth Night:* The Limits of Festivity?' *Studies in English Literature* 22 (1982): 223–238.

Macdonald, Ronald R. *William Shakespeare: The Comedies*. Twayne's English Authors Series. Ed. Arthur F Kinney. New York: Twayne, 1992.

Ovid. *The Metamorphoses*. Trans. Allen Mandelbaum. San Diego: Harcourt Brace, 1993.

Scragg, Leah. *Discovering Shakespeare's Meaning*. Totowa, New Jersey: Barnes & Noble, 1988.

Shakespeare, William. *Twelfth Night*. The Riverside Shakespeare. Ed. G. Blakemore Evans. Boston: Houghton, 1974.

Slights, Camille Wells. *Shakespeare's Comic Commonwealths*. Toronto: University of Toronto Press, 1993.

Spencer, Theodore. *Death and Elizabethan Tragedy: A Study of Convention and Opinion in the Elizabethan Drama*. New York: Pageant, 1960.

Turner, Frederick. *Shakespeare and the Nature of Time: Moral and Philosophical Themes in Some Plays and Poems of William Shakespeare*. Oxford: Oxford University Press, 1971.

Weiss, Theodore. *The Breath of Clowns and Kings: Shakespeare's Early Comedies and Histories*. New York: Atheneum, 1974.

Williams, Porter, Jr. "Mistakes in *Twelfth Night* and Their Resolution: A Study in Some Relationships of Plot and Theme." *PMLA* 76 (June 1961): 193–199.

LINDA WOODBRIDGE

# Country Matters: As You Like It and the Pastoral-Bashing Impulse

Audiences delight in *As You Like It*, but critics often get twitchy about it, which seems odd. The play after all features cross-dressing, the biggest female speaking role in all of Shakespeare, an intriguingly intimate friendship between two women, an exploited agricultural laborer, and a set speech on animal rights—one would think that this comedy offered satisfactions for gender theorists, feminists, queer theorists, Marxists, and ecocritics alike. What's not to like in *As You Like It*?

The answer, I think, is fairly straightforward: what's not to like is the pastoralism. For a couple of centuries now but especially in recent decades, a wide spectrum of critics has heaped scorn upon the bucolic realm of pastoral, and Shakespeare's most pastoral play has come in for its share of scorn. Shakespeare being who he is, critics are seldom as hard on him as on other writers of pastoral, and some exonerate him entirely by recasting *As You Like It* as itself a sneer at pastoral: Shakespeare is not himself conventional, but uses conventions playfully, self-consciously, mockingly. He writes not pastoral but antipastoral. This move in itself, of course, drives another nail into pastoral's coffin. Excavating the cultural meanings of the critical vendetta against pastoral, and exploring how it plays out in *As You Like It*, may give us not only a fresh perspective on the play, but a route into the enigma of pastoral bashing and what it says about our culture.

*Re-Visions of Shakespeare: Essays in Honor of Robert Ornstein.* Evelyn Gajowski (ed. and introd.) (Newark, Del.: University of Delaware Press, 2004): pp. 189–214. Copyright © 2004 Associated University Presses and Linda Woodbridge.

## *As You Like It* and Critical Antipastoralism

Critics often complain of a lack of action in *As You Like It,* beginning in act 2. It's not so much that they get bored when the wrestling match is over as that they feel uneasy at being invited to share in a pastoral life that seems, as well, lazy. In this relaxed world, exiled lords entertain each other with songs or gaze thoughtfully into brooks, lovers pin poetry to trees, and Jaques and Celia go off to take naps—troubling evidence of a lack of purposeful action in Arden. Peter Lindenbaum excoriates pastoral in general for its "life of leisure and freedom from the cares and responsibilities of the normal world," sternly averring that responsible Renaissance writers recognized that "in this world of ours man simply has no time for relaxation or even momentary escape from the pressing activity of day-to-day living"; Sidney in *Arcadia* and Shakespeare in *As You Like It* "lodge an objection to the whole prospect of life in a pastoral setting, to a cast of mind that either seeks an easy, carefree existence anywhere in our present world or indulges overmuch in dreams of better times and better places, thereby avoiding full concentration upon the facts of man's present existence."[1] The shepherd's reprehensible life of ease has offended so many critics that A. Stuart Daley feels he must explain the habits of sheep to excuse all the slacking that goes on in an early Arden afternoon: "At midday, after a long morning of nibbling on the herbage, the animals needed complete rest, and lay down to ruminate. At noon, a shepherd such as those in *As You Like It* could expect two or three hours of comparative freedom. Indeed all English workers had the right to a midday rest, according to a statute of 1563."[2] The play's adjournment from the court into a rural world of ease is often belittled as an escapist fantasy. To avoid being charged with advocating escapism, a responsible author must "insist upon the need to leave Arcadia," Lindenbaum dictates;[3] Richard Helgerson insists, "the pastoral world is meant to be left behind."[4] Critics assume that characters in Arden scramble to get back to the court: Daley writes, "With the zeal of a reformed sinner, Celia's fiancé resolves to 'live and die a shepherd'; but his aristocratic calling obviously forbids the abandonment of his lands and great allies to the detriment of the commonweal."[5] Critics seem untroubled that *As You Like It* nowhere articulates this ideal of public service, or that the play not only leaves open the question of whether Oliver and Celia will stay in the country, but insists that Duke Frederick and Jaques opt to stay in Arden—Jaques' decision to stay is given an emphatic position at the very end of the play. Ignoring all of this and focusing on characters who do leave the pastoral world, Lindenbaum, who is pretty hard on Duke Senior for using banishment as an excuse for lolling around in the woods, readmits him to favor when he makes the crucial decision "to leave Arcadia":

His pastoral dream proves by the end to have been that of a basically good man on vacation. His essential moral health is affirmed at the play's end by his unhesitating willingness to return to court and take up responsible active life in the political world again. This final act reflects the whole play's anti-pastoral argument. The forest is initially a play of ease, idleness, and escape from normal cares and responsibilities, but that view provides the stimulus for Shakespeare's eventual insistence upon a more active stance.[6]

Albert Cirillo expresses approval that once characters have straightened out their lives, "they can return to the court"; far from pastoral's challenging court values, he sees it the other way around: "the Forest needs the contrast with the court and worldly values to clarify the consciousness of the audience as to the essential illusory quality of the pastoral world."[7]

Renato Poggioli's belief that "the psychological root of the pastoral is a double longing after innocence and happiness, to be recovered not through conversion or regeneration, but merely through a retreat" rings false in *As You Like It*, where Frederick is converted, Oliver regenerated.[8] You'd think the discomfort of Arden, with its wintry wind, would obviate charges of escapism, but critics instead read this as Shakespearean contempt for pastoral. Daley notes that "characters who express an opinion about the Forest of Arden utter mostly dispraise"; taking at face value Touchstone's gripes and Rosalind's "saucy lackey" impertinences, he pronounces "the local women . . . vain and foul and the backwoods dialect lacking in grace and beauty"; the "consistent dispraise of the country" shows that Shakespeare did not intend "a traditional contrast between court and country."[9] But *did* such dispraise indicate Shakespeare disdained the country? Traditionally, pastoral figures gain moral authority through asceticism; in pastoral, country harshness obviates charges of hedonism that would undermine pastoral's ability to critique the corruptions of a world of power. Lindenbaum reads dispraise of the country as unhappiness with pastoral, born of frustrated golden-world expectations, of finding country life "no different from life at court or in the city,"[10] Svetlana Makurenkova generalizes about Shakespeare's career, "one may trace throughout the corpus of Shakespeare's work a certain dethroning of idyllic pastoral imagery."[11]

Taking the play's realism for antipastoralism, critics create a no-win situation. Pastorals *do* speak of rural harshness—Meliboeus's dispossession from his farm in Virgil's first eclogue or, in *As You Like It*, Corin's low wages from a churlish absentee master (2.4.75–78) and description of shepherds' hands as greasy, work-hardened, and "tarr'd over with the surgery of our sheep" (3.2.50–51, 59–60).[12] But such details don't make critics revise their belief that pastoral ignores "real difficulties and hardships" and shuns "realistic description of the actual conditions of country life"; instead, critics consider such realism as "anti-pastoral sentiment" attributable to frustration at the genre's artificiality and escapism. Cirillo says "every force which would lead to the acceptance of life in Arden as a perfect world is negated by the intrusion of a harsher reality";[13] but the idea of Arden as a perfect world comes only from Cirillo's stereotype that pastorals deal in escapist golden worlds. For such critics, when a pastoral doesn't fit the stereotype, it doesn't negate the stereotype but becomes evidence of the author's unhappiness with pastoral. This resembles the way that the Renaissance decried as unnatural woman who didn't fit its stereotypes, thus preserving the stereotypes, intact.

Touchstone finds shepherding "a very vile life" (3.2.16) and many think that his name, implying a test of genuineness, declares him the play's voice of truth. Yet his plans to wriggle our of his marriage discredit him: and anyway, a clown's-eye view of the action is never the whole story in Shakespeare. Against Touchstone's view we have Corin's sensible cultural relativism: "Those that are good manners at the court are as ridiculous in the country as the behavior of the country is most mockable at the court" (3.2.43–46). Touchstone's witty equivocation on "manners" shows how anti-rural prejudice works: "If thou never wast at court, thou never saw'st good manners; if thou never saw'st good manners; then thy manners must be wicked; and wickedness is a sin, and sin is damnation. Thou art in a parlous state, shepherd" (3.2.38–42). The pun has lost its force, since "manners" now means only "etiquette"; in Shakespeare's day it also meant "morals." Considering country etiquette uncouth, courtiers assume that country morals as loose too. Touchstone discovers this untrue of country wench Audrey, who declares (to his disappointment) "I am not a slut" (3.3.35). Orlando too mistakes country manners, expecting violent inhospitality: "I thought that all things had been savage here" (2.7.71). Orlando, says Rawdon Wilson, "fails to understand the nature of Arden"; exiled courtiers need "a period of adjustment to Arden"[14]—a time to revise prejudices about country life?

The play has sometimes been attacked on aesthetic grounds, with complaints that the satiric and the bucolic are awkwardly joined and tonally disjunctive, especially in the person of Jaques, whom critics virulently attack, often on the assumption that a satiric voice doesn't belong in a choir making mellow pastoral music. But satiric voices have always spoken in Arcadia—satire is one thing pastoral is all about. Unwillingness to stomach Jaques echoes criticism of Spenser and Milton for letting sharp attacks on abuses intrude into a pastoral setting. Shakespeare is not alone in being scorned for writing pastoral or praised for allegedly resisting pastoral: the whole pastoral mode has been inimical to our general cultural climate for a good many years now.

## New Historicists versus Pastoral: The Passion for Power

It's hard to think of another genre that has been described so patronizingly, attacked so virulently, dismissed so contemptuously over many years. Samuel Johnson called *Lycidas* "a pastoral, easy, vulgar, and therefore disgusting."[15] W. W. Greg said of one of Spenser's eclogues "only a rollicking indifference to it own inanity . . . saves it from sheer puerility," and considered eclogues "the type of all that is frigid and artificial in literature," announcing that a "stigma . . . attaches to pastoral as a whole," that even the best pastorals suffer from lack of originality, and that even *Lycidas,* the best pastoral since Virgil, is so defective that "the form of pastoral instituted by Virgil and handed down without break from the fourteenth century to Milton's own time stand[s] condemned in its most perfect flower."[16] Peter Lindenbaum, disgusted with Sannazaro's representation of Arcadia as "a soothing dwelling place for the troubled human spirit," charges that "the pastoral mode in Sannazaro's hands threatens to become a vehicle for mere indulgence in sentimental feeling."[17] Spenserian retreat from aspiration, Louis Montrose calls "resignation to the poetry of pastoral triviality."[18] Renato Poggioli says pastoral "reduces all human intercourse to an everlasting tête-à-tête."[19] P. V. Krieder thinks the "susceptibilities" of "inexperienced writers" makes them "silly victims of an unnatural pastoralism"; he denounces "the tawdry allurements of pastoralism."[20] Feminists too have attacked pastoral: as Lisa Robertson puts it, "Certainly, as a fin de siecle feminist, I cannot in good conscience perform even the simplest political identification with the pastoral genre . . . [wherein] the figure of woman appears as eroticized worker— the milkmaid or the shepherdess."[21]

It seems the genre can't put a foot right. If it's political, it is taxed with toadying to repressive regimes; its very attacks on such regimes are inscribed in ideological structures it can't escape. If it speaks of love and spring, it is escapist and trivial. If it treats politics *and* love, its tone is disjunctive. If its authors are thriving courtiers, they are indicted for hypocrisy in that they praise retired life while living a public life; if they are out of political favor, living in the country, they have a sour grapes attitude. If pastoral life is highly artificial, ignoring agricultural laborers' harsh life, it is suppressing socioeconomic reality; if it includes gritty details of sheep tending, it is called antipastoral, and made an accomplice to its own undoing. Pastoral's very popularity is held against it: the astounding receptivity of readers to legions of Corins, Colins, and Dorindas over centuries—nay, millennia—provokes not praise for the genre's wide appeal and staying power but condemnation for repetitious unoriginality. The charge that pastoral is repetitious is fair in a way, though the sensation of being waterlogged in a sea of oaten piping mainly afflicts those who survey the whole genre; is it fair to adduce against individual pastorals the fact that there are too many pastorals in the world? It would be hard *not* to be repetitious in a mode that has had such a long run as pastoral has—from the ancient Greeks and Romans right through the 1960s. Anyway, the charge is brought selectively against pastoral: other numbingly repetitive genres are tolerated—satire, epigram, sonnet, sermon, or (later) commentaries on football games. The aesthetic complaint about pastoral's repetitiousness seems to mask other causes for distaste. Why the contempt for pastoral? What are the cultural meanings of this vendetta?

The most obvious point of entry into the question is pastoral's relation to the world of power, a feature of the discourse about pastoral since its Greek and Roman beginnings, but most recently of lively interest to new historicists such as Louis Montrose, whose influential essays on Elizabethan pastoral posit its inscription within the ideology of state power. Focusing on court pageants and pastorals produced for Elizabeth on progresses, and extending his critique to all pastorals, Montrose argues that pastoral performs the cultural work of justifying autocratic government, that its authors are state propagandists, encomiasts, sycophants, that Renaissance pastorals mingled "*otium* and *negotium,* holiday and policy"; "Elizabethan pastorals of power combin[ed] intimacy and beginity with authoritatiranism."[22] Pastoral professions of power's hollowness, Montrose dismisses as cynical attempts to dissuade lower orders from wanting to share power.

Do propagandistic pageants fairly represent pastoral? It is true that Queen Elizabeth used royal progresses through the countryside to intimate "a beautiful relation between rich and poor," in Empson's sardonic formulation of pastoral's primary mystification. But the pastoral mode can also be dissident and oppositional, attacking specific power abuses.[23] Over centuries, many authors have used pastoral to criticize politics, to attack political and clerical abuses and meddle in current affairs. Virgilian pastoral had implications for current events of its day—civil wars between Brutus and Cassius. Mantuan's pastorals attack abuses of the Roman Church; Naldo Naldi wrote eclogues on the house of Medici; Ariosto wrote an eclogue on the 1506 conspiracy against Alfonso d'Este; Spenser in *The Shepheardes Calender* criticizes the proposed French marriage of Queen Elizabeth; Francis Quarles's eclogues dealt with current religious controversies. Pastoral's country cousin, the Georgic, was indeed employed in eighteenth-century justifications of imperial colonization, but it was also employed to criticize such colonization, as in the ending of "Autumn" in James Thomson's *The Seasons,* 1746.[24] The sixteenth century assumed that pastorals critiqued power: George Puttenham wrote that eclogues "under the veil of homely persons, and in rude speeches insinuate and glance at greater matters, and such as perchance had not been safe to have been disclosed in any other sort."[25]

And pastoral not only attacks specific abuses of power but challenges the power ethic itself. It has a long tradition of discrediting the supposed pleasures of power. The first set of pastoral eclogues in English, by Alexander Barclay, begins with three eclogues on the miseries of court life; the subtitle features "the Miseries of Courtiers and Courts of All Princes in General."[26]

New historicists have also read pastoral as an attempt to curry favor with those in power by justifying that power for them. When pastoral is not read as outright propaganda, as is the case with Queen Elizabeth's pastoral entertainments, it is often read as some courtier's sycophantic bid for career advancement. From Virgil's praise of Caesar onwards, pastoral *has* at times been encomiastic, and no one would deny that the pastoral mode has its sycophantic face. *Iam redit et Virgo, redeunt Saturnia regna; / iam nova progenies caelo demittitur alto* might be a motto for the Elizabethan age: "the Virgin and the rule of Saturn are now returning; a new offspring is now sent from heaven." The words are Virgil's, but just as Christianity took this image from Virgil as a prophecy of the Virgin Mary, so Elizabeth appropriated for herself his image of the Virgin Astraea, and mythmakers heralded her reign as a return of Saturn's golden, pastoral age. This crucial iconography comes from a pastoral, Virgil's fourth eclogue; through it, the Elizabethan explosion of pastoral was implicated in the machinery of state propaganda.

But granted that the Elizabethan propaganda machine did absorb some pastoral writers, the question remains, why pastoral? Why not use trappings of epic or lyric in royal entertainments, rather than shepherds? I think pastoral needed to be co-opted because of its great potential for criticizing governmental abuses, the centralizing policies at the heart of the Tudor project, and the power ethic itself. An autocratic regime that feared criticism needed to disable pastoral. But it was less successful at this than many think. Pastoral has served many purposes that new historicists ignore: why have they gazed so exclusively upon pastoral's more sycophantic face, generalizing to the entire mode from one unsavory posture, seeing "royal pastoral" as contaminating the whole mode?

For example, Montrose and others have read *The Shepheardes Calender* as Spenser's bid for royal favor and career advancement; but much evidence in the poem points in a contrary direction. This pastoral actually criticizes Queen Elizabeth, treading on dangerous ground in its references to Catholic perfidy in the 1572 Huguenot massacre by Charles IX, brother of the duke of Alençon with whom Elizabeth was currently contemplating marriage (*May* eclogue), and the *July* eclogue criticizes the Queen for repressive policies, particularly the house arrest of Archbishop Grindal.[27] As Paul Alpers says, "a poet who praised [Grindal's] virtues and lamented his misfortunes was not playing it safe."[28] Montrose astonishingly recognizes *July* as "a boldly explicit allusion to Elizabeth's reprimand for Grindal's outspokenness that is thoroughly sympathetic to the Archbishop" without modifying his contention that the *Calender* is politically sycophantic; he simply reasserts that the repressive regime curtailed free speech, leaving the reader to wonder why it did not curtail *July*.[29] Further, Montrose shanghais the *February* eclogue into the tradition of sycophancy toward the Tudors by reading the oak/briar fable, I think, upside down: ignoring plain signs identifying the oak with the Catholic Church, the briar with the Tudors, he takes the oak as the Tudor establishment.[30] That so penetrating and logical a writer as Louis Montrose would have risked such strident misinterpretations bespeaks a kind of desperation—this poem *must* be discredited at all costs. *The Shepheardes Calender* appears to me to be a dissident poem, criticizing specific abuses of power and challenging the power ethic itself, condemning those who, prompted by too much "prosperitie," "gape for greedie gouernaunce / And match them selfe with mighty potentates, / Lovers of Lordship" (*May*, 117–124).

Some pastorals, like *The Shepheardes Calender*, challenge the power ethic; others simply evade the world of ambition, offering country contentment as a mute alternative to ambition's frantic frenzies. A move like Montrose's, which relocates the dissident *Shepheardes Calender* within a power-hungry world, makes its protestations against ambition appear merely hypocritical. The whole genre suffers when such major texts are discredited as bids for preferment, inscribed in a court culture of ambitious strivings; this move disables pastoral's challenge to the world of ambition. Why new historicists need to do this is obvious: their whole program is predicated on the assumption that power is what matters in human affairs. As an antipower genre, pastoral is an enemy.

The hypocrisy ascribed to pastoral authors—using an antipower genre to curry favor with the powerful—has rubbed off on the shepherds, undermining their moral authority. This matters to pastoral more than to other modes: pastoral's critique of worldly values depends on the moral authority its speakers gain by refusing participation in the world they indict. As Paul Alpers says, "The literary shepherd's sufficiency to great matters is due to his simplicity and innocence; these confer on him a moral authority."[31] We are seldom interested in the moral authority of a sonnet speaker or the narrator of a prose fiction; but in pastoral it is everything. If a pastoral persona is implicated in the world of power and ambition, the pastoral crumbles.

Even when a pastoral is acknowledged to be oppositional, its dissidence has often been judged politically wrongheaded. Opposition to a centralized court has been seen as atavistic—as powerful central governments emerged all over Europe, the Tudor centralizing project worked to break the baronial power based in the country. Pastoral satire on the court's emasculated aristocracy is dismissed as nostalgia for "real" feudalism. Even if a pastoral is admittedly political and its political heart is conceded to be in the right place, it may stiffer a final dismissal as being ineffective as a means of protest. Some argue that pastoral emasculates itself by indirectness, especially by allegory. Alpers argues that giving moral authority to the powerless renders such authority toothless, since the powerless must speak with impotent indirection. And indirection, for Montrose, spells duplicity: though allegory is "an obfuscation necessary to circumvent governmental hostility to all expressions of dissent or controversy,"[32] he still despises pastoral for such obfuscations.

It's easy to be brave at our historical remove. John Stubbs had his hand cut off for publishing a criticism of the Queen's contemplated French marriage, a criticism that Spenser—in the same year and with the same printer—got away with making in *The Shepheardes Calender*, which was couched in allegory. Montrose judges pastoral "a literary mode specialized to the conditions of a complex, contentious, and authoritarian civilization—a fallen world of duplicity and innuendo. Its enforced deceptiveness epitomizes the very condition it seeks to amend."[33] He concludes that such ignominious "indirection and dissimulation are the rhetorical techniques of poetry and policy."[34] In assuming that only direct frontal assaults really count as dissent, Alpers and Montrose insist on a brash courage I'm not sure we have a right to demand of those living in a repressive society. And dismissing indirection as a literary technique disables not only pastoral but a good deal of literature. Is "A Modest Proposal" less effective dissent than an outraged letter to the authorities? Swift *tried* straightforward polemical pamphlets; but after the failure of such frontal assaults he took up a more potent weapon, irony.

I have argued that pastoral figures gain moral authority by refusing participation in the world they indict. Removal from the court to the country is paradoxically a condition of making credible critiques of the court. Failure to accept this necessary doubleness, this absent presence in the world of power, helps account for persistent complaints about pastorals' uncouth diction and tonal disunity. Pastoral is damned if it does and damned if it doesn't: couched in artificial court language, it is denounced for evading the material reality of peasant life; couched in rustic diction, it is dismissed as lacking the decorum of serious literature.[35] Dr. Johnson dismissed Spenser's rustic diction as a "studied barbarity"[36] and complained of Milton's using religious allegory in a pastoral: the disjunction of Lycidas's being "now a feeder of sheep, and afterwards an ecclesiastical pastor" is "indecent." It was "improper," Johnson decreed, "to give the title of a pastoral to verses in which the speakers, after the slight mention of their flocks, fall to complaints of errors in the church and corruptions in the government."[37] The unity issue is crucial: readers from Johnson on have faulted pastoral for yoking together by violence bucolic contentment and satire on abuses. Yet the two are intimately linked: it is by eschewing power and comfort that one gains authority to attack the powerful and comfortable. One must depart from power's premises to find the perspective and authority to unmask power's abuses, pretenses, futility. Seeing artistic disunity in pastoral's double tone—contentment in a simple life and criticism of the powerful—destroys the pastoral mode.

The pastoral persona occupies a subject position uniquely suited to challenging the power ethic: a shepherd's critique had moral weight because s/he wasn't implicated in power. But didn't that mean forgoing power? Creating "pastoral counter-worlds," Montrose argues, "is always suspect—potentially dangerous, escapist, or regressive. To make poetry a vehicle of transcendence is tacitly to acknowledge its ethical and political impotence."[38] The dilemma of corrupt implication in power versus irresponsible evasion of power is familiar to those who try to get women into positions of power where they can influence events: they risk reproducing the oppressive, unequal system they oppose. Those who believe that women can oppose the power system only by opting out of it risk lacking the means to change anything. They argue that lack of power is a catastrophe only in a power-obsessed society; the only way to reduce society's obsession with power is for individuals to avoid obsession. But won't the powerful oppress those who eschew power? Others faced with this dilemma, advocates of unilateral disarmament, have argued that someone has to make the first move. However imperfect, co-optable, exploitable the pastoral genre, its merit is that for dismantling oppressive power structures, it offers a position from which to make the first move. It is not a perfect position—it risks political toothlessness—but it is more credible than the position of the powerful. And even if some implicated in power—courtiers or preferment-seekers—choose this subject position, does that necessarily nullify their criticisms or make it less valuable to imagine a less power-obsessed world?

Attacking both royal power and pastoral's critique of royal power creates a damned-if-you-do-and-damned-if-you-don't situation. New historicists cut the ground from under any oppositional stance—one cannot be truly oppositional if one has ever sought social advancement, or values relaxation, or uses irony. As Anne Barton has summed up Stephen Greenblatt's mode of disabling dissent, "what looks to us like subversion in the art of the past is merely something orthodoxy makes strategic use of."[39] Does new historicism really demystify authority, or does it grant authority a mysterious, near-omnipotent power?

Can't criticizing power or articulating an ideal be valuable no matter *who* does it, no matter what their motives or personal lives? It is said that U.S. voters attend not to candidates' policies but to their personalities or private lives, and the same might be said of critics who discredit pastoral if its authors have any link with the world of power. Even Golden Age myths, an extreme manifestation of the pastoral impulse, are not without value—*is* what is irrecoverable in the past (or never existed) necessarily unattainable in the future? Can an ideal, however unrealistic, not at least *correct* reality, creating a synthesis out of the thesis of hierarchical authoritarianism and the antithesis of a classless Golden Age? And if an ideal is worth articulating, how much does it matter who articulates it or how pure his motives?

We are hard on pastoral, but how credible a position for demystifying power do *we* occupy? We are quick to indict the Elizabethan elite, but are we in our tenured positions not ourselves an elite compared to the vast underclasses of our own society? We are nimble at decoding from Elizabethan prefatory epistles the complicity of their authors in a system of court patronage; yet the acknowledgment pages of our scholarly books advertise the elite institutions at which we teach, grants supporting the research, colleagues at prestigious universities who read the manuscript—the appearance of their names is our equivalent of commendatory verses. One can decode such stuff easily enough—authors published by the most prestigious presses, with the most famous friends reading the manuscript, the best fellowships and grants, are those with power in our profession. They are often those who deplore the power and patronage of Elizabeth's tune. Does pastoral, that challenger of the life of power and influence, threaten us because it hits too close to home?

## Other Motives for Pastoral Bashing

In recent times, literary study has become less preoccupied with power, but other incentives to pastoral bashing remain. Foremost among them is class prejudice. Do we take seriously the passions and opinions of farm hands? Even Marxist critics accord high seriousness to genres populated by kings and dukes. A variant is city prejudice against the rural. Urban villains get more respectful attention than kindly rustics. Krieder sniffs at Audrey and William in *As You Like It*: "These bumpkins are actual shepherds whom, in delusion, the élite social groups are imitating; the crude life, gross manners, and dull wits of these uncouth simpletons represent the state of society to which courtly ladies and gentlemen, in their ignorance, believe they should like to revert."[40] We don't say aloud that Audrey and William are only rednecks, but if we aren't too worried about their being taken advantage of by a courtier, their rustic status—so unlike our own sophistication—is perhaps not wholly irrelevant.

Second, repugnance for pastoral is the unexamined reaction of a capitalist, consumer society to a land posited as indifferent to material goods. Poggioli heaps scorn on pastoral's uncommercial mentality: "Foremost among the passions that the pastoral opposes and exposes are those related to the misuse, or merely to the possession, of worldly goods"; it opposes to "an acquisitive society" the ideal of "contained self-sufficiency," ignoring "industry and trade."[41] For opposing or ignoring capitalist developments, which indeed were happening on its bucolic doorstep, pastoral is called reactionary. But pastoral's unworldliness is often strategic, a mode of critiquing the crass materialism of a protocapitalist society. Scorn for pastoral's anticapitalism emanates most obviously from the political and economic right; but even opponents of capitalism sometimes judge the countryside an ineffective platform from which to launch salvos against the ills of an urban society.

But why? Going outside one's own culture can be a precondition for analyzing its ills. Edward Said argues that Auerbach's exile in Turkey helped him see European culture with new eyes.[42] And if the outside place is imaginary, so much the better: the Renaissance took an interest in utopias and the possibility of perfect worlds existing out in space,[43] and during the sixteenth century, as Sandra Billington shows, "Misrule entertainments began to draw on the possibilities of *alterae terrae* for their settings, and the *mundus inversus* changed from a reductive to an improving concept."[44] Sir Thomas More, in *Utopia,* went outside Europe *and* reality to reach a standpoint from which to critique Tudor England's economic and legal ills. Pastoral realms can operate as such *alterae terrae.* And even when Tudor pastoral left the world of urban ills behind, there were plenty of economic ills in the country—enclosures, low agricultural wages, depressions in the textile industry, rural depopulation. Pastoral does not always ignore these—the low wages of Corin the shepherd are an issue in *As You Like It.*

A third root of antipastoralism: our workaholic age suffers entrenched resistance to relaxation. In its early days, the Protestant work ethic was still more countercurrent than mainstream: Elizabethans still celebrated some one hundred holidays a year. We moderns have a much worse case of work anxiety than they did. Early modern workers, who put in very long hours, understandably created fantasies of ease. Like the Land of Cockaigne, work-free pastures were a cherished dream, attended with much less guilt than we accord them. Renaissance comedy values sleep; sleeplessness is a plague suffered by *tragic* heroes. Berowne in *Love's Labor's Lost* is aghast at the King's proposed ascetic regimen, which curtails life's most agreeable activities: "O, these are barren tasks, too hard to keep, / Not to see ladies, study, fast, not sleep!" (1.1.47–48). Dogberry speaks for the spirit of comedy in roundly declaring, "I cannot see how sleeping should offend" (*Much Ado* 3.3.40–41). But listen to what modern critics say about ease. Poggioli sneers at the convention that "redeems [the shepherd] from the curse of work. Literary shepherds form an ideal kind of leisure class"; "the pastoral imagination exalts the pleasure principle at the expense of the reality principle."[45] Lindenbaum decrees that for Milton, "not even Eden is exempt from strictures against a life of uncomplicated ease and retirement which many in the English Renaissance found suspect."[46] But was it the Renaissance that found ease and retirement suspect, or is it us? Here the Yankee nationality of so many pastoral bashers (Cirillo, Daley, Helgerson, Montrose, Lindenbaum) is suggestive: Americans are infamous for having the longest work week and fewest holidays of any civilized nation on earth.

A grim suspicion of relaxation, inherited from Puritan forebears, disables pastoral for us. But the Renaissance didn't condemn shepherds for luxurious ease. Some pastoral writers saw shepherding as real work; others found it a life of ease but didn't condemn that. Shepherds in *The Shepheardes Calender* work long hours guarding sheep, suffer bitterly from winter while working outside, agonize about whether to take a break to enjoy the holiday sports of May; before they can relax enough to tell a moral fable, they must arrange for a lad to guard their flocks. It looks like work to me; the poem takes it seriously as an important responsibility, both in its literal agrarian sense and its allegorical sense as ministerial or governing duties. That looking after sheep isn't work is probably the attitude of those who have never tried looking after sheep; the same goes at the allegorical level, where shepherds represent bishops or secular administrators. Governing is hard work. Other pastoral writers do represent sheep-tending as a relatively easeful, stress-free life, and they aren't at all bothered by this. What with our high-pressure, high-achieving modern sensibility, such an attitude drives us crazy. Many charge that when pastoral shepherds (unlike real peasants) moon around feeling lovelorn or unproductively carping at the clergy, their fantasy world reproduces the idle court from which pastorals emanated—leisured aristocracy, disdainful of manual labor. Poggioli is outraged by this dream of bucolic idleness: "Wishful thinking is the weakest of all moral and religious resorts," he fulminates, and pastoral is but a "retirement to the periphery of life, an attempt to charm away the cares of the world through the sympathetic magic of a rustic disguise."[47] By all means, we must focus squarely on "the cares of the world" at every waking moment!

The issue is not only laziness but also a morally reprehensible evasion of an everyday reality full of trouble. Lindenbaum dubs pastoral a "realm of wish-fulfillment"; he disdains its wishing away of evil, its "miraculous events" such as "the immediate conversion of (Shakespearean) villains as soon as they enter a forest."[48] Pastoral is, in short, escapism.

Well, so what? The Renaissance, I think, wasn't nearly as hard on escapism as we are. If life is harsh and intolerable, why not escape? In Shakespearean comedy Orlando, Camillo, Pericles, and many others find happiness by running away from trouble. Human history is a tale of great escapes, from the biblical exodus to the great refugee migrations of our day, and escaping heroes populate myth and literature—the holy family's flight into Egypt, Aeneas's flight from Troy, the heroes of American literature forever lighting out for the territories. To assume that life is dreadful and then to dictate that we must stay where we are and face up to its full dreadfulness at all times, not even yielding to an occasional fantasy of escape, is bleak doctrine indeed. There is something disturbingly humorless, regimented, and censorious about views

that approve only of pastorals that manfully resist the escapist urge, decreeing
that the shepherd "is morally obligated to leave his pastoral bower."[49]

A fourth impetus to pastoral bashing is our valorization of public over
private life. Poggioli denounces pastoral's concern with private life as narcis-
sistic solipsism; Montrose equates private life with "the comforts and safety
of mediocrity."[50] Such devaluing of private life has gender implications: the
domestic sphere has long been constructed as female and great ideological
work has gone into confining women to the home. In this gendered sche-
ma, pastoral's opting out of the world of power and public life is effeminiz-
ing, emasculating. Pastoral, especially compared with epic or tragedy, has a
strongly valorized female presence—shepherdesses, milkmaids, shepherds in
love with lasses. The shepherd's job is a nurturing one, a kind of ovine baby-
sitting—and we all know how society values child care. Women writers, too,
were especially attracted to pastoral: as Josephine Roberts points out, "the
seventeenth century witnessed an . . . outpouring of pastoral writing by such
figures as Aemilia Lanyer, Mary Wroth, Elizabeth Brackley, Jane Cavendish,
An Collins, Margaret Cavendish, Katherine Philips, Elizabeth Wilmot, and
Aphra Behn."[51]

As the female is often devalued, some read pastoral love lyrics allegorically because they can't believe poets would attend to anything as lowly as
love—reading "private" allegorically as "public" seems to make it worthier of
their attention. Montrose deems the public life the only important life. That
Queen Elizabeth was female obscures what a masculine definition of the important life this is: most Renaissance women had no access to public careers.
*The Shepherd's Calender's* concerns, Montrose says, are "erotic desire and social
ambition," but erotic desire, inhabiter of a private realm, is really a displacement of ambition, which belongs to the public world. What seems to be love
is really politics; private is really public. The assumption is that public life
alone merits attention. Montrose extends this widely, finding "an encoding
principle that is undoubtedly operative in much of Elizabethan literature:
amorous motives displace or subsume forms of desire, frustration, and resentment other than the merely sexual."[52] Elizabethans would leap on a facile reduction of love to "the merely sexual"—Hamlet's "country matters"; but what
startles me is not the "sexual" so much as the "merely," which dismisses everything in life but politics and public striving, erasing at a stroke nearly every
woman from early modern history. It translates much Renaissance literature
too—the loves of Romeo and Juliet, Othello and Desdemona, the Duchess of
Malfi and Antonio, become politics in disguise; the merely sexual, the merely
private, is not important enough to be a subject of literature.

Helgerson shows how those with a gentleman's education were expected
to give up the youthful folly of writing poetry (especially love poetry) in favor of public service, but this expectation was hardly impossible to resist. As

Helgerson shows, Spenser during a life of public service never gave up poetry and love. Shakespeare had no gentleman's education, and his characters don't speak of an ideal of public service. Does anyone in Shakespeare counsel that it is anyone's *duty* to seek office? (Volumnia, perhaps; but does *Coriolanus* endorse her views?) Shakespeare presents political power more as a desired good than a public duty; only once in office do rulers discover that it isn't as much fun as in fairy tales. No one needs to urge others toward a duty of power: there are plenty of candidates. If one or two potential or former rulers shirk in a sheepcote or forest, nobody minds.

A fifth cultural obstacle is our preference for action over contemplation, related to the public/private issue because public was linked with action, private with inaction. Lindenbaum ascribes Sidney's alleged "opposition to pastoralism" to the "kind of Humanist training he had received, designed to prepare him for active service to his state and disposing him against any kind of life that might resemble inactivity."[53] Again, anxiety about ease: even though we inhabit the pastorally tinged groves of academe, for us contemplation (unless dignified by a title like basic research) doesn't seem like work. Hallett Smith shows how the Renaissance identified the generic poles of epic and pastoral with the active and contemplative lives;[54] the Renaissance usually (though not always) valued active over contemplative, and here we have outdone them. And again the gender issue—the active life has always been masculine, with women often seen as a drag on purposive activity.

The Renaissance placed literary genres on a spectrum from active to contemplative. The preference for action relegated pastoral to the bottom rung, but it was still a serious genre. Here is Sidney's hierarchy of genres from *The Defense of Poesy:* (1) heroical (i.e., epic); (2) lyric; (3) tragedy; (4) comedy; (5) satire; (6) iambic; (7) elegiac; (8) pastoral.[55] The first three genres belong to the sphere of action (lyrics here are songs praising memorable manly actions). Pastoral, the most reposeful, least action-packed genre, droops at the bottom of the ladder. But while Sidney places pastoral lowest among canonical genres, he defends it stoutly, and it is possible to see pastoral's low position not simply as a value judgment but also as a strategic location from which to make comment on the high.

Bakhtin posits that canonical genres have shadows: noncanonical genres (mimes, satyr plays) are their parodic doubles, with lower-class characters and diction that challenge the values of high literature.[56] We might also see a shadow effect within high literature itself. Genres in the lower half of Sidney's hierarchy are parodic doubles of genres in the upper half, standing apart from and commenting on the upper tetralogy's world of action, on its strivings after power, fame, glory, wealth, and love. Pastoral, I suggest, is a parodic double of epic. Writers often couple the two: Sidney shows how pastoral paints the epic strivings of Alexander the Great as amounting to no more than a pastoral singing match; Spenser, in the *October* eclogue, writes of a conflict between pastoral and epic. Pastoral looks at the launching of a thousand ships, at the death of Hector, at Cyclops, Sirens, battles, underworld journeys—and asks in its mood of repose what it's all worth. No wonder mighty men who strive and mighty epic poets feel compelled to push pastoral to the bottom of the generic heap.

Seeing pastoral as carnivalized epic—like carnival, it is ruled by lower-class characters and has the values of *otium* or holiday—sheds light on disagreements over the effectiveness of pastoral's critiques: when some critics see its assaults on the court as potentially effective while others think the court co-opted pastoral for its own uses, what we have is exactly the old "subversion/containment debate" visible in other manifestations of the carnival spirit. The difference is that with pastoral, those arguing for containment have gone almost unopposed by subversionists.

Finally, a Freudian take on our cultural resistance to pastoral might look closely at the long cultural practice wherein male authors wrote pastorals as a first step toward writing epics. In this career trajectory, pastoral occurs at the stage where a boy begins to break away from mother. Nurturing images persist—loving care for sheep—beside images of inaccessible, rejecting women (Rosalind in *The Shepheardes Calender*) or dead women (Dido in the same poem). Poets came of age by writing a pastoral, after which a strong poet might eventually work his way up to that task of manhood, epic. Steven Marx finds signs of coming-of-age rites in pastoral: youth/age conflict, isolation, instruction by elders.[57] If pastoral is partly a dream of childhood, of a world before Mother was lost, then the sternness with which (especially male) critics reject pastoral reflects the way male identity is formed by cutting itself off from Mother and a world of women. Examining responses to pastoral by male and female readers is beyond my scope here; but my impression is that the most vehement pastoral haters have been male. One of the best writers on pastoral, one sympathetic to its aims, is a woman, Annabel Patterson.[58] Montrose finds Spenser's dead Dido (a Queen figure, of course) as a "radical solution" to resentment of Elizabeth's authority: "kill the lady."[59] Boy children, subordinated poets, perhaps even literary critics, experience the matricidal urge to establish male identity by striking out at the Queen, at female Authority, at Mother.

If pastoral, then, speaks to some of our cherished fantasies and needs, it also triggers some of our cultural prejudices. Wildly popular in its own day, Renaissance pastoral has largely been assailed and discredited in later centuries. Nobody listens to this Cassandra among genres. Even in its most oppositional moments, it has been cast as a tool of the establishment. In a protocapitalist age, pastoral attacked the passion for worldly goods. In an urbanizing age, it celebrated country life. In an age of centralized government, it spoke for a decentering, centrifugal force. In an autocratic age, it challenged obsession with power. But this important cultural work has been disallowed.

Is it still possible to resist the tyranny of our own culture and rasp away encrustations of centuries of antipastoralism? Let us have another look at the pastoralism of *As You Like It*.

## Sermons in Stones and Good in Every Thing

Pastoral's challenge—sometimes overt, sometimes implicit in its withdrawal from the frantic world—is to the assumption that power, public life, hard work, and success are everything. *As You Like It* represents the world of power in Frederick's court as literally repulsive: having banished Duke Senior and his followers, Frederick now banishes Rosalind and sends away Oliver. Through that great tool of patriarchy, male competitive sport, the Duke enacts a public semiotics of power in a scenario of invader-repulsion: the populace is invited to combat Charles the wrestler. The Duke's tyranny betrays paranoia: he banishes Rosalind because her "silence and her patience / Speak to the people, and they pity her," seemingly fearful that "the people" might rise up on behalf of Rosalind and her father (1.3.79–81). Do those who come to wrestle Charles represent for the Duke the challenge he fears? Does he invite it precisely to demonstrate that he can defeat such challenges? Frederick and Le Beau call Orlando "the challenger," though when asked "have you challenged Charles the wrestler?" Orlando answers "No, he is the general challenger" (1.2.169–178). That the court issues a challenge and then feels *it* is being challenged betrays a paranoid insecurity that it tries to assuage by violence.

A pivot between the court and Oliver's household, Charles the wrestler flags the sibling competition that is festering in each place. Both paranoid tyrants, Duke Frederick and Oliver, project onto powerless siblings their own murderous impulses. Both keep the brother/competitor at bay by rustication—pushing him into a countryside that prejudice has encoded loathsome. Duke Frederick has pushed his brother Duke Senior into forest banishment, and Oliver has pushed his brother Orlando into a neglected life in a country home. Our initial view of the country is resentful: in the play's opening speech Orlando complains, "my brother keeps me rustically at home, or stays me here at home unkept; for call you that keeping for a gentleman of my birth, that differs not from the stalling of an ox? His horses are bred better. He lets me feed with his hinds" (1.1.3–18). A hind was a farm hand; it is appropriate that the word later occurs in its other meaning, "deer," for this passage superimposes peasant life on animal life. The servant Adam is pushed into the animal kingdom, called "old dog" (1.1.86). Frederick too has pushed his brother/competitor into the countryside, where he sleeps outside like an animal. Challengers must not rise; they are pushed out into the country, down among animals. The despised realm is that of peasants and animals, the world of shepherds: pastoral.

Rustication was a Tudor political punishment: noblemen fallen from grace often retreated to a country estate, remaining there under house arrest, an echo of the way pastoral poets were pushed out of the upper canon's polite society into a rustic underworld, for challenging the world of power. But Duke Senior's first speech defends country living and attacks the court, with its artificiality, danger, and competitiveness: "Hath not old custom made this life more sweet / Than that of *painted pomp*? Are not these woods / More free from *peril* than the *envious* court?" (2.1.2–4; emphasis mine). Any fear that his forest society might merely reproduce structures of authority, dominance, and competition of Frederick's court are immediately allayed by Duke Senior's style, a striking departure from Frederick's. By the time we meet Duke Senior in act 2, we are accustomed to Frederick's mode of communication, which like the speech of the early King Lear is performative, his speeches curt and peppered with commands ("Bear him away" [1.2.211]); "Dispatch you with your safest haste / And get you from our court" (1.3.39–40); "Open not thy lips" (1.3.80); "You, niece, provide yourself" (1.3.85); "Push him out of doors" (3.1.15). In act 1, the average length of Frederick's speeches is less than three lines, mainly short sentences of staccato monosyllables, His longest flight, a twelve-line speech in act 3, is clogged with curt imperatives: "*Look* to it: / *Find* out thy brother. / *Seek* him with candle; *bring* him dead or living / or *turn* thou no more / To seek a living in our territory" (3.1.4–8). Frederick's curt, choppy, commanding language recreates the haste and arbitrariness of his acts—banishing Rosalind, turning Orlando out of favor, dispatching Oliver and seizing his lands. In contrast, Duke Senior's first words are egalitarian: "Now, my co-mates and brothers in exile" (2.1.1). Where Frederick's typical utterances are commands, Duke Senior's are questions: "Hath not old custom made this life more sweet? . . . Are not these woods / More free from peril?" (2.1.2–4); "Shall we go and kill us venison?" (2.1.21); "What said Jaques? / Did he not moralize this spectacle?" (2.1.43–44,); "Did you leave him in this contemplation?" (2.1.64); "What would you have?" (2.7.101). Further, Duke Senior listens to the answers. Inquiring rather than commanding, he listens attentively to people, replacing Frederick's banishments and repulsions with hospitable welcomes: "Sit down and feed, and welcome to our table" (2.7.104). Speeches are longer than at court: Duke Senior's first is seventeen lines long, and his courteous questions elicit two unhurried nineteen-line answers. The verse grows relaxed and flowing, its complex sentences and run-on lines a relief after Frederick's tense verbal jabbings. The anthropomorphosed deer, prominent in this first forest scene, is an important reversal: in act 1 humans were pushed down into the animal kingdom, but in Arden, animals rise to the human level.

The exiles, suffering "the icy fang/ of the winter's wind" (2.1.6–7), are not luxuriating in sloth; but their life is wholesomely easeful. It is simply not the case that the court is presented as the brisk, responsible world of action, the country as an irresponsible life of ease: the court is paranoid, twitchy, a world of hasty political decisions, its frenetic pace neurotic, born of the knowledge that its power is illegitimate. Its pace is so brisk as to abrogate both justice and courtesy. The relaxed movement, language, and song in the play's pastoral world have the rhythm of a livable environment.

Pastoral, always the wealth-eschewing genre, was well placed to be oppositional to the new capitalism; in the early scenes, set in "a commercial world of exchange and transaction," even good characters speak its language: "Orlando's initial lines (1.1.1–27) are strewn with references to types of change and exchange; and some of the same terminology is repeated in Celia's protestation of love to Rosalind . . . (1.2.17–25). Such words as 'bequeathed,' 'will,' 'profit,' 'hired,' and 'gain' are particularly suggestive."[60] In Arden, such language ebbs.

One of Arden's lessons is how little the world of power matters once it is out of sight. A bracing effect of the time-honored human strategy of running away from trouble—escapism—is that nobody in the new land has *heard* of our local tyrant, which shows the world of power striving in a whole new light. Our exiles have arrived where nobody has heard of Duke Frederick's power grab. Corin never speaks of Frederick's usurpation, and the fact that Duke Senior, presumably his former ruler, is living in exile in the immediate neighborhood is something Corin never mentions.

Before his exile, was Duke Senior too a tense, paranoid, competitive ruler? Was it rustication that taught him patience, courtesy, humaneness, relaxation—a conversion as stunning as Frederick's later conversion? We can't know—the play doesn't say what he was like before. If the Duke hasn't changed, if he was always a good, humane man, it might make us uneasy about the vulnerability of patient, courteous, humane, relaxed rulers—but the play doesn't invite us to worry about this, as *The Tempest* does. It doesn't matter what kind of ruler Duke Senior was and will be: the play loses interest in that, and directs our attention elsewhere.

The segregation of *As You Like It*'s twelve pastureland scenes from its four forest scenes makes it possible to drop Duke Senior after act 2—he reappears only in the last scene. The play moves from the real court to the forest court, to a pastureland with no court. As the play progresses, politics, which comes on strong at first, is entirely replaced by love. Interest is deflected from public to private. Was Shakespeare's pretended interest in the lesser spheres of politics, power, and authority all along a sublimation of his real interest, love and women? To paraphrase Montrose, political motives here displace or subsume forms of desire, frustration, and resentment other than the merely political.

Strongly approving Rosalind's and Orlando's return to court, Lindenbaum declares, "the pastoral sojourn was not strictly necessary; the love of Rosalind and Orlando was well under way even at the troubled court,"[61] but their return to court isn't strictly necessary either. Theirs is a world-peopling comedic destiny; one can procreate anywhere. The move from court to country prefigures the shift in the play's center of gravity from politics to love. The exclusionary circle tyranny drew around itself when Frederick forbade Rosalind to come nearer than twenty miles (1.3.41–43) yields to an inclusive circle: Rosalind reigns in "the circle of this forest" (5.4.34). Though many will return to the court, the play doesn't stage the return but ends with *everyone* in Arden, Duke Frederick and all; the court as the play ends is entirely empty. The ending dwells not on resumption of power or return to responsible public service but on living happily ever after in a world of love. Country matters.

As Edward Said's Orientalist is outside the Orient, so most pastoral writers have been outside the country, assuming, like Orientalists, that city writers must represent the country, since it cannot represent itself.[62] But where Orientalism projects onto the Orient the West's disowned qualities, creating a worse self against which the West defines itself, pastoral does the opposite. Its rustic is an antienemy, an antiscapegoat: one on whom to project not one's most loathed but one's best qualities, or desired qualities. Like Browning's Setebos, a city writer created in country folk "things worthier than himself," made them "what himself would fain, in a manner, be." Pastoral writers created a standard against which to measure the value of contemporary striving. The potent pastoral dream recurred amid the Industrial Revolution, where it helped spawn Romanticism, and amid the malaise of the industrialized, urban twentieth century—there was a good deal of pastoralism in 1960s counterculture. However we mock and condemn it, pastoralism will likely keep reemerging, disquietingly indicting the way we live by holding out an ideal more attractive than the world we have created.

Country matters. Doesn't it?

## NOTES

1. Peter Lindenbaum, *Changing Landscapes: Anti-Pastoral Sentiment in the English Renaissance* (Athens: University of Georgia Press, 1986), 1, 3, 17.
2. A. Stuart Daley, "Where Are the Woods in *As You Like It*?" *Shakespeare Quarterly* 34 (1983): 176–177.
3. Lindenbaum, *Changing Landscapes,* 96.
4. Richard Helgerson, "The New Poet Presents Himself: Spenser and the Idea of a Literary Career," *PMLA* 93 (1978): 906.

5. A. Stuart Daley, "The Dispraise of the Country In *As You Like It*," *Shakespeare Quarterly* 36 (1985): 307.

6. Lindenbaum, *Changing Landscapes,* 110.

7. Albert Cirillo, "*As You Like It:* Pastoralism Gone Awry," *ELH* 38 (1971): 24.

8. Renato Poggioli, *The Oaten Flute: Essays on Pastoral Poetry and the Pastoral Ideal* (Cambridge: Harvard University Press, 1975), 1.

9. Daley, "Dispraise," 306–307, 311–312.

10. Lindenbaum, *Changing Landscapes,* 1.

11. Svetlana Makurenkova, "Intertextual Correspondences: The Pastoral in Marlowe, Raleigh, Shakespeare, and Donne," *in Russian Essays on Shakespeare and His Contemporaries,* ed. Alexandr Parfenov and Joseph G. Price (Newark: University of Delaware Press, 1998), 194.

12. William Shakespeare, *Complete Works,* ed. David Bevington, 4th ed. (Glenview, Ill.: Scott, Foresman, 1992), 292–325. All references to Shakespeare plays are to this edition.

13. Cirillo, "*As You Like it,*" 27.

14. Rawdon Wilson, "The Way to Arden: Attitudes Toward Time in *As You Like It,*" *Shakespeare Quarterly* 26 (1975): 22, 18.

15. Samuel Johnson, "Milton," in *Lives of the English Poets,* ed. Arthur Waugh (Oxford: Oxford University Press, 1906), 1:116.

16. W. W. Greg, *Pastoral Poetry and Pastoral Drama* (New York: Russell and Russell, 1959), 30, 87, 134, 69, 130, 135.

17. Lindenbaum, *Changing Landscapes,* 12.

18. Louis Montrose, "'The perfecte paterne of a Poete': The Poetics of Courtship in The *Shepheardes Calender,*" *Texas Studies in Literature and Language* 21 (1979): 49.

19. Poggioli, *The Oaten Flute,* 21.

20. P. V. Krieder, "Genial Literary Satire in the Forest of Arden," *Shakespeare Association Bulletin* 10 (1935): 21.

21. Lisa Robertson, "How Pastoral: A Manifesto," in *A Poetics of Criticism,* ed. Juliana Spahr, Mark Wallace, Kristin Prevallet, and Pam Rehm (Buffalo, N.Y.: Leave, 1994), 279.

22. Louis Montrose, "'Eliza, Queene of Shepheardes,' and the Pastoral of Power," *English Literary Renaissance* 10 (1980): 169, 180.

23. William Empson, *Some Versions of Pastoral* (London: Chatto and Windus, 1935), 11–12.

24. Karen O'Brien, "Imperial Georgic, 1660–1789," in *The Country and the City Revisited: England and the Politics of Culture, 1550–1850,* ed. Gerald MacLean, Donna Landry, and Joseph P. Ward (Cambridge: Cambridge University Press, 1999), 169.

25. George Puttenham, *The Art of English Poesy,* ed. Gladys Doidge Willcock and Alice Walker (Cambridge: Cambridge University Press, 1936), 38.

26. Alexander Barclay, *Eclogues* (London: P. Treveris, 1530; first published ca. 1523).

27. Edmund Spenser, *The Shepheardes Calender,* in *The Poetical Works of Edmund Spenser,* ed. J. C. Smith and E. De Selincourt (London: Oxford University Press, 1912).

28. Paul Alpers, "Pastoral and the Domain of Lyric in Spenser's *Shepheardes Calender*" in *Representing the English Renaissance,* ed. Stephen Greenblatt (Berkeley and Los Angeles: University of California Press, 1988), 166.

29. Montrose, "'The perfecte paterne of a Poete,'" 48.

30. Louis Montrose, "Interpreting Spenser's *February* Eclogue: Some Contexts and Implications," *Spenser Studies* 2 (1981): 70.

31. Alpers, "Pastoral and the Domain of Lyric," 166.

32. Montrose, "'The perfecte paterne,'" 47.

33. Louis Montrose, "Of Gentlemen and Shepherds: The Politics of Elizabethan Pastoral Form." *ELH* 50 (1983): 435.

34. Ibid., 439.

35. One refreshing exception is Robert Lane, who argues persuasively that Spenser's casting of *The Shepheardes Calender* in country dialect is a radical sociopolitical move in a milieu wherein theorists such as Puttenham were "establish[ing] the court and its elite as the standard in language use" (*"Shepheards Devises": Edmund Spenser's* Shepheardes Calender *and the Institutions of Elizabethan Society* [Athens: University of Georgia Press], 35).

36. Samuel Johnson, "Principles of Pastoral Poetry," in *The Rambler,* ed. S. C. Roberts (London: Dent, 1953), 84.

37. Johnson, "Milton," 116.

38. Montrose, "'The perfecte paterne,'" 54.

39. Anne Barton, "Perils of Historicism," Review of *Learning to Curse,* by Stephen Greenblatt, *New York Review of Books,* 28 March 1991, 55.

40. Krieder, "Genial Literary Satire," 213.

41. Poggioli, *The Oaten Flute,* 4–5.

42. Edward Said, *The World, the Text, and the Critic* (Cambridge: Harvard University Press, 1983), 5–9.

43. William Empson, "Donne the Space Man," in *William Empson: Essays on Renaissance Culture,* vol. 1, ed. John Haffenden (Cambridge: Cambridge University Press, 1993), 98.

44. Sandra Killington, *Mock Kings in Medieval Society and Renaissance Drama* (Oxford: Clarendon, 1991), 38.

45. Poggioli, *The Oaten Flute,* 6, 14.

46. Lindenbaum, *Changing Landscapes,* 18.

47. Poggioli, *The Oaten Flute,* 2, 11.

48. Lindenbaum, *Changing Landscapes,* 92.

49. Ibid., 5.

50. Montrose, "'The perfecte paterne,'" 49.

51. Josephine Roberts, "Deciphering Women's Pastoral: Coded Language in Wroth's *Love's Victory,*" in *Representing Women in Renaissance England,* ed. Claude J. Summers and Ted-Larry Pebworth (Columbia: University of Missouri Press, 1997), 163.

52. Montrose, "Of Gentlemen," 440.

53. Lindenbaum, *Changing Landscapes,* 19.

54. Hallett Smith, *Elizabethan Poetry: A Study in Conventions, Meaning, and Expression* (Cambridge: Harvard University Press, 1952), chap. 1.

55. *The Prose Works of Sir Philip Sidney,* ed. Albert Feuillerat (1912; reprint, Cambridge: Cambridge University Press, 1962), 3:3–46.

56. Mikhail Bakhtin, *The Dialogic Imagination,* ed. Michael Holquist, trans. Caryl Emerson and Michael Holquist (Austin: University of Texas Press, 1981).

57. Steven Marx, *Youth Against Age: Generational Strife in Renaissance Poetry, with Special Reference to Edmund Spenser's "The Shepheardes Calender"* (New York: Peter Lang, 1985), 208 ff.

58. See Annabel Patterson, *Pastoral and Ideology: Virgil to Valéry* (Berkeley and Los Angeles: University of California Press, 1987).

59. Montrose, "'The perfecte paterne,'" 54.

60. Wilson, "The Way to Arden," 20.

61. Lindenbaum, *Changing Landscapes,* 127.

62. Edward Said, *Orientalism* (New York: Pantheon, 1978), 8.

EMILY DETMER-GOEBEL

# *Agency and the Threat of Cuckoldry in* As You Like It *and* Merchant of Venice

It is a commonplace notion that Renaissance women give up power and agency when they marry. Prior to marriage, however, desirable single women seem to have limited power during courtship rituals; she is to be the gatekeeper to sexuality, to keep at bay both suitable and unsuitable men until consent can be granted by her and/or by her father. After marriage, each partner, at least in theory, gives up the right to refrain from sexual intimacy with the other; their consent to marriage created a "marriage debt" to the other. Similarly, their marriage oath insists on their giving up "all others" as well. What are we to make, then, of two likeable heroines such as Rosalind and Portia, each joking about the likelihood of taking a lover while married? Since one is not yet married and the other only recently so, these characters seem playfully to insist that they retain the single woman's power to consent (to a new sexual partner). Yet, instead of simply seeing these cuckold jokes as indicative of women's fearful power to "unman" the male characters by threat of cuckoldry, as Stephen Cohen has recently argued, I want to explore how these jokes highlight an agency patriarchy depends on. While the threat is there, these scenes, ironically, also confirm the need for married women's agency in matters of consent and withholding of consent.

In Act IV of *As You Like It*, Rosalind disguised as a man jests with Orlando about the chastity of a wife like his Rosalind. When Orlando asks

*Kentucky Philological Review,* Volume 20, Numbers 4–5 (March 2005): pp. 14–19. Copyright © 2005 Emily Detmer-Goebel.

47

Ganymede if Rosalind will have him, her answer is "Ay, and twenty such" (4.1.112). After the mock-marriage, she asks Orlando how long he would keep her, after he has "possessed her" (137). When he answers "For ever and a day," she tutors him: "Say 'a day,' without the 'ever'" because "Maids are May when they are maids, but the sky changes when they are wives" (138, 141). Rosalind councils that not only is it likely that wives will become even more willful after marriage, she goes as far as to suggest that a husband is likely to find his wife in his neighbor's bed (161). One standard reading of this scene is that Rosalind is testing Orlando.[1] Rosalind presents the nightmare version of a wife to discover Orlando's response. Is he tainted by the misogynist culture that sees women in this negative way? When Orlando responds that he doesn't believe his Rosalind could ever act this way, his faith in her is understood as a sign of their future happiness. In this reading, the jokes about cuckoldry allow her to test Orlando's inclination for misogyny at the same time that Rosalind's male disguise allows her to enter into the fraternal arena where joking about women's sexual will is routine.

Jacques and the lords establish a similar fraternal bond as they sing about the inevitability of "wear[ing] the horn" (4.2.11). While Rosalind's jests emphasize the power a wife has in a marriage, here the men embrace their lack of power. Louis Montrose sees Jacques's song as a moment of transformation in the play: "the threat that the power of insubordinate women poses to the authority of men is transformed into an occasion for affirming and celebrating patriarchy and fraternity" (50). Building on Montrose's observations, Cohen traces the rise and fall of what he sees as a short-lived phenomenon in which there is a positive "valorization of a community of cuckolds" (Cohen 15).

Cohen speculates that this emphasis on community or fraternity is in response to a male cultural anxiety surrounding a court headed by a powerful woman. Powerful woman characters like Rosalind (and Portia and Beatrice), so the argument goes, represent an Elizabethan political climate where men feel subordinate to singular, exceptional women like Queen Elizabeth. Cohen argues that the community of cuckolds acts as a kind of "psychological recompense" by "preservation of a fragile marginal space of male-solidarity" (15, 16). Even so, while these arguments explore how "fraternity can defend against the threat men feel from women" (Montrose 51), I find it interesting that the play does not spotlight powerful women as particularly threatening.

On the contrary, the most unruly woman in the forest seems to play at using this power. Rosalind's wit, intelligence, and good-natured jesting with herself as the "butt of her own jokes" about cuckoldry might disarm the audience, as Claire Claiborne Park has argued (108). Rather than a moment that feeds into a culture's fear of women's sexual appetite, Rosalind's assertions might be taken as only jest.[2] In addition to seeing this use of humor as a way to contain women's power, I want to suggest that the audience is invited to acknowledge a wife's power to put horns on her husband in order to admire her when she virtuously refrains front doing so. In other words, Rosalind's jests about what she might do underscore her choice. We are meant to agree with Orlando that his Rosalind will not cuckold him. Many recent commentators focus on the loss of power Rosalind experiences once she becomes a married woman. Rather than see Rosalind's marriage as a point when she gives up the power, we are invited to imagine that Rosalind retains agency. If she refrains from cuckolding Orlando, it is a choice rather than passive obedience (which would look more like . . . "I have no choice; it is my duty.")

Near the end of *The Merchant of Venice,* Portia, like Rosalind, seems to make reference to her agency when she jokes about cuckolding her new husband, Bassanio. I want to consider how her jokes about sleeping with the Doctor act as a reminder to Bassanio of the agency located in a woman's choice. Not just the choice of husband (which Portia's father takes front her), but also the choice to remain a chaste wife. But before we look at the cuckold jokes, I want first to explore the ways that *Merchant* seems to be a play that is particularly interested in the agency located in choice and consent.

Portia's father leaves a will that requires Portia's suitor to choose the correct casket, thereby, not allowing Portia a customary right of consent: I cannot choose one, nor refuse none" (1.2.25–26). Acting as a kind of dramatic foil, Jessica's consent to elope underscores the consent that Portia seems to lack about choosing a husband: While Portia's father fails to trust Portia with the important choice of a husband, Jessica clearly accepts her father's trust to protect their house and goods, only to abuse it when she chooses to steal away with Lorenzo. While we might focus on the fact that Shylock's comments seem to focus more on the actual goods that she steals, Shakespeare's audience would potentially find her elopement as a comment on a cultural debate regarding marriage and consent. Historians disagree to what degree early modern culture saw parental power of consent as absolute. Some modern historians such as Martin Ingram note that eloping couples were on the rise; he cites the numerous tracts written by both divine and secular commentators regarding the need for more legal intervention to protect parental rights (135). He also points to the Canons of 1597 and 1604 which attempt to shore up the need for parental consent without being absolute. Richard Greaves counters that "parental domination in the choice of marital partners is easily overstated, except for the nobility and gentry" (156). While it may be unclear how much the culture believes in the necessity of parental consent, the practice of marriage without a parent's consent seems to be widespread enough to cause a great deal of debate. I believe that what is at stake in this debate is not merely the question of parental versus individual rights to "make a marriage." I see this controversy connected to a shift in the perceived agency located in women's consent, both to marriage and to sex.

The tension between varying cultural attitudes about the agency located in women's consent can be examined in texts about the controversy over parental rights. John Stockwood, a religious writer whose tract on the subject is entitled *A Bartholmew Fairing for Parents . . . showing that children are not to marrie without the consent of their parentes* (1589) laments that the problem of clandestine marriage is such that it warrants a whole book. In the preface, he notes that such are the "miseries of our times" that the "too usual bad custom" of children marrying without the consent of their parents has been "laughed and jested at" (7). He calls for more legal control from magistrates for this "heinous and notorious crime . . . for all such disobedient and unruly children . . . have forestalled the right of their godly parents" (94). Apparently, it became common for couples to defend their elopement with the fact that the woman consented. Stockwood ridicules such defense, since it not only acts as a confession of the man's fault in attempting the "maiden" without parental consent, but also reveals how the "thief" caused the women to "cast off and sunder the cords of due obedience unto her father or mother . . . which the Lord will not suffer unrevenged" (91). Not surprisingly, Stockwood refuses to see this hypothetical woman's consent as valid and as representing her own choice to act; her consent is only a register of her own moral fault, caused by the said "thief." Using the language of theft recalls a time when rape and abduction were legally considered the same crime: a property crime. In these cases, as in Stockwood's example, a woman's consent did not authorize the abductor/seducer. Yet, that Stockwood has to make this argument shows that this narrow notion of women's consent is coming under pressure in early modern England.

One sign of this change can be seen in statute law. In 1558, for example, a new statute (4 & 5 Philip & Mary, cap 8) discussed the problem of proper-tied women under the age of 16 who were "secretly allured and wonne to contract matrimony with the said unthrifty and light personages" (*A Collection* 997). The historical importance of this statute relates to the absence of the conflated charge of rape. While this law is still concerned with marginalizing women's consent, it is significant that the age limit is 16. In other words, statute law seems to acknowledge the power of adult women's consent to make a bad marriage (with an "unthrifty or light" person). As we see in Stockwood's text, some people clearly want to grant more authority to a woman's act of consent. Shakespeare's Jessica seems to evoke the latter; her choice to become a "Christian and a loving wife" (2.3.21) grants her a kind of authority to act that goes beyond simple disobedience. This subplot shores up the concept of women's consent as relating to woman's agency.

At the heart of *The Merchant of Venice,* there are at least two other crucial acts of consent or withholding of consent: Antonio consents to be Bassanio's bond, and Shylock refuses to consent to accept the money and be merciful. In both of these moments it could be argued that the agency located in choice is constructed as an act of importance, and one that reveals something about the individual's integrity. Portia's cuckold jokes, on the other hand, have been seen as either moments that are unimportant or as moments when Portia seems to lose a bit of integrity. I'd like to challenge that interpretation.

Early in the play when Nerissa asks Portia what she thinks of the men who come to court, Portia jokes twice about cuckoldry. Since the Neapolitan prince is so enamored of horses, Portia jokes, "I am much afeard my lady his mother played false with a smith" (1.2.42–43). This seems an innocent joke at the Neapolitan prince's expense. Carol Cook, examining the relational structure of the cuckold jokes in *Much Ado About Nothing*, points out (with a little help from Freud) that the act of cuckolding makes the women the active and powerful player in the humiliation of her husband. The telling of the joke, on the other hand, can restore the male prerogative if told by a man to another man because it "returns the woman to silence and absence, her absence authorizing the male raconteur to represent her in accordance with particular male fantasies, and produces pleasure through male camaraderie" (189). Interestingly, this first cuckold joke is told by a woman to a woman. Here is does seem to establish Portia's power, but as a means to balance the traditional power of choosing a husband that has been stripped of her by her father's will.

While Portia lacks the power to choose or refuse who she might marry, she believes she still has some power. She tells Nerissa that if she were forced to marry someone she didn't care for, she says she would choose anew: "If I should marry him, I should marry twenty husbands" (1.2.60–61). Her joke reminds us that her consent matters. Forced to marry against her will, Portia suggests that she might feel inclined to choose new sexual partners. These early references to infidelity and cuckoldry evoke Portia's confidence and mastery of herself.

Yet, Shakespeare makes clear that Portia does indeed consent to Bassanio, even before he picks the correct casket: "One half of me is yours, the other half yours" (3.2.16). After he has won her, Bassanio also wants her consent "confirm'd, sign'd, [and] ratified by [her]" (148). As a way to assure him of her consent, she acknowledges her submission of her past power as a single woman who was "Queen" of herself (169). In this way, the play suggests a direct correlation between a wife's consent and her future fidelity.

Since the love between Bassanio and Portia is presented as mutual and given freely, Portia's taunts about her possible infidelity at the end of the play seem somewhat puzzling, given the harmony surrounding the three couples.[3] Lisa Jardine rightly points to the ambiguity surrounding both the above-mentioned speech of submission and the jokes about cuckoldry at the end of the play. She argues that the play "diffuses the tension" in Portia's power due to her education, wealth, and class, by making it clear that the riddle is revealed to be a story of non-cuckoldry. Jardine finds the husbands' threatened power "reinscribed" by the final joke of the play which affirms the "husband's ownership and control of his wife's 'ring'" (17). While I agree that patriarchal power is firmly in place at the end of the play, I want to consider how that power system does not depend on women feeling powerless.

Portia's ring accumulates more meaning than a symbol of her love, and as Karen Newman points out, when Bassanio gives it away, he "opens his marriage to the forces of disorder" (28). Portia seems to celebrate her own unruliness when she questions Bassanio about the ring. Once he admits that he gave it away to the lawyer that saved Antonio's life, she cautions her new husband:

> Let not that doctor e'er come near my house—
> Since he hath got the jewel that I loved,
> And that which you did swear to keep for me,
> I will become as liberal as you,
> I'll not deny him any thing I have,
> No, not my body, nor my husband's bed.
> Know him I shall, I am well sure of it. (5.1.223–229)

Portia seems to be telling Bassanio that by losing the ring, he loses the "male privileges the exchange of women and the rings insured" (Newman 31). In other words, if the ring represented a pledge of fidelity, the loss of the ring might authorize infidelity. She pretends that she might be powerless to the charms of the Doctor that was able to get the ring from Bassanio.

Portia then complicates the situation by presenting a riddle to Bassanio when she presents her ring. When he exclaims that it is the same ring he gave to the Doctor, Portia tells him: "I had it of him; pardon me Bassanio / For by this ring the doctor lay with me" (5.1.258–259). Doubling the riddle, Nerissa presents her ring which she says she got in a similar fashion. This joke is capped by Gratiano's quip: "What, we are cuckolds ere we have deserv'd it?" (5.1.265). Soon Portia reveals that what she says is true; she lay with the Doctor because she was the Doctor. Bassanio forgives and acknowledges her innocence with another play on the idea that Portia can sleep with the Doctor: "Sweet doctor, you shall be my bedfellow,— / When I am absent then lie with my wife." (5.1.284–285). Just as Bassanio must acknowledge that he and Antonio owe their safety to Portia's agency which took her to Venice in the guise of Balthazar, Bassanio also acknowledges that Portia's chastity is well protected by Portia herself when he is not nearby.

Newman persuasively argues that Portia's power is neither (limited to) the festive inversion of the "women on top" which is ultimately contained or that which reverses the cultural expectations of gender hierarchy. She claims the final scene interrogates the ways in which power is assigned in early modern sex/gender systems (33). Portia's playful threats don't register as the quid pro quo to which Gratiano's joke refers. Instead, her riddle mimics the riddle of women's consent in patriarchal culture. Husbands count on women defending themselves (their honor and their husband's honor) when they are not present by withholding consent from opportunities which present themselves. While one aspect of the culture uses humor to demonize women who fail to do so as whores, Shakespeare's comic heroines seem to celebrate the heroics of marriage by maintaining their chastity.[4]

Rosalind's and Portia's jokes about cuckolding their husbands can be read as contributing to the culture's understanding of women's agency. It's not that women are "naturally" whores as the misogynist thinkers insist, nor are they only temporarily "on top" as in the festive mood of the comedies. Instead, Rosalind and Portia represent patriarchy's celebration of married women's power to remain chaste. Patriarchy needs for women, both single and married, to feel empowered to withstand the persuasions of other men, even the persuasive Doctor.

Another woman in Shakespeare's canon jokes about cuckolding husbands. In *Othello*, Emilia playfully admits to Desdemona that she would cuckold her husband for "the whole world" (4.2.77). Reminiscent of Gratiano's quip about deserving to be cuckolded, Emilia claims that when women cheat, their husbands are to blame: "The ills we do, their ills instruct us so" (106). In striking contrast, Rosalind's and Portia's jokes acknowledge women's power to cuckold their husband. In the world of these plays, Rosalind and Portia can joke about women's power to cuckold, not because they are forced to look elsewhere for love and comfort, but because we in the audience believe they would refuse to do so. Rather than simply dramatizing the agency in granting consent to marry, these two plays glance at women's agency to grant consent (in the case of cuckoldry) or to withhold consent from men other than their husbands. In conclusion, let me point out that while I argue that the plays celebrate this agency, it should not be assumed that this is a proto-feminist stance. This agency is always circumscribed; this needful agency is in service of patriarchy and not a single or married woman's sexual autonomy.

## Notes

I would like to thank the Huntington Library fellowship program for providing funding for research at their excellent library.

1. Cf. Carol Thomas Neely's fascinating essay which demonstrates the relationship of Rosalind's behavior with early modern treatises about ways to cure lovesickness.

2. As many critics have explored, in the tragedies the power to choose anew (husband or sex partner) is presented as a real threat as we see in *Othello* or *The*

*Winter's Tale.* See also Jyotsna Singh's work on early modern treatises on the dangers of female sexuality.

3. See Barber who concludes "no other final scene is so completely without irony about the joys it celebrates" (187) Cf. Newman 32.

4. See Mary Beth Rose's analysis of the increasing role of love (and consent) and marriage in Protestant marriage tracts and in Shakespeare's plays.

## Works Cited

Barber, C. L. *Shakespeare Festive Comedy.* Princeton: Princeton University Press, 1959. Paperback Edition, 1972.

Cohen, Stephen. "No Assembly but Horn-beasts: The Process of Cuckoldry in Shakespeare Romantic Comedies," *Journal for Early Modern Cultural Studies* 4.2 (2004): 5–34.

*A Collection of Sundry Statutes.* Fardinando Pulton, ed. (London, 1640).

Cook, Carol. "The Sign and Semblance of her Honor: Reading Gender Difference in *Much Ado About Nothing*," *PMLA* 101 (1986): 186–202.

Cressy, David. *Birth, Marriage, & Death: Ritual, Religion, and the Life-Cycle in Tudor and Stuart England.* Oxford: Oxford University Press, 1997.

Greaves, Richard L., *Society and Religion in Elizabethan England.* Minneapolis: University of Minnesota Press, 1981.

Ingram, Martin. *Church Courts, Sex, and Marriage in England, 1570–1640.* Cambridge: Cambridge University Press, 1987.

Jardine, Lisa. "Cultural Confusion and Shakespeare's Learned Heroines: These are old paradoxes," *Shakespeare Quarterly* 38 (1987): 1–18.

Montrose, Louis. "The Place of a Brother in *As You Like It:* Social Process and Comic Form," *Shakespeare Quarterly* 32 (1981): 28–54.

Neely, Carol Thomas. "Lovesickness, Gender, and Subjectivity: *Twelfth Night* and *As You Like It*," *A Feminist Companion to Shakespeare.* Dympna Callaghan, ed. Oxford: Blackwell Publishers, 2000. 276–298.

Newman, Karen. "Portia's Ring: Unruly Women and Structures of Exchange in *The Merchant of Venice*," *Shakespeare Quarterly* 38 (1987): 19–33.

Park, Clara Claiborne. "As We Like It: How a Girl Can Be Smart and Still Popular," *The Women Part: Feminist Criticism of Shakespeare.* Carolyn Ruth Swift Lenz, Gayle Green, and Carol Thomas Neely, eds. Urbana: University of Illinois Press, 1980. 100–116.

Rose, Mary Beth. *The Expense of the Spirit: Love and Sexuality in English Renaissance Drama.* Ithaca: Cornell University Press, 1988.

Shakespeare, William. *The Complete Works of Shakespeare.* David Bevington, ed. 4e. New York: Longman, 1997.

Singh, Jyotsna. "The Interventions of History: Narratives of Sexuality," *The Wayward Sisters: Shakespeare and Feminist Politics.* D. Callaghan, L. Helms, J. Singh, eds. Oxford: Blackwell, 1994. 7–58.

Stockwood, John. *A Bartholmew Fairing for Parents . . . showing that children are not to marrie without the consent of their parentes.* London, 1589.

ELIZABETH RIVLIN

# *Mimetic Service in*
# The Two Gentlemen of Verona

*T*he *Two Gentlemen of Verona* includes one of William Shakespeare's most intensive considerations of servant characters and their relationships with masters. Thirteen of the twenty scenes in the First Folio *Two Gentlemen* feature speaking parts for servant characters, not including the scenes in which Julia appears disguised as a male page. At least in part because of the centrality of servant/master relationships, literary criticism through the centuries has not been kind to the early comedy.[1] While it is true that the servant-clown figures of Speed and Launce (not to mention the latter's infamous dog, Crab, about whom more later) have traditionally earned the lion's share of critical approbation, they have also been accused of distracting from the courtly love and friendship plot.[2] Buried within the traditional critique of *Two Gentlemen* as one of Shakespeare's immature efforts lies a critical anxiety about the prominent place the play assigns to servant characters.

Such criticisms ignore, however, the way in which Shakespeare maps servant/master relations onto bonds of romantic love and friendship, so that far from detracting from the play's conceptual unity, service underwrites its governing interest in how interpersonal relationships shape the individual subject. Specifically, servants and masters in *Two Gentlemen* share an imitative bond that consolidates broader concerns about the role of imitation in constructing social identity. The servant acts as his master's proxy, an iterative

*ELH*, Volume 72, Number 1 (2005): pp. 105–128. Copyright © 2005 The Johns Hopkins University Press.

function, but one that allows him to exploit the space between will and its fruition. The imitative relationship of servant and master is thus informed by difference as well as similitude. In this sense, it resonates with Philip Sidney's definition of poetic mimesis, but with the key proviso that Shakespeare portrays the mimetic function in a social register alien to Sidney's conception. It is in that social register that servants in *Two Gentlemen* highlight two conflicting ideas of elite identity. The first of these ideas, put into practice by the play's courtiers, suggests that imitations reproduce and naturalize homogenous social positions.[3] The second, based on performances of identity that are simultaneously imitative and creative, has its locus in domestic servants. In contrast to the circumscribed, fixed concept of the elite subject posed by the first model, the second model of identity proves heterogeneous and mutable, capable of accommodating the shifting influence of multiple social positions. By bringing the relation of servants and masters in *Two Gentlemen* to the forefront and discussing the theatrical and poetic connotations of mimesis, I argue that the mimetic servant/master dynamic both shows the potential of Renaissance servants to rearrange social identities and reflects on the capacity of Shakespeare's theater to generate and dismantle such identities.

*Two Gentlemen* redefines elite identity through the service of Julia, the gentlewoman who cross-dresses as a page boy in the final two acts. Although the play recognizes the pervasiveness of socially aspirant desires, Shakespeare displays little interest in the upward mobility of either domestic servants or courtiers. Rather, it is Julia's downward mobility that opens up a narrative of the elite subject achieving potency through subservience. In the heroine who "change[s] . . . shapes," Shakespeare offers a subject shaped not only by a gender differential, but also by the asymmetrical social dynamic of mistress and servant.[4] The implications of locating the servant's agency in an elite subject are twofold, for even as this move implies that members of the elite classes were best positioned to appropriate the servant's productive mimesis, it also demonstrates that such performances undercut the stability of social hierarchies by presenting elite identities as multifaceted and theatricalized. In other words, elite identities are no less performative and contingent than the service roles that these subjects at times assume.

To sharpen and clarify this conception of the elite subject, Shakespeare draws comparisons and contrasts between the personal and domestic functions of Launce, Speed, and Lucetta, and the courtly service in which Proteus and Valentine engage. Both forms hinge on imitation, but where the domestic servants deploy their potential to parody, alter, and sometimes produce their masters' wills, the courtiers strive to emulate their peers and rivals, putting an emphasis on similitude that ironically undercuts each courtier's desire for singularity. To illustrate this contrast, I will juxtapose scenes in which Julia's waiting woman Lucetta at once reflects and reconstructs Julia's desires with scenes where courtiers' self-replicating exchanges of wit largely cancel themselves out. I argue that Julia adapts the examples of domestic servants, and that the generativity and inclusivity of her imitations in turn offer Shakespeare's rebuttal to normative courtly identities that fail to admit of multiple and heterogeneous social constituents. To that end, I look closely at moments at which, in disguise as the page boy Sebastian, Julia's character invokes a heterogeneous identity formed through the interaction of servant and master personae.

The theatricality of servant/master mimesis also points outward to the social function of the Renaissance theater. As has been often noted, players in late sixteenth-century London were technically servants, who carried the livery of their companies' patrons—like any servants of a nobleman's household—in exchange for sponsorship and (when necessary) protection from the authorities.[5] And of course, they often played the parts of servants onstage. These lines of connection between players and servants bound together the institutions of service and theater, a bond that their common use of mimetic representation helped to cement on a conceptual level. Like the servants in *Two Gentlemen,* players in the theater operated as proxies, in the sense that their embodied performances interpreted and reconstituted the play text. If within the play's fictional world servants manipulate the space between their masters' will and its replication, the theater analogously exploited that space to promote a sense of a heterogeneous and changeable elite subject. Public theaters in London were sites of social diversity, and plays like *Two Gentlemen* dramatized to audiences a version of their own cross-class alliances and amalgamations.[6] Seen from this perspective, mimetic service in the play becomes an important mechanism for reflecting and projecting the changing social identities of playgoers. At the same time that *Two Gentlemen*'s metatheatricality calls attention to the aesthetic component of assuming a role in the social hierarchy, it demonstrates the theater's relevance to the creation and transformation of social identities. In sum, focusing on the category of service shows that subjectivity has both social and aesthetic registers and that these two registers prove mutually reinforcing.

An important context for the play's portrayal of mimetic service is the multiplicity of services in Renaissance England. "Servant" could mean not only "a personal or domestic attendant, one whose duty it is to wait upon his master or mistress," but more broadly, "one who is under the obligation to render certain services to, and to obey the orders of, a person or a body of persons, especially in return for wages or salary." This second definition encompasses those in governmental service or in service to a nobleman at court, as would be the case with Proteus and Valentine at the court of the Duke of Milan. Finally, "servant" refers to the courtly lover's submission to his mistress, "a professed love; one who is devoted to the service of a lady."[7]

Accordingly, Silvia's first word, addressed to Valentine, is "Servant!" (2.4.1). A single character in *Two Gentlemen* occupies the subject positions of both servant and master, sometimes simultaneously and sometimes in temporal sequence. Proteus, for example, is the master of Launce and servant to the Duke of Milan; he is also the servant of Julia and Silvia, though never at the same time. Even the lowly Launce is both servant and master, although he enacts his mastery parodically in scenes with his dog, Crab. And finally, Julia begins the play as mistress to Lucetta and later transforms herself into Proteus's servant boy. The classification of these roles under the broad rubric of service testifies to the ubiquity and fungibility of service roles in Elizabethan society, and consequently the difficulty of defining the servant in fixed, nonnegotiable terms.[8] The social flexibility of servants makes them fit agents in the play for interrogating established social categories.

The presumption, expressed in contemporary household and service manuals, was that, regardless of the nature of their service or their own social status, servants would imprint and enact the will of their masters.[9] For example, in *The Servants Dutie* (1613), Thomas Fosset states that the servant should have "no will of his owne, nor power over him selfe, but wholly to resign himselfe to the will of his Master, and this is to obey."[10] Fosset thus suggests that displaying and fulfilling the master's will is the servant's first duty. He must vacate his own will and desires, becoming, in this sense, more his master than himself. But Richard Barnett's study of William Cecil's (later Lord Burghley) household reveals the other side of servants' submission: "Their security was the health, success, and gratitude of their master. The story of these times is the tale of endless maneuver by people anxious to get what they could while they could from whomever they could."[11] Barnett's point here is that the mimetic function of servants was entirely compatible with self-interested motives. Through appropriating the master's interests, servants served themselves; or to put it another way, in looking after their own interests, servants served their masters as well. This characterization of Burghley's household gives a less sinister tint to Iago's assertions about serving Othello: "I follow him to serve my turn upon him," and, "In following him I follow but myself" (1.1.42, 58). Though Iago's intent is to give Othello only "shows of service," the historical context suggests that, at least in theory, masters' and servants' interests were inextricably bound.[12]

The mimetic imperative that underwrote Renaissance service encouraged the confusion of distinct class identities, as Barnett's case study suggests. Shakespeare makes this process explicit by putting both servants and masters in the position of imitator and, on a broader scale, by depicting mimesis as a force for production, rather than simply reproduction. The anthropologist Michael Taussig's discussion of colonial mimesis—the reciprocal imitations of the colonized subject and the colonizer—makes a case for the productive

properties of mimesis that also has explanatory power for the relation of servants and masters. Taussig's thesis is that colonized subjects resist their colo-
nizers by copying them. To enact this resistance, the copy alters the original
(the colonizer) even as it appears to reproduce it, turning the colonizer into a
copy of an altered copy.[13] Similarly, in *Two Gentlemen,* servants represent—in
the sense of reproducing to the world—their masters, at the same time as they
serve as their masters' representatives, distorting their intentions and creating
an altered pattern for them to follow.

But there are limitations to how fully Taussig's colonial model can account for servant/master mimesis. Whereas his analysis of "a space between"
the colonizing self and the colonized other presumes (and then deconstructs)
a dichotomy of self and other, Renaissance hierarchies operated on the principle of a social spectrum.[14] Although servants in the play may at first appear
as their masters' reflective others, they cannot realistically be disassociated
from the self, not least because many of the characters play both master and
servant. The pervasiveness of service in *Two Gentlemen* precludes any a priori
distinction between self and other and undercuts Taussig's insistence on an
oppressed underclass. Instead, for Julia to become a servant produces new
possibilities for elite subjectivity. That Julia's service is a performance complicates Taussig's argument that imitation is a source of political resistance. *Two
Gentlemen* seems rather to suggest that the performativity of service works
to the advantage of an elite subject such as Julia, who can manipulate the
servant's imitative faculty without facing the social restrictions of the domestic servant. At the same time, by making the positions of subordination
and mastery unstable and contingent, the play displays an interest in how
the mimetic performances of service affect and alter the elite subject who
undertakes them.

Domestic servants, who most obviously function as their masters' copies in the play, participate in a dialectical relationship with their masters that
puts copy and original in dialogue with one another. A few preliminary examples illustrate how the servant's reproductions disrupt the master's originary
authority and generate a sense of a mutually produced, even collaborative,
agency. In Act 1, scene 1, Proteus tries to prove to Speed, Valentine's servant,
that Valentine is the shepherd and Speed the sheep, an apparent affirmation
of the hierarchical separation between master and servant. But Speed's response, "Why then, my horns are his horns," stresses the inseparability of the
master's and servant's interests and effectively demotes Valentine to the status
of sheep, or worse, a cuckold (1.1.78). By Proteus's own logic, what belongs to
the servant belongs equally to the master. Later, Launce assigns a derogatory
epithet to Speed rather than to Valentine, then reverses himself: "Why, fool,
I meant not thee, I meant thy master" (2.5.41). Launce's apparent distinction
between servant and master is undercut by the ease with which the epithet is

transferred between them: master and servant are interchangeable referents. If anything, these moments in the text suggest that low qualities spread from domestic servants to their masters, so that the horns of the sheep are inflicted on the shepherd. Both passages invoke the extent to which domestic servants act as their masters' doubles and exemplars, the latter going against the grain of the servant's dependency on the master.

Lucetta and Julia's scenes in the first half of *Two Gentlemen* most clearly exhibit the mutual production of servant and mistress. Lucetta both provides the copy to her mistress's original and complicates the terms of that copying; it is not overstating the case, I think, to say that her mimetic functions make possible Julia's later adoption of mimetic service.[15] In this sense, the critic Charles Hallett was not far off the mark when he commented of Act I, scene 2 that "Shakespeare gives the maid the best lines."[16] This scene and subsequent ones give Lucetta a controlling position. She has intercepted Proteus's letter to Julia: "I being in the way / Did in your name receive it" (1.2.39–40). Though the apparent meaning is that she has subsumed herself in order to receive the letter in Julia's name, it is clear that Lucetta actually mediates between Julia and the letter. The servant's substitutability for her mistress is manifested in the stichomythia between them, which involves frequent plays on "I" and "you." When Julia asks, "What think'st thou of the fair Sir Eglamour?" Lucetta answers, "As of a knight well-spoken, neat, and fine, / But were I you, he never should be mine" (1.2.9–11). Her phrasing offers an alternative to Iago's statement: "Were I the Moor I would not be Iago" (1.1.57), which opposes the master's identity to the servant's. Where Iago betrays fear that Othello will subsume and consume him, Lucetta uses the conditional as an opportunity to rehearse an appropriate response for her mistress. The scene highlights the imagination's ability to double between the positions of mistress and servant.

The mirroring and symmetry of Julia and Lucetta's exchanges depend, paradoxically, on the asymmetry of their respective social roles. So, for example, Lucetta's claim that she is unworthy to pass judgment on Julia's suitors—"'Tis a passing shame / That I, unworthy body as I am, / Should censure thus on lovely gentlemen"—only highlights her continual interference (1.2.17–19). And later in the scene, the difference in Lucetta's and Julia's social degrees becomes the occasion for a series of musical puns that emphasize the essential harmony between servant and mistress. First, Lucetta says she is too low to respond to Proteus's letter, a sentiment Julia reinforces several times by chastising Lucetta for her sauciness and her "unruly bass," a pun on her base rank (1.2.97). But Lucetta also asserts that Julia needs "a mean to fill your song," indicating that their dialogue has produced its own kind of mean (1.2.96). The discrepancies that mark their "song" evoke the asymmetries of theatrical performance, where the identifications between common players, elite roles, and socially mixed audiences created heterogeneous forms. By the same token, their dialogue is imbued with an awareness of how the theatricality of the servant/master relationship creates bonds that cross social barriers.

The other scene featuring Lucetta and Julia reinforces the hierarchical, yet collaborative, nature of the servant/mistress relationship by showing that the servant's imitations are simultaneously reflective and generative. Thus, Lucetta takes the part of both text and author, evidenced in this passage where Julia implores her servant's help:

> Counsel, Lucetta. Gentle girl, assist me,
> And e'en in kind love I do conjure thee,
> Who art the table wherein all my thoughts
> Are visibly charactered and engraved,
> To lesson me, and tell me some good mean
> How with my honour I may undertake
> A journey to my loving Proteus.
>
> (2.7.1–7)

Whereas in Act 1, scene 2, Lucetta reveals that she has substituted for her mistress in receiving the letter from Proteus in Julia's name, here she becomes both a blank slate and a mirror reflecting the character(s) of Julia's thoughts. The image is appropriate, given that the primary meaning of "to character" was "to inscribe or write."[17] The notion of servant as conduit is further emphasized by the idea that Julia "conjure[s]" Lucetta, implying that the servant is a supernatural creature wholly at the master's bidding. But "to character" could also mean "to represent, symbolize, portray," which implies a more active role.[18] Accordingly, Lucetta is asked to "lesson" Julia, and in this sense to assume a pedagogical function. In the first acts, Julia is situated wholly within the court of Verona; she looks to Lucetta to access and interpret those wider spheres from which she is insulated because of her rank and gender. Ironically, the "table" of Lucetta's mind seems to write the letter of Julia's thoughts. The passage suggests that even as the servant offers a mimetic, textual record of her mistress's will, she also participates in authoring that text.

The interpretive, textualized functions that servants perform have been likened by Jonathan Goldberg and Richard Rambuss to the work of the Renaissance secretary, who records and disseminates his master's will. In arguing that character is conceived as a textual entity in *Two Gentlemen* and other Shakespearean plays, Goldberg asks if "when a letter transcribes intention, does it indite absent meaning?"[19] The suggestion is that while copying the writer's will, the letter constructs it. Lucetta embodies, conveys, and helps to author the letter.[20] In enacting these multiple roles, the servant or secretary becomes what Rambuss has termed a "simulacrum" of his master, and though Rambuss does not say so explicitly, a simulacrum that produces a new version of the master he duplicates and transcribes.[21] As Goldberg and Rambuss maintain, the text's otherness helps to determine the master's character. By this logic, Lucetta gives Julia a mimetic other through which Julia is enabled to reconstitute her self.

The mimetic servant/master relationship established in Act 2 catalyzes Julia's transformation in the second half of the play. Julia absorbs Lucetta's lessons in the power of mimetic service and puts them to practice in her own stint as servant. As noted earlier, it is suggestive that Shakespeare puts this tool in the hands of an elite subject who deliberately simulates a subordinate position. In this sense, Julia's performance at once echoes and complicates Frank Whigham's assertion that in Elizabethan England "movement across the gap between ruling and subject classes was becoming increasingly possible, and elite identity had begun to be a function of actions rather than of birth—to be achieved rather than ascribed."[22] Like Whigham's opportunistic subjects, Julia achieves her aims through service; unlike them, she moves down the social ladder to do so. Whigham's survey of courtesy literature does not account for the phenomenon of masked downward mobility, although in this play it functions as a platform for social agency. In the guise of a male servant, Julia gains opportunities for active modes of intervention in her own affairs.[23] And in her development, the otherness of the servant reveals itself to be illusory, for the other is continually reintegrated into the self of the mistress. And yet, while the servant/master relationship does not emerge as an oppositional one, the role of the servant offers a route of self-definition different from that pursued by either Whigham's or Shakespeare's ambitious courtiers.

*Two Gentlemen* sets Julia's unorthodox narrative of mobility against the more conventional social and romantic expectations associated with courtly service, revealing the inefficacy of such expectations.[24] One of the major assumptions supporting courtly service is that the budding courtier will "be in eye of every exercise / Worthy his youth and nobleness of birth" (1.3.32–33). In other words, courtly service figures as a series of performances that reveal native worth. Because these performances are presumed simply to reproduce qualities inherent to courtiers, they are intended to affirm the fixity and stability of preexisting social privilege.

In practice, however, the iterative function of courtly service exposes its own pitfalls, particularly in the arena of courtly love, which absorbs much of the attention of *Two Gentlemen*'s courtiers. The specific performances associated with courtly love shape service at the court of Milan and drive the rivalries that unfold between Valentine and Proteus, as well as among the supporting cast of courtiers. Courtly love offers another version of servant/master relationships, in that the lovers represent themselves as servants to a love object, the mistress. As suggested by the metamorphic and mimetic connotations of Proteus's name, however, these servants change their affections with some frequency, rendering the mistress a fungible commodity.[25] The fragility that underlies mastery is strongly articulated in the particular situation of the mistress of courtly love. Silvia, who is the object of court rivalries in Milan, enters with the imperative "Servant!" on her lips; but although her suitors assume obsequious stances, her lack of actual authority over them becomes quickly apparent, culminating in her near rape by Proteus.

Mimesis has an object in courtly love relationships different from that in other forms of service. While Lucetta's—and later Julia's—domestic service stresses the servant's mimetic influence over the master, the play's courtly servants direct their energies towards mimetic rivalry with their peers. Critics such as Jeffrey Masten and Lorna Hutson have suggested that, in this kind of scenario, the mistress acts as a vehicle for a reproductive process that occurs between and for men.[26] The lover's subordination to his courtly mistress is the thinnest of veils for his assertions of mastery.

The play undercuts such declarations of authority and control, however, for the nature of the game forces the courtiers into a single mold. Competition and emulation empty out identity and prove the flip side of Julia's increasingly dense subjectivity. This self-destructive mechanism becomes evident in a dialogue between Valentine and Thurio that shows the limits of the courtiership discourse. Like Lucetta and Julia, Valentine and Thurio verbally spar, but where mistress and servant suggest a sense of subjective interchange, the courtiers' dialogue reveals the irony of each character's desire to set himself apart within a system that enforces conformity. Thurio's retort to Valentine, "Sir, if you spend word for word with me, I shall make your wit bankrupt," has the unintended effect of revealing the bankruptcy of his own wit as well as Valentine's (2.4.36–37). As René Girard has argued, rivalry derives not from difference but from the similitude of desire, a similitude that threatens to eradicate distinct identities.[27] The more that the courtiers strive to outdo one another at the game of service, the less distinct from one another they become.[28]

Shakespeare implies, then, that the methods of self-promotion used in courtly service make impossible the singularity that might enable the courtier's success. In analyzing Thomas Wilson's *Arte of Rhetorique,* a prominent courtesy book of the period, Whigham says: "He effectively uncouples the existing order from transcendent authority and refounds it on the sheerly formal, learnable, vendible skills of persuasion."[29] While Whigham ascribes social domination to the use of courtly rhetoric, *Two Gentlemen* is preoccupied with the threat of self-nullification. The cliches of courtly service and love that absorb the play's courtiers void subjectivity of the productive irregularities that characterize cross-class mimesis. Singularity of character, the play suggests, may instead be a product of asymmetry and multiplicity.

In the wonderfully comic scenes that feature Launce, Shakespeare strengthens this critique of courtly service and illustrates the contrasting potential of domestic service. These scenes suggest that domestic service forces a reevaluation of the master's identity and reveals, in Proteus's case, its contingency and lack of self-sufficiency. While Lucetta serves as impromptu teacher to Julia, the clowns Launce and Speed educate the audience by parodically replicating their masters' social affectations. Launce, in particular, exposes and distorts Proteus's motives by making unsettling connections between his own brand of domestic service and Proteus's courtly service. This intertwining of servant and master may help to explain the traditional structuralist interpretation of the clowns. Harold Brooks, for example, tried to resolve the seeming incompatibility of servant and master plots by claiming that "the relation between the clown episodes and the leading themes, of love and friendship, becomes simpler to describe; for it rests quite evidently throughout on the principle of comic parallelism."[30] Parallelism implies narratives and issues that run alongside one another but that do not meet or influence one another; it does not account for how mimesis affects perceptions of the character who is imitated, breaking down the invisible barrier Brooks would construct between servant and master. Launce infects what Erich Auerbach called the "aesthetic dignity" of Shakespeare's noble characters and forces increased scrutiny of the substance—or more accurately, the insubstantiality—of Proteus's desires.[31]

Launce's two monologues display the options for creative imitation that the domestic attendant was well suited to exploit, while highlighting the theatrical artifice of the roles of servant and master. When Launce, aided by his unresponsive dog Crab, reenacts his leave-taking from his family, he echoes Proteus's overwrought departure from Julia, placing himself in the master's position. In his histrionic relationship with his dog/servant, Launce both recreates and parodies the servant's mimetically derived control over his master. The monologues function in dual fashion: they reinforce the dynamics of mimetic service elsewhere in the play, and they reduce the relation of servant and master to an absurd, animalistic one, alluding thereby to the falseness of claims that hierarchical distinctions are natural rather than performed.

That the roles of master and servant seem close to arbitrary in Launce's staging only enhances the sense of their performativity. Launce breezes through the casting of parts in his family melodrama until he comes to one of the central dramatic figures, "this cruel-hearted cur" Crab, whom he accuses of having "no more pity in him than a dog" (2.3.8–9). Launce thus analogizes a dog to a dog. But who, then, will play the dog?: "I am the dog. No, the dog is himself, and I am the dog. O, the dog is me, and I am myself" (2.3.18–20). This entanglement of identities initially involves Launce trying to play the dog (the faithless, heartless servant), and the dog playing himself. He then resolves it, or so he thinks, by having the dog stand in for him while he maintains his own identity. But Launce recognizes neither tautology nor contradiction in establishing an equivalence between himself and his alleged servant. On another level, the humor comes from the dog's passive resistance to being anything other than dog. Crab refuses to imitate, a defiance that becomes strikingly apparent in Launce's final, frustrated comment: "Now the dog all this while sheds not a tear nor speaks a word. But see how I lay the dust with my tears" (2.3.26–28). The dog is a stable fixture of nonrepresentation: both within the fiction and its representation, Crab does nothing and issues no response.[32] The metaphor of servant as dog breaks down at the point where the dog is most a dog and least a performer of a theatrical role.

Launce, on the other hand, finds himself deeply affected by the staged drama and responds mimetically—and tearfully—to his own plight. He foreshadows Julia/Sebastian's narration of an imaginary performance that makes its audience weep from feelings of sympathetic identification, an important moment to which I will return shortly. Launce and Julia are similar in that each responds to him or herself as if to another, an externality fostered by the doubled stance of servant and master. But it is also true that the hyperbolic, metatheatrical quality to Launce's maneuvering between subject positions makes an unsettling background to Julia's performance of downward mobility. Launce's parody insinuates that social roles and relationships emerge from performances that have no natural or stable basis; the only nonparticipant in the social world is Crab, who cannot act. By extension, the theatricality and performativity of social roles and relationships make it difficult to police elite identity, which Launce's comic improvisations have unmoored from its mode of self-authorization.

In staging his unseemly submission to his dog, Launce's second monologue exemplifies the breakdown of servant's and master's discrete identities. Launce gestures towards the effects on Proteus of his own insouciant role-playing: "When a man's servant shall play the cur with him, look you, it goes hard" (4.4.1.2). Launce has played the role of the cur with his master, outwitting and overstaging him, and now he finds himself mirroring his master's folly.[33] It turns out, actually, that he has done Proteus one better, having taken a literal whipping for his dog's transgressions. (Crab micturated in Silvia's dining chamber.) "How many masters would do this for his servant?" wonders Launce finally (4.4.25). Good question. Despite, or maybe because of, his resistance to playing the part of the faithful servant, Crab seems to gain an infectious mimetic power over Launce, forcing Launce into conformity with Crab's dogged dogginess. Launce's debasement in imitating his dog concretizes the process of debasement to which Proteus submits himself in the quest for dominance at court. Earlier, Launce has observed that his master "is a kind of a knave," an epithet that, in its connotations of a lowborn villain, might more predictably apply to a domestic servant than to a courtier (3.1.261).[34]

It seems appropriate, then, that as Proteus and the disguised Julia enter, bringing an end to Launce's clowning in this scene, Proteus is preoccupied with servants and service. Always alert to the advantages that service might bring, Proteus now seeks a servant—a reliable second self—to execute his desires in his name. Julia, disguised as the page boy Sebastian, fits the bill. This part of the scene also marks Launce's dismissal, enforced until he can recover Proteus's missing dog. Julia/Sebastian essentially replaces Launce. Like Cordelia and Lear's fool, Julia and Launce never interact, although they do briefly share the stage. (Ruth Nevo reads Launce as a "foil for Julia, his unconquerable good nature acting not to undercut but to underwrite Julia's 'folly.'")[35] Julia is in the unique position of playing both sides of the servant/master equation, not as Launce does through parodic role-playing, but by shifting her role from that of mistress in the earlier scenes with Lucetta (who conveniently disappears from the play after Act 2) to that of Proteus's servant and finally back to mistress in the final scene. She alone has the opportunity to play the role of the clever, creative domestic servant from the vantage point of elite privilege. Julia incorporates in her single, but also multiple, character the mimetic tension that animates relations between servants and their masters. As a result, Acts 4 and 5 press hard on questions about the interrelationship of subjectivity and social position.[36]

Proteus chooses to retain Sebastian's services because Sebastian appears at once to be a gentleman and a socially submissive youth. This coupling is important, as Proteus requires a servant with good breeding to be his proxy in wooing Silvia, but one who is also wholly subservient to his will. Thus, Proteus announces that he has retained Sebastian "chiefly for thy face and thy behaviour, / Which, if my augury deceive me not, / Witness good bringing up, fortune, and truth" (4.4.59–61). But he fails to notice that there is a contradiction between the proxy and reproductive aspects of the servant's status as copy. He orders Sebastian to deliver Julia's ring to Silvia, assuming the servant's mandate to act as a transparent replication of his master while ignoring the power of representation that accompanies the proxy role. His failure to recognize Julia in a male servant's clothes merely literalizes the broader problem facing masters who trust their servants to transcribe their wills and not to transform or alter them.

Thus, Proteus misreads the role his servant plays. Earlier in Act 4, Julia says that Proteus's betrayal has made her into a "shadow"; this self-characterization seems to fit her for the role of obedient servant, a shadow of her new master (4.2.121). Her very presence in Milan, however, bespeaks her decision to turn her shadowy position to advantage: "Alas, poor Proteus, thou hast entertained

/ A fox to be the shepherd of thy lambs," an echo of Speed and Valentine's riffing on sheep and shepherds, servants and masters (4.4.84–85). She reveals her intention to substitute her own agency for Proteus's, under cover of carrying out his wishes:

> I am my master's true-confirmèd love,
> But cannot be true servant to my master
> Unless I prove false traitor to myself.
> Yet will I woo for him, but yet so coldly
> As, heaven it knows, I would not have him speed.
>
> (4.4.96–100)

Unlike Silvia and her suitors, Julia resists folding love into a discourse of service; her true love for Proteus opposes itself to the figure of the true servant. She sees the conventional expectations attached to servitude as entailing a falseness to the self, in that the servant is obliged to make the master's desires her own. Julia's idea of service instead entails placing her own will and desires before those of Proteus, while simultaneously exploiting the entanglement of wills between servant and master. The passage shows Julia to be aware of the potential space that the servant's position as copy creates for her own desires and for a reshaping of those of Proteus.

The redevelopment of Julia's identity in Act 4 is defined not so much by the imposition of servant copy over mistress original, as by their mimetic interplay and joint performativity. As Proteus's emissary, she pays a visit to Silvia, who greets her with curiosity about Proteus's former lover, Julia herself. Julia as Sebastian is put in the strange position of discoursing about herself in the third person, detached from both her original subject position and the one she acts out here. Sebastian tells Silvia that he once played "the woman's part" in a Pentecost pageant: "And I was trimmed in Madam Julia's gown, / Which servèd me as fit, by all men's judgements, / As if the garment had been made for me" (4.4.153–155). At this moment, a Renaissance audience would have watched a boy actor playing a gentle female character disguised as a servant boy who conjures up a vision of himself as a gentlewoman. The context recalls Stephen Orgel's discussion of the fact that boy actors who played women onstage were also apprentices to older male actors. Orgel makes the point that economic, social, and erotic analogies linked male apprentices to women, so that in performing the woman's part the boy actor crystallized both homosexual and heterosexual modes of desire.[37] In evoking a performance that overlays the male servant and the female gentlewoman, Julia manipulates a recognition of their cultural equivalence, deploying the power of a transgendered image over male spectators ("by all men's judgements") and inviting a renewal of that erotic gaze. But Julia also makes herself an implicit spectator of Sebastian's performance, suggesting both an internalization and a mutuality of gaze: Julia watched Sebastian, and Sebastian watched Julia watching him, while all along the audience knows that Julia has fabricated the entire spectacle, and in this sense, that she watches both personae. As the mistress, she imitates the role of the servant, while as servant she envisions wearing the garment of her mistress. In effect, her self has become an evolving product of multiple performances and spectators.

To the erotics of this compound identity, one might add such a figure's potential to generate control from a position of submission and imitation. It is worth noting, along these lines, that the specific spectators in this scene, both imagined and actual, are women. Orgel has argued that "for a female audience ... to see the youth in skirts might be ... to see him not as a possessor or master, but as companionable and pliable and one of them."[38] But here, the servant boy also models for elite women the successful use of the mimetic faculty, activating frustrated desires. In contrast to Silvia, Julia recognizes that more influence resides in the role of servant than in the constricting part of a mistress of courtly love.

The pressure that service puts on conceptions of mastery and elite identity occurs in an explicitly theatrical context in Act 4, reinforcing the sense in which the theater allows identity to be packaged as a product of aestheticized representations and interpretations. Sebastian describes his participation in the Pentecost pageant in a way that underscores the collaboration between servant and mistress, and that simultaneously represents Proteus's interests in a fashion he had not intended:

> And at that time I made her weep agood,
> For I did play a lamentable part.
> Madam, 'twas Ariadne, passioning
> For Theseus' perjury and unjust flight;
> Which I so lively acted with my tears
> That my poor mistress, movèd therewithal,
> Wept bitterly; and would I might be dead
> If I in thought felt not her very sorrow.
>
> (4.4.157–164)

Sebastian so convincingly emotes that Julia is moved to imitate his tears; he, in turn, reacts to his mistress's response to the performance. As if all this were not sufficiently dense, the play within a play also moves Silvia, who mimetically enacts the same process as the imagined Julia: "Alas, poor lady, desolate and left. / I weep myself to think upon thy words" (4.4.166–167). The benefits of this staging for Julia are tangible. She usurps Proteus's authority and further alienates Silvia from Proteus. And she vents her self-pity while maintaining critical detachment, so that she incorporates female lamentation without being dominated by it. Julia's integration of servant and mistress taps into a theatrical and cultural resource that, by virtue of a shared position in the society, allows the servant's performance to articulate and translate the desires of the gentlewoman. The effect is one of a hall of mirrors, endlessly reflecting images of servant and mistress back onto themselves and confusing the discrete identity of each.

If Act 4, scene 4 marks a radical conjoining of service, performance, and subjectivity in Julia/Sebastian's character, *Two Gentlemen*'s last act seemingly restores Julia to her former position. Domestic servants are noticeably absent from the comic resolution hastily precipitated by Proteus's attempted rape of Silvia and then Valentine's proposed sacrifice of Silvia to Proteus.[39] The final show of social unity excludes characters outside of Valentine's elitist vision: "One feast, one house, one mutual happiness" (5.4.170). In the process, Julia's downward mobility is swiftly corrected, and she nominally returns to her status as a gentlewoman of the court and the beloved of Proteus. Accordingly, Masten has proposed that the ending reinforces "the homogeneity of the gentlemanly subject," inscribed through a network of homosocial relations.[40] Masten makes readers aware of how *Two Gentlemen* privileges and normalizes an explicitly male, erotic, and collaborative principle of social reproduction that tends to subsume heterosexual unions and render women invisible. While the play supports the argument that social imitation was a linchpin of Renaissance English subject formation, Masten's emphasis on reproduction underplays the role of transformative imitations that depend on cross-class difference. The courtier's drive to imitate his peers does imply a reproduction of the homogenous subject, but I have argued that Shakespeare presents such self-replications as portending nihilism rather than strengthening hegemonic structures. On the other hand, I have pointed out places in the play where servant/master mimesis opens the elite subject to heterogeneous social positions and undercuts its naturalized claims to authority and dominance.

For these reasons, it is significant that Julia ends the play still in the layered, now inseparable, roles of mistress and servant. Though she eventually falls silent, she does have extensive lines to speak in the scene and remains onstage throughout in her page boy's costume. The visible residue of her servant persona lingers, leaving her permanent identity in suspension. The closure of *Two Gentlemen* does not allow for a restabilization of elite identity; to the contrary, it underscores its contingency and insecurity. The male courtiers may well be celebrating the ostensible perpetuation of a tightly circumscribed courtly culture, but Julia's presence exposes the flimsiness of such claims and continues to pose an alternative.

Shakespeare's persistent emphasis on the performativity of identities reinforces the connection between servant/master relationships in *Two*

*Gentlemen* and theatrical mimesis. It also opens for consideration some of the distinctions between Shakespeare's use of mimesis and Sidney's influential definition in *The Defence of Poesy*. While I have argued that Shakespeare's construction of mimesis emphasizes the provisional and multiple nature of identity, Sidney's version rests on an assumption of characters' stability and permanence. For Sidney, "representing" and "counterfeiting" are closely intertwined aspects of imitating "the divine consideration of what may be and should be."[41] The transformation of the actual "brazen" world into a divinely imaged "golden world" is thus essential to the poet's mandate.[42] But Sidney is careful to stress that the transformative properties of mimesis do not apply to theatrical and social realms, where gratuitously "mingling kings and clowns" destroys a drama's decorum and thus its ability to depict the golden world.[43] Sidney's concept of representation depends on maintaining social and generic hierarchies that would seem to preclude servants' socially disruptive imitations.

Seen through the lens of *Two Gentlemen,* the Renaissance theater mediates between social and aesthetic realms, an intervention in which performances of service play an integral part. *The Defence of Poesy* suggests that plays, like other forms of poetry, deploy the transformative component of mimesis to simulate an ordered version of the social world; by contrast, *Two Gentlemen* suggests that the theater uses that transformative component to confuse further the categories of an already unidealized social world. The performativity that informs service in Shakespeare's play puts the theatrical production into contact with social practice in a way that Sidney's poetic theory seems unable (or unwilling) to compass. At the same time, theater's intermediary position reflects on the aesthetic implications of social roles. That is, Sidney's conception of mimesis as an artist's tool casts Julia's manipulation of the roles of servant and mistress as a form of artistic control.

Thus, while Sidney's theory denies any transaction between poetic mimesis and social imitation, it nevertheless makes it possible to conceive of servants' bodies and identities as a theater for refashioning elite identities. As envisaged in *The Two Gentlemen of Verona*, theater is first and foremost a conceptual space where aesthetic and social modes of representation converge. It is no accident, then, that at the moment of Julia and Silvia's charged interaction, when questions of social identity appear most dense and intractable, Shakespeare turns to a metatheatrical conceit to formulate the intertwined relationship of servant and mistress, suggesting both that the artifice of performance erodes the fixity and sanctity of social roles and that opportunity and power develop from exploiting this insecurity. In this early work of Shakespeare's, the theater is not only the site for experiments in the aesthetics of identity and the social effects of the aesthetic, but also and more importantly, the condition of possibility for such innovations.

# Notes

I would like to thank Susanne Wofford, whose seminar provided the genesis for this essay, and who was instrumental in nurturing it through many stages of development. Thank you, too, to the anonymous journal readers whose comments and suggestions helped to tighten the argument considerably. And special thanks go to Michael LeMahieu, for his willingness to read multiple drafts and his always keen insights.

　　1. The critical history of *The Two Gentlemen of Verona* has not been especially glorious. Alexander Pope, writing in 1725, helped instigate the tradition of doubting that Shakespeare could be fully responsible for "the lowest and most trifling conceits" expressed in the play. See Pope's *Preface to Shakespear's Work* (1725), excerpted in *Shakespeare: Early Comedies,* Casebook Series, ed. Pamela Mason (London: Macmillan, 1995), 141. Pope excuses Shakespeare from full responsibility for less desirable scenes in the play by asserting that several were "interpolated by the Players." Arthur Quiller-Couch, writing in 1921, displays even more incredulity in pronouncing the final scene to be "vitiated . . . by a flaw too unnatural to be charged upon Shakespeare" (*Shakespeare: Early Comedies,* 144).

　　Until the last twenty years, even more common was the tendency to explain, and to some extent excuse, the deficiencies of *The Two Gentlemen of Verona* on the grounds that it belongs to the category of Shakespeare's early comedies; clearly, in the words of Stanley Wells, "he still has much to learn about the mechanics of his craft" (Wells, "The Failure of *The Two Gentlemen of Verona,*" in *Shakespeare: Early Comedies,* 169). See also H. B. Charlton in *Shakespeare: Early Comedies,* 145–147; Harold F. Brooks, "Two Clowns in a Comedy (To Say Nothing of the Dog): Speed, Launce (and Crab) in *The Two Gentlemen of Verona,*" in *Shakespeare: Early Comedies,* 149–159; Inga-Stina Ewbank, "'Were Man but Constant, He Were Perfect': Constancy and Consistency in *The Two Gentlemen of Verona,*" in *Two Gentlemen of Verona: Critical Essays,* ed. June Schlueter (New York: Garland, 1996), 91–132; Charles A. Hallett, "'Metamorphosing Proteus': Reversal Strategies in *The Two Gentlemen of Verona,*" in *Two Gentlemen of Verona: Critical Essays,* 153–177; and Ruth Nevo, *Comic Transformations in Shakespeare* (New York: Methuen, 1980), 53–67, esp. 66.

　　2. Hallett complains about 1.1, for instance, that "an audience will be far more aware of Speed's wit than of Proteus's purpose and, further, that the less important character, Speed, seems to dominate to the point of obscuring the love plot" (Hallett, 160). He extends this critique to the play's overall structure, arguing that characters' motivational reversals, necessary for dramatic effect, are repeatedly undercut by the intrusion of low comedy and comic characters. These kinds of structural or spatial analogies have frequently been used to convey the usurpation of the high love plot in *Two Gentlemen* by low clowning and comedy. Charlton, for example, claimed that Launce "has no real right within the play, except that gentlemen must have servants, and Elizabethan audiences must have clowns. But coming in thus by a back-door, he earns an unexpected importance in the play" (Charlton, 145). Charlton thus implies that servants and clowning comedy belong together, outside the play; even the image of Launce entering through the "back-door," as through the servants' entrance, bespeaks his auxiliary, subordinate status.

　　3. My work on mimesis in service relationships represents an extension of Jeffrey Masten's important discussion of the mirroring structure of male friendship

and collaboration in *Two Gentlemen*. Masten's has been one of the primary voices advocating for a radical rereading of the play's treatment of power, sexuality, and intimacy. Although homosocial and erotic relationships feature less prominently in my argument, I see my essay as producing insights complementary to Masten's, in that I too am interested in the tension between social reproducability and difference in the construction of Renaissance subjectivities. Further, service and friendship are closely connected in Renaissance discourses, as Masten suggests. Where I differ is in the efficacy and value that I believe Shakespeare assigns to irreducible social differences, as exemplified in the play's servant/master relationships. See Masten, *Textual Intercourse: Collaboration, Authorship, and Sexualities in Renaissance Drama* (Cambridge: Cambridge University Press, 1997), 37–48; and Masten, "*The Two Gentlemen of Verona:* A Modern Perspective," *The Two Gentlemen of Verona*, The New Folger Library Shakespeare, ed. Barbara A. Mowat and Paul Werstine (New York: Washington Square Press/Pocket Books, 1999), 199–221.

    4. William Shakespeare, *The Two Gentlemen of Verona*, in *The Norton Shakespeare*, ed. Stephen Greenblatt and others (New York: Norton, 1997), 5.4.107. All references to this text and other plays by Shakespeare are hereafter cited parenthetically by act, scene, and line numbers.

    5. See Andrew Gurr, *The Shakespearean Stage, 1574–1642*, 3rd ed. (Cambridge: Cambridge University Press, 1992), 29. See also Michael Neill's discussion of the similarities between players and marginalized servants, both of whom he says had "a sense of shared proteanism" as well as an ambivalent relation to authority ("Servant Obedience and Master Sins: Shakespeare and the Bonds of Service," *Putting History to the Question: Power, Politics, and Society in English Renaissance Drama* [New York: Columbia University Press, 2000], 18). Gurr and Neill point out that players were not bound to their patrons in quite the same way as traditional servants, the usual practice being for companies to use their own judgment in running their commercial affairs and making artistic choices, relying on their patrons only in rather unusual circumstances.

    6. Jean-Christophe Agnew says that the theater was perceived as both describing and "anatomiz[ing]" changing social forms and relationships, another way of expressing the double-sided nature of theatrical mimesis. *Worlds Apart: The Market and the Theater in Anglo-American Thought, 1550–1750* (Cambridge: Cambridge University Press, 1986), 59.

    7. *OED*, definitions 1, 2a, and 4b.

    8. Mark Thornton Burnett has completed the most extensive study to date of literary representations of servants in Renaissance England, covering apprentices, tradesmen, male domestic servants, maidservants, and servants in the noble household. Burnett emphasizes the expansiveness and lack of precision that attended designations of servant (*Masters and Servants in English Renaissance Drama and Culture: Authority and Obedience* [New York: St. Martin's Press, 1997], 2). Neill also points to the universality of service in the Renaissance as "a defining condition of social order" (19).

    9. Susan Dwyer Amussen gives an account of the reciprocal duties that in Elizabethan society were standard for master and servant to fulfill. In return for the servant displaying the kind of obedience a child owes a parent, the master was expected to protect the servant and provide "a moral and practical education" (*An Ordered Society: Gender and Class in Early Modern England* [Oxford: Blackwell, 1988], 40). It should be noted, however, that Amussen concentrates mostly on middle-class

English families of the period rather than the noble households portrayed in *Two Gentlemen*.

10. Thomas Fosset, *The Servants Dutie, or the Calling and Condition of Servants* (London, 1613), 22.

11. Richard C. Barnett, *Place, Profit, and Power: A Study of the Servants of William Cecil, Elizabethan Statesman* (Chapel Hill: University of North Carolina Press, 1969), 11. Gentlemen servants were a common feature of noble households in the Renaissance. Burnett devotes the final chapter of his study to the figures of the steward and gentleman-usher who oversaw households and often had intimate access to the noble master and mistress.

12. Barnett, 52.

13. Michael Taussig draws on ethnographic evidence from indigenous cultures to theorize mimesis in a colonial context. The mimetic similarity of the original (the colonizer) and copy (the colonized) hinges on the contact between them: "I want to dwell on *this notion of the copy, in magical practice, affecting the original to such a degree that the representation shares in or acquires the properties of the represented.*" *Mimesis and Alterity: A Particular History of the Senses* (New York: Routledge, 1993), 47–48.

14. Taussig, 78. See also 71.

15. It is not clear how great a disparity of rank exists between Julia and Lucetta. While Lucetta seems to perform at least some of the duties of a domestic servant, the First Folio designates her "waiting-woman to Julia." This description could indicate the comparatively genteel social status of a lady-in-waiting, similar to Maria's (listed as "Olivia's gentlewoman") in *Twelfth Night*. The *OED* defines "waiting-woman," first in use in the sixteenth century, as "a female servant, or personal attendant," which does not clear up the ambiguity, insofar as personal attendants to the aristocracy could be drawn from the ranks of the relatively genteel, including, for example, poorer but still wellborn relatives. The haziness of their respective social positions resembles that which Burnett ascribes to an early seventeenth-century account of Lady Magdalen, Viscountess Montague's youthful service to the Countess of Bedford. That account "identifies the place of a 'gentlewoman' and a 'chambermaid' in the household hierarchies" but then "goes on to blur the distinctions between the two offices as part of its commendatory imperative" (126). The uncertainty over Lucetta's status reinforces the tension between hierarchical distinction and emotional intimacy in servant/master relationships.

16. Hallett, 162.

17. *OED*, definition 1. For similar readings of the image of Lucetta as "table," see Frederick Kiefer, "Love Letters in *The Two Gentlemen of Verona*," in *Two Gentlemen of Verona: Critical Essays*, 133–152, esp. 149; and Jonathan Goldberg, "Shakespearean Characters: The Generation of Silvia," *Shakespeare's Hand* (Minneapolis: University of Minnesota Press, 2003), 10–47, esp. 25.

18. *OED*, definition 2.

19. Goldberg, 24.

20. Goldberg makes this point about Lucetta by observing that "it is her character to be a letter, to bear the letter, and to return what is inscribed as a lesson" (25). Goldberg argues for the inseparability of character in Renaissance drama from textual inscription. In related fashion, an essay by Elizabeth Pittenger explores the correlations between the failure of the ideal of Shakespeare's originary text and the failure of human transmissions of knowledge. "Dispatch Quickly: The Mechanical Reproduction of Pages," *Shakespeare Quarterly* 42 (1991): 389–408. Both Goldberg

and Pittenger are interested in the materiality and textualization of Renaissance character. Their theories offer a comparison to the theatrical constructions of character that I take up in this essay and, to me, suggest some of the connections between the mimetic mediums of text and drama, not least the ways in which Shakespeare integrates elements of both.

21. Richard Rambuss, "The Secretary's Study: The Secret Designs of the *Shepheardes Calender*," *ELH* 59 (1992): 319.

22. Frank Whigham, *Ambition and Privilege: The Social Tropes of Elizabethan Courtesy Theory* (Berkeley: University of California Press, 1984), 5. On what he argues is the increasing weight placed on worth over birth in the early modern period see Michael McKeon, *The Origins of the English Novel, 1600–1740* (Baltimore: The Johns Hopkins University Press, 1987), 131–175. For accounts of changing patterns of social mobility, especially increases in the size of the gentry and nobility, see David Underdown, *Revel, Riot, and Rebellion: Popular Politics and Culture in England 1603–1660* (Oxford: Clarendon Press, 1985); and Keith Wrightson, *English Society 1580–1680* (New Brunswick: Rutgers University Press, 1982).

23. An analogous phenomenon consisted of courtiers masquing as shepherds and other rustic folk in Renaissance pastoral entertainments performed for the Queen. Louis Montrose has explored this subject in "Of Gentlemen and Shepherds: The Politics of Elizabethan Pastoral Form," *ELH* 50 (1983): 415–459. He argues that such performances were informed by a tension between affirming gentility and undercutting it, a similar dynamic to that which I see animating Julia's disguise as servant.

24. Camille Wells Slights reads *Two Gentlemen* as critiquing Proteus and Valentine's corruption of the courtly ideal. It seems to me more accurate to say that the play critiques the ideal of courtly service itself ("Common Courtesy in *The Two Gentlemen of Verona*," in *Shakespeare's Comic Commonwealths* [Toronto: University of Toronto Press, 1993], 57–73, esp. 67–69). Also see Ewbank, who views the play as walking a fine line between celebrating and criticizing the world of the courtly romance (Ewbank, 107–108).

25. Proteus appears in book 4 of Homer's *Odyssey*, as well as in Virgil's *Georgics*. In the *Odyssey*, Proteus is a wily old sea god who will not yield his knowledge until he is forcibly prevented from changing shapes. There is a compulsive quality to his shape-shifting that resonates with Shakespeare's Proteus, who continually reconstitutes himself in the image of whoever is closest to him. But where Homer's Proteus assumes the likeness of a leopard, a tree, and other non-human entities, Shakespeare's Proteus takes on the likeness of other characters, a form of mimesis that seems to trap both him and his objects. See *The Odyssey*, trans. Robert Fitzgerald (New York: Vintage, 1990), 4.377–614.

26. Masten argues that *Two Gentlemen* features "a homosocial circuit of writing" in which women act as pretexts and texts, but not as agents of circulation (*Textual Intercourse*, 43). In a similar vein, Lorna Hutson makes the case that the English humanist program trafficked in women to propagate a male line of property and capital. See her *The Usurer's Daughter: Male Friendship and Fictions of Women in Sixteenth-Century England* (London: Routledge, 1994), 64–76.

27. René Girard's theory stresses the triangularity of mimetic desire, a structure in which the female character—here, Silvia—mediates desires of her male suitors which are fundamentally directed towards one another. Like other readers of the play, Girard is not very attentive to moments where this symmetrical mirroring

fractures and allows an asymmetrical dynamic to take shape. See Girard, "Love Delights in Praises: A Reading of *The Two Gentlemen of Verona*," *Philosophy and Literature* 13 (1989): 231–247. See also Girard, *Deceit, Desire, and the Novel: Self and Other in Literary Structure*, trans. Yvonne Freccero (Baltimore: The Johns Hopkins University Press, 1965).

28. At first glance, the minor character Eglamour seems to present an exception to the norms of courtly service, which it turns out he does only insofar as he embodies a different cliche of service: the faithful servant. He represents himself to Silvia as "your servant and your friend. / One that attends your ladyship's command" (4.3.4–5). Trapped in this construct of unreflective obedience much as Proteus, Valentine, and Thurio are in their own, Eglamour lacks the generative and creative properties possessed by domestic servants in the play. Where they exploit the space implied by the mimetic relationship, Eglamour closes off that space, collapsing imitation into reproduction. He seems constitutionally incapable of giving the kind of instruction to his mistress in which Lucetta, Launce, and Julia herself specialize, and perhaps as a result, Silvia ends up in the forest in the company of outlaws, at the point of being raped by Proteus. Eglamour's version of courtly service proves an unsatisfactory alternative, as empty in its mechanical courtesy as are the other courtiers' frenetic machinations.

29. Whigham, 3.

30. Brooks, in *Shakespeare: Early Comedies*, 153.

31. Erich Auerbach, *Mimesis: The Representation of Reality in Western Literature*, trans. Willard R. Trask (Princeton: Princeton University Press, 1953), 314. Auerbach's seminal work contains a chapter on Shakespeare ("The Weary Prince") that concentrates on the plots and generic characteristics consistently associated with highborn characters in the tragedies. Although Auerbach is alert to the "stylistic lapses" of noble characters in Shakespeare's plays, he posits these occurrences merely as exceptions to the general rule that Shakespeare is not interested in "everyday" or common characters and subjects (328). William Empson's important study of double plotting in Renaissance literature, *Some Versions of Pastoral* (London: Chatto and Windus, 1935), 27–86, esp. 28, is more interested in the "comic interlude" and its impact on the structure of the whole. But Empson anticipates Auerbach's tendency to make strong separations between the main and subplots. Both Auerbach and Empson validate, even if inadvertently, the bifurcation of class and representation they analyze.

32. The commentary on mimetic representation becomes more complex when we factor in how Crab might be represented in performance. As John Timpane suggests, there is comic potential both in the use of a live dog and in the substitution of a stuffed animal. See Timpane, "'I Am but a Foole, Looke You': Launce and the Social Functions of Humor," *Two Gentlemen of Verona: Critical Essays*, 189–211, esp. 202. In a discussion with the director and actors at the Newberry Library in November 2000, following a production of *Two Gentlemen* by the Chicago Shakespeare Repertory Theater Company, it was explained that the owners of the dog playing Crab had been at the previous evening's performance, causing the dog to bark unpredictably during his time onstage and reinforcing Crab's failure to play his part. The audience found his bad behavior hilarious. In this context, one might consider Wittgenstein's question: "Why can't a dog simulate pain? Is he too honest?" (*Philosophical Investigations*, 3rd ed., trans. G. E. M. Anscombe [New York: Macmillan, 1958], §250.) On the other hand, in a production in which a prop

stands in for the dog, the prop's lack of sentience (similar to the shoes, hat, and staff) could also be very funny, emphasizing Crab's obdurate refusal to signify in literal fashion.

33. Timpane writes of the effect on an audience of this scene that "[d]og is king, servant is still servant, and master becomes—irrelevant" (198). This is a somewhat useful way of putting it, but Timpane is thinking mostly of Proteus as master, even in this scene where Launce so clearly serves as the proxy master.

34. "Knave" could refer to both base behavior and low birth, the latter particularly attached to "a male servant or menial in general" (*OED*, definitions 2, 3). In Act 2, scene 2 of *King Lear*, Kent deliberately evokes both senses when he (repeatedly) calls Oswald a knave.

35. Nevo, 62.

36. Most critics who have discussed the cross-dressing of Shakespeare's comic heroines have taken gender, rather than social status, to be the primary object of metamorphosis. Several critics have suggested, however, that cross-dressing maps the dependency of boys onto that of women, amplifying the eroticism of their shared submissive position in the culture, but also gesturing towards the constructedness of this position. See Lisa Jardine, "'As Boys and Women Are for the Most Part Cattle of This Colour': Female Roles and Elizabethan Eroticism," *Still Harping on Daughters: Women and Drama in the Age of Shakespeare* (Sussex: Harvester Press, 1983), 9–36; and Jardine, "Twins and Travesties: Gender, Dependency and Sexual Availability in *Twelfth Night*," in *Erotic Politics: Desire on the Renaissance Stage*, ed. Susan Zimmerman (New York: Routledge, 1992), 27–38; Stephen Orgel, "Call Me Ganymede," in *Impersonations: The Performance of Gender in Shakespeare's England* (Cambridge: Cambridge University Press, 1996), 53–82; Peter Stallybrass, "Transvestism and the 'Body Beneath': Speculating on the Boy Actor," in *Erotic Politics*, 64–83. An influential essay on the feminist potential of cross-dressing is Jean Howard, "Cross-Dressing, the Theater, and Gender Struggle in Early Modern England," in *Crossing the Stage: Controversies on Cross-dressing*, ed. Lesley Ferris (New York: Routledge, 1993), 20–46.

37. See Orgel, 70. Comparisons between servants and wives occur with some frequency in Renaissance service and household manuals. See, for example, I. M.'s *A Health to the Gentlemanly Profession:* "For in these dayes what greater loue could almost be found, then betwixt the Maister and the Seruant: it was in maner equall with the Husbandes to the Wyfe, and the Childes to the Parent." I. M., *Shakespeare Association Facsimiles* No. 3 (London: Oxford University Press, 1931), C2v.

38. Orgel, 81.

39. See Masten, *Textual Intercourse*, 45–48, for a synopsis of critical attitudes towards the play's controversial final scene.

40. Masten, *Textual Intercourse*, 48.

41. Philip Sidney, *The Defence of Poesy*, in *Sir Philip Sidney: The Major Works*, ed. Katherine Duncan-Jones (Oxford: Oxford University Press, 2002), 217–218. Sidney's definition of mimesis reads: "Poesy therefore is an art of imitation, for so Aristotle termeth it in the word *mimesis*—that is to say, a representing, counterfeiting, or figuring forth—to speak metaphorically, a speaking picture—with this end, to teach and delight."

42. Sidney, 216.

43. Sidney, 244.

ROY ERIKSEN

# The Taming of a Shrew:
## *Composition as Induction to Authorship*

Who is the author of *A Pleasant conceited Historie, called The Taming of a Shrew* (1594), or what can his craftsmanship reveal about his identity? The fact that Shakespeare's *The Taming of the Shrew*, published for the first time in 1623, but written somewhere between 1590 and 1594 (Bullough 2002: 1: 57–58; Thomson 1984: 1–9), has a shorter precursor with an approximately identical title has until fairly recently hindered serious consideration of *A Shrew* in its own right.[1] When editors and critics of Shakespeare have compared it to *The Shrew*, the majority has—not surprisingly—found it to be inferior in most respects.[2] If we add to the deemed inferiority that *A Shrew* is shorter than many Elizabethan plays, it was early relegated to the slippery category of 'bad quartos.'[3] The problem is however that the comedy is remarkably 'good' in terms of plot structure, the quality of the dialogue, and—I would argue—even in terms of some aspects of style.[4] In *A Shrew* there are no blatant loose ends or obvious gaps, whereas in *The Shrew* the metadramatic Sly material does not survive the Induction. In view of its relative shortness, *A Shrew* may have been cut for provincial acting during the plague of 1592–1594, but then the cuts were arguably executed with discernment. Still, the play's Italianate integration of plots is advanced even for the year of its publication while its style of speech construction, I propose, strongly suggests that it antedates 1590 and is by a playwright intimate with

*NJES: Nordic Journal of English Studies*, Volume 4, Number 2 (2005): pp. 41–63. Copyright © 2005 University of Gothenburg, Sweden and Roy Eriksen.

the compositional techniques of Marlowe. Then, too, the play has by many been dubbed 'Marlovian' and its style 'Marlowesque' in view of its multiple echoes and half-quotes from Marlowe's work, a fact used to undermine the status of the text further, because it was assumed that only an incompetent hack would have relied so heavily upon the period's leading playwright. Still we know that Marlowe is notorious for his propensity to quote and echo his own work (Levin 1961, 30, 60, 111–112; Eriksen 1987: 195–199). Moreover, the craftsmanship that went into the composition of *A Shrew* is such as to throw serious doubt on the idea that it is a 'bad' version of a now lost ur-version of the play, which in turn would have been the one Shakespeare could have drawn on. Considering this unsettled state of affairs, may not *A Shrew* quite simply be the original play and the heavy Marlovian presence in it be explained as the work of Marlowe himself? The compositional characteristics of the play point in that direction and there is empirical evidence to suggest that this is so.

Critics have however primarily been worried about the anonymous play's relationship to *The Taming of the Shrew*. Although the two plays share the same action and theme, in actual fact the texts hardly share a single line and only the names of Katherine (Kate) and Sly (Slie) occur in both texts. The male protagonist in Shakespeare's play, Petruchio (a servant's name in *Supposes*), is termed Ferando in the quarto. The plays are nevertheless sufficiently similar to invite comparison of in terms of quality. Stephen Miller is typical when he characterises *The Shrew* as "the more verbally brilliant text" (2000: 282). However, when Loughrey and Holderness (1992: 24–26) examine passages which are close in content in *A Shrew* and *The Shrew*, they convincingly argue against what they term the "tradition of comparative condemnation" (15), demonstrating greater richness of metaphor and referentiality in the passages in *A Shrew*. I believe that the same claim is valid for other passages as well. Leah S. Marcus makes a similar point,[5] but on the other hand she emphasizes that

> *The Shrew* is wittier and would have appeared more refined and up to date than the farcical Marlovian *A Shrew*, which was very old fashioned by the time of *The Shrew*'s publication in 1623. (Marcus 1996: 128)

But does the fact that part of the humour and intertextual games of *A Shrew* would have seemed dated in 1623 really detract from its efficiency as a comedy when it was first written and acted? Contemporaries appear to have reacted differently, because the play was reprinted in 1596 and 1607.[6] Nor does the outdated humour of *A Shrew* with regard to the 1623 horizon cancel out the fact that the earlier and shorter play is superior in other respects.

Leo Salingar has observed that Slie has more 'aristocratic' and 'academic' tastes than Shakespeare's tinker, and throughout the play "remains attentive and draws a moral at the end from what he has seen," and that "[r]ather than being a dunce,"

> he knows what a comedy is and it is the Players who blunder, whereas in Shakespeare (himself an Actor) the point seems precisely that his actors are wasted on spectators like Sly (1972: 272).

The dramatist behind *A Shrew* hence does not sympathize with the actors, but rather distances himself from them, in the way we would expect a university wit to do. For instance, he skilfully uses metadramatic effects to baffle and entertain the audience when Slie comments directly on and interferes with the action.

Still, these dissimilarities apart, why is the structurally more finished *A Shrew* so relatively short? The plague of 1592–1594 threw the London stage into a state of disorganization. The theatres were completely closed for long periods, companies were dispersed or had to downsize or regroup to meet the changed situation. The vogue for producing 'large' plays with many actors and spectacular effects that had been dominant since 1588 came abruptly to an end. One strategy of survival during the crisis was to leave London to tour in the provinces with purposely adapted and shortened versions of popular plays to fit a smaller and less expensive company. It goes without saying that only well-established companies with a certain amount of popular success, and with some financial backbone, could have managed to carry out such tours. Paul Werstine's attempt to reduce such travel to a minimum in his attack on W. W. Greg's 'narrative' about bad quartos does not seriously affect the fact that such travel is documented, but it may raise important questions about what constitutes 'badness' (Werstine 1998: 45–66; Urkowitz 1988: 204). Richard Hosley long ago discussed *A Shrew* suggesting that its badness was 'abnormal' and that the play does not really fit into the category (Hosley 1964).

One of the companies that performed outside London was the Earl of Pembroke's Men, probably originally formed in 1590, and which after suffering much hardship during the various outbreaks of the plague, or in the uncertainty that followed, became amalgamated with the Lord Admiral's Men in 1597. In the spring and summer of 1593 the company which had been one of the four companies producing 'large' plays (Gurr 2000: 122)—in a downsized version and still under the patronage of the Earl of Pembroke—went on an unsuccessful provincial tour and in 1595–1596 they also acted in Oxford (Boas 1923: 20; Greg 1950: 62). Three, if not five plays, which are extant in bad quartos very probably belonged to the Earl of Pembroke's Men (Greg 1950: 61). These are *Edward II* (1593) and *Doctor Faustus* (1593?), *2* and *3 Henry VI* (1594 and 1595), and the anonymous *The Taming of a Shrew* (1594). Two of these plays—*Doctor Faustus* (A) and *The Taming of a Shrew*—survive in what could be abridged versions intended for provincial performances.

Let me consider the case of *Doctor Faustus* (A) briefly. In a number of articles Tom Pettitt has brought the methods of folklore studies to bear on Elizabethan drama and Marlowe's plays in particular. In a paper originally read to the Marlowe Society of America, he presents empirical data from *The Massacre at Paris* and *Doctor Faustus* (A and B) which document beyond doubt that the A-text has been subjected to processes of oral transmission.[8] Pettitt's ground-breaking empirical evidence not only bears on the status of the A-text and the longer B-text, but applies indirectly in the case of *A Shrew*, as well.[9] The evidence demonstrates

> that [the] A-version of *Doctor Faustus* reflects the impact of oral transmission (memorization and reproduction from memory) on a play whose original text, *where they have material in common*, is better represented by the B-text (Pettitt 2006: 24ms).

Pettitt's findings are interesting also because they present a parallel to the clear departures in the A-text from certain of Marlowe's compositional habits which are better reproduced in the material it shares with the B-text,[10] compositional traits which also abound in *A Shrew*. So in addition to illustrating how "a single reading in one version must, beyond any possibility of alternative explanation, have preceded the reading in the other" (Bradley 1991: 9), these departures in the A-text could be signs of accommodation to new conditions and—possibly—acting in the provinces. W. W. Greg wrote about the shorter version that it

> [a]ppears to be a version prepared for the less critical and exigent audiences of provincial towns, and prepared not in an orderly manner by making cuts and alterations in the authorized prompt-book, but by memorial reconstruction. (1950: 60)

Although we are less willing today to accept the view that provincial audiences necessarily were "less critical and exigent," the play-text must have been cut to down to a more manageable size to suit a smaller company.[11] Yet, I think Greg's secondary proposal concerning "the dwindling resources of the company" would have played a far greater role in the process than the need to cater to "a vulgar audience."

In *A Shrew*, therefore, the lack of manifest signs of textual corruption or 'contamination' strongly suggests that the extant play never went on tour, or if it did the experience did not rub off on any extant version of the play. Besides, if the need for a longer performance would have arisen, it could easily have been expanded by means of "fond and frivolous jestures" of the kind that Richard Jones, the printer of *Tamburlaine*, decided to omit from that text (1592: sig. A2). Be this as it may, the tight structure of the comedy certainly suggests that the text printed in the 1594, 1596 and the 1607 editions is close to the play as written. Let us therefore turn to the play's artful over-all structure and its relationship to Marlowe's compositional style.

### Construction at plot level

Editors and critics have tried to explain away the "puzzling relation" (Salingar 1972: 272) of *A Shrew* to *The Shrew* by claiming that the former's more integrated ending is "mangled" (Blakemore Evans 1997: 140) when compared to that in a hypothetical but lost version of *The Shrew* (Bullough 2000: 57). Richard Hosley who believes that *A Shrew* is an adaptation of Shakespeare's play thinks, for instance, that

> [i]t is doubtful whether by 1594 any English dramatist other that Shakespeare was sufficiently skilled in plot-construction to write a carefully and subtly integrated triple-action play as we should have to suppose a lost original to be if *A Shrew* were derived from it in the manner envisaged by modern textual theory (Hoseley 1981: 31).

To accept such inventive explanations would entail forgetting for instance that Marlowe and other university-educated dramatists ever existed and, for example, Ann Thompson rightly observes that "[t]he combination of three plots is a remarkably sophisticated example of dramatic structure for the early 1590s" (1984: 166). For need complexity and structural finesse be attributed to Shakespeare alone? Consider for instance the carefully crafted loco-temporal structures of *Doctor Faustus* (B) which give ample evidence of how accurately Marlowe organised the scenes and plot material of his generically mixed play (Eriksen 1985: 49–74 and 1987: 103–167). The intricate plot structure of *A Shrew* similarly reveals that its playwright, too, is one who can handle at least three, if not five, plots simultaneously.[12]

The dramatist introduces the main action of the play by a metadramatic device based on the traditional comic motif according to which a drunken man, here named Slie, is duped into believing that he is a lord. The jesting nobleman, who assumes the role of a servant, instructs his servants to wait on Slie and to entertain him with a comedy entitled "The taming of a shrew"

(1.63). The main body of the play is thus lodged within a comic framing device based on role reversal, and the author upholds the metadramatic effect throughout by making Slie comment on the action four times from his privileged position on the stage, before he is carried off after falling asleep (15.127–133). By means of these interruptions the dramatist disrupts the illusion of reality and repeatedly brings the audience 'to its senses' reminding us that the play itself is doubly distanced from the 'real' world. What we get is simply not what we get.

The first plot encountered inside the frame is not the taming plot, but what sets it going: an intricate comic subplot of deception and disguise known from Latin and Italian comedy. Aurelius who is the son of the Duke of Cestus, has come to Athens to visit his friend, Polidor. The two young men fall in love with the two youngest daughters of the rich merchant Alonso, Emelia and Phylema. Due to the different social status of duke and merchant, the young nobleman decides to pose as a merchant's son in order to be accepted by Alonso:

> Tell him I am a Marchants sonne of *Cestus*,
> That comes to traffike unto Athens heere,
> And heere sirha I will change with you for once,
> And now be thou the *Duke of Cestus*, sonne,
> Revell and spend as if thou wert my selfe,
> For I will court my love in this disguise. (4.59–63)

By making Aurelius a prince, the dramatist imports a theme from romance and romantic comedy: love between young people from different social classes. As pointed out by Stephen Miller, social conflict in *A Shrew* is an integral part of the obstacles to young love and threatens the creation of a new and more inclusive society at the end of the comedy. The harsh reaction of the Duke of Cestus on discovering that Aurelius has married a merchant's daughter and persuaded a merchant to pose as his father to secure Alonso's approval (12 and 16) makes the reality of this threat clear enough:

> Turne hence thy face: oh cruell impious boy,
> Alfonso I did not thinke you would presume,
> To match your daughter with my princely house[.] (16.63–65)

Rather than being simpler than the corresponding plot in *The Shrew*, therefore, the dramatist responsible for *A Shrew* introduces greater thematic complexity and conflict into the play. Miller surprisingly interprets this greater complication as an indication that "*A Shrew* is an adaptation of *The Shrew*" (Miller 1998),[13] but one could argue that the reduction of the number of sisters from three to two in *The Shrew* also may imply complication and concentration of focus, because Bianca is provided with three rivals. This practice would be in keeping with Shakespeare's way of handling sources.

The prime obstacle to young love nevertheless is the unjust requirement imposed upon Emilia and Phylema by their father, who

> hath solemnlie sworne,
> His eldest daughter first shall be espowsed,
> Before he grauntes the yoongest leave to love . . . (4.16–18)

However, the true obstacle in *A Shrew* is the headstrong and independent character of Kate, who is repeatedly referred to as "a skould" and "the divell himselfe" (4.22; 23). The wooing and taming of the intractable eldest sister is the main plot while the champion of the seemingly futile task is the adventurous Ferando, a man of "wealth sufficient" and much mirth. When we first meet him he is already on his way to Kate after having been approached both by his would-be father-in-law with a promise of 6000 crowns if he marries her, and by Polidor's servant on the same topic. We conceive that the wooing takes the form of a wager between Alonso and Ferando, and this is matched by Kate's intention in an aside to the spectators that she will agree to the marriage and put Ferando's manhood to the test (5.40–42). So throughout the taming the audience already knows Kate's true intentions. Thus *The Taming of a Shrew* has a structure of plot-within-plot-within-plot, the innermost being the most important one and presenting the essential drama, which when seen through the perspective of the Slie framework "enables the audience to acquire a self-conscious, metadramatic awareness of the illusion" offered by the inner play (Holderness and Loughrey 1992: 21).

The plot structure of the play suggests a more than common knowledge of literary composition. The beginnings and conclusions of the plots are arranged with neat symmetry. After the Slie material in the beginning of the play (scenes 1–2), the lovers' plot is initiated when Polidor welcomes Aurelius to Athens (scene 3), the second love plot (i.e. the taming) begins when Ferando enters together with his man Saunders (scene 4). The two comic intermezzi between Polidor's Boy and Saunders form no real plot and the minor characters speak for the last time in scene 15 (Sanders) and scene 18 (Boy). When the principal characters leave at the end of the play in reverse order, Ferando and Kate exit first (18), to be followed by the other lovers (18), before Slie is carried on in his own clothes for the final scene (19):

1. Slie plot (1–)
    2. The lovers' plot (3–)
    3. The taming plot (4–18)

2. The lovers' plot (18)
1. Slie plot (19)

In view of this controlled structure, it comes as no surprise that the author has constructed the play's 'places of action' in a comparable over-all design.

The first scene is set in the evening outside an alehouse, where Slie is discovered sleeping before the action moves to an unspecified hall in the Lord's manor. Here the performance of the taming of the shrew (3–18) takes place. The setting of that play is Athens and remains so till Ferando and Kate leave for the country house after the wedding in scene 8. From then on the acting space changes eight times between Ferando's country house and Athens, before the action returns to the space outside the alehouse encountered in the first scene. In the following figure we see how these settings are distributed symmetrically:

FIG. 1  *A SHREW:* 'PLACES OF ACTION'

| outside an ale-house | | | | | | | | outside an ale-house |
|---|---|---|---|---|---|---|---|---|
| 1 | | | | | | | | 19 |
| inside the lord's house --------------------------------------------------------------------------I | | | | | | | | |
| 2 | | | | | | | | |
| Athens | country | Athens | country | Athens | country | Athens | country | Athens |
| 3–8 | 9 | 10 | 11 | 12 | 13 | 14 | 15 | 16–18 |

The dramatist expertly places the protagonist's arrival at Ferando's country house, the site of the taming school, exactly halfway through the play (in scene 9), so at the heart of the comedy we enter if not the 'green world' of Shakespearean comedy, at least a site for game and play where Ferando deliberately acts the fool. Saunders's account of his master's dress and behaviour tells it all:

He puts on an olde
Jerkin and a paire of canvas breeches down to the
Small of his legge and a red cap on his head and he
Lookes as though wilt burst thy selfe with laffing
When thou seest him. He's ene as good as a
Foole for me . . . (9: 11–16)

He is dressed in other words to be "even like a madman" (9: 8) and fool in the upcoming scenes in the taming school. The audience would therefore have expected farce and extravagant behaviour in the country house scenes,[14] and the on-stage spectator Slie correctly identifies Ferando as "the Fool" when he enters in scene 15. His outrageous behaviour at the country house suggests that he plays the part of the *homo sylvarum,* or wild man (Laroque 1993: 11), typical of summer festivals. That he is deliberately play-acting is clear when he, in a soliloquy addressed to the audience, announces that "This humour must I holde me a while." The use of a symbolic, if not festive, setting for the taming shows us the dramatist's thoughtful control of settings and plots as the action shifts between town and country and the action flits between parody of Romantic comedy and plain farce. In the world of the taming school, Ferando is Lord of Misrule and everything is turned upside down. Abuse masks as love, brutality as care, the moon becomes the sun, and an old man becomes a maid. The dramatist's command is no less than impressive, and to my mind it is matched only by the carefully plotted structure of settings in *Doctor Faustus* (B)[15] or by the simpler five-fold structure of *A Midsummer Night's Dream* where the odd matches and transformations also take place in the central scenes in the dark forest (Rose 1972: 18–19).

The conspicuous artifice in the distribution of plots and settings is foregrounded in the way the dramatist keeps us aware of his metatheatrical device throughout. When in the very last scene he brings the action back to the locale of the opening scene, he again underlines the return and the frame by making the Tapster's speech upon discovering Slie sound asleep—

> *Now that the darksome night is overpast,*
> And dawning day apeares in *cristall sky,*
> Now must I hast abroad: . . . (19: 1–4; my italics)

—repeat images from the Lord's grandiloquent opening speech:

> Lord.               Now that the gloomie *shaddow* of the night, /
> . . .
> Longing to view Orions drisling lookes,
> Leaps from th'antarticke World unto the skie
> And dims the Welkin with her pitchie breath,
>         And *darkesome night oreshades* the christall heauens[.]
>                 (1: 10–14; my italics)

Again the dramatist parodies himself, and we are brought back as if by magic, the illusion has been broken. The play's action, the events of several days, was—as Slie puts it—a mere "dreame" taking place between nightfall and dawn. Albeit on a different level, we are reminded of the double time scheme in *Doctor Faustus,* where in the longer and more complete B-text the protagonist's twenty-four years of pleasure are circumscribed a symbolic 'day' of twenty-four hours running from morning to morning (Eriksen 1985: 55–56).[16] It is perhaps symptomatic of the play's relationship to Marlowe that the long quote from *Doctor Faustus* in the Lord's first speech comes from the first part of a similar framing-device in the B-text.[17]

The exact repetition of words from the Lord's speech in the Tapster's speech at 19.1–5 constitutes a large-scale example of *epanalepsis,* or circular return, that shows us a dramatist that is highly conscious about his art. In other words he is not lowering his aim to cater to vulgar audiences, but constructing his play according to the book.[18] When this is said, is the same degree of authorial control that can be documented in the loco-temporal structure of *A Shrew* evident in the way the dramatist builds his speeches? This issue is important for the question of authorship, too, because Marlowe developed a new kind of speech composition with well-defined characteristics which are easy to check empirically. By carrying out a simple pattern recognition analysis of *A Shrew* and comparing the results to Marlowe's data, we will get important information about the provenance of the play.

### Construction at speech level

In *Tamburlaine the Great* Marlowe established a style of speech composition by means of "a poetics by contrivance and artful combination" (Eriksen 1996: 111), which was to serve as a model for his contemporaries and Shakespeare in particular. This style involved creating strongly jointed speeches by treating them as if they were complete rhetorical periods. In brief, a speech consisting of several periods, or complete sentences, was given holistic rhetorical patternings that emphasized the speech as a finished unit of communication with a well-defined beginning, middle and end.[19] Let me give one example of the type of speech I am referring to, Tamburlaine's five-line speech to Cosroe in *Tamburlaine:*

> Hold thee, Cosroe; wear two *imperial crowns.*
> Think thee invested now as *royally,*
> Even by the mighty hand of Tamburlaine,
> As if as many *kings* as could encompass thee
> With greatest pomp had *crown'd* thee *emperor.* (2.5.1–5; my italics)

Here we note that the repetitions and parallelisms (abc/cba) encircle the image of sovereignty in the middle line ("the mighty hand of Tamburlaine"). The speaker is in a strong position and has complete control over the flow of words. A large-scale example in the same play of the same architectural technique is the famous "Nature that fram'd us of four elements" speech (2.7.12–29), which I have discussed in detail elsewhere (1987: 69–71). There the topoi of Tamburlaine's quest for power are arranged symmetrically within a strongly marked rhetorical frame constituted by the repeated thematic keywords "sweetness/sweet" and "crown" (12; 29). In these speeches in *Tamburlaine,* Pt. 1 the Aristotelian formula for wholeness has been applied to create a dynamic whole. Despite the dialectic and progressive linearity that naturally inheres in dramatic dialogue, the separate elements in its processual flow form one well-disposed verbal construct, "one poem's period" (5.2.107). The speech and others of its kind behave like a stanza, one of the "rooms" of poetry, and therefore can be analysed in terms of spatial form by a simple method of pattern recognition.

But not all speeches are as elaborate in their rhetorical patterning as the cited speech, albeit some are more highly wrought, many more considerably less patterned or not at all. What nevertheless characterises Marlowe's compositional style in *Tamburlaine* is that as many as 31% of the speeches in Part 1 and 24% of the speeches in Part 2 have structures of this kind (cf. Appendix 1). The author of *A Shrew,* too, closely adheres to this style for the play abounds with speeches patterned in this fashion.

The following six examples taken from scenes 1, 16, and 19 in *A Shrew* illustrate the type of patternes involved. Repetitions are underscored in the text and single letters placed in the margin signal the repetitions of identical words and derivations, whereas letters in brackets signal synonyms (pot *vs.* cushen; view *vs.* see).

1) *Slie.* Tilly vally, by crisee *Tapster* Ile fese you anon.    a
   *Fils* the tother *pot* and ails paid for, looke you    b (c)
   I doo drinke it of mine own Instegation,
   *Heere* Ile *lie* a while, why *Tapster* I say,    d a
   Fils a fresh cushen heere. *Omne bene*[20]    b (c)
   Heigh ho, *heers* good warme lying. (1.10–20)    d

2) *Lord.* Now that the gloomie *shaddow* of the *night,*    a b
   Longing to *view Orions* drisling lookes,    (c)
   Leapes from th'antarticke World vnto the skie
   And dims the Welkin with her pitchie breath,
   And darkesome *night oreshades* the christall heauens,    b a
   *Here* breake we off our hunting for to *night,*    d b
   Cvppe the hounds and let vs hie vs home,
   And bid the huntsman *see* them meated well,    (c)
   For they haue all deseru'd it well to daie.
   But soft, what sleepie fellow is this lies *here?*    d
   Or is he dead, *see* one what he doth lacke?    (c)

3) *Ferando.* Why so, did I not tell thee I should be the man,
   Father, I leave *my* lovelie *Kate* with you,    a

*Provide* your selves against our marriage daie,                  b
For I must hie me to my countrie house
In haste, to see *provision* may be made,                         b
To entertaine *my Kate* when she dooth come. (5.47–52)  a

4) *Alfonso.* Let me give thankes unto *your* royall *grace*,      a
    For this great honor don to me and mine,
    And if *your grace* will walke unto my house,         a
    I will in humblest maner I can, show
    The eternall service I doo owe *your grace*.            a

5) *Duke.* Thanks good *Alonso:* but *I came alone,*               a
    And not as *did beseeme* the *Cestian Duke,*          b
    Nor would I have it knowne within the towne,
    That I was here and thus without my traine,
    But as *I came alone* so will I go,                   a
    And *leave* my son to solemnise his feast,           c
    And ere't belong Ile come againe to you,
    And do him honour as *beseemes* the son
    Of mightie Jerobell the *Cestian Duke,*               b
    Till when Ile *leave* you, Farewell *Aurelius.*       c

6) *Tapster.* Now that the darksome *night* is overpass,           a
    And dawning day apeares in cristall sky,
    Now must I halt abroad: but soft whose this?
    *What Slie* oh wondrous hash he laine here *allnight,*   b a
    Ile *wake* him, I thinke he's starved by this,          d
    But that his belly was so stuft with ale,
    *What* how *Slie,* Awake for shame.                    b d

I will briefly comment on the holistic repetitions in the six speeches, which however humble do contribute to stringing the speeches together on a formal level: Example 1 presents a combination of *epanalepsis* (Fils . . . cushen vs. Fils . . . pot) with double *epanados* (Tapster . . . Here Ile lie vs. Tapster . . . heers . . . lying). The following more developed speech by the Lord (Example 2) reveals a combination of the three defining repetitions, arranged so as to give the speech a peripety of its own in 1.15 ("Here breake we off . . ."). The initial mythological half of the speech (10–14) which is built around the image of the hunter Orion, is considerably more patterned and stylistically artificial than the second half,[21] but its basic image is echoed in the hunting imagery that introduces the Lord's theatrical sport. There is of course deep

irony in letting the soaked Slie be introduced by the image of "Orions drisling lookes." The speech is clearly not the result of badly jointed shards.

Example 3, Ferando's farewell to Alsonso in 5.47–52, presents an example of antimetabole (ab . . . ba), where exact words (my . . . *Kate*) and a
derivation (provide vs provision) gives balance, framing his intention declared
in the central line to leave for his country house. My fourth example, Alonso's
speech of thanks at 17.111–115) provides a simple example of *epanalepsis* in
which a formula of address "my grace" is repeated in the initial, central, and
final verse of his speech. The difference between the merchant and the prince
is seen in the fifth example, the Duke's response to Alonso (17.116–125). In
a highly formalised reply he rejects the informality of the situation and the
breach of princely decorum by marshalling his words into a rigid pattern that
emphasizes his own singularity ("But as I came alone so will I go"). The repetitions are multiple examples *epanados* and *epanalepsis* ("not as did beseeme
the *Cestian Duke*" vs "as beseemes . . . the *Cestian Duke*"). As observed in examples 1, 3, 4, and 5 titles and names are frequently used to provide linking
in speeches, and so it is in my sixth and final example, the Tapster's discovery
speech (19.1–7). Here Slie's name (4; 7) and references to the night (1; 4) in-
terlock with the repetition of "wake . . . awake" (5; 7) to a configuration where
instances of *epanados* emphasize the beginning, middle and end of the speech,
as seen in most of the cited speeches. As a point of general importance, characters of authority (the Lord and the Duke) or in a powerful position exhibit
more rhetorical repetitions (cf. Eriksen 1996: 123–125).

The practice revealed in these examples, and they are sufficiently many
to be accepted as typical of the dramatist's style of composition, we can term
mannerist, because it corresponds well with the mannerist aesthetic principle of "order with more ornament" put into use in written compositions
and visual art (Eriksen 2001: 79–109; 164–167). Such practice went against
contemporary academic and 'classical' views of period composition, and was
thus severely criticised by Scaliger, who warns against creating "false periods."
For a sentence does not become a true period merely because it is endowed
with rhetorical ornaments connecting it beginning and end. "Falsos autem
nomine ipsos puto, quum [periodeia] non in motu, sed in spatio posuere"
(1561: 4: 197, c.2). Marlowe, who in Dido and *Tamburlaine* established the
practice of creating what Harry Levin terms "verse sentences" by piling cause
on clause, also composed with extrasyntactic but architecturally plotted verbal
repetitions, did not heed such warnings and created speeches bound together
by verbal ornaments. The technique caught on and although Shakespeare is
the dramatist who learned most from Marlowe's technique in this respect, the
author of *A Shrew* apparently was an even more eager follower.

By applying the method—based on Renaissance prescriptions and practice—developed for my study of *Doctor Faustus* (B) to the speeches in *A Shrew*

and *The Shrew* interesting patterns emerge (see Appendix 1). For instance, there is twice as much holistically patterned text, meaning speeches that in terms of repetitions are treated as periods, in *A Shrew* than in *The Shrew;* 31% versus 15%. Besides, *A Shrew* has more than twice as many complex segments, i.e. speeches with two or more of the verbal figures identified: 29 versus 12. This means that *A Shrew* presents figures that are very close to Marlowe's early plays, and more particularly *Tamburlaine* (31% and 24%), whereas *The Shrew* is closer, for example, to *The Comedy of Errors* (12.7%), *I Henry VI* (12.9%), *Titus Andronicus* (13.0%), and *Romeo and Juliet* (15.8%). We can safely conclude that Shakespeare did not write *A Shrew* and that it is probable that *A Shrew* was composed before 1590.

The frequency with which the author of *A Shrew* patterns his speeches is in itself not sufficient to identify the author. This type of evidence must be supplemented by other types of evidence such as parallel passages and verifiable linguistic preferences. Borrowings in *A Shrew* from plays by Marlowe are legion as indeed they are internally between works within the Marlowe canon. I do not think, therefore, that it is "incredible that Marlowe would mimic himself so crudely" (Bulloughs 2000: 1: 58). In fact, as Levin pointed out (1961: 148–149) such mimicking is in keeping with Marlowe's practice in *Doctor Faustus* (B), and elsewhere.[22]

Let me conclude by offering four examples drawn from *Doctor Faustus* and *A Shrew* that elaborate on one particular formula, a phenomenon that is quite common in the Marlowe canon (Eriksen 1987: 192–199). When Faustus requests a wife, Mephostophilis instead promises him a courtesan

> As *chaste* as was Penelope,
> As *wise* as Saba, or as beautiful
> As was *bright* Lucifer before his fall. (B 545–547; my italics)

A similar passage with a series of three comparisons, but in a somewhat expanded version, crops up in *A Shrew* when Aurelius tells Valeria that he has

> A *lovely love*,
> As *bright* as is the heaven cristalline,
> As *faire* as is the milke white way of Jove,
> As *chaste* as Phoebe in her sommer sportes
> As softe and tender as the *azure* downe,
> That circles Cithereas silver doves. (10.1–6; my italics)

The properties of chastity, wisdom, and beauty are transformed to brightness, beauty and chastity in *A Shrew*, but the reference to Venus, or Lucifera, in the mention of bright Lucifer is kept in varied form in "Cithereas silver doves". The underlying reference to Paris's choice between the three goddesses is obvious, and so the first version of the topos becomes a fitting anticipation of Helen:

> Clad in the *beauty* of a thousand stars.
> *Brighter* art thou *than* flaming Jupiter
> When he appeared to hapless Semele,
> *More lovely than* the monarch of the sky.
> In wanton Arethusaes *azurde* armes. (B 1888–1892; my italics)

We note that a number of elements are repeated and new are added, but in principle the same image cluster is repeated with a halo of related images; in this instance Jupiter takes the place of Jove and the azure down of Venus's unchaste doves are transmuted into "wanton *Arethusaes* azurde armes," as the author forages in his treasure house of classical reference. A fourth reworking of the same cluster comes in *A Shrew*, when Aurelius praises Phylema and Emelia:

> Those lovelie dames
> *Richer in beawtie then* the orient pearle,
> *Whiter then* is the Alpine Christall mould,
> And farre *more lovelie then* the terean plant,
> That blushing in the aire turns to a stone. (5.121–125; my italics)

The topoi of beauty and the turn of phrase in the comedy are virtually indistinguishable from those in *Doctor Faustus* and related ones found in *Tamburlaine*. The similarities are such striking examples of the Marlovian idiom that it becomes hard to distinguish between the passages, and when we accept that self-parody was not beyond Marlowe, it appears more than likely that he was responsible for all four.

Therefore, when we add this observation on the close relationship of the discussed passages to the well-organised plot structure of *A Shrew*, including the special formal features it shares with *Doctor Faustus* (B), and new empirical data that show that the former displays a high frequency of patterned speeches of the kind introduced by Marlowe, the conclusion seems inevitable: Marlowe had a hand in *A Shrew*, and most likely he alone was responsible for penning it. His style can be documented on all levels of composition. As is evident from the brevity of this article, more work needs to be done on this topic, particularly on the use of farce and parody in the play. Still, one preliminary result seems clear: the author of *A Shrew* is no longer anonymous.

NOTES

1. The great watershed in the attitude to *A Shrew* was brought about by Holderness and Loughery 1992 and 2003: 13–36, and Marcus 1992: 177–200 and 1996: 101–131.

2. Marcus summarizes the situation tellingly: "In all modern editions of the authorized text, *A Shrew* is treated not as an artistic structure with its own patterns of meaning and its own dramatic logic, but as a heap of shards thrown together by ignorant actors with no capacity for coherence" (1992: 183).

3. See for instance Werstine 1998; Urkowitz 1988: 204; and Maguire 1996.

4. Michael J. B. Allen and Kenneth Muir did not include the play among the 'bad quartos,' because they found it "longer and more coherent than the texts of the other 'bad quartos'" (1981: xv).

5. Commenting on sig. E2ᵛ, page 74 of *A Shrew*, Marcus, argues that "*A Shrew*'s version . . . is less explicit, but would hardly be regarded as corrupt if it were allowed to stand on its own: it is editorially suspect only because it does not replicate every nuance of *The Shrew*" (1996: 118).

6. For the minimal variants between the three editions see Boas 1908: 1–8.

7. This ties in well the basic conflict between a mercantile class and the aristocracy. Slie ironically has more aristocratic and academic tastes than Shakespeare's tinker.

8. Thomas Pettitt, "Towards the *Zielform:* Oral Transmission and the Reshaping of Marlowe's Plays" (finally forthcoming in *Comparative Drama*). I am grateful to Dr. Pettitt for letting me see both the original paper and the revised article in manuscript. See also Pettitt 1980 and 1988.

9. Had Pettitt's article been printed when originally planned, its conclusions would have seriously undermined the basis of "the current orthodoxy," seen in e.g. Bevington and Rasmussen 1993 and Maguire 2004. Maguire argues that the A-text "has none of the verbal symptoms of memorial construction" (49).

10. Patterns of rhetorical composition typical of Marlowe's style are better and more completely preserved in the B-text (Eriksen 1987: 220–221).

11. But see Werstine, who thinks the evidence is inconclusive when it comes to deciding the size of companies. "[T]here remains a wide gap between the results and the recorded sizes of touring troupes around 1600. The gap does not prove that the 'bad quartos' cannot be touring texts, but it does prove that the 'bad quartos' cannot be shown to be touring texts." "Touring and the Construction of Shakespeare Criticism" (1998: 58). See Pettitt's findings on this topic, however, which strongly indicate that the A-text is a touring text.

12. The two comic intermezzi with Boy and Sanders can hardly be said to constitute an independent plot, but prepare us for Sanders's treatment of Kate in the scenes at the country house. The minor of plot where Phylotus poses as Aurelius's father really forms a part of the romantic plot.

13. The passages he compares would not stand the sort of test Pettitt applies to the A- and B-texts of *Doctor Faustus,* and *A Shrew* does not reveal signs of memorial contamination.

14. It is symptomatic that the transformation of Kate takes place outside the city and in the topsy-turvy mood of a country festival.

15. The settings in *Doctor Faustus* (B) are distributed as follows, when the misplaced comic scene between Rafe and Robin is restored to its correct position:

| Wittenberg | Papal court | Wittenberg | Imperial court | Wittenberg | Ducal court | Wittenberg |
|---|---|---|---|---|---|---|
| 1–7 | 8–9 | 10 | 11–14 | 15 | 16–17 | 18–20 |

See Eriksen (1987: 60–65) and for the misplaced comic scene (Eriksen 1981: 249–258). This placing is now universally accepted, e.g. by Bevington and Rasmussen, who arrived at the conclusion "independently" (1993: 288). They do not however address the structure of settings in the B-text.

16. The double time frame is as follows:

| outer frame (1–2) morning/dinner | inner frame | the 24 years of the compact (5–19) | inner frame | outer frame (20) morning |
|---|---|---|---|---|
| | midnight (5) | | supper/midnight (18–19) | |

The outer frame breaks down in the A-text which does not have the final discovery scene the morning following Faustus's death at midnight.

17. I refer to Faustus's incantation at midnight (B 227–) and its echo when on the night the compact expires the devils come to watch his futile final conjurations (B 1895–), The central notions of "the *gloomy* shadow of the *night*" (B 227) and the ascent from darkness (i.e. the leap "from th'Antarcticke World vnto the skie" "to view *Orions* drisling looke" are echoed in the reference to "This *gloomy night*" and the description how "from eternall *Dis*" the devils "ascend to *view*" their subject Faustus (B 1896), who like Orion is a hunter who becomes the hunted.

18. See the recommendations of the Byzantine rhetorician Hermogenes (1614: 1.2.337), whose works were revived by Torquato Tasso and others.

19. The repeated lexical items can be presented as follows, where the letters a, b, c refer to the words:
   1) epanalepsis (/a . . . a/)
   2) epanalepsis with antimetabole/chiasmus (/ab . . . ba/); and
   3) epanados with antimetabole and /or epanalepsis (/ab . . . a . . . ba/)
   The verbal signs repeated are single examples or combinations of these types:
   1) Identity (grace . . . grace; lord . . . lord)
   2) derivations and inflexions (come . . . coming . . . came)
   3) Synonyms (house . . . abode . . . hovel)

20. The opening words of the Latin drinking chant are placed in the margin after 1.6 in the quarto, whereas it appears to belong in 1.8.

21. For the stark stylistic contrasts, see Holderness and Loughery 1992: 23–24.

22. For more self-parody internally in *Doctor Faustus* (B), see Eriksen 1987: 175–177.

# Works Cited

Allen, Michael J. B. and Muir, Kenneth (eds). 1981. *Shakespeare's Plays in Quarto: A Facsimile Edition of Copies Primarily from the Henry E. Huntington Library.* Berkeley: University of California Press.

Bevington, David and Rasmussen, Eric (eds). 1993. *Doctor Faustus: A- and B-texts* (1604, 1616). Manchester: Manchester University Press.

Boas, F. S. (ed). 1908. *The Taming of A Shrew.* London: Chatto and Windus.

Bradley, David. 1991. *From Text to Performance in the Elizabethan Theatre.* Cambridge: Cambridge University Press.

Bullough, Geoffrey (ed). 2002. *Narrative and Dramatic Sources of Shakespeare.* 8 vols. London and New York: Routledge.

Dolan, Frances E. (ed). 1996. *The Taming of the Shrew: Texts and Contexts.* Boston and New York: Bedford/St. Martin's.

Eriksen, Roy. 1981. "The Misplaced Clownage-Scene in *The Tragedie of Doctor Faustus* (1616) and Its Implications for the Play's Total Structure." *English Studies* 17. 249–258.

Eriksen, Roy. 1985. "'What resting place is this?' Aspects of Time and Place in *Doctor Faustus* (1616), *Renaissance Drama.* 16: 49–74.

Eriksen, Roy. 1987. *The Forme of Faustus Fortunes: A Study of The Tragedie of Doctor Faustus (1616).* Oslo and Atlantic Highlands, Conn.: Solum and Humanities Press.

Eriksen, Roy. 1996. "Ars Combinatoria: Marlowe and the Art of Framing." *Variations sur la lettre, le mètre e la mésure: Shakespeare* Ed. Dominique Goy-Blanquet. Amiens: CRDP de l'Academie d'Amiens. 111–126.

Eriksen, Roy. 2001. *The Building in the Text: Alberti, Shakespeare, Milton.* University Park, Penn.: Penn State Press.

Greg, W. W. (ed.). 1950. *Marlowe's Doctor Faustus, 1604–1616.* Oxford: Clarendon Press.

Hermogenes. 1614. "Ars oratoria absolutissima, et libri omnes." G. Laurentius (ed). *Coloniae,* n.p.

Holderness, Graham and Loughery, Brian (eds). 1992. *A Pleasant Conceited Historie, Called The Taming of A Shrew.* Eastbourne: Pearson Education.

Hosley, Richard. 1964. "Sources and Analogues to *The Taming of the Shrew.*" *Huntington Library Quarterly* 27: 289–308.

Hosley, Richard, (ed.). 1981. *The Taming of the Shrew.* Gen. ed. Alfred Harbage. *Complete Pelican Shakespeare: The Comedies and the Romances.* Harmondsworth: Penguin.

Laroque, Francois. 1993. *Shakespeare's Festive World: Elizabethan Seasonal Entertainment and the Professional Stage.* Cambridge: Cambridge University Press.

Maguire, Laurie E. 1996. *Shakespearean Suspect Texts: The 'Bad' Quartos and Their Contexts.* Cambridge: Cambridge University Press.

Maguire, Laurie E. 2004. "Marlovian text and authorship." Ed. Patrick Cheney. *The Cambridge Companion to Christopher Marlowe.* Cambridge: Cambridge University Press. 41–54.

Maguire, Laurie E., and Berger, Thomas L. (eds.) 1998. *Textual Formations and Reformations.* Newark: University of Delaware Press.

Marcus, Leah. 1992. "The Shakespearean Editor as Shrew-Tamer." *English Literary Renaissance* 22.2: 177–200.

Marcus, Leah. 1996. *Unediting the Renaissance: Marlowe, Shakespeare, Milton.* London and New York: Routledge.

Marlowe, Christopher. 1592. *Tamburlaine the Great.* London: Richard Jones.

Miller, Stephen. 1998. "*The Taming of a Shrew* and the Theories; or, 'Though this be badness, yet there is method in' t,'" in Maguire and Berger (eds). 251–263.

Pettitt, Thomas. 1980. "The Folk Play in Marlowe's *Doctor Faustus*." *Folklore* 91: 72–79.

Pettitt, Thomas. 1988. "Formulaic Dramaturgy in *Doctor Faustus*. Eds. Kenneth Friedenreich et al. *"A poet and a filthy play-maker": New Essays on Christopher Marlowe*. New York: AMS, 167–191.

Pettitt, Thomas. 2006. "Towards the *Zielform:* Oral Transmission and the Reshaping of Marlowe's Plays." *Comparative Drama* (forthcoming).

Rose, Mark. 1972. *Shakespearean Design*. Cambridge, MA: Harvard University Press.

Salingar, Leo. *The Traditions of English Renaissance Comedy*. Cambridge: Cambridge University Press.

Scaliger, J. C. 1561. *Poetices libri septem*. Lugduni, n.p.

Shakespeare, William. 1997. *The Riverside Shakespeare*. Gen. ed. G. Blakemore Evans. Boston: Houghton Mifflin.

Thompson, Ann (ed). 1984. *The Taming of the Shrew*. New Cambridge Shakespeare. Cambridge: Cambridge University Press.

Urkowitz, Stephen. 1988. "Good News about Bad Quartos." Ed. Maurice Charney. *'Bad' Shakespeare: Revaluations of the Shakespeare Canon*. London and Toronto: Associated University Presses.

Werstine, Paul. 1998. "Touring and the Construction of Shakespeare Textual Criticism," in Maguire and Berger (eds). 45–66.

## *Appendix 1*

(A) here refers to the percentage of the text found in patterned speeches, (B) the total of patterned speches, and (C) the number of speeches with a combination of two or three verbal figures:

|  | A | B | C |
|---|---|---|---|
| 1 Tamburlaine | 31.1 | 59 | |
| 2 Tamburlaine | 24.7 | 42 | |
| Dido | 21.2 | 29 | |
| The Massacre at Paris | 25.4 | 39 | |
| Doctor Faustus (B) | 18.7 | 37 | |
| Edward the Second | 17.0 | 52 | |
| The Jew of Malta | 12.0 | 38 | |
| | | | |
| **A Shrew** | 31.2 | 66 | 29 |
| The Shrew | 15.0 | 32 | 12 |
| The Comedy of Errors | 12.7 | 23 | 13 |
| 1 Henry VI | 12.9 | 35 | |
| 2 Henry VI | 21.8 | 72 | |
| 3 Henry VI | 22.9 | 58 | |
| Titus Andronicus | 13.0 | 40 | |
| Romeo and Juliet | 15.8 | 53 | |

PHILIP D. COLLINGTON

# "Stuffed with all honourable virtues": Much Ado About Nothing *and* The Book of the Courtier

In a 1901 article published in *PMLA*, Mary Augusta Scott suggested that Shakespeare modeled the "merry war" of wits between Benedick and Beatrice on the verbal sparring between Castiglione's Gaspare Pallavicino and Emilia Pia, yet since then few critics have explored correspondences between *Much Ado About Nothing* (1600) and *The Book of the Courtier* (1528).[1] This neglect is surprising, for as Peter Burke documents, Castiglione's book was widely read by Shakespeare's contemporaries, whether in Italian, in Thomas Hoby's 1561 English translation, or in subsequent Latin versions; and figures as varied as Roger Ascham, Francis Bacon, John Florio, King James I, Ben Jonson, John Marston, Thomas Nashe, George Puttenham, and Thomas Whythorne read and/or owned *The Courtier*.[2] Eighteenth-century forger William Ireland even signed Shakespeare's name in a 1603 edition of *The Courtier* (now in the British Library), prompting Burke to wonder: "Why did he do this? Did he consider Castiglione, like Shakespeare, to be a representative of the Renaissance?"[3] Whatever Ireland's motives, the association of these two authors is well-founded. As Daniel Javitch explains, for Elizabethans seeking self-improvement, "Castiglione's perfect courtier had become an important and appealing model of civilized conduct"; and Walter Raleigh notes that, for writers in particular, *The Courtier* "proved an excellent book to steal from."[4] Recent studies have uncovered indebtedness

*Studies in Philology*, Volume 103, Number 3 (Summer 2006): pp. 281–312. Copyright © 2006 The University of North Carolina Press.

to Castiglione in a host of other plays, ranging from *Love's Labor's Lost* and *Measure for Measure* to *Hamlet* and *Othello*.[5] Yet when it comes to *Much Ado,* little sustained commentary has been attempted since Scott: Geoffrey Bullough briefly notes how the scenes in which Benedick and Beatrice are duped into falling in love (2.3, 3.1) recall Lodovico Canossa's tale of a woman falling for a man upon hearing "the opinion of many" attesting to his worthiness (3.67); Barbara K. Lewalski devotes several pages to the play's links to Castiglione in debating matters of desire, knowledge, and neoplatonic love; and A. R. Humphreys acknowledges that *Much Ado* mirrors Castiglione's appreciation for verbal wit, decorum, dancing, and music.[6]

I believe that Shakespeare does more with *The Courtier* than simply borrow character types, rework stock situations, or rehash humanist clichés about rhetoric and the arts, but I reopen this comparative project in the face of scholarly resistance. For although Scott praises *The Courtier* as a work that has "borne . . . well the judgment of time," the same cannot be said for her article (475–476). According to Burke, her list of correspondences "fail[s] to carry conviction" and should serve as a warning of "the danger of seeing Castiglione everywhere"; Humphreys considers the resemblances outlined by Scott "merely general parallels, sometimes quite loose, and not specific enough to prove a direct debt owed by Shakespeare to Castiglione"; and in a 1983 study, Louise George Clubb scoffs that Scott's argument "smacks of that desperation which is an occupational hazard to source hunters, especially Shakespearean ones."[7] Others, when they mention links between *Much Ado* and *The Courtier,* dismiss them in passing and without substantiating their objections.[8] My point is not to exhume a century-old study in order to vindicate a critic charged with methodological naïveté, sentimental characterology, or worst of all, "Fluellenism"—a term coined by Richard Levin after the Welsh captain who argued that salmon in the rivers of Monmouth and Macedonia proved Henry V was descended from Alexander the Great.[9] Instead, a reading of *Much Ado* alongside *The Courtier* evinces the English dramatist's skeptical examination of the source's courtier-ideal, presented in an accessible dramatic form. I will counter Burke's misplaced caution about "the danger of seeing Castiglione everywhere" and his contention that the two texts share little besides a general sense of style and wit.[10] There is more to an intertextual matrix than verbal parallels or one-to-one correspondences between characters like Beatrice and Emilia Pia. Castiglione *is* "everywhere" in *Much Ado,* an intellectual presence to which Shakespeare responds in profound and hitherto unexamined ways.

In the paragraphs that follow, I will demonstrate how issues debated in *The Courtier* reappear as a number of thematic controversies in Shakespeare's comedy. After a brief elaboration of some of the "remarkable correspondences" proposed by Scott (502), I will turn to *Much Ado*'s profound intellectual engagement with *The Courtier's* debates concerning gender, laughter, friendship, service, and *sprezzatura*. I will argue that, despite his initial loutish behavior as the play's scorner-of-love, Benedick comes to represent Castiglione's courtier-ideal by embracing this author's "middle way," striking balances between homosocial friendship and heterosexual love; between soldierly roughness and courtly refinement; between adherence to literary precepts and acceptance of social exigencies; and between self-advancement and service to his prince. Scott hints at this transformation in her identification of the amendment of faults as an important theme in both works (497) and in her acknowledgment that "Gaspare, for all his chaff, is, like Benedick, eminently reasonable and practical" (495). But the latter character is not always so; Scott merely scratches the surface of a complex process dramatized in Shakespeare's comedy. Paradoxically, the character who comes to exemplify Castiglione's ideal is not the play's ranking prince (Don Pedro's failings will be detailed below), but Benedick —the man ironically introduced as "A lord to a lord, a man to a man, stuffed with all honourable virtues" (1.1.54–55). Benedick may not end up a "stuffed" man, but he does ultimately surpass his peers in his capacity to reject impossible standards and the interpersonal intolerance that ensues therefrom and instead to accept personal imperfection, social compromise, and uncertainty in love.

## I

Scott concludes her seminal article by identifying a number of correspondences between Shakespeare's comedy and *The Courtier* (see 491–502). She points out that the general setting of Messina in *Much Ado* resembles the leisurely world of Urbino, where pastimes include witty conversation, composing verse, masking, dancing, and playing games, but where warfare is an omnipresent offstage reality.[11] When it comes to the courtly games, both settings of Urbino and Messina operate as de-facto matriarchies in which the highest-ranking females, Elisabetta Gonzaga and Hero, cede their central place to—and defer to the livelier intellects of—their closest friends and confidants, Emilia and Beatrice. Emilia "was endowed with so livelye a wytt and judgement . . . [that] she seemed the maistresse and ringe leader of all the companye" (1.4); likewise, Don Pedro compliments Beatrice's "merry heart," and Antonio marvels that, unlike Hero, she will not "be ruled" (2.1.310, 49).[12] Scott likens Beatrice's ongoing competition with Benedick for the last word ("You always end with a jade's trick. I know you of old" [1.1.140–141]) to Emilia's periodic quelling of Gaspare's antifeminist flights of fancy. Scott also notes the Italian precursor closes *The Courtier* by demanding that her rival "stand to triall" for speaking ill of women (4.73), while Beatrice demands justice for the slander of Hero. Moreover, as with Beatrice's heightened sense of verbal decorum ("I wonder that you will still be talking, Signor Benedick; nobody marks you" [1.1.112–113]), Emilia doesn't suffer long-winded fools gladly, as she terminates Fra Serafino's "triflyng tales" (1.9) and Lodovico's "verge tedyouse" disputation on classical rhetoric (1.39). Scott likens Benedick's complaint of Beatrice's witty barbs ("I stood like a man at a mark, with a whole army shooting at me" [2.1.245–246]) to the ladies' comic assault on Gaspare "as [though] they wold have buffeted him and done as the wood women did to Orpheus" (2.96).

Scott does not explore the way both play and courtesy book frequently liken courtship to military exercises: Bernardo Accolti (a.k.a. Unico Aretino) recommends that suitors attempt "to winn the fortresse of [her] minde, to breake in peeces those most harde Diamondes . . . that lye many times in the tender brestes of these women" (2.94), and Giuliano de' Medici warns that ladies' eyes "lye lurkinge like souldiers in warre lyinge in wayte in bushment" (3.66). Such passages anticipate Don Pedro's proxy wooing of Hero ("in her bosom I'll unclasp my heart / And take her hearing prisoner with the force / And strong encounter of my amorous tale" [1.1.312–314]) or Claudio's nervous aggression on their (second) wedding day: "Which is the lady I must seize upon?" (5.4.53). These verbal echoes emphasize the heightened masculine anxiety and the barely repressed mistrust of women exhibited by a variety of men in both Urbino and Messina.[13] As mentioned above, Scott does note that courtesy book and play share preoccupations with the amendment of faults, especially the enumeration of the ideal lady's and gentleman's graces. Finally she spots verbal echoes in Hoby's translation, such as the phrase "much ado" (anticipating the play's title)[14] or in such adages as "he that loveth much, speaketh little," which recurs in *Much Ado* in Claudio's line, "Silence is the perfectest herald of joy" (2.1.303). At this point, however, her argument peters out and does not consider the implications of the intertexts beyond a suggestion that Beatrice and Benedick derive their "vividness" from the fact they were "originally real [sic] persons" (502).[15]

I would elaborate upon Scott's character correspondences by comparing Urbino's bedridden Duke Guidobaldo (who must absent himself from each evening's debates) to Messina's relatively ineffectual governor, Leonato (whose impotent fury is mocked by Hero's accusers in 5.1). Castiglione compliments Duchess Elisabetta's patience in the face of her husband's debilitating illness, saying that although her virtues "would perhaps have lien hid a space, fortune . . . thought good with many adversities and temptatyons of miseries to disclose them, to make trial therby that in the tender breast of a woman, in companye wyth synguler beawtye, there can dwell wysdome, and stoutenes of courage, and all other vertues that in grave men them selves are most seldome" (1.4). In *Much Ado*, Leonato's wife is apparently no longer living, but the play dramatizes the testing of his daughter's virtue by afflicting Hero with adversity and misery (highlighting, in the process, the failings of "grave" men). And although Leonato ranks only as a local governor, he runs his household like a miniature court in which visiting princes are "royally entertained" (1.3.41).

If anything, Scott only shows the tip of the iceberg of correspondences. In addition to those identified by Bullough, Lewalski, and Humphreys, I propose the following: Item. Castiglione dedicated *The Courtier* to his close friend Alfonso Ariosto; Shakespeare borrowed plot materials from *Orlando Furioso* by his relative Ludovico Ariosto.[16] Item. Like Shakespeare, Castiglione was a man of the theater, possibly composing prologues for comedies and producing plays for the pope.[17] And just as Shakespeare may have taken bit parts in his own plays (e.g., playing Friar Francis in *Much Ado*), Castiglione inserts himself twice into *The Courtier*.[18] Both men characterize the world as a stage on which identity is more performance than essence. Item. *The Courtier*'s Bernardo Bibbiena boasts that his grace and beauty cause "many women [to] burne for the love of me, as you knowe" (1.19), anticipating Benedick's ridiculous claim to Beatrice that "it is certain I am loved of all ladies, only you excepted" (1.1.120–121). Item. Bernardo Bibbiena later tells a "dishonest and shamefull" jest about a woman who decorated her door with "the heades of the wielde beastes that [she] killeth everie daye in huntinge" (2.93), which reappears as Beatrice's query, "how many hath [Benedick] killed? For indeed I promised to eat all of his killing" (1.1.41–43).

And Item. Shakespeare may pay homage to his Italian source by naming the play's singing servant Balthasar. To be sure, there are Balthasars in other plays, but unlike the merchant from *The Comedy of Errors*, the footman in *Romeo and Juliet*, and the letter-carrier in *The Merchant of Venice*, Balthasar in *Much Ado* participates in several popular *Courtier*-like pastimes: dancing (e.g., with Margaret), debating (e.g., women's "ill qualities"), uttering social adages (e.g., about the folly of "wooers"), composing witticisms (e.g., his punning on "note"), and playing music (e.g., his song "Sigh No More, Ladies").[19] When Balthasar modestly declines Don Pedro's initial request for a song, the Prince gently chides him in lines that encapsulate the spirit of the courtesy book: "It is the witness still of excellency / To put a strange face on his own perfection" (2.3.46–47). Burke dismisses this exchange as merely poking fun at the "exaggerated modesty" of a theatrical "fop."[20] Yet there is more to this passage than a satirical jibe; it emphasizes qualities of modesty, refinement, and grace which pervade the courtesy book. Is it really just a coincidence that Balthasar (= Baldassare Castiglione) discusses with Don Pedro (= the play's courtly prince) the signal importance of "perfection"? Right from the opening quip about Benedick being "stuffed" with virtues, the play debates which qualities constitute an ideal courtier's identity.

The same scene in which Balthasar reluctantly sings opens with Benedick's private meditation on hypocrisy and human folly: "I do much wonder that

one man, seeing how much another man is a fool when he dedicates his be-
haviours to love, will, after he hath laughed at such shallow follies in others,
become the argument of his own scorn by falling in love" (2.3.8–12). Here is
how Castiglione's Cesare Gonzaga introduces a similar topic for debate:

> Whoso wyll diligentlye consider all our doynges, he shall fynde
> alwayes in them sundrye imperfections. . . . where one man
> knoweth that an other knoweth not, and is ignoraunte in the
> thyng that the other hath understandynge in, eche man doth
> easilye perceyve the errour of hys felow, and not hys owne; and
> we all think oure selves to be verye wyse and peradventure in that
> poynt most, wherein we are most foolysh. (1.8)

Where Gonzaga cites as examples men who, once incited, "wexed foolish in
verses, some in musicke, some in love, some in daunsinge, some in makynge
antiques" (30), Benedick cites as evidence the sudden transformations in
Claudio, such as the latter's new taste in music ("the tabor and the pipe"),
fashion ("a new doublet"), and rhetoric ("His words are a very fantastical
banquet") (2.3.8–21). Rather than merely posit such passages as verbal
parallels between Shakespeare and Castiglione, I propose that the rest of
this particular scene confirms the validity of Gonzaga's conclusion, that
"for certeine . . . in everye one of us there is some seede of folye, the which
beyng stirred may multiplye (in a maner) infinite" (30–31). For once the
seed of love is planted by his peers in the garden scene, it likewise multiplies
with "infinite" rapidity in Benedick: "I will be horribly in love with her"
(2.3.232). This passage typifies Shakespeare's intertextual engagement with
*The Courtier:* rather than being much ado about *nothing,* the play probes the
shifting foundations of personal and social identity through characters who
proffer advice, debate virtues, and question received wisdom about gender,
love, marriage, and service.

## II

Reading Castiglione's courtesy book alongside *Much Ado* can elucidate some
of the play's more puzzling passages, one of which, ironically, stresses the
inutility of proffering advice. Yet Shakespeare may be defending, not biting,
the source-hand that feeds him. At the opening of act 5, Leonato upbraids
his brother Antonio for offering consolatory advice—"preceptial medicine"
(5.1.24)—regarding a daughter that both know is not really a fornicator and
not really dead. "Give me no counsel," Leonato says (three times), castigat-
ing hypocritical scholars who would "patch grief with proverbs": "there was
never yet philosopher / That could endure the toothache patiently, / However they have writ [in] the style of gods" (3–33, 35–37). While both men

are understandably distraught over Hero's slander, playgoers and readers would be justified in questioning the appropriateness of the lengthy charade (30+ lines) in which the two speak of her—in private, unusually, and not for the benefit of eavesdroppers—as if she were dead: "Bring me a father that so *loved* his child, / Whose joy of her is overwhelmed like mine, / And bid him speak of patience" (8-10, emphasis added). Hero is alive: should he not *love* (present tense) her? This odd passage may stem more from the playwright's engagement with Castiglione than with fidelity to consistent characterization. As Burke's study of the European reception of *The Courtier* documents, by Shakespeare's day the dialogic complexities of the book had been ironed smooth by pedantic editors and simplistic paratexts (such as Hoby's handy appendices summarizing "the chiefe conditions and qualities" of courtiers and ladies), reducing *The Courtier* to a kind of "recipe book" or "instruction manual."[21] Indeed, Hoby himself writes that his translation may be employed generally as "a storehouse of most necessary implements for the conversacion, use, and training up of mans life with Courtly demeaners."[22] Leonato's overwrought diatribe, while emotionally manipulative and potentially misleading with respect to the plot of *Much Ado,* is *thematically* appropriate in the way it rejects England's contemporary practice of mining scholarly texts for proverbs, behavioral maxims, and other forms of "preceptial medicine." Thus Shakespeare reaffirms *The Courtier*'s original insight that human interactions are too complex, provisional, and dissimulative for simple precepts to apply.

Another puzzling aspect of Much Ado that may be elucidated by *The Courtier* is the way in which the two scorners-of-love list qualities of manly or womanly perfection, not as criteria they wish to see fulfilled, but as a defensive posture by which the impossibility that the other could attain such ideals serves as a pretext for not falling in love. Benedick is the first to articulate his proviso: "One woman is fair, yet I am well [i.e., not lovesick]. Another is wise, yet I am well. Another virtuous, yet I am well. But till all graces be in one woman, one woman shall not come in my grace" (2.3.27–30). He goes on to note that until he finds a bride who is rich, fair, mild, noble, "of good discourse," and "an excellent musician," he will remain a bachelor (30–35). His demands correspond to the composite ideals debated in *The Courtier,* particularly its third book, which outlines desirable qualities in a woman: beauty, honesty, discretion, chastity, and so forth. Earlier on, Lodovico specifies that while cleanliness, white teeth, and soft hands are desirable, more "natural" attributes evince womanly perfection:

How much more then doeth a man delite in [a woman] . . . that is manyfestlye seene [that] she bath nothinge upon her face, though she be not so white nor so red, but with her naturall colour somewhat wan, sometime with blusshinge or through other chaunce dyed with a pure rednes, with her hear by happe out of order and ruffled, and with her simple and naturall gestures, without shewing her self to bestow diligence or study, to make her faire? This is that not regarded pureness which best pleaseth the eyes and mindes of men, that stande alwayes in awe to be deceived by art. (1.40)

Being attractive without "diligence or study" (e.g., through the application of cosmetics) is the essence of womanly *sprezzatura;* that is, seemingly effort-less beauty, that "not[-]regarded pureness." Lodovico's ominous-sounding mention of how men "stande alwayes in awe" (are always afraid) of being deceived by appearances resurfaces in Claudio's repudiation-scene tirade in which he accuses Hero of dishonesty: "Would you not swear— / All you that see her—that she were a maid, / By these exterior shows? But she is none" (4.1.38–40). Claudio goes on to accuse her of looking as "chaste" as Diana but being as "intemperate" as Venus (56–61); in other words, of concealing sexual promiscuity using art. It is worth pointing out that Shakespeare devotes an entire scene (3.4) to Hero's prewedding preparation, unremarkable in and of itself, except that Hero's irritability with Ursula and Margaret over the choice of "rebato" (collar) and "tire" (headdress), com-bined with her boasting of the "excellent" perfume of her gloves and that her gown "exceeds" that recently worn by the Duchess of Milan, constitute the antithesis of womanly *sprezzatura.* Hero tries too hard to be beautiful, perhaps even tinting her hair, as Margaret notes: "I like the new tire within excellently, if the hair were a thought browner" (12–13).

My point is not that Hero's slander stems from her elaborate trous-seau, but that Claudio's belief in this slander may be enabled by her penchant for studied elegance, whereas Benedick's conversion to loving Beatrice stems from her relative carelessness about her physical appearance. Right from the first scene, Claudio seems attracted to images, whereas Benedick concerns himself with essences:

*CLAUDIO:* In mine eye she [i.e., Hero] is the sweetest lady that ever I looked on.

*BENEDICK:* I can see yet without spectacles, and I see no such matter. There's her cousin, an she were not possessed with a fury, exceeds her as much in beauty as the first day of May doth the last of December.

(1.1.183–187)

I disagree with Lewalski's suggestion that this exchange shows Benedick's superficial "attraction to his lady's physical beauty"; his concern with

Beatrice's apparently bad-tempered essence takes precedence over his grudging acknowledgment of her natural beauty (i.e., she is likened to spring).[23] For example, elsewhere Benedick does not seem attracted to artfully tinted hair; rather, his love's "hair shall be of what colour it please God" (2.3.34–35) During his eavesdropping scene, Benedick is reassured that Beatrice does exhibit enough ideal qualities to warrant his affection: she is "excellent," "sweet," "out of all suspicion," "virtuous," "exceeding wise," and so forth (2.3.162–165). The garden scene trick succeeds, not just because Beatrice unexpectedly conforms to his defensive composite ideal, but also because she reportedly loves Benedick genuinely and without artifice: "Counterfeit? There was never counterfeit of passion came so near the life of passion as she discovers it" (110–112). Just as *sprezzatura* has been variously interpreted as the art of concealing art, nonchalance, or effortlessness, "conspicuously false modesty," or "the ability to disguise what one really desires," Beatrice's outward fury is interpreted as concealing depths of passion within.[24] In other words, the less she acts as though she were in love, the greater her actual capacity for loving may prove. To wit, she does not boast of her own beauty, virtue, fidelity or passion; yet the existence of these can be inferred from outward signs, a principle Benedick illustrates when he interprets her curt invitation: "Ha. 'Against my will I am sent to bid you come in to dinner.' There's a double meaning in that. . . . If I do not take pity of her I am a villain" (2.3.254–259). Not to pick up on her apparent signals would be imperceptive; not to reciprocate her love would be ungentlemanly.

Beatrice's parallel blazon of a perfection superficially supports Castiglione's espoused ideal of the golden mean (more on this below), but her eschewing of excess merely functions as a defensive posture, one readily apparent to onlookers:

BEATRICE: He were an excellent man that were made just in the midway between [Don John] and Benedick. The one is too like an image and says nothing, and the other too like my lady's eldest son, evermore tattling.

LEONATO: Then half Signor Benedick's tongue in Count John's mouth, and half Count John's melancholy in Signor Benedick's face—

BEATRICE: With a good leg, and a good foot, uncle, and money enough in his purse, such a man would win any woman in the world, if a could get her good will.

LEONATO: By my troth, niece, thou wilt never get thee a husband. . . .

(2.1.6–18)

Though Benedick does tame his tongue, he never appears as the patchwork Frankenstein wittily envisioned here. Instead, the deception and conversion of Beatrice in her eavesdropping scene (3.1) succeeds because, as Lodovico observes in *The Courtier*, "There may be other thinges also that beside beawty often times enflame our mindes, as maners, knowleage, speach, gestures and a thousand mo . . . and above all the knowing a mans self to be beloved" (1.53). Not only does Beatrice overhear that Benedick is wise, noble, young, handsome, and "For shape, for bearing, argument, and valour / . . . foremost in report through Italy" (3.1.96–97), but most importantly that he "loves Beatrice . . . entirely" (37). She learns that he only conceals his passion in order to avoid being mocked. Again, not to reciprocate would be, in her case, unladylike and occasion further censure from her peers.

That these parallel provisos undone by gentle deceptions generate a truly compatible love affair is illustrated in the way, moments before their wedding, rather than fussing about their clothes or appearance, they engage in a witty game analogous to that proposed by Gaspare:

> to have everye manne open what vertues he would principally the persone he loveth should be indowed with all. And seeying it is so necessarilye that we all have some spotte, what vyce he woulde also have in hym: to see who can fynde out most prayse woorthye and manlye vertues, and most tollerable vyces, that shoulde be least hurtefull bothe to hym that loveth, and to the wyghte beloved. (1.7)

This same game is initiated twice in *Much Ado*, once by Balthasar and Margaret (his playful itemization of "ill qualities" while dancing with Margaret [2.1.98–110]), and then later by Gaspare's proposed counterpart, Benedick:

BENEDICK: I pray thee now tell me, for which of my bad parts didst thou first fall in love with me?
BEATRICE: For them all together, which maintained so politic a state of evil that they will not admit any good part to intermingle with them. But for which of my good parts did you first suffer love for me?
BENEDICK: "Suffer love"—a good epithet. I do suffer love indeed, for I love thee *against my will*.

(5.2.59–66, emphasis added)

Thus Benedick subtly echoes the "double meaning" he (mis)perceived in Beatrice's earlier invitation *against her will* to bid Benedick come in to dinner. Despite the surface mockery, she may have loved him then; he certainly loves her now.[25] Gaspare's parlor game acknowledges the inevitability of personal imperfection ("some spotte") and the importance of limiting vices to those which would inflict minimal harm on the beloved. This spirit of compromise enables participants to aspire to a literary courtly ideal but reconcile themselves in the real world to personal failings and social exigencies (such as the necessity of getting along with an imperfect spouse). Lodovico later interrupts the seemingly endless discussions of desirable traits by observing that "there is never a vessell in the worlde possible to be founde so bigge that shalbe able to receive al the thinges that you wil have in this Courtyer," to which Pietro da Napoli jokingly replies that a fat man would therefore have an unfair advantage over slender opponents in the race to attain courtly perfection (1.46). Whereas achieving the courtier-ideal is impossible, slight imperfections may prove beneficial.

Once Benedick's glaring imperfection (his hostility towards women, love, and marriage) is exposed to him, his physical appearance, social allegiances, and personal philosophy all undergo a dramatic shift towards Castiglione's courtier-ideal: "Happy are they that can hear their detractions and can put them to mending. . . . I will be horribly in love with her" (2.3.226–232). Before this conversion to love, however, Benedick exhibited behaviors roundly discouraged by a variety of speakers in *The Courtier*. For example, upon his return from the war he jokingly asks whether Leonato was "in doubt" about Hero's paternity (implying that his host is a cuckold). Leonato deflates the awkward moment by stating he was not, "for then were you a child" (and not yet the seducer he boasts of being now [1.1.102–104]). Beatrice is not so gracious and reprimands Benedick for his inappropriate comment in lines cited earlier (i.e., "nobody marks you" [112–113]). Castiglione's Federico Fregoso states categorically that such behavior is unbecoming of a courtier, that he should "refrain from praising himself out of purpose, from using a noysome sawcinesse, from casting out otherwhile a worde thinking to make men laughe, which for that it is spoken out of time will appeare colde and without any grace" (2.6). Federico later adds that men who utter "filthie" words "in the presence of honourable women" in order to "bee counted good felowes" should be shunned from polite company (2.36). Benedick's anxious clamoring for acceptance by male comrades is further suggested by Beatrice's observations that "He hath every month a new sworn brother," that "He wears his faith but as the fashion of his hat," and that he hangs upon companions "like a disease" (1.1.68–82). As Bernardo Bibbiena observes, there is nothing so uncourtly as "commune jesters and parasites, and such as with fonde matters move menne to laughe" (2.57). Beatrice castigates Benedick for this tendency in her stinging rebuke, "he is the Prince's jester. . . . None but libertines delight in him" (2.1.137–139; more on this below).

While the popularity of *The Courtier* and *Much Ado* can be attributed to the great variety of subtle witticisms, crude jests, practical jokes, and off-color anecdotes contained therein (e.g., the courtesy book's tale of pregnant nuns and lusty friars [2.61], or the play's incessant bawdy punning, e.g., on horns, bulls, and cuckolds 15.4.43–51]), Castiglione's inclusion of such materials has been historically controversial. Fears that the book's anticlerical jokes and sexual innuendo could land it on the papal *Index* of prohibited works occasioned a number of expurgated editions in the sixteenth century.[26] Dain A. Trafton explains that the second book's lengthy discussions of surface appearances and joke-telling represent the "nadir of courtiership [as it is] devoted to mere *sprezzatura*," a deliberately misleading sidetrack by which Castiglione satirizes contemporaries who viewed telling jokes and winning "drawing room" amusements as the essence of courtly service. Jokes, clothes, and other forms of surface frivolity are largely abandoned by book 4, where Castiglione turns to more serious matters such as service to one's prince.[27]

*Much Ado* presents a similar structure in charting Benedick's character development and social refinement in stark contrast with Claudio and Don Pedro's personal stasis and increasing boorishness. The latter men's first appearance after the repudiation-scene "death" of Hero is marred by their insensitivity towards grieving Leonato and Antonio. "We had liked to have had our two noses snapped off with two old men without teeth," quips Claudio, before taunting Benedick about the latter's impending wedding: "when shall we set the savage bull's horns on the sensible Benedick's head?" (5.1.114–115, 177–178). Moreover, Don Pedro's belabored story about how Beatrice recently "trans-shape[d Benedick's] particular virtues" (172–173) must seem inappropriate to playgoers who have just witnessed the forthright private conference in which she declared her love for him and he agreed to avenge Hero's slander (4.1.255–335). What might have been amusing in act 1 is simply gauche by act 5. Benedick castigates his former friend and master for their uncourtly behavior: "I will leave you now to your gossip-like humour. You break jests as braggarts do their blades" (5.1.182–183). Benedick's willingness to defend a wronged lady's honor, even to the point of defying his prince, distinguishes him as having achieved the highest level of service outlined in *The Courtier*.

## III

By aligning himself with Beatrice, challenging Claudio to a duel, and abandoning Don Pedro's service—all because of Hero's slander—Benedick illustrates three important thematic subjects elaborated in *The Courtier:* the complexity of masculine honor, the sacrosanct nature of a woman's reputation, and the importance of advising one's prince.

In adjusting his own behavior to conform to a more refined courtly ideal, Benedick is mocked for becoming effeminate. Don Pedro scoffs at his new-found fondness for imitating foreign dress ("a Dutchman today, a Frenchman tomorrow"), shaving ("he looks younger than he did by the loss of a beard"), applying perfume ("civet") and cosmetics ("paint"), and learning to play music ("his jesting spirit . . . is now crept into a lute-string, and now governed by the stops" [3.2.30–56]). Certainly such foppish excesses come under fire in Castiglione's Urbino, where Lodovico would outlaw ostentatious refinement: "[I will] have our Courtyer . . . not so softe and womanishe as many procure to [be], that do not onely courle the hear, and picke the browes, but also paumpre themselves in every point like the most wanton and dishonest women in the worlde" (1.19).[28] The courtier should avoid the slavish imitation of foreign fashions (French, Dutch, Spanish) and the wearing of fancy clothing with decorations that make him look like—again, the dreaded term—a "commune jestar" (2.26–27). And according to Gaspare, he should avoid such "womannishe" delicacies as the playing of music—though this last point is quickly refuted by Lodovico, who is "not pleased with the Courtyer if he be not also a musitien" (1.47). Indeed, Claudio's joke about Benedick's government-by-lute-string may echo a passage in *The Courtier* in which Federico Fregoso praises this instrument as most flattering to the individual singer ("to sing to the lute is muche better, because al the sweetenesse consisteth in one alone") and the innovation of pitched frets as producing the most harmonious sounds ("all instrumentes with freates are ful of harmony, because the tunes of them are very perfect" [2.13]). Thus for a lover to be "governed" by a lute-string is ridiculous if he plays badly but admirable if he aspires to the highest attainable level of artistic refinement. The mockery Benedick incurs from his peers stems from his previous rejection of these qualities (e.g., his satiric description of "Monsieur love" [i.e., Claudio] and his criticism of Balthasar's singing [2.3.36, 83–87]) but more so from the rapidity and extent of Benedick's current transformation. One simply cannot acquire courtly grace, personal style, and musicianship overnight. However, Benedick could be forgiven his lack of *sprezzatura* in this scene because he undergoes such a laborious change, not in the interest of political or social advancement, but in the hope of repairing the damage done by his tyranny towards ladies in general and of winning Beatrice's heart in particular. Benedick fulfills Castiglione's ideal of a courtier capable of quick adaptation, as outlined by Wayne Rebhorn: "He wants his ideal courtier to become an eternally flexible, protean actor of many masks, *an intrinsically moral man* who continually refashions his beautiful image to fit the myriad scenes he finds in the great theatre of his world."[29]

If anything, Benedick's sudden transformation evinces *nonconformity*, making him a laughingstock in danger of ostracism in Messina. "I hear what they say of him," Don Pedro intones ominously—enlisting the peer pressure of an anonymous "they" to correct Benedick's outlandish appearance (3.2.53–54). In love, he is not dressed for success, but dressed to excess; a significant flaw according to Sir Frederick: "a man should frame himselfe to the custome of the moste. . . . I woulde love it the better yf it [i.e., his dress] were not extreme in anye part" (2.26–27). It takes considerable courage to change from soldier and scorner-of-love to lover and recipient of soldiers' scorn. But Benedick risks established membership in the homosocial (and homogeneous) peer group in order to refashion his identity and join another—a leap of faith by the play's erstwhile "heretic in despite of beauty" (1.1.226–227):

> BENEDICK: I may chance have some odd quirks and remnants of wit broken on me because I have railed so long against marriage, but doth not the appetite alter? A man loves the meat in his youth that he cannot endure in his age. Shall quips and sentences and these paper bullets of the brain awe a man from the career of his humour? No. The world must be peopled.
>
> (2.3.232–239)

To ease the transition, Benedick takes the purported emasculation caused by love and service to a lady (decried again in book 4 as "matters belonginge to enterteinment of women and love . . . [which] do many times nothinge elles but womannish the mindes" [4.4]) and reimagines these as hypermasculine service in which he potently "peoples" the world in the face of quasi-military dangers. In fact, by echoing Saint Paul (i.e., "When I was a child, I spoke as a child . . . but when I became a man, I put away the things of a child"[30]), Benedick implies that to cling to the peer group and refuse to marry and reproduce would be retrograde, immature, even immoral. As *The Courtier* repeatedly asserts, falling in love is age-appropriate behavior for the young: off-limits to the elderly ("in olde men love is a thing to bee jested at" [2.13]), but perfectly acceptable for a bachelor like Benedick. The observance of decorum is everything to Castiglione's courtier: "let him consider wel what the thing is he doth or speaketh, the place wher it is done, in the presence of whom, in what time, the cause why he doeth it, his age, his profession, the ende whereto it tendeth, and the meanes that may bring him to it" (2.7). After much deliberation, Benedick determines that it is *time* to fall in love.

Furthermore, when Benedick initially balks at Beatrice's demand that he "kill Claudio" for slandering her cousin, she excoriates him in terms which suggest that effeminacy stems, paradoxically, from misplaced loyalty to the male peer group, not from the "entertainment" of love or ladies: "Count Comfit, a sweet gallant, surely. O that I were a man for his sake! Or that I had any friend would be a man for my sake! But manhood is melted into curtsies, valour into compliment, and men are only turned into tongue, and trim ones too" (4.1.316–321). Thus she encourages Benedick to prove himself a true courtier by defeating effeminate pseudo-courtiers using martial valor. For while good breeding, social grace, *sprezzatura,* and so forth are all desirable qualities, ultimately what distinguishes a courtier is his willingness to fight for a worthy cause: "I judge the principall and true profession of a Courtyer," Lodovico declares, "to be in feates of armes" (1.17). Beatrice's bitter sarcasm stems less from virago-like aspirations on her part than from frustration at her own social limitations. When Gaspare quips that "generallye everye woman wisheth she were a man" in order to attain that perfection denied to her because of her sex, Giuliano de' Medici counters that "The seelie poore creatures wish not to be a man to make them more perfect, but to have libertye, and to be ridd of the rule that men have of their owne authoritie chalenged over them" (3.15–16). Beatrice demands restitution for a gross miscarriage of justice in which two princes and a count abuse their authority and destroy the reputation of an innocent young lady, offences the gravity of which is underscored by Leonato's own withering sarcasm: "I thank you, Princes, for my daughter's death. / Record it with your high and worthy deeds. / 'Twas bravely done" (5.1.262–264). A worthy deed would have been to defend Hero's honor, a fact which motivates the explosive aggression exhibited by Leonato, Antonio, and Benedick in act 5; on the other hand, an unworthy deed would be to shrink from combat like so many pseudo-courtiers, "Scambling, outfacing, fashion-monging boys, / That lie and cog and flout, deprave and slander, / Go anticly, and show an outward hideousness" (5.1.94–96). Beatrice wishes she were a man because she wants Benedick to punish those who merely pretend to be men. Thus she goads him towards an appropriately militarized behavioral ideal. Giuliano de' Medici recommends such a reciprocal arrangement: "as she is made perfect by the man, so doeth she also make him perfect" (3.16).

On this topic, Benedick in love differs substantially from his friend Claudio. The latter keeps the realms of love and war separate, as in his confession to Don Pedro that he loves Hero:

CLAUDIO:    When you went onward on this ended action

I looked upon her with a soldier's eye,

That liked, but had a rougher task in hand

Than to drive liking to the name of love.

But now I am returned, and that war-thoughts

Have left their places vacant, in their rooms

Come thronging soft and delicate desires. . . .

(1.1.286–292)

To Claudio, war and desire represent incompatible spheres of masculine endeavor, like tenants in a building who may never share a room. Before his conversion to love, Benedick also shared this mistaken notion that love somehow impedes military valor, as seen in his initial contempt for Claudio's abandonment of drums, armor, and plain-speaking in favor of pipes, fashionable doublets, and "fantastical" rhetoric (2.3.13–22). Yet following Claudio's repudiation of Hero at the altar, Benedick takes a considerable risk by not exiting the church with his military comrades (at 4.1.112), remaining with the civilian women, elderly men, and other guests. Even before Beatrice's searing admonition that he "be a man" (255ff), Benedick distinguishes himself by coming to Hero's defense when even her father assumes the worst and berates her with unrelenting cruelty. Benedick promises, "though you know my inwardness and love / Is very much unto the Prince and Claudio, / Yet, by mine honour, I will deal in this" (245–247). Thus while the two military heros claim that Hero's purported infidelity has besmirched their reputations ("I stand dishonoured, that have gone about / To link my dear friend to a common stale," Don Pedro petulantly complains [64–65]), Benedick is the first man to come to the fallen woman's aid (112) and the first to vow *on his honor* to help restore her reputation. If the military men are wearing dress uniforms, the splitting of the group presents a stark visual emblem: three soldiers angrily depart the scene of marriage, while a fourth deserts his regiment and commanding officer to succor the seemingly defeated camp. When Benedick next encounters Claudio and Don Pedro, he reminds them that they are mistaken and that "In a false quarrel there is no true valour" (5.1.119), before formally resigning Don Pedro's service ("I must discontinue your company") and challenging his peer to a duel ("For my Lord Lackbeard there, he and I shall meet " [185–189]).

Benedick's insult, "Lackbeard," may seem hypocritical (after all, he likewise shaved to impress Beatrice), but he has come to transcend such superficial binaries as war = manly = beard *vs.* love = effeminate = shaved. Benedick can be a soldier and a lover, refined yet ferocious, as Claudio discovers to his great surprise:

*DON PEDRO:* He is in earnest.

*CLAUDIO:* In most profound earnest and, I'll warrant you, for the love of
    Beatrice.

*DON PEDRO:* And hath challenged thee?

*CLAUDIO:* Most sincerely.

*DON PEDRO:* What a pretty thing man is when he goes in his doublet and
    hose and leaves off his wit!

                                                        (5.1.191–197)

Their quips after Benedick's departure barely conceal their nervous apprehension that, even in his foppish civilian dress, Benedick has never been so fierce or frightening as he is *for the love of Beatrice*. Many of *The Courtier*'s key passages concerning military valor center on precisely this issue of whether a man in love may be an honorable and effective soldier. Cesare Gonzaga argues that falling in love provides, not an impediment, but a catalyst to martial valor:

> as touchinge the understanding of great matters . . . they [i.e., women] do not stray our wittes, but rather quicken them, and in warr make men past feare and hardie passinge measure. And certesse it is not possible, that in the hart of man, where once is entred the flame of love, there should at any time reigne cowardlynesse. . . . Therefore whoseo coulde gather an armie of lovers, that shoulde fight in the presence of the ladies they loved, shoulde subdue the wholl world, onlesse against it on the contrarie part there were an other armie likewise in love. (3.51)

Benedick has little to fear from his adversary, for while Claudio is a soldier who once performed "the feats of a lion" (1.1.15), he is not a soldier *in love*. Remaining with the ladies at the altar and challenging Hero's accuser to a duel are unlikely to be mentioned in the annals of great military feats, yet as Lodovico points out, "we wyll holde oure selves contented . . . with the uprightnesse of a well meaning minde, and with an invincible courage, and that he alwaies shew himself such as one: for many times men of courage are sooner knowen in small matters then in greate" (1.17). In defending Hero against the authority of the prince's slander, Benedick embarks on one of the most delicate and controversial actions one may perform: defying his superior officer. For in agreeing to obey Beatrice's order to "kill Claudio," Benedick would also be correcting the egregious error of his prince. As Ottaviano suggests, "whan he [i.e., the courtier] knoweth his [i.e., the prince's] minde is bent to commit any thinge unseemlie for him, [he should] be bould to stande with him [i.e., stand up to him] in it, and . . . to disswade him from everie ill pourpose, and to set him in the waye of vertue" (4.5).

Now it may be objected that Benedick never truly approaches Castiglione's courtier-ideal, that his behavior in 5.2 proves that he remains in essence an unrefined scorner-of-love. For example, he banters with Margaret using military imagery that reduces love to crude sexual coupling: when Margaret tells him to "Give us the swords; we have bucklers of our own," Benedick replies, "If you use them, Margaret, you must put in the pikes with a vice" (5.2.18–21)[31] Yet here he is not in the presence of a courtly lady but merely an aspiring "upper servant," one linked with the lowlife villain Borachio (a man so lacking honor or refinement that he commits slander for hire then confesses his crime in a drunken stupor).[32] Benedick needn't bother minding his manners in such company. Moreover, in the same scene Benedick has difficulty expressing his love in a sonnet for Beatrice: "I cannot show it in rhyme. I have tried. I can find out no rhyme to 'lady' but 'baby'—an innocent rhyme; for 'scorn' 'horn'—a hard rhyme. . . . No, I was not born under a rhyming planet" (5.2.35–40). Perhaps neither was Castiglione's Unico Aretino, who recites an extempore sonnet interpreting the emblematic letter "S" embroidered on Elisabetta's headpiece only to have the narrator expose the artifice behind his apparent feat of poetic *sprezzatura:* "many judged [the poem] to be made at the first sight. But bicause it was more witty and better knitt then a man would have beleved the shortnes of time required, it was thought he had prepared it before" (1.9). Benedick is not a very good poet; he lacks an appreciation for music; his jokes are poorly timed; he is an awkward dancer and an ineffectual masker; and his dress and toilet tend to the outlandish. Yet somehow none of this really matters, because when it comes to what Cesare Gonzaga refers to as "the understanding of great matters," Benedick displays unparalleled loyalty in love, chivalry in defending Hero's honor, and determination in correcting his prince's errors. As Raleigh archly observes, "Nothing great was ever accomplished by one whose ruling passion was self-improvement."[33]

What more could Messina ask from a courtier? Lodovico considers "armes to be his principall profession, and al the other good qualities [merely] an ornament thereof" (1.44). In this Benedick differs substantively from Claudio. "Thus far I can praise him," remarks Don Pedro, concerning the former man; "he is of a noble strain, of approved valour and confirmed honesty" (2.1.374–376). The Prince is not damning Benedick with faint praise: these are the core qualities that a courtier should exhibit. Claudio, in contrast, displays more of the superficially refined qualities: "his nice fence and active practice, / His May of youth and bloom of lustihood" (5.1.75–76). Here Leonato *is* damning Claudio with faint praise. "[T]he most exquisite Claudio;" as Don John enviously calls him (1.3.48), cuts an attractive figure and knows all the latest fencing techniques, but he lacks the essential qualities of an honorable soldier. By making Benedick consistently fail to achieve minor ideals found in *The Courtier*, Shakespeare exposes the dangers inherent in attaching disproportionately high values to superficial details, which eclipse the book's major criteria for courtly perfection.

The Claudio-Hero plot of *Much Ado* illustrates the disastrous consequences of sexual slander and poor leadership, two major topics of concern in Castiglione's third and fourth books. With respect to personal reputation, Count Lodovico articulates the prevailing gendered social ideals, ones which prove so damaging in *Much Ado;* namely, that "even as in women honestye once stained dothe never retourne againe to the former astate: so the fame of a gentleman that carieth weapon, yf it once take a foile [i.e., a blemish] in any litle point through dastardlines or any other reproche, doeth evermore continue shameful in the worlde and full of [ignominy]." Immediately after making this categorical statement, Lodovico backpedals and qualifies his position, saying that "the more excellent our Courtyer shalbe in this arte, the more shall he bee worthy praise" and that "I judge not necessarye in hym so perfect a knowledge of thynges and other qualities" (1.17). The problem, of course, is that one cannot be more or less "perfect" or "excellent" (both adjectival superlatives), just as one cannot be "a little bit pregnant" or, in the case of Hero and Claudio, a little bit suspected of unchastity or dishonor. Honor is an absolute: it either exists entirely, or it vanishes into air; and because of its essential fragility, *The Courtier* recommends against the application of inflexible criteria to the evolving complexities of human affairs. But since he understands that such criteria will persist, Castiglione warns against treating these with anything other than cautious reverence. In particular, a woman's chastity should remain off-limits when recounting "meerie jestes": "to speake a woorde which should seeme to come of a readinesse of witt . . . [by] staynynge of a woorthie gentilwomans honesty . . . is a verie naughtie matter and woorthie sore punishment" (2.83). Impugning a woman's honor in earnest is an even more grave offense.[34]

Claudio's hypersensitivity about his own honor and his cautious inquiries about Hero's (e.g., "Is she not a modest young lady?" [1.1.160]) produce a volatile mixture which ignites when exposed to narrative catalysts suggested by *The Courtier*. In the first, Pietro Bembo declares that the most "bitter" pain imaginable arises out of suspicion: "I have . . . seene the woman whom I served, stirred against me, eyther upon a vain suspicyon that she conceyved her self of my trustinesse, or elles upon some other false opinyon that had bine put into her head by some mennes report to my hindraunce, so that I beleaved no grief might be compared to myne" (1.11). Whether the suspicion stems from mistaken apprehensions or false reports, the result is incomparable pain. Claudio experiences such misgivings twice: first when Benedick mocks him for losing Hero to the proxy Don Pedro ("the Prince hath got your Hero" [2.1.192–193]), a mistake which induces "melancholy" and a "jealous complexion" in Claudio (214, 292); and a second time when he witnesses Margaret dressed in Hero's clothes speak to a man out of her chamber window, inducing a reaction more akin to the smoldering rage that stems from wounded pride ("in the congregation where I should wed, there will I shame her" [3-2.118–119]).[35]

His susceptibility to repeated deception is a phenomenon suggested by the second narrative catalyst discussed in *The Courtier*. Bernardo Bibbiena observes that "Trulye the passions of love bringe with them a great excuse of everye fault" and that, because a lover is more susceptible to error and because the gravity of any resulting errors will be mitigated by the circumstances of being in love, he must therefore exercise extreme caution in his dealings with others and *be above reproach himself:* "a Gentilman that is in love, ought aswell in this point as in all other thynges to be voide of dissimulation, and of an upright meaninge" (2.94). A lover is like a walking time bomb—more likely explode than another man and more likely expect forgiveness when he does. That Claudio feels entitled to leniency is suggested by his behavior following the exposure of Don John's slander plot. Claudio's offer to make restitution to Leonato sounds more like defiance than remorse. "Choose your revenge yourself," he challenges; "Yet sinned I not / But in mistaking" (5.1.266–269). And his willingness to wed Hero's supposed cousin, sight unseen, contradicts his earlier vow to "lock up all the gates of love" and never marry another (4.1.104). In light of this quick second wedding, Claudio's speech at the first visit to her burial monument ("her fame . . . never dies" [5.3.6]) seems merely an empty gesture.

It could be said, in Claudio's defense, that in each regrettable action he merely follows the lead of his prince. Time and again, Don Pedro is present to support the mistaken decisions taken by his impressionable charge. For example, Don Pedro is present for Don John's first mention of Hero's infidelity, and after making only minimal protest— "I will not think it" (3.2.112)—he quickly swallows the bait in spite of his half-brother's limited credibility: "I will join with thee to disgrace her" (120–121). Don Pedro is also present to witness Hero's supposed midnight assignation and lends his authority to Claudio's charges in church the following day:

DON PEDRO:                          Upon mine honour,
              Myself, my brother, and this grievèd Count
              Did see her, hear her, at that hour last night
              Talk with a ruffian at her chamber window,
              Who hath indeed, most like a liberal villain,
              Confessed the vile encounters they have had
              A thousand times in secret.

                                                   (4.1.88–94)

Strangely, there is no mention elsewhere in the play that either man confronted or interrogated the "liberal villain"; nor could the supposed confession of a thousand midnight assignations be true, given the fact that Beatrice has been Hero's constant bedfellow (4.1.149). In the next act, Don Pedro persists in his error: "My heart is very sorry for your daughter's death, / But on my honour she was charged with nothing / But what was true and very full of proof" (5.1.103–105). Thus he destroys the honor of a bride and her family on the flimsiest of evidence, by swearing the truth of an improbable piece of hearsay, gathered from unreliable third parties. As many soldiers do when accused of causing a wrongful death, Claudio's best defense would be to say that he was only following his commander's lead—that he was only following orders.

This is where Shakespeare's engagement with *The Courtier* becomes most profound. As Trafton's study emphasizes, Castiglione's book is structured as a "progressive exploration" which builds up to two climactic discussions in book 4, one concerning the courtier's primary function as effective advisor to his prince and the second exploring the operations of neoplatonic love; in other words, the signal philosophical issues of truth and beauty.[36] By making Don Pedro vouch for the veracity of such obvious fabrications, with such disastrous results, Shakespeare illustrates warnings about princely authority set forth in *The Courtier*. For example, Lodovico writes that when princely errors occur, "there are diverse causes and among other the obstinatenes of princes, whiche to prove mastries [i.e., to show that they can work miracles] oftentimes bend themselves to favor him, that to their seeming, deserveth no favour at all, and manye tymes in deede they are deceyved" (1.16). In prematurely readmitting to his trust his defeated bastard brother, Don Pedro shows off his own forgiveness and magnanimity. The action backfires, though, as the humiliation of receiving ostentatious charity from his captors motivates Don John's slander. "I had rather be a canker in a hedge than a rose in his grace" (1.3.25–26), he growls, though he resents Claudio's success as well: "That young start-up hath all the glory of my overthrow" (63–64).

To be fair, Don Pedro is not aware of his half-brother's plot, but here too the prince is in dereliction of his office. As Ottaviano Fregoso explains, it would be his duty to know such things as the qualities of those in his immediate circle: "a good judgement is verye necessarye in a Prince to descern who deserveth to be put in trust, and who not" (4.41). Such attitudes stem from a simple, quasi-Machiavellian axiom: "ignorance hurteth, whereof springe all vices" (4.25).[37] Unlike for Claudio, for Don Pedro to err—even if only "in mistaking"—represents a very serious failing. For as Castiglione's duchess observes, an individual who is misled into committing a crime should receive a "double punishmente," first for the crime itself and second for allowing himself to be led by one who gives an "yll example" (1.23). Because of the high stakes involved, political savvy is more important than all other courtly graces combined:

LODOVICO: You may see that ignorance in musike, in daunsinge, in
    ridinge hurteth no man, yet he that is no musitien is ashamed and

aferde to singe in the presence of others . . . but of the unskilfulnes
to govern people arrise so mane yvelles, deathes, destructions, mis-
cheeffes and confusions, that it may be called the deadliest plagu[e]
upon the earth. And yet some princes most ignorant in government, are
not bashfull nor ashamed to take upon them to govern. . . .

(4.8)

Don Pedro's problem is that he governs his followers unwisely and with
faulty intelligence; the Friar quickly perceives that "[t]here is some strange
misprision in the princes," and Benedick agrees that their "wisdoms [have
been] misled" (4.1.185–187). The antithesis of Lodovico's "bashfull" prince,
one who acknowledges his limitations, Don Pedro confidently repeats his
mistakes loudly and in public. To make matters worse, the one courtier who
could represent the voice of reason amid all the mischievous talk of Hero's
infidelity, Benedick, is mocked each time he approaches his prince (in 3.2.,
5.1., 5.4). In fact, in the first instance, had Benedick not been driven off the
stage by the superficial barbs of "these hobby-horses," Don Pedro and Claudio (3.2.68–69), he would have been present to hear Don John's explosive
imputations concerning Hero shortly thereafter (74—128). Benedick's exit
is dramatically expedient, for Shakespeare must get him off the stage during
this exchange; unlike other yes-men in Don Pedro's retinue, Benedick is too
apt to ask questions and too quick to confront individuals in error. When
Claudio quips that he "knows" who loves Benedick and Don Pedro chimes
in, "That would I know, too. I warrant, one that knows him not" (3.2.59–61),
the irony is that neither man is a sound judge of character; it is Don Pedro,
not Beatrice, who "knows him not"— though the prince doesn't know Don
John, either, for that matter.

    In the dying moments of the play, Benedick assumes the mantle of the
courtier-ideal not because he has achieved a high degree of superficial courtly
refinement but because he chooses love over suspicion and service over slander. Indeed, Benedick determines to marry in spite of the powerful influence
exerted by his superior officer: "I'll tell thee what, Prince: a college of wit-
crackers cannot flout me out of my humour. Dost thou think I care for a satire
or an epigram? No, if a man will be beaten with brains, a shall wear nothing
handsome about him" (5.4.100–104). It used to be Benedick who was chided
for ill-timed and inappropriate jesting; now it is tempting to interpret his
parting jibe about the "college of wit-crackers" as Shakespeare's dismissal of
the scurrilous jesting and artificial niceties of Castiglione's books 1 and 2, and
his dramatic advocacy of the more serious recommendations in books 3 and
4. Indeed, Benedick's final onstage actions are (1) to stand by his decision to
marry; (2) to forgive his friend ("live unbruised, and love my cousin"); (3) to

lead a dance ("First, of my word! . . . play, music"); (4) to advise Don Pedro ("get thee a wife. There is no staff more reverend than one tipped with horn"); and (5) and to mete justice out to the enemy of his prince (5.4.97–128). Benedick has come a long way from merely functioning as "the Prince's jester," a stinging term that both wounded the aspiring courtier's pride ("The Prince's fool! . . . I am not so reputed" [2.1.137, 205–207]) and recalls Hoby's favorite term for the antithesis of the courtier: "commune jestar" (2.27). Benedick no longer proposes ridiculous services like fetching a "tooth-picker" from "the Antipodes" (2.1.261–269); now he can perform more constructive employments for his prince. Although there is no line in which Benedick expressly resumes his service to Don Pedro, the fifth action listed above implicitly confirms that he has rejoined the prince's retinue: "I'll devise thee [i.e., for you, Don Pedro] brave punishments for him [i.e., your enemy, Don John]" (5.4.127–128).

In marrying *and* rejoining the military, and in recommending that his military commander "get" a wife to gain social prestige, Benedick strikes that elusive balance between social and political finesse, and, in the process, achieves personal happiness, political advancement, and social stability in Messina.[38] This is the much touted "golden mean" so valued in countless Renaissance advice manuals; as Lodovico phrases it, "betwene thys excellent grace, and that fonde foolyshnesse there is yet a meane, and they that are not by nature so perfectly furnished, with studye and diligence maye polishe and correct a great part of the defaultes of nature" (1.14).[39] Benedick has charmed playgoers and readers for four centuries because, more than any other character in *Much Ado,* he amends as many faults as he is able and accepts those that cannot be remedied. In so doing, he achieves a kind of comic *sprezzatura:* effortless yet charming imperfection. If Ottaviano Fregoso's prioritization may be taken as representative, that "as musike, sportes, pastimes, and other pleasaunt facions, are . . . the floure of Courtlines, even so is the traininge and the helping forward of the Prince to goodnesse and the fearinge him from yvell, the frute of it" (4.5), then Benedick (and Beatrice) provide the most fruitful service of all. While *Much Ado* begins as a "merry war of wits" between one couple, the conflict gradually turns outwards to defeat the real enemies of peace, love, women, and their prince.

## IV

In her introduction to Hoby's translation of *The Courtier,* Virginia Cox observes that the courtesy book was initially presented (and subsequently received) as a light game or "trivial pursuit": "*The Courtier* has been its own worst enemy: the urbanity and lightness of tone of Castiglione's dialogue . . . have often obscured, especially for readers remote in place and time from the society that produced it, the scope and moral gravity of the . . . questions it raises."[40] The same could be said for Shakespeare's frivolously titled comedy.

Of course the playwright was much closer in time, if not in place, to the fictional Urbino of the early sixteenth century, and yet the likelihood that his play was written in response to the Italian courtesy book is still downplayed. The critical response to the comparative project initiated by Scott has been condescending and dismissive, as if to read *The Courtier* as a "hypotext" (original/source) to Shakespeare's richly allusive dramatic "hypertext" (subsequent borrowing text) were to indulge in a kind of quaint Victorian parlor game (e.g., "spot the verbal parallels," or "find the English character's Italian predecessor").[41] Yet intertextuality is not a marginal issue in Castiglione and Shakespeare studies; it is of central importance, largely because in listing and then illustrating desirable and undesirable qualities and behavioral patterns, Castiglione demonstrates how human identity is also a composite, a pastiche, a collection of acquired attributes: "even as the bee in the greene medowes fleeth always aboute the grasse chousynge out flowres: so shall our Courtyer steale thys grace from them that to hys seming have it, and from ech one that percell that shal be most worthy praise" (1.26). The elision in Hoby's translation of the individual "Courtyer" and the book's title *Courtier* underscores the degree to which writing, like identity, is profoundly intertextual; and Castiglione's pollen-collecting metaphor for composite identity anticipates modern conceptualizations of the "relational self" as a palimpsest of internalized narratives and introjected objects.[42] *Much Ado* is thus no mere dramatized roman-à-clef, keyed to the *dramatis personae* found in Castiglione; nor is it a slavish imitation of the earlier author's comic anecdotes or witty dialogue. Rather, *Much Ado* represents a profound thematic and philosophical engagement with Castiglione's text in which Shakespeare exposes as false the distinction between the self-fashioning of the aspiring courtier in the private realm and the selfless devotion of the advisor who serves his prince in the political realm.

A related misconception in Shakespeare criticism holds that an aspiring gentleman's relationship with his homosocial peer group and with his prince took precedence over his love relationships, that the two were mutually exclusive—a false dichotomy we can dispense with upon reading Castiglione. In his preface to the Norton edition of *The Courtier*, Javitch invokes Norbert Elias's concept of the "civilizing process," one in which the transition from feudalism to early capitalism necessitated new behavioral codes to preserve existing hierarchies and ensure enduring loyalties. Javitch argues that *The Courtier* quietly furthers this process, cynically functioning as a conformist manual in which "prince-pleasing" becomes "one of the book's central but deliberately inconspicuous considerations."[43] David Quint proposes a second and equally "central" consideration: namely, the crucial role played by courtly ladies in these civilizing and "pacifying" processes. By providing a "rival audience for whom, as well as for the Prince, the courtier puts on display [his] exquisite accomplishments," ladies allied with their prince could enhance his control over unruly males.[44] As the case of Beatrice's intervention demonstrates, this "rival audience" can just as effectively contest the authority of a prince determined to be ruling unwisely or in a tyrannical manner.

Shakespearean critics have also debated the degree to which Elizabethan culture's pervasive misogyny reflects resentment over disruptions occasioned by men being forced (by the hetero-patriarchal imperative to marry) to transfer their energies and allegiances from peers in the male spheres of politics and war to seek "grace" from ladies instead.[45] Men should be serving the court, but instead they must court the ladies. Yet as the example of *Much Ado* illustrates, it is Benedick—the male who comes to align himself most strongly with the ladies—who upholds such ideals as civic order, social justice, and family honor. Benedick's repetition of the term "grace" in his initial proviso, "til all graces be in one woman, one woman shall not come in my grace" (2.3.29–30), points to its meaning as both *quality* and *reward* as defined in the Italian treatise. For as Quint argues, a Renaissance prince and a lady being wooed exerted analogous powers over men: "each [was] the recipient of the courtier's devoted attention, each the bestower or withholder of 'grazia.'"[46] Benedick's most egregious error lay not in itemizing extravagant demands but in arrogating the power to bestow or withhold grace in the first place. Benedick discovers that grace is not his to give to himself: it can only come from his prince, his lady, or ideally, from both. Benedick also, despite his antifeminist quips and antimatrimonial barbs, upholds the sanctity of marriage, concluding that no staff (symbol of authority) is "more reverend than one tipped with horn" (symbol of cuckoldry) (5.4.123–124). In stark contrast, Claudio's continued allegiance to the unmarried prince Don Pedro—at the expense of his relationship with Hero—is presented as retrograde and unwise. And Claudio's humorless inability to accept compromise and uncertainty in love goes entirely against the practical spirit of Castiglione's Gaspare, who advocates tolerance of the "spottes" of imperfection when these appear in the beloved (1.7). "Surely as I live," Hero assures her groom, "I am a maid," to which her father anxiously adds, "She died, my lord, but whiles her slander lived" (5.4.64, 66). In Claudio's uncourtly world-view, slander can kill; but in Benedick's more refined understanding of the inevitability of "spottes," slander merely injures, and it is the perpetrators—not the victims—who should receive correction.

Castiglione's elaborate codes of gentlemanly refinement serve both the political and the romantic spheres, and Shakespeare's primary insight as a reader of *The Courtier* is his dramatic demonstration that these two spheres need not be mutually exclusive. In fact, the very garden bower in which Benedick and Beatrice are tricked into falling in love is likened to a court rife with unctuous flatterers. As Hero describes the garden, "There honeysuckles, ripened by the sun, / Forbid the sun to enter, like favourites / Made proud by princes, that advance their pride / Against the power that bred it" (3.1.8–11). Benedick does not oppose his prince because he has been made proud by the acquisition of courtly grace; instead, Benedick is emboldened by love to serve Don Pedro more effectively. The best way to serve one's prince is to "get" oneself (and, if possible, one's prince also) a wife. As Cesare Gonzaga explains in an axiom borne out by Benedick's success (and by Don Pedro's failure), the surest way to attain courtly perfection is to fall in love, "For he that loveth, alwaies coveteth to make himself as lovely as he can" (3.51).[47]

## Notes

1. Scott, "*The Book of the Courtyer:* A Possible Source of Benedick and Beatrice," *PMLA* 16 (1901), 475–502 (hereafter cited parenthetically). Quotations from Castiglione and Shakespeare are taken from the following editions and will be cited parenthetically in my text: *The Book of the Courtier,* trans. Thomas Hoby, ed. Virginia Cox, Everyman ed. (London: J. M. Dent, 1994); and *Much Ado About Nothing,* ed. Sheldon P. Zitner, Oxford World Classics (Oxford: Oxford University Press, 1998). In his introduction to an earlier edition of Hoby's *Courtier* (the one used by Scott), Walter Raleigh charted Castiglione's influence on Elizabethan literature in general terms: "it is not clear that Shakespeare knew THE COURTIER," Raleigh argued, but Italian courtesy books may have inspired the wit of "Beatrice and Benedick, of Rosalind and Orlando" (Raleigh, ed., *The Book of the Courtier From the Italian of Count Baldassare Castiglione: Done into English by Sir Thomas Hoby ANNO 1561,* Tudor Translations 23 [1900; repr., New York: AMS Press, 1967], lxxix, lxxxiv).

2. Burke, *The Fortunes of the "Courtier": The European Reception of Castiglione's "Cortegiano"* (University Park, PA: Pennsylvania State University Press, 1995), passim; see especially "Appendix 2: Readers of the Courtier before 1700," 163–178. Raleigh points out that four editions of Hoby's translation were printed during the reign of Elizabeth: 1561, 1577, 1588, and 1603 (introduction to *The Book of the Courtier,* Tudor Translations edition, lix–lx).

3. Burke, *The Fortunes of the "Courtier,"* 132.

4. Javitch, preface to *The Book of the Courtier: The Singleton Translation,* Norton Critical Editions (New York: Norton, 2002), vii; Raleigh, introduction, *The Book of the Courtier,* Tudor Translations edition, lxxviii.

5. See Donatella Baldini, "The Play of the Courtier: Correspondences between Castiglione's *Il libro del Cortegiano* and Shakespeare's *Love's Labour's Lost*," *Quaderni d'Italianistica* 18 (1997) 5–22; C. L. Gent, "*Measure for Measure* and the Fourth Book of Castiglione's *Il Cortegiano*," *Modern Language Review* 67 (1972): 252–256; Barbara A. Johnson, "The Fabric of the Universe Rent: *Hamlet* as an Inversion of *The Courtier,*" *Hamlet Studies* 9 (1987) 34–52; Mitchell Allen Sutterfield, "'Courtier, Soldier, Scholar': Self-Fashioning in Castiglione's *Courtier* and Shakespeare's *Hamlet*" (Ph.D. diss., George Washington University, 1992); Viviana Comensoli, "Music, *The Book of the Courtier,* and Othello's Soldiership," in *The Italian World of English Renaissance Drama: Cultural Exchange and Intertextuality,* ed. Michele Marrapodi (Newark: University of Delaware Press, 1998), 89–105. Other studies

of note include Cajsa C. Baldini, "A Courtier or a Prince: Shakespeare's *Richard II* as a Dramatization of Conflicting Paradigms of Political Craftsmanship," *Forum Italicum* 37 (2003): 56–69; Maurice Hunt, "Ways of Knowing in *The Merchant of Venice*," *Shakespeare Quarterly* 30 (1979) 89-93; and Camille Wells Slights, "Common Courtesy in *The Two Gentlemen of Verona*," in *Shakespeare's Comic Commonwealths* (Toronto: University of Toronto Press, 1993) 57-73.

   6. Bullough, *Narrative and Dramatic Sources of Shakespeare. Volume II: The Comedies, 1597–1603* (London: Routledge and Kegan Paul, 1958), 79–80; Lewalski; ed., *Much Ado About Nothing*, Blackfriars Shakespeare (Dubuque, IA: William C. Brown, 1969), xiv–xvi; Humphreys, ed., *Much Ado About Nothing*, Arden Shakespeare (London: Methuen, 1985), 16–19.

   7. Burke, *The Fortunes of the "Courtier,"* 27, 82; Humphreys, ed., *Much Ado*, Arden edition, 16 n. 2; Clubb, "Castiglione's Humanistic Art and Renaissance Drama," in *Castiglione: The Ideal and the Real in Renaissance Culture*, ed. Robert W. Hanning and David Rosand (New Haven: Yale University Press, 1983), 191. Clubb's own study traces correspondences between *The Courtier* and later Italian stage-comedies—source-hunting, to be sure, but at least it's not *Shakespearean* source-hunting! Bullough finds "no very close resemblances" between the two works but concedes that Castiglione's book provides an "interesting analogue" to *Much Ado* (*Narrative and Dramatic Sources of Shakespeare*, 78–80). Without specifying which play(s) he has in mind, George Bull writes that Shakespeare's jokes and witticisms "renew the jokes and puns recommended by Castiglione" (introduction to *The Courtier*, trans. Bull, Penguin Classics edition [London: Penguin, 1976], 14).

   8. F. H. Mares's introduction to the New Cambridge Shakespeare edition may be taken as representative in this respect: after summarizing the preliminary findings of Scott, Bullough, and Lewalski, the editor dismisses their proposed parallels as "distant" hints and counters that Shakespeare's "real originality" lay in using the Benedick-Beatrice plot to comment on the Claudio-Hero plot borrowed from Bandelloind Ariosto (*Much Ado About Nothing*, New Cambridge Shakespeare [Cambridge: Cambridge University Press, 1988], 6–7).

   9. Levin, *New Readings vs. Old Plays: Recent Trends in the Reinterpretation of English Renaissance Drama* (Chicago: University of Chicago Press, 1979) 209–229.

   10. Burke, *The Fortunes of the "Courtier,"* 82–83.

   11. Cf. Wayne A. Rebhorn, who argues that the idealized setting of *The Courtier* is placed "against a backdrop of war, destruction, cut-throat competition, and unprovoked malice," exterior realities which occasionally intrude into Urbino's polite conversations (*Courtly Performances: Masking and Festivity in Castiglione's "Book of the Courtier"* [Detroit: Wayne State University Press, 1978], 121).

   12. Bull (introduction to *The Courtier*, Penguin edition, 15) reports that Emilia Pia's death in 1528 occasioned some scandal in Rome because of reports that, rather than receiving the sacraments on her deathbed, she discussed passages from *The Courtier*—a theological insouciance revived in Beatrice's own cavalier attitude towards the afterlife: "there [i.e., at the gate of hell] will the devil meet me like an old cuckold with horns on his head" (2.1.42–43).

   13. On masculine anxieties explored in (and elicited by) *The Courtier*, see Jennifer Richards, "'A wanton trade of living'? Rhetoric, Effeminacy, and the Early Modern Courtier," *Criticism* 42 (2000): 185–206; on *Much Ado*, see Janice Hays, "Those 'Soft and Delicate Desires': *Much Ado* and the Distrust of Women," in *The Woman's Part: Feminist Criticism of Shakespeare*, ed. Carolyn R. S. Lenz, Gayle

Greene, and Carol Thomas Neely (Urbana: University of Illinois Press, 1980), 79–99; and Carol Cook, "'The Sign and Semblance of Her Honor': Reading Gender Difference in *Much Ado About Nothing*," *PMLA* 101 (1986): 186–202.

14. According to Lewalski's count, the phrase occurs "at least three times" in Hoby (*Much Ado*, Blackfriars ed., xiv).

15. On the degree to which the events which transpire at Urbino in *The Courtier* (and its characters, purportedly drawn from life) form an "elaborate fiction"—an ideal reconstruction rather than an accurate transcription—see Rebhorn, *Courtly Performances*, 53–56.

16. See Bull, "Characters in *The Courtier*," in *The Courtier*, Penguin ed., 23; on Shakespeare's borrowings from *Orlando Furioso*, see Zitner, ed. *Much Ado*, Oxford ed., 11; and Bullough, ed., *Narrative and Dramatic Sources of Shakespeare*, 62–105. Neither editor notes the coincidence in dedicatee/source.

17. Clubb, "Castiglione's Humanistic Art and Renaissance Drama," 191–192; Ralph Roeder, *The Man of the Renaissance: Four Lawgivers: Savonarola, Machiavelli, Castiglione, Aretino* (New York: Viking Press, 1933), 318. On the theatrical underpinnings of the courtly ideal, see Rebhorn, *Courtly Performances*, 23–51.

18. *The Courtier* excuses Castiglione's absence from the Urbino dialogues in the early pages (1.1), but Octavian promises a cameo appearance by "our Castillo" upon the author's return from the court of Henry VII (4.38). For ongoing speculation concerning Shakespeare's acting career and minor roles he may have played, see Park Honan, *Shakespeare: A Life* (Oxford: Oxford University Press, 1999) 204–205 and sources cited there. Stephen Greenblatt supports Nicholas Rowe's contention that Shakespeare performed an autobiographical Ghost in *Hamlet:* "it would have been his best role" (*Will in the World: How Shakespeare Became Shakespeare* [New York: Norton, 2004], 322). Castiglione, on the other hand, was mocked by contemporaries for "identifying himself with his model" (Raleigh, introduction to *The Courtier*, Tudor Translations edition, xii–xiii).

19. See Balthazar's brief appearances in *Much Ado* (2.1.98–110, 2.3.44–93, and 5.3.12–21). Zitner discusses the singer's "aristocratic pretensions" yet makes no comment on the similarity in name (*Much Ado*, Oxford edition, 44–45).

20. Burke, *The Fortunes of the "Courtier*," 110.

21. Ibid., 43–44; Hoby's appendices are in Cox, ed., *The Courtier*, Everyman ed., 367–374.

22. Hoby, "Epistle to Lord Henry Hastinges," in Cox, ed., *The Courtier*, Everyman ed., 4–5.

23. Lewalski, introduction to *Much Ado*, Blackfriars ed., xv.

24. On Castiglione's controversial *mot clef*, see Harry Berger Jr., "Sprezzatura and the Absence of Grace," in Javitch, ed., *The Book of The Courtier*, Norton edition, 295–307, quotations on 296–297. Cf. Rebhorn, *Courtly Performances*, 33–40; and Javitch, "*Il Cortegiano* and the Constraints of Despotism," in *Castiglione*, ed. Hanning and Ronsand, 17–28; reprinted in *The Courtier*, Norton ed., 319–328, especially 324–326.

25. To Jean H. Hagstrum, this passionate, if combative, friendship makes Beatrice and Benedick Shakespeare's most exemplary young couple, inasmuch as they evoke "the mutuality that arises between two good and compatible minds, possessing the same kind of goodness and force" (*Esteem Enlivened by Desire: The Couple from Homer to Shakespeare* [Chicago: University of Chicago Press, 1992], 369).

26. See Burke, *The Fortunes of the "Courtier,"* 99–106; and Bull, introduction to *The Courtier,* Penguin edition, 15.

27. Trafton, "Structure and Meaning in *The Courtier,*" *English Literary Renaissance* 2 (1972): 290–291. Cf. JoAnn Cavallo, "Joking Matters: Politics and Dissimulation in Castiglione's *Book of the Courtier,*" *Renaissance Quarterly* 53 (2000): 402–424.

28. Citing this passage from Castiglione, David Kuchta argues that English courtiers walked a social tightrope in which excessive refinement might link them with effeminacy, homosexuality, or worse: "Overdressing was a form of semiotic prostitution . . . an exchange muddled by an immoderate attention to materiality" ("The Semiotics of Masculinity in Renaissance England," in *Sexuality and Gender in Early Modern Europe: Institutions, Texts, Images,* ed. James Grantham Turner [Cambridge: Cambridge University Press, 1993], 239).

29. Rebhorn, *Courtly Performances,* 29, emphasis added; on Castiglione's view of subjective "pliability," see also Valeria Finucci, *The Lady Vanishes: Subjectivity and Representation in Castiglione and Ariosto* (Stanford: Stanford University Press, 1992), 9–10.

30. *The Holy Bible,* Douay Version (Douay 1609 / Rheims 1582), 1 Corinthians 13:11.

31. On swords and bucklers as symbols of phalluses and pudenda, see E. A. M. Colman, *The Dramatic Use of Bawdy in Shakespeare* (London: Longman, 1974), 186, 217.

32. On social class, see Zitner, introduction to *Much Ado,* Oxford ed., 42–44. Alexander Leggatt aptly describes the actions of Borachio and Margaret as "a piece of shabby knavery, done in the dark for money" in *Shakespeare's Comedy of Love* (London: Methuen, 1974), 158.

33. Raleigh, introduction to *The Courtier,* Tudor Translations ed., lxviii.

34. On the centrality of chastity, the only "attribute of femininity on which both defenders and detractors of women agree" in *The Courtier,* see Finucci, *The Lady Vanishes,* 49–73, quotation on 64.

35. It goes without saying that, in this second instance, Hero's grief at the abortive ceremony also confirms Pietro's observation.

36. See Trafton, "Structure and Meaning in *The Courtier,*" 289–297, quotation on 284.

37. Cf. Marlowe's prologue spoken by "Machevill," which asserts that in politics "there is no sin but ignorance" (*The Jew of Malta* [ca.1590], in *The Complete Plays,* ed. J. B. Steane [London: Penguin Classics, 1986], 15).

38. Benedick's political ascendancy is subtly indicated by his shift in address to Don Pedro, from tentative requests and deferential forms (e.g., "you" and "your grace" at 2.1.216, 234, 261, 264, 269), to the blunt, jocular, and informal "Prince [sic], *thou* art sad. Get *thee* a wife" in the last scene (5.4.122, emphasis added).

39. For a detailed study of this ideal, see Joshua Scodel, *Excess and the Mean in Early Modern English Literature* (Princeton: Princeton University Press, 2002). Scodel writes that Hoby's comments on seeking balance in such areas as fashion, joke-telling, and dancing are "typical" of the period's many courtesy books (53).

40. Cox, introduction to *The Courtier,* Everyman edition, xvii.

41. The terms are from Gérard Genette, *Palimpsests: Literature in the Second Degree,* trans. Channa Newman and Claude Doubinsky (Lincoln: University of Nebraska Press, 1997), 5.

42. On the narrative self, see Roy Schafer, *The Analytic Attitude* (New York: Basic Books, 1983), chapters 13–15; on the relational self, see Stephen A. Mitchell, *Relational Concepts in Psychoanalysis: An Integration* (Cambridge: Harvard University Press, 1988), passim.

43. Javitch, introduction to *The Courtier*, Norton edition, viii–ix. This recapitulates his earlier essay, "*Il Cortegiano* and the Constraints of Despotism."

44. Quint, "Courtier, Prince, Lady: The Design of the *Book of the Courtier*," in Javitch, ed., *The Courtier*, Norton ed., 354–355.

45. See, for example, Janet Adelman, "Male Bonding in Shakespeare's Comedies," in Shakespeare's *"Rough Magic": Renaissance Essays in Honor of C. L. Barber*, ed. Peter Erickson and Coppélia Kahn (Newark: University of Delaware Press, 1985), 73–103; Carol Thomas Neely, "Broken Nuptials in Shakespeare's Comedies," in ibid., 61–72; and Shirley Nelson Garner, "Male Bonding and the Myth of Women's Deception in Shakespeare's Plays," in *Shakespeare's Personality*, ed. Norman N. Holland, Sidney Homan, and Bernard J. Paris (Berkeley: University of California Press, 1989), 135–150.

46. Quint, "Courtier, Prince, Lady," 356.

47. A version of this paper was presented to the Canadian Society for Renaissance Studies (University of Manitoba, June 2004). Funding for the project was provided by a Niagara University Research Council Summer Research Stipend, 2004. The author also acknowledges the continued financial support of the Dean of the College of Arts and Sciences and the Department of English, Niagara University.

KENT CARTWRIGHT

# Language, Magic, the Dromios, *and* The Comedy of Errors

Discussions of Shakespeare's *The Comedy of Errors* eventually tend to find their way to Dr. Pinch: although Pinch is "lean-fac'd," he casts a wide shadow.[1] He may appear only in one scene and speak only some dozen lines, but he registers an impression so lingering as to suggest something characteristic about the imaginative structure of the play.[2] Whether he is a "doting wizard," a schoolmaster, or a quack doctor familiar from dramatic tradition, he carries onto the stage, nonetheless, an aura slightly disturbing, even eerie (IV.iv.56). That sense of disturbance emanates not from his gaunt frame or "saffron face"; it derives, rather, from the way that Dr. Pinch becomes the physical manifestation of an idea, an anxiety, and an obsession (IV.iv.59). In him, the play's imaginings of demonic possession have finally called forth their bizarre material counterpart. Dr. Pinch thus enters the action from a realm more of fantasy than of narrative, and he stands for the fear that what one utters—by its own mere agency—might just turn into reality. As the proverb says, "Speak of the Devil and he will appear."[3]

But I am getting ahead of my story, and this is a story that involves a variety of characters, especially the Dromios, and, more broadly, the workings of language in the play. My argument is that words and thoughts in *The Comedy of Errors* unexpectedly acquire a certain magical agency and that the magical and the fantastical also acquire a certain potential for truth. I would

*SEL: Studies in English Literature, 1500–1900*, Volume 47, Number 2 (Spring 2007): pp. 331–354. Copyright © 2007 The Johns Hopkins University Press.

suggest, that is, that the play delves beyond its own overt empiricism toward a substructure of fantasy and enchantment that conveys, paradoxically, a sense of the "real." This argument points toward a residual medievalism in Shakespeare, identifiable in elements such as fairies and sympathetic bewitchment. The magical resonates importantly, too, in *The Comedy of Errors*'s expressions of *copia* and festivity. Instances of amplitude, doubleness, and repetition eddy through the scenic structure and language of the play as if bearing witness to some uncanny agency. The Dromios are the characters most sensitive to the magical, and, in their festivity and unruly speech and their earthiness and responsiveness, they enhance the sense of magic's odd realism. At the end, the rationalism of the denouement will draw a certain power from the penumbra of the magical.

The idea of magic arises in the action, of course, from the disturbing possibility that different characters might share the same identity. That possibility cannot be explained, at least initially, by empirical sense impressions: "What error drives our eyes and ears amiss," asks the alien Antipholus (II. ii.184). With sense impressions baffled, the characters are launched into a "green world" of Ephesian enchantment—made that much more numinous by the reputation of Ephesus in the New Testament as a place of magic.[4] Conversely, in the last act's resolution, Egeon's declaration that his eyes and ears "cannot err" will help to bring the city back to its senses (V.i.317). Thus, rational empiricism will finally unravel the truth, while magic will be understood as the false explanation for, as the Abbess puts it, "this sympathised one day's error" (V.i.397).[5] But, of course, the very idea that an "error" could be "sympathised," that is, spread from character to character by some psychic force, does not seem itself altogether rational or empirical. Despite the play's Providential and Pauline denouement, magic acquires, I want to suggest, a certain agency and validity, a truth value.

## Aspects of Magic

Three aspects of magic stand out for our purposes: sympathy, language, and possession. Sympathetic magic in the Middle Ages and the Renaissance identified the belief that effects could be created on a remote being by performing them on another object representative of that being.[6] Dromio of Syracuse alludes to one form of sympathetic magic when he explains that devils usually ask for "the parings of one's nail, a rush, a hair, a drop of blood, a pin, a nut, a cherry-stone" (IV.iii.69–71). With one such domestic trifle, a witch can work vicarious effects.

A related form of sympathetic magic involves what today we think of as voodoo dolls. A number of English witch trials in the years just before *The Comedy of Errors* give evidence of witches who configured wax effigies of their enemies and then mutilated them—for example, by stabbing the effigy in the midsection with stiff hairs in order to cause stomach pains in the victim.[7] Likewise, in 1591 the possibly deranged William Hacket was executed for seeking the queen's death in that he "did trayterously raze a certaine picture of the Q. Maiesties . . . and . . . did maliciously and traiterously put in and thrust an yron Instrument into that part of the sayde picture, that did represent the Brest and Hart of the Q. Majestie."[8] In April 1594, the year of *The Comedy of Errors*'s first probable performance, Ferdinando Stanley, the fifth Earl of Derby died from bewitchment, according to some reports. Shakespeare surely had specific knowledge of the earl, the patron of Lord Strange's Men with whom Shakespeare was connected.[9] Surrounding the earl's death were peculiar events associated by some with bewitchment or Catholic revenge or both. The earl's demise reportedly involved a wax effigy, a wizard, and an apparition; and near to the earl during his illness, allegedly, was a "mumbling" woman who "seemed to be able to ease him of his vomiting and hiccough, but whenever she did so, became troubled in the same way herself."[10] *The Comedy of Errors* has no wax effigies or mumbling women, but it does have telepathic effects, especially between corresponding characters, in that the fears for the self that one character expresses can produce real afflictions for another. In this play, thoughts have the potential for sympathetic agency.

Magic also has a historic and histrionic association with language: spells, charms, incantations, and prayers. "The whole of Elizabethan culture testifies to the power imagined in words," states Jane Donawerth, but word magic inspired opposing judgments in contemporary rhetorical treatises and also on the stage.[11] Although radical thinkers such as Marsilio Ficino and Henry Cornelius Agrippa could argue for thaumaturgic effects in language, many Elizabethan rhetoricians were suspicious of word magic, given the attack by Protestants on what they considered the witchcraft of the Catholic Mass.[12] A dramatist such as Christopher Marlowe, however, could claim that eloquence has the power to bewitch. In *Tamburlaine*, for example, Theridamas finds himself charmed by Tamburlaine's blandishments: "What stronge enchantments tice my yeelding soule," he asks (I.ii.224).[13] In Shakespeare's *Henry VI, Part 1*, Joan la Pucelle's word magic is both defended and denied by other characters—and never quite discredited. More extensively in *The Comedy of Errors*, words take on magical lives of their own; they migrate and double; and they infuse themselves into and dominate the minds of characters.

Such a version of word magic might recall the idea of possession, perhaps the most extreme form of bewitchment, wherein an alien force inhabits and controls one's body. Possession, for Protestants, constituted a difficult subject. Just as Reformers rejected relics, pardons, intercessions by saints, and most forms of priestly mediation between God and man, they also tended to reject the efficacy of exorcisms. Many Protestants, nonetheless, still considered demonic possession possible.[14] In the late 1580s and early 1590s, numerous

cases occurred of apparently demonic possession, even mass possessions, especially of children, often taking the form of trances, wild hallucinations, and
involuntary utterances.[15] As just one example, in 1593—close to the time of
*The Comedy of Errors*'s probable composition—a sensational pamphlet detailed
the notorious case of five Throckmorton sisters and seven maidservants from
Warboys, all possessed by demons. For this virtually communal or "sympathised" act of possession, three accused witches were tried by the Bishop of
Lincoln and hanged in 1592.[16] Possession seemed capable of spreading within
a household like a contagion, observes Philip C. Almond of cases from 1574
to 1597.[17] As *The Comedy of Errors* reached the stage, demonic possession was
in the air, and it constitutes one of the ideas iterated most often in the play.[18]
The resident Antipholus even comes to exhibit what others perceive as the
signs of demonic possession—frightful countenance, nonsensical talk, and
physical violence. The alien Antipholus and his Dromio, for their part, feel
mutually bewitched and even transformed in their first encounter with Adriana, and, in general, they believe themselves beset by "enchanting" "witches,"
afflicted with the "imaginary wiles" of "sorcerers," and made to "wander in
illusions" (III.ii.160, 155; IV.iii.10–11; IV.iii.41).

### *Copia*, Amplification, and Dilation

Alongside magic, I would like to place a different set of terms that will lead
us later to the Dromios. Let me begin with a somewhat artificial distinction
between, on the one hand, narrative, and, on the other, "amplification," a
term that I take from Thomas Wilson's *Art of Rhetoric* (1560).[19] When we
discuss narrative, we generally have in mind plot lines and actions, causal
relationships among events in time, motivations and desires, degrees of
agency, and the like. Yet, often imbedded in narrative is a kind of coun-
terforce, what we might call "amplification," or, to borrow from Desiderius
Erasmus, "*copia*," or, to use Patricia Parker's term, "dilation."[20] Amplification, according to Wilson, is augmentation in language or in substance. It
makes possible endless variations on a theme or a convention; thus the fit-
ness of Erasmus's term *copia*, from which the verb "to copy" derives, and thus
Parker's sense of dilation as delay and doubling.[21] Amplification "mov[es]"
the "affections," says Wilson, and stimulates the mind.[22] In Terence, for
instance, multiple variations on a character type or a predicament—compared, likened, or differentiated—make possible a range of engaging and
edifying distinctions.[23] Erasmus also emphasizes in *copia* a certain liveliness:
"Nature herself especially rejoices in variety," and "the mind always eagerly
examines whatever it sees as new," he argues.[24] Thus Erasmus typically
discusses *copia* through images of abundance, splendor, pleasure, and vividness. Doubling in *The Comedy of Errors*—of characters, of events, of experiences—generates fundamentally the delight and vitality of *copia*.

Amplification and *copia* evoke additional values associated with the Renaissance and its drama, such as play, clowning, festive misrule, and carnivalesque inversion, the domain, in *The Comedy of Errors,* of the Dromios. Thus, in a work such as *The Comedy of Errors,* characters who stand for or express festivity often do so by means of amplification. Syracusan Dromio's speech about "the parings of one's nail" illustrates that convergence. The rejuvenating, pun-drenched wit contest between Antipholus and Dromio of Syracuse, concerning whether or not "there's a time for all things," offers an episode of rhetorical amplification and dilation that prolongs the time and delays the plot (II.ii.63–64).[25] Simultaneously, it overthrows Antipholus's violent anger toward his slave, induces laughter and delight, and elevates Dromio to at least intellectual and spiritual parity with Antipholus. Indeed, the brothers Dromio could be described (as we shall see) as themselves figures of amplification.

*Copia* and festivity also share a Renaissance kinship with magic. Rhetorical embellishments and flourishes, for example, were often criticized by medieval and Renaissance theologians, as John O. Ward shows, because their effects resembled those of magic.[26] From a broader perspective, Stuart Clark identifies demonology as an aspect of European intellectual history and demonstrates that magic, witchcraft, and possession were values that Renaissance thinkers connected with cognates such as parody, festive misrule, and hierarchic inversion in an intellectual model of complementary and opposed terms. Amplitude, festivity, and magic, that is, cluster on one side of an encompassing binarial system in contrast to values such as restraint, work, order, rule, rationality, and sacrament. Such clustering and associating of terms is important, for witchcraft beliefs could be credible only because they "were sustained by a whole range of other intellectual commitments." Thus, Clark observes, one could "move from the festive to the demonic without any sense of elision."[27] In that spirit, *The Comedy of Errors* links the domains of comedy, copiousness, and conjuration. In the hilarious "lockout" scene, for example, when the resident Dromio calls out the names of a half-dozen maidservants, the other Dromio taunts him: "Dost thou conjure for wenches, that thou call'st for such store" (III.i.34). "Such store": Ephesian Dromio's runaway replication of names itself suggests demonic incantation. Amplitude in language—in a scene already colored with comedic hierarchical disruption—raises the associated specter of magical agency. We are now in a position to see how instances of *copia* can suggest eerie effects.

### Reiteration, Possession, and Materialization

In the very first scene of *The Comedy of Errors,* amplification and dilation lead to a sense of possession as characters imitate an emotion that finally takes on its own life. This pattern emerges as Solinus, Duke of Ephesus, listens to the condemned Egeon tell the tale of his shipwreck and the separation of his family. Inside the shipwreck story, passion is already presented as infectious, for the wife's "incessant weepings" at the sea storm migrate to the "piteous plainings" of the babies, who "mourn'd for fashion," and finally to Egeon, moved "to seek delays" from drowning because of the others' cries (I.i.70, 72, 74, 73). Outside the shipwreck story, Egeon's narration of pity and dilation has, similarly, a contagious effect on Solinus, for the Duke, who first "excludes all pity" from his decree, now comes to feel "pity" for the sufferings of Egeon and his family and, climactically, makes himself Egeon's "advocate" by granting him a daylong reprieve (I.i.5, 97, 145). Solinus's pity and delay mirror Egeon's own pity and delay with the theme of imitation ("mourn'd for fashion") enunciated by Egeon and enacted by Solinus, each character possessed in turn by the same prior emotion.[28] Sympathy has become "sympathised."

At work, too, is another, odd displacement of feeling, for Solinus expresses more desire to save Egeon's life than does Egeon himself. In his opening lines, Egeon had taken comfort from the Duke's "doom of death"; in the sea storm, he had embraced the prospect of death; and in the closing lines of the scene, he repeats his world weariness: "Hopeless and helpless doth Egeon wend, / But to procrastinate his lifeless end" (I.i.2; I.i.157–158). Egeon experiences himself already as the walking dead, so that the Duke's urge to rescue his life ignores, almost comically, Egeon's embrace of his own demise. Here imitative pity, once aroused, expatiates, acquires its own life, takes possession of the mind, and reads itself back, even mistakenly, into its object. Such amplification might be considered the play's very first error; it is also a source of its vitality, its inner life, since Solinus's pity will reshape events.[29]

We have, then, the striking demonstration of a feeling migrating, spreading, and transferring as if it were self-powered, automotive. The process appears already a little magical, and it will come to embrace words, phrases, sounds, and patterns of action, which will seem capable of wandering from episode to episode. Indeed, Solinus's dilating pity creates a dramaturgical field of associative or telepathic energy, for it calls forth, as if magnetically, the entrance of Egeon's son in the next scene with a bag of potentially redemptive money. There the First Merchant, with apparently preternatural knowledge, informs the alien Antipholus that a countryman has been "apprehended" and will die "ere the weary sun set in the west," echoing the vowels and consonants, as well as the temper, of Egeon's closing speech just seconds before as he "wend[s]" toward "his lifeless end" (I.ii.4, 7). A drift of phonemes and feelings from one scene to another has begun. Instances of shared language put the traveler Antipholus (in scene ii) and his long-separated father Egeon (in scene i) in uncanny synchronicity. Antipholus describes himself as a "drop of water" falling in the ocean, "inquisitive" for his fellow, and he concludes, "So I, to find a mother and a brother, / In quest of them, unhappy, lose myself" (I.ii.35–40).

Because Adriana's later appropriation of the same water image is so distinct, critics tend to ignore Antipholus's repetition of Egeon's prior diction. Egeon had also described this son as "inquisitive" and in "quest" of "his brother," and Antipholus's "unhappy" enjoys all sorts of variations in Egeon's previous narrative: "happy but for me," "happy . . . in my timely death"—until the old man receives from Solinus the defining epithet, "Hapless Egeon" (I.i.125, 129, 126; I.i.37, 138, 140; see also I.i.38, 113). Finally, Antipholus's "lose myself"—not only a phrase in the speech but also a motif in the play—recalls Egeon's earlier "I hazarded the loss of whom I lov'd" (I.i.131). These resonances create a psychic kinship, as if, as G. R. Elliott says, the "very air" of the second scene "is felt to be *fathered* by Aegeon's" first scene, or as if one episode had the power to call forth the next, or as if moods and words from one scene could wash into another, the scenes becoming strangely "sympathised."[30]

The same effect now repeats and complicates itself, for, in the next scene, the women's language echoes not only that of the Antipholus scene (I.ii) but also that of the earlier Egeon scene (I.i). The charged epithet "slave" perambulates from the end of the second to the beginning of this third scene (I.ii.104; II.i.1). Luciana's talk of merchants and marts evokes the immediately prior action, and the women's discussion of men's "liberty" recalls Antipholus's preceding alarm at Ephesian "liberties of sin" (II.i.4–5; II.i.7, 10, 15; I.ii.102). Words are on the move—but the most surprising channeling occurs between this third scene and Egeon's first scene. Adriana's claim about men's "liberty," of course, recalls ironically Egeon's loss of it. Various of the women's other phrases and images also recall Egeon's story: "Time" as men's "master" (II.i.8), "lash'd with woe" (II.i.14; cf. I.i.2), "heaven's eye" (II.i.16; cf. I.i.66, 88), "bound" (II.i.17; cf. I.i.81), and "wild wat'ry seas" (II.i.21; cf. I.i.63). The connections tighten as Adriana dilates upon her own unhappiness. Her image of "A wretched soul bruis'd with adversity" evokes the conflict between "adverse towns" that threatens to bruise mortally the wretched Egeon (II.i.34; I.i.5, 15). Likewise her recognition of her own "helpless patience" recalls the adjective's last use by Egeon in a pointed couplet as he exits, patient but "helpless" (II.i.39; I.i.157). Still other verbal fragments drift from Egeon to Adriana, such as "complain" (II.i.37; cf. I.i.72) and "bereft" (II.i.40; cf. I.i.115). Likewise, when Adriana insists that others would grieve as she does if they were "burden'd with like weight of pain," she catches the tenor of Egeon's "burdened / With lesser weight, but not with lesser woe" (II.i.36; I.i.107–108). The words and feelings of Egeon's narrative seem to have defined the form and color of Adriana's grief. Bits of his language double in hers, hers vary upon his, as if his dilations had conjured forth the possibilities of her expression, the characters possessed by a linguistic field with its own magical life.

Language has acquired here a structural and instrumental function. Often, of course, a Shakespearean play will reiterate certain words, phrases, and images, such as the terms of sickness in *Hamlet,* that lend ambiance and meaning to a play. Most instances of recurrent words and images do not require or invite the notion of magical agency to explain them; rather, we think of them as indices to the special nature of the dramatic world before us. In a play such as *The Comedy of Errors,* however—in which magic is a primary subject, in which characters share images whose presence seems to be flagged (such as the "drop of water"), and in which a mediating figure identifies a universally "sympathised" misprision —in such a play, thinking about language as possessing a kind of magical agency seems more than fair. Word magic in *The Comedy of Errors,* moreover, produces a metadramatic effect, the impression that we are watching the action, in some sense, create itself. In *The Comedy of Errors* language both communicates and enacts the play's special nature.

Words and figures of speech can repeat and preternaturally amplify previous ones. Such a repetition makes Syracusan Antipholus's encounter with Adriana slightly uncanny. It also casts doubt on his infatuation with Luciana.[31] Antipholus and Adriana share the thrilling water imagery of dissolution and recombination. Antipholus has likened himself to "a drop of water / That in the ocean seeks another drop" (I.ii.35–36). Adriana, appearing to have read his mind, claims at their first meeting that he could no more divide himself from her than he could let "fall / A drop of water in the breaking gulf, / And take unmingled thence that drop again" (II.ii.125–127).

That strangely shared sense of deliquescence is recaptured in the bewitching "mist" that Adriana, upon their first meeting, has cast over Antipholus: "I'll . . . / in this mist at all adventures go," he proclaims, yielding, as he follows her inside (II.ii.215–216). Antipholus's eventual distaste for Adriana notwithstanding, her "mist" identifies an aura of enchantment and potential transformation.[32] In that mist, Antipholus will be able to fall in love by imagining Luciana as a thing "divine," a "mermaid," a "god" with the power to change men (III.ii.32, 45, 39). "Mist" is associated with "mystification" and with magic, as a line from Stephen Gosson suggests: "The Iuggler casteth a myst to work the closer."[33] Adriana's mist creates, I argue, the necessary state of enchantment—and for Antipholus, the sense of wonder—that makes his extravagant vision of Luciana possible. The first enchantment by Adriana haunts the second by Luciana.

Adriana's language from the prior scene (II.ii) has possessed Antipholus, evident as he attempts to woo Luciana in the subsequent one (III.ii). Although he recoils from being drowned in the "weeping" Adriana's "flood of tears," Antipholus yet embraces drowning if he could be pillowed in Luciana's "golden hairs" "Spread o'er the silver waves," as if his romantic imagining of Luciana were conditioned on his impressions of her sister (III. ii.42, 46, 48). Indeed, the very vision of a drowning lover had entered the play in an earlier speech by Adriana: "I'll weep what's left away, and weeping die" (II.i.115).

When Antipholus tells Luciana, furthermore, that she is "mine own self's better part," he repeats exactly the idea and phrasing used by Adriana, who had spoken of herself to him as his "dear self's better part" (III.ii.61; II.ii.123). While Antipholus labors for rapturous sincerity in his courting of Luciana, he speaks in imagery partly inspired by the sister-"witch" Adriana—as if her earlier language had mothered some of his. Antipholus affects authenticity, but the play's diction invites a certain doubt about its depth and even truth. The magical, possessive power of language allows us to hover wonderingly between the immediate moment and its resonant context.[34]

Numerous words also migrate and circulate through the play as a whole: words such as "bound," "liberty," "wander," "marks," "hand," "warrant," and "merry." As a case in point, *merry* shows how a word can acquire almost talismanic properties. Early on, Antipholus of Syracuse tells the First Merchant that Dromio "Lightens my humour with his *merry* jests" (I.ii.21; emphasis mine, here and below). The idea of merriment now takes possession of Antipholus's mind as an explanatory paradigm, for in his subsequent contretemps with the wrong Dromio, he insists, despite mounting evidence to the contrary, that his servant must be joking, and so he threatens to break Dromio's "*merry* sconce" (I.ii.79). Later, reconnecting with his own Dromio, Antipholus asks, "is your *merry* humour alter'd" and, faced with the latter's bafflement, can only grow ineffectually enraged (II.ii.7). The idea of Dromio's "*merry* humour," once fixed, predetermines Antipholus's perceptions. The same paradigm repeats itself with Angelo, as *merry* begins to wander errantly through the world of Ephesus. The resident Antipholus, shut out of his house, vows to Angelo that he still "mean[s] to be *merry*" (III.i.108). Thus, when Angelo gives the chain to the wrong Antipholus, who hints that he might not pay for it, Angelo blurts out almost automatically the lame explanation, "You are a *merry* man, sir" (III.ii.177). Later, deflecting the resident Antipholus's adamant denial of having the chain, Angelo continues to insist that the former is only affecting a "*merry* humour"—duplicating unconsciously the other Antipholus's earlier depiction of Dromio (IV.i.27). The same weak rationale for bizarre behavior repeats itself with other characters, such as Dromio of Syracuse and the Courtesan (IV.iii.56). *Merry* migrates copiously from character to character even though it patently fails as an explanation, so that the word finally seems to arise less from situation than from some compulsion, a part of the "sympathised one day's error," the collective trance or "mist," the act of possession, that afflicts Ephesus.

Let us turn from haunted scenes and wandering language to an even more disconcerting telepathic condition in Ephesus: the power of words, fears, desires, and thoughts to produce real effects—sometimes upon the speaker, sometimes upon someone else. *The Comedy of Errors* offers a satirical example late in the play when Antipholus of Syracuse becomes convinced that he and

Dromio are "distract" and "wander in illusions," and he thus prays, "Some blessed power deliver us from hence!" (IV.iii.40–42). Responding instantly to that invocation, the seductive Courtesan enters, and Antipholus recoils in horror that "Satan," "the devil," has appeared in answer to "tempt" him (IV. iii.46–48). Other thoughts also manifest the power to call forth actions, as if utterances could have prophetic power—a feature that might recollect *Henry VI, Part 2*.[35] Mistaking the traveler Antipholus for her husband, Adriana argues that when he "play[s] false," she herself is then "possess'd with an adulterate blot," since husband and wife "be one" (II.ii.142, 140). Furthermore, she asserts, were she "licentious," as is he, he would "tear the stain'd skin off [her] harlot brow" (II.ii.131, 136). These extravagant imaginings find a certain prophetic fulfillment later in the play, when her real husband, having been locked out from home, accuses her of being a "harlot" (IV.iv.99; see also IV.iv.58–62; V.i.205); he later threatens to "scorch," or gash, her face and to "disfigure" her (V.i.183; see also IV.iv.102). The husband's accusation of harlotry is, of course, wrong in spirit, but the question is left open about what happened between Adriana and the alien Antipholus when she led him away to "dine above" and to "shrive" him (II.ii.207, 208).[36] Adriana's imagined recriminations, declared to one brother, find fulfillment in the threats and gestures of the other. If in her husband's mind, Adriana has now acquired her own "adulterate blot," then her Pauline, metaphysical claim that husband and wife are one also has been realized unexpectedly.

One more example of the verbal engendering the material returns us to Dr. Pinch. Antipholus of Syracuse early in the play expresses his horror of falling victim to Ephesian "nimble jugglers," "Dark-working sorcerers," and "prating mountebanks" (I.ii.98, 99, 101). Although Antipholus comes to experience something of what he fears—"Soul-killing witches," for example—the malefactors whom he itemizes make their fullest visitation not upon him but upon his twin, in the figure of Dr. Pinch (I.ii.100). Indeed, the resident brother describes his persecutor, Pinch, as exactly what the alien Antipholus had earlier feared: "a mountebank, / A thread-bare juggler and a fortune-teller," "A living dead man," and "a conjurer" (V.i.239–240, 242, 243). The fears of the first brother are materialized, made manifest, in the sufferings of the second, as if the twins shared a kind of psychic reciprocity, a sympathy, whereby the thoughts of one might fashion or conjure forth the experiences of the other: hence, the uncanniness that plays against the comedy of Dr. Pinch that I described earlier in this essay. Just as in *Othello*, for example, Iago's salacious imaginings of Desdemona and Othello making love eventually conjure forth its physical emblem, the bed, so, too, in *The Comedy of Errors*, the fraught imaginings of demonic possession eventually call forth, require, the wizard-exorcist. It is in just that sense that Dr. Pinch is a creature of fantasy more than of narrative.

Dr. Pinch serves a further symbolic function since his repudiation as a fraud constitutes perhaps the necessary condition for Egeon's redemption from the role of sacrificial victim.[37] But the aura of the exorcist cannot be erased completely, for he and Egeon bear an unnatural resemblance. Antipholus of Ephesus describes Pinch as a "lean-fac'd," "needy," "hollow-ey'd," "living dead man" (V.i.238, 241, 242). Moments later, Egeon describes himself in like terms: "defeature[d]" by time, "crack'd and splitted" in voice, "dull[ed]" in senses, and assuredly needy; we have already noted his death wish (V.i.300, 308, 316). Most likely, Pinch and Egeon were both originally played by the same tall, lean, pale actor, John Sinklo.[38] If so, then the repressed Pinch (killed by Antipholus as the messenger feared?) makes his uncanny return in the person of Egeon. Shakespeare may even be calling attention to this doubling by means of the unnecessarily long description of Pinch and Egeon, the language making provision for the exorcized Pinch, reiterated in his double, still to haunt the scene and trouble our consciousness.

Utterances have power. In fact, characters in *The Comedy of Errors* repeatedly pay tribute to the power of speech to create, to transform, or to dominate reality, a feature seldom noted by critics. That point is stated explicitly in the climactic "lockout" scene in act III. Balthazar urges resident Antipholus not to break into his own home, as he loudly threatens to do. "A vulgar comment will be made of it," says Balthazar, that will supplant Antipholus's

> yet ungalled estimation,
> . . . . . . . . . . . . . . . . . . . . . . . . . . . . . . . . .
> And dwell upon your grave when you are dead;
> For slander lives upon succession,
> For e'er housed where it gets possession.
>
> (III.i.100–106)

Once slander takes possession of a reputation—and the word *possession*, pointedly rhymed, is no accident—such slander acquires its own life, dwells upon one's grave like a body snatcher, and fixes one's identity forever, the power of speech made demonic. In the very next scene, Luciana reinforces that sense of the possessing power of language as she warns alien Antipholus of the perils of bad reputation: "Ill deeds is doubled with an evil word," she says (III.ii.19–20). Evil words of detraction make one's malefactions twice as bad, and the image of doubling suggests both amplification and twin existence. Speech, it would seem, constitutes a kind of second domain of reality with its own life and with the power to magnify (or diminish) the literal or empirical.

Words can displace the living, can double reality, and can possess the house. Tudor humanist rhetoricians, of course, celebrated the power of speech to move, sway, and even violate people. As Wilson puts it in *The Art of Rhetoric*, "what greater delight do we know than to see a whole multitude with the only talk of a man ravished and drawn which way him liketh best to have them?"[39] That tribute to rhetoric is enlarged in *The Comedy of Errors* with the sense that utterances possess magical or prophetic power. They migrate through the play as if under their own motive force, they take possession of their hearers and blind judgments, they evoke physical manifestations, and they refashion selves. While the narrative of *The Comedy of Errors* seems absorbed with the visual, with mistakes of identity and related sight gags, a certain dilatory substratum of the play makes room for the more dreamlike, associative, and telepathic agency of thoughts and words. At a time when antitheatrical polemicists were fretting over the power of iconography, demonlike, to possess its viewers, *The Comedy of Errors* hints, ironically, that at least co-equal to the power of the visual is the magical and amplifying power of the verbal.[40]

## Magic and the Dromios

To the discussion of amplification as magic belong the brothers Dromio, for it is the Dromios who provide the greatest access to the realm of magic, who fold it into the action, and who help to validate it.[41] Those effects happen in part because the Dromios occupy a theatrical ontology separate from that of the Antipholi. The masters are characters in some proper, narrative sense; they have longings, through-lines, and stories. Not so the Dromios, for whom incidents alone prompt desires—Ephesian Dromio's for manumission, Syracusan Dromio's for bachelorhood. In contrast to the brothers Antipholus—one romantic, the other mercantile—the Dromios seem more alike than different. If the Antipholi illustrate the emerging bourgeois individualism that we associate with the early modern, the Dromios claim the residual presence of qualities more anachronistic, reflective of a medieval division of experience between order and festivity.[42] Liminal figures, they function as audience surrogates who, in Robert Weimann's famous formulation, stand slightly outside the *locus,* the self-contained theatrical illusion, and provide ironic commentary to the playgoer.[43]

The Dromios' responses to events bespeak two seemingly contradictory mentalities: realism and fantasticality. In the first regard, the Dromios display the clown's typical plebian realism in their physicality and their distrust of romance, heroics, and intellectualism. That realism generates many of *The Comedy of Errors*'s liveliest moments. The twin servants introduce, of course, the play's most concrete language, as when Ephesian Dromio first enters chattering of capons burning, clocks striking, pigs falling from the spit, and a sixpence given "o' Wednesday" for "my mistress' crupper"—a vivid world already there (see I.ii.44–45, 55–56). They also account for almost all of the play's quite extensive and audience-engaging topical allusions, as in their references to syphilis (see, for example, II.ii.83–84). To those contributions, we can add another dimension of realism linked to sympathy. Dromio of Ephesus achieves various moments when the slapstick falls away and he suddenly inspires pathos as an example of a servant beaten by his master to excess. In the most strongly registered of those, after Ephesian Antipholus has called him "sensible in nothing but blows," Dromio launches into a sustained and rhetorically powerful set piece detailing how he has had "nothing at [his master's] hands for [his] service but blows" (IV.iv.25, 29–30). This lengthy, self-contained, and affecting lament strikes with a sudden seriousness; it illustrates the emotive power of amplification and dilation—and Shakespeare allows its critique to stand unanswered. Maurice Hunt even suggests that the Dromios' outcries against their beatings constitute a criticism of those Elizabethans whose harsh brutality toward servants compared to that of slaveholders.[44] Beyond supplying domestic verisimilitude and topicality, then, the Dromios can also sometimes break through the slapstick illusion and present their sufferings as intensely real.

But the Dromios, in the second regard, enlarge the imaginative dimension of the play. I have in mind not the clown's Utopianism that Weimann finds, say, in Lear's Fool, but, rather, a special capacity for representing vividly and fantastically the fears and desires of other characters.[45] The Dromios, in this aspect, tread on the borders of the dream world and hold a light to the play's anxieties about identity and the dissolution of the self. They stand here for shape shifting and metamorphosis, a quality signaled by their trademark punning. Indeed, the Dromios' quibbling, argues Eamon Grennan, sets up a realm of "linguistic anarchy" that repudiates any convention of a fixed relationship between language and a "non-linguistic reality."[46] Thus, the Dromios' puns remind us that experience is ambivalent, and reality fluid and elusive, perhaps unknowable.[47] So it is that the servant-twins, even while they stand for a kind of plebeian realism, will open up the play to elements of fantasticality and magic.

The Dromios—particularly Dromio of Syracuse—evince the wildest imaginations in *The Comedy of Errors*. Syracusan Dromio's description to Adriana of the Officer who arrests her husband provides an example of amplification run riot to the point of fantasticality: Dromio calls the Officer, in turn, a Tartar, "devil," "fiend," "fury," "wolf," "fellow all in buff," "back-friend," "shoulder-clapper," "hound," and a monster from the morality plays who "carries poor souls to hell," all within nine lines (see IV.ii.32–40). We might at first think of such allusions as overwhelming in their anarchic copiousness, as if they had begun to self-replicate or to conjure themselves. But Dromio is also speaking associatively and allegorically, in terms of a familiar, interconnected set of dualistic and often biblical archetypes. In describing the Officer, furthermore, he links the figure of a demon carrying souls to hell to disturbing contemporary accounts of aggressive and corrupt bailiffs preying upon victims who are to be confined in filthy and disease-ridden Elizabethan debtor's prisons. Dromio's demonic phantasmagoria rides, paradoxically, upon convincing realism, so convincing that an audience might even begin to see the otherwise mild-mannered Officer as possibly dangerous.[48] The Dromios' sense of the gritty underwrites their sense of the demonic, and that effect constitutes one of their key contributions to the play.

If Syracusan Dromio's representation of demonism emerges as oddly realistic, his earlier dilation upon fairies and folk magic approaches hyperrealism. When Adriana mistakes Antipholus of Syracuse for her philandering husband, Antipholus wonders if he "married . . . her in my dream," "[o]r sleep I now," or if his "eyes and ears" misperceive (II.ii.182–184). But Dromio reacts with a more extravagant impressionability: he calls for prayer beads; "cross[es himself] for a sinner"; declares that he is in "fairy land" with "goblins, [elves,] and sprites"; claims to be "transformed" in mind and shape; and suspects that he is an "ape" (II.ii.187–190, 195, 198). When Luciana counters that he is instead an "ass," he embraces her depiction as "true" (II.ii.199–200). In fact, as soon as Dromio starts to reinterpret himself in Luciana's terms, he begins to feel viscerally transformed, as if to imagine something intensely were also suddenly to experience it psychosomatically. He has become possessed. Dromio's impressionability also sharply increases the anxiety of Antipholus, who now wonders if he is "in heaven, or in hell," "mad or well advis'd," known to others but disguised to himself (II.ii.212–213). Despite their shock, however, Antipholus and Dromio experience in this scene a heightened awareness of themselves and others, apparent in Antipholus's eager embrace of "this offer'd fallacy" (II.ii.186).

Enchantment, the sense of being possessed, entails, for them, the unexpected correlative of excitement, intensity, and vividness, a new immediacy of experience that might be taken as a value in its own right. That new-found intensity will be evidenced in Antipholus's wooing of Luciana and Dromio's horror at Nell. According to the *Malleus Maleficarum* (ca. 1489), witches can inspire men to immoderate sexual passion.[49] Likewise, in popular medieval folklore, fairies can be seductresses—and the Syracusans' encounter with Adriana and Luciana is weighted especially with images of fairyland. As C. S. Lewis points out, fairies can possess concentrated beauty, glamour, and colorfulness, qualities that the exotic Ephesian women may exhibit on stage. Fairies, in this view, are doubles of humans, but more intense. As Lewis puts it, "Their life is, in one sense, *more* 'natural'—stronger, more reckless, less inhibited, more triumphantly and impenitently passionate—than ours."[50] Fairies are versions of us, but more vivid, more real (indeed, some such values must inhere in the image of Elizabeth as the Faerie Queene).[51] The Ephesian women inspire this sense of a magical hyperreality, and the idea of it takes hold first in Dromio. The Dromios are the most responsive, impressionable, and sympathetic characters in the play, and, as such, they amplify and confirm a world of experience that is apparently demonic and bewitched but also more exciting, vivid, and real than the rationalist world of mistaken identity.

The Dromios not only infect the Antipholi with their hyperbolic imaginations, they also function as their masters' alter egos, mirrors as well as agents.[52] Recent criticism has emphasized the Dromios' kinship with the play's female characters, since both sets occupy positions of servitude to the Antipholi.[53] Indeed, the Dromios' sensibilities exhibit those qualities—such as associative logic, imaginativeness, or sympathy—linked to the feminine here and elsewhere in Shakespeare (for example, *Henry VI, Part 1*). Yet the fears and responses of the Dromios also constitute fantastical and slightly uncanny versions, doubles, of their masters' anxieties about women. Dromio of Syracuse makes a good example. His witty set piece speech to Antipholus about Nell the kitchen wench pictures her as a veritable globe, monstrous, oozing rheum or grease, and intent on possessing him: she "claims" him, "haunts" him "as a witch" who would "transform" and emasculate her victim (III.ii.80, 143, 145).[54] Precisely that hyperbolic description convinces Antipholus in earnest that both Adriana and Luciana are witches and that he has come perilously close to surrendering his identity to the latter's "enchanting presence" (III.ii.160). Even as we understand it as parody, Dromio's blazon expresses Antipholus's actual fear of being engulfed, suffocated, and possessed by women. Dromio's fantasy contains Antipholus's psychological reality, so that the demonic acquires a kind of primitive authenticity. A parallel argument could be made about the way that the resident Dromio's desire for freedom from indenture to the abusive Antipholus echoes his master's desire for liberty from the demanding Adriana.[55]

Any suggestion that the Dromios have a special proximity to "the real" must acknowledge the problematic nature of that term. The idea of the real— as in "the touch of the real"—has been employed by new historicist critics to identify the power of the anecdote to bring to life past human experiences that resist the abstracting and objectifying narratives of official histories.[56] For them, the anecdote can thus illuminate "the accidental, suppressed, defeated, uncanny, abjected, or exotic," and those exorcized occurrences can serve, in turn, to revivify the "*grands récits*."[57] Implicitly, in this account, the real is something more than the illusory "reality effect" of a semiotic system, as viewed by Roland Barthes, or the empty simulacrum of mass and electronic media, as depicted by Jean Baudrillard.[58] For theorists such as Barthes and Baudrillard—and preeminently Jacques Lacan—the "real" becomes fundamentally inaccessible. Notwithstanding, Renaissance humanism took an interest in the experience of something like the "real" derived from writing or art, perhaps best expressed by terms such as *enargia* and *energia* that suggest an image of unusual vividness and immediacy, one so lively that it creates the sense of its own reality.[59] Those terms echo on the rhetorical level the larger humanist interest in how literature moves, inspires, and enflames its readers, sometimes evoking, at its extreme, a sense of transcendence; such a literary experience contains a special authenticity or truth value. The Dromios exhibit a dramaturgical realism that partakes of this special sense of vividness, liveliness, and energy. Their peculiar ontology and heightened responsiveness generate an immediacy and a concentration of characterological consciousness that privilege their perspectives.[60] More than any other of the characters, the Dromios represent spontaneity, demonstrate authenticity, and stand for a Renaissance vividness akin to "the real." As both comic realists and nightmare fantasists, furthermore, they constitute part of the world of amplification and doubleness, for they can be defined as metaphoric extensions, exaggerations, or parodies of others. They are figures who are essentially figurative, and they and their paradoxical realism cannot be recuperated easily within a world of rationalism or individualism. Farce is sometimes dismissed by critics, but as its prime agents, the Dromios illustrate the enigmatic and liminal domain that farce can explore. It is the domain of anxiety, sympathy, association, permeability, transformation, and linguistic anarchy, of words that can migrate and possess the mind, and of thoughts that can call forth reality; it is the domain of the magical.

### Conclusion

A certain Baconian empiricism may generate the resolution in *The Comedy of Errors*, but the magical world cannot be rejected so easily. The ending, for example, can never comprehend the uncanny workings of language and speech in the play's structure. Despite the denouement's empiricism, various facts are left unresolved, perhaps irresolvable. Is the traveler Antipholus—like Demetrius in *A Midsummer Night's Dream*—left, in his love for Luciana, still transformed by Adriana's "mist" of enchantment, for example? I would claim that the sense of religious or Providential wonder that infuses the ending of *The Comedy of Errors* draws its strength and credibility from the already present and unsettled sense of the magical.[61] The survival of the realm of sympathy and possession, despite the rationalist triumph, may be part of what makes the conclusion satisfying—because it is not allowed to be reductive. If the magical in *The Comedy of Errors* privileges the Providential, then treating it as an error is itself an element in the comedy of errors. But my point is not simply to valorize magic—or amplification or the carnivalesque—against their opposites. I think, rather, that Shakespeare is attempting to mark out a suggestive, mutual terrain somewhere between religion and magic, narrative and amplification, between the visual and the verbal, and the literal and the metaphoric. It is that ambivalent space in *The Comedy of Errors*, a space of wondering and wandering, where Protestant empiricism and rationalism become vivified with a medieval otherworldliness, that constitutes, I would suggest, the true ground of the "real."[62]

## NOTES

1. Shakespeare, *The Comedy of Errors,* ed. R. A. Foakes, Arden Shakespeare (London: Methuen; Cambridge MA: Harvard University Press, 1962), V.i.238. Hereafter, quotations from this text will appear parenthetically by act, scene, and line numbers.

2. The power of Dr. Pinch to haunt the imagination is suggested by the characters themselves: the Messenger and Antipholus of Syracuse devote an impressive amount of attention and energy in the last scene to recalling Dr. Pinch and his misadventures offstage with Antipholus; see V.i.169–177, 237–246. Dr. Pinch's evocative power is also demonstrated in the number of terms used to describe him: a *"Schoolmaster"* (stage direction, IV.iv), a "conjurer" (IV.iv.45; V.i.177, 243), a "doting wizard" (IV.iv.56), a "doctor" (V.i.170),

> a hungry lean-fac'd villain;
> A mere anatomy, a mountebank,
> A thread-bare juggler and a fortune-teller,
> A needy-hollow-ey'd-sharp-looking-wretch;
> A living dead man. This pernicious slave.

(V.i.238–242)

3. Morris Palmer Tilley, *A Dictionary of the Proverbs in England in the Sixteenth and Seventeenth Centuries: A Collection of the Proverbs Found in English Literature and the Dictionaries of the Period* (Ann Arbor: University of Michigan Press, 1950), p. 154, under D294.

4. On the "green world," see Northrop Frye, *Anatomy of Criticism: Four Essays* (Princeton: Princeton University Press, 1957), pp. 182–184.

5. Critics have often felt that *The Comedy of Errors* takes a skeptical view of magic. Stephen Greenblatt, representatively, sees *The Comedy of Errors*—unlike the *Henry VI* plays—as adopting a position toward magic comparable to that of Reginald Scot's *The Discovery of Witchcraft* (1584) ("Shakespeare Bewitched," in *Shakespeare and Cultural Traditions: The Selected Proceedings of the International Shakespeare Association World Congress, Tokyo, 1991,* ed. Tetsuo Kishi, Roger Pringle, and Stanley Wells [Newark: University of Delaware Press; London and Toronto: Associated University Presses, 1994], pp. 17–42, 28–31, 33).

6. "Sympathy" had a long life as a medieval medical term; sympathy identifies, as Ernest B. Gilman puts it, "an attraction or mutual response between two separate bodies" ("The Arts of Sympathy: Dr. Harvey, Sir Kenelm Digby, and the Arundel Circle," in *Opening the Borders: Inclusivity in Early Modern Studies: Essays in Honor of James V. Mirollo,* ed. Peter C. Herman [Newark: University of Delaware Press; London: Associated University Presses, 1999], pp. 265–297, 265; see also p. 275).

7. This form of magic has its religious counterpart in the widespread pre-Reformation practice among sick people of leaving "wax or metal images of arms, legs, hearts and other diseased bodily parts" at the shrines of saints hoping for cures in their own or others' bodies (Carole Rawcliffe, *Medicine and Society in Later Medieval England* [Phoenix Mill, Gloucestershire UK: Alan Sutton Publishing,

1995], p. 22). Officials counted thousands of such images and other devotional objects at English shrines.

8. Richard Cosin, *Conspiracie, for Pretended Reformation: viz. Presbyteriall Discipline* (London, 1592) (STC 5823), p. 67.

9. See J. J. Bagley, *The Earls of Derby, 1485–1985* (London: Sidgwick and Jackson, 1985), pp. 63–75. On Shakespeare and Strange's Men, see Lawrence Manley, "From Strange's Men to Pembroke's Men: *2 Henry VI* and *The First part of the Contention,*" *SQ* 54, 3 (Fall, 2003): 253–287. Andrew Gurr places Shakespeare, by mid-1592, with Pembroke's Men, rather than Strange's (*The Shakespearian Playing Companies* [Oxford: Clarendon Press, 1996], pp. 270–272).

10. C. L'Estrange Ewen, *Witchcraft and Demonianism: A Concise Account Derived from Sworn Depositions and Confessions Obtained in the Courts of England and Wales* (London: Heath Cranton Limited, 1933), p. 175; see also Bagley, pp. 66–67.

11. Jane Donawerth, *Shakespeare and the Sixteenth-Century Study of Language* (Urbana: University of Illinois Press, 1984), p. 38; see pp. 38–46. According to John O. Ward, the Renaissance "humanist movement marked a revival of the Greek sophistic notion of rhetoric as magic" (p. 109). Ward sees the Renaissance overall as a period of heightened interest in, and tension between, competing concepts of rhetoric as technique or control and rhetoric as magic ("Magic and Rhetoric From Antiquity to the Renaissance: Some Ruminations," *Rhetorica* 6, 1 [Winter 1988]: 57–118).

12. See Judith H. Anderson, *Words that Matter: Linguistic Perception in Renaissance English* (Stanford: Stanford University Press, 1996), pp. 137–141.

13. Christopher Marlowe, *Tamburlaine the Great, Part 1,* ed. David Fuller, in *The Complete Works of Christopher Marlowe,* 5 vols. (Oxford: Clarendon Press, 1998), 5:4–77. The magic of rhetoric was conventional enough that John Lyly could parody it in *Galatea,* in which Rafe crosses himself and his hair stands on end when the Alchemist's boy, Peter, chants out the terms of his master's art; see Lyly, *Galatea, Midas,* ed. George K. Hunter and David Bevington, Revels Plays (Manchester and New York: Manchester University Press, 2000), II.iii.18–19, 30.

14. Barbara Rosen, *Witchcraft in England, 1558–1618* (Amherst: University of Massachusetts Press, 1969), p. 228.

15. Rosen, pp. 32–33; see also Rossell Hope Robbins, s. v. "Possession," *The Encyclopedia of Witchcraft and Demonology* (New York: Crown Publishers, 1959), pp. 392–398.

16. *The Most Strange and Admirable Discovery of the Three Witches of Warboys* (London, 1593) (STC 25019); for a modernized edition, see Philip C. Almond, *Demonic Possession and Exorcism in Early Modern England: Contemporary Texts and Their Cultural Contexts* (Cambridge: Cambridge University Press, 2004), pp. 75–149; for a summary, see Ewen, pp. 169–173.

17. "And it was 'contagious.' Agnes Briggs became a demoniac the same night that she saw Rachel Pinder's behaviour. Possession spread like the plague among the Throckmorton children . . . Among the Starkie family it began with one son and daughter, and eventually spread to another five people" (Almond, p. 40).

18. For a discussion of possession from a medical perspective, see Jonathan Gil Harris, "Syphilis and Trade: Thomas Starkey, Thomas Smith, *The Comedy of Errors,*" in *Sick Economies: Drama, Mercantilism, and Disease in Shakespeare's England* (Philadelphia: University of Pennsylvania Press, 2004), pp. 29–51. Rosen makes the

point that possession, as a symptom, can be applied to various causes (p. 227). As a number of critics have noted, "possession" also has mercantile associations.

19. Thomas Wilson, *The Art of Rhetoric (1560),* ed. Peter E. Medine (University Park: Pennsylvania State University Press, 1994), pp. 146–167.

20. See Patricia Parker, "The Bible and the Marketplace: *The Comedy of Errors,*" in *Shakespeare from the Margins: Language, Culture, Context* (Chicago: University of Chicago Press, 1996), pp. 56–82.

21. *OED,* s. v. "copia"; see also Parker, pp. 56–67.

22. Wilson, p. 160.

23. Desiderius Erasmus of Rotterdam, *On Copia of Words and Ideas (De Utraque Verborum ac Rerum Copia),* trans. Donald B. King and H. David Rix (Milwaukee: Marquette University Press, 1963), book 2, method 5, pp. 47–55, 52. See also Joel B. Altman, *The Tudor Play of Mind: Rhetorical Inquiry and the Development of Elizabethan Drama* (Berkeley and London: University of California Press, 1978), pp. 165–174.

24. Erasmus, p. 16.

25. See Parker, pp. 61–65.

26. Ward, pp. 70–110.

27. Stuart Clark, *Thinking with Demons: The Idea of Witchcraft in Early Modern Europe* (Oxford: Clarendon Press, 1997), pp. viii, 21. See, for example, chap. 2, "Festivals and Sabbats," pp. 11–30.

28. On dilation in this scene, see Parker, pp. 57–59.

29. The pattern reveals itself, of course, as reassuringly benign and optimistic: Solinus appropriates Egeon's pity, not his death wish.

30. G. R. Elliott, "Weirdness in *The Comedy of Errors,*" in *The Comedy of Errors: Critical Essays,* ed. Robert S. Miola (New York and London: Garland, 1997), pp. 57–70, 61; see also Parker, p. 59.

31. On the relationship between Antipholus, Adriana, and Luciana, see Kent Cartwright, "Surprising the Audience in *The Comedy of Errors,*" in *Re-Visions of Shakespeare: Essays in Honor of Robert Ornstein,* ed. Evelyn Gajowski (Newark: University of Delaware Press, 2004), pp. 215–230, 220–224.

32. See William C. Carroll, *The Metamorphoses of Shakespearean Comedy* (Princeton: Princeton University Press, 1985), p. 69.

33. *OED,* s. v. "mist," 2b; *The Schoole of Abuse by Stephen Gosson. A Reply to Gosson's Schoole of Abuse by Thomas Lodge. With Prefaces . . . by Arthur Freeman* (London, 1579; rprt. New York: Garland, 1973), A2r.

34. Any doubt about Antipholus's sincerity here might reinforce doubt about Luciana's really falling in love with Antipholus later. Her affections are most deeply moved for Antipholus when she watches him harassed, bound, and deported as mad in IV.iv—when, comically, she sighs and suffers for the wrong brother.

35. In *Macbeth,* Shakespeare explores the same power of utterances to produce actions; see Kent Cartwright, "Scepticism and Theatre in *Macbeth,*" *ShS* 55 (2002): 219–236, 225–228.

36. See Laurie Maguire, "The Girls from Ephesus," in *Comedy of Errors: Critical Essays,* pp. 355–391, 367–368 and nn53–54.

37. Foakes, "Introduction," pp. xlix–l.

38. John Sinklo (or Sincklo or Sincler) was noted for his thinness; he is named in *Henry VI, Part 3, The Taming of the Shrew,* and *Henry IV, Part 2* (Edwin Nungezer, *A Dictionary of Actors and of Other Persons Associated with the Public Representation of*

*Plays in England before 1642* [New Haven and London: Yale University Press, 1929], pp. 326–327).

39. Wilson, pp. 35–36.

40. On fears about the iconic power of theater, see Huston Diehl, *Staging Reform, Reforming the Stage: Protestantism and Popular Theater in Early Modern England* (Ithaca: Cornell University Press, 1997), e.g., pp. 1–66.

41. The Dromios are frequently mentioned in criticism but seldom discussed in detail. For an excellent recent exception, see Maurice Hunt, "Slavery, English Servitude, and *The Comedy of Errors,*" *ELR* 27, 1 (Winter 1997): 31–56.

42. On the clown, see David Wiles, *Shakespeare's Clown: Actor and Text in the Elizabethan Playhouse* (Cambridge: Cambridge University Press, 1987), especially pp. 1–10.

43. Robert Weimann, *Shakespeare and the Popular Tradition in the Theater: Studies in the Social Dimension of Dramatic Form and Function,* ed. Robert Schwartz (Baltimore and London: Johns Hopkins University Press, 1978), see especially pp. 73–85.

44. Hunt, p. 39. See also Maguire, pp. 372–378. Miola notes that Dromio's speech has comic antecedents in Plautus (*Shakespeare and Classical Comedy: The Influence of Plautus and Terence* [Oxford: Clarendon Press, 1994], p. 23). The effect in Shakespeare's play, however, seems to transgress the comedic.

45. Weimann, pp. 42–43.

46. Eamon Grennan, "Arm and Sleeve: Nature and Custom in *The Comedy of Errors,*" *PQ* 59, 2 (Spring 1980): 150–164, 158. Anarchic language, maintains Grennan, outfits the Dromios with a "weapon of comic revenge" against the figures of authority who abuse and victimize them (p. 159).

47. Ibid.

48. Foakes suggests that by the time that Dromio sees Antipholus in the next scene (IV.iii), his quibbling about the Officer as a devil has become "earnest"; Foakes argues that a movement from jest to sincerity "is a characteristic of the word-play of the Dromios" (p. xlvii).

49. Heinrich Institoris and Jakob Sprenger, *Malleus Maleficarum,* trans. Montague Summers (London: Pushkin Press, 1948), pp. 47–48; the putative witch, Joan la Pucelle, has such an effect on the Dolphin Charles in *Henry VI, Part 1,* I.ii.108–112; all citations are taken from Shakespeare, *King Henry VI, Part 1,* ed. Edward Burns (London: Arden Shakespeare, 2000).

50. C. S. Lewis, *The Discarded Image: An Introduction to Medieval and Renaissance Literature* (Cambridge: Cambridge University Press, 1964), pp. 122–138, 133. Shakespeare is drawing upon a medieval concept of fairies, the kind that might be expected to have persisted in rural England.

51. Shakespeare elsewhere associates a character's heightened vividness or "realness" with a heightened sense of spiritual presence. Talbot's heroic loss to the French is described in just such terms: he rose "above human thought," "[e]nacted wonders," sent hundreds "to hell," and was "exclaimed the devil" while the army stood "agazed" at "his undaunted spirit" (*Henry VI, Part 1,* I.i.121–127).

52. Just as the Dromios' reactions and emotions often mediate between the audience and the stage, they also affect the judgments of their masters. They can activate sympathy. With the Syracusans, for example, Dromio's conviction that they are in fairyland engages Antipholus; Dromio's description of the monstrous Nell

also moves his master to believe that "none but witches do inhabit here" (III.ii.155); and his railings at the Courtesan intensify Antipholus's belief that she is a demon.

53. Maguire, pp. 372–378; Hunt, pp. 47–48.

54. Dromio's later horror at the way the Officer has laid hands on Antipholus of Ephesus recapitulates his exaggerated fear of possession.

55. Dromio of Ephesus perhaps acquires his liberty by assisting Antipholus in escaping Dr. Pinch. If so, Dromio transforms, in an extended sense, from Antipholus's "bondman" into "his man, unbound" (V.i.289, 291). (Messenio in the Plautine source play acquires his freedom by sorting out the twinship of the brothers Menaechmus.) The idea of liberty, of course, is associated with the male realm early in the play: "A man is master of his liberty," affirms Luciana (II.i.7). The idea infuriates Adriana, who resents her husband's sexual wanderings because they imply Antipholus seeks liberty from her. On Ephesian Antipholus's aversion to home, see Mary Thomas Crane, *Shakespeare's Brain: Reading with Cognitive Theory* (Princeton and Oxford: Princeton University Press, 2001), p. 49.

56. See, for example, Stephen Greenblatt, "The Touch of the Real" and Catherine Gallagher, "Counterhistory and the Anecdote," in *Practicing New Historicism*, ed. Gallagher and Greenblatt (Chicago and London: University of Chicago Press, 2000), pp. 20–48, pp. 49–74.

57. Gallagher, p. 52.

58. Roland Barthes, "The Reality Effect," in *The Rustle of Language*, trans. Richard Howard (New York: Hill and Wang, 1986), pp. 141–148; on simulacra, see Jean Baudrillard, *Simulacra and Simulation*, trans. Sheila Faria Glaser (Ann Arbor: University of Michigan Press, 1994), especially pp. 1–42.

59. On *enargia* and *energia*, see, for example, Richard A. Lanham, *A Handlist of Rhetorical Terms*, 2d edn. (Berkeley and Oxford: University of California Press, 1991), pp. 64–65.

60. See Robert Nozick, "Being More Real," in *The Examined Life: Philosophical Meditations* (New York and London: Simon and Schuster, 1989), pp. 128–140.

61. For an influential religious reading of *The Comedy of Errors*, see Arthur F. Kinney, "Shakespeare's *Comedy of Errors* and the Nature of Kinds," in *Comedy of Errors: Critical Essays*, pp. 155–181. The 1996 Royal Shakespeare Company production of *The Comedy of Errors*, directed by Tim Supple at the Other Place in Stratford-upon-Avon, was particularly successful at evoking the play's sense of wonder (Miola, "The Play and the Critics," in *Comedy of Errors: Critical Essays*, pp. 3–51, 34–35).

62. *Henry VI, Part 1* displays related interests. According to Edward Burns, "The play is informed by a clash between two readings of events—broadly describable as French/Catholic/Magical/Female and English/Protestant/Rational/Male" ("Introduction," in Shakespeare, *King Henry VI, Part 1*, ed. Edward Burns [London: Arden Shakespeare, 2000], pp. 1–103, 36).

## ACKNOWLEDGMENT

I am indebted, for various forms of assistance with this essay, to Iska Alter, Anannya Dasgupta, Elizabeth Driver, Sean Keilen, Attila Kiss, Bernice Kliman, Kathleen Lynch, Lawrence Manley, Ágnes Matuska, Edward Rocklin, William Sherman, and György Szönyi.

# MICHAEL STEPPAT

# *In Mercury's Household:*
# The Merry Wives of Windsor

FALSTAFF. [ . . . ] I can construe the action of her familiar style, and the hardest voice of her behaviour—to be Englished rightly—is "I am Sir John Falstaff's". (I.3.43–45)[1]

EVANS. I pray you have your remembrance, child: *accusativo hing, hang, hog.*

QUICKLY. "Hang-hog" is Latin for bacon, I warrant you. (IV.1.40–42)

## I

As Shakespeare's "English comedy", *The Merry Wives of Windsor* has been one of his most popular theatre pieces for centuries. The two passages just quoted, with their context, have had anything but a joint share in this strength, since the improvised Latin lesson in Act IV Scene 1, which is only given in the Folio and not in the Quarto version of 1602, has not often been performed. Yet the two passages have an inner connection which, even apart from the theatre, invites exploration in greater depth. As the first signals, an impoverished Sir John Falstaff plots to fleece a wealthy burgher housewife by seduction; in and around the second, the Welsh parson and schoolmaster is teaching young Will Page some Latin with waggish comments from Mrs. Quickly. In the first, Falstaff's fantasized grammar of

*Cahiers Élizabéthains*, Volume 72 (August 2007): pp. x, 9–19. Copyright © 2007 Michael Steppat.

body language conjugates a possessive relationship, joining the external subject into his own signifying chain and provoking questions about the construing of ownership, the propriety of property. In the second, almost a mirror to the first, Welsh hog-Latin is "Englished rightly" into a domestic commodity of the kind an early, modern housewife would be expected to manage—to own—and prepare for her family. Criticism now tends to think of the "English comedy" as "the Comedy of English", or "the Comedy of Language", as Giorgio Melchiori puts it,[2] its distinctive features being what he calls "linguistic experimentation" and what Patricia Parker describes as "dizzying wordplay".[3] How does this chime with the play's now common classification (as against earlier somewhat puzzled assignments to the realm of farce) as Shakespeare's only citizen comedy?

A fresh orientation of research has built on earlier statements such as H. C. Hart's that *Merry Wives* is about "mistresses of households in a well-to-do class" and in "hospitable homes, all in a gallimaufry"[4] or Jeanne Roberts's that it is "a true domestic drama".[5] Scholars have for a few years now been looking more closely at the anti-aristocratic discourse of early modern domesticity and the conduct expected of housewives, usually of the middle or lower middle classes, as a paradigm for understanding this rather singular play. At issue is Shakespeare's attitude toward the rising middle or burgher class of his day, and of his country—perhaps not the least among aspects to be considered for any construction of the bard as an individual within a sociocultural texture. Almost unanimously, scholars and critics see *Merry Wives* reassuringly warranting the value of middle-class management and supervision of domestic property together with linguistic discipline. But how does this assessment square with exuberant linguistic experimenting? Does the scopic register's determinacy match the implications of the play's vocatory fields? What verbal and social economy—or lack of it—does the play address? I will argue that we should question the critical warrant and seek an answer in the signifying energy of the theatre as it interrogates a middle-class obsession with matters of ownership and, having turned the accusative into the masculinity of a castrated beast in the hands of a housewife's "husbandry", invites a hearing of the *genitive* case as a snare, a flirting *Jenny*'s.

On the surface, "property" in *Merry Wives* appears not so much a preoccupation as a matter of disparagement, possibly of anxiety. In the romanticizing "main" plot, which in the manner of citizen comedy is sketched somewhat lightly, the Folio's Fenton is the aristocratic young lover of bourgeois Anne Page, against her parents' wishes. In a decorous if somewhat tepid verse of courtship he admits that her father has objected to his "riots past" and "wild societies" which have emptied his purse, "And tells me 'tis a thing impossible / I should love thee; but as a property" (III.4.8–10), to gain access to—what else?—the Page fortune. To win Anne, Fenton declares he has outgrown the motive which had first prompted him, and proclaims:

> I found thee of more value
> Than stamps in gold or sums in sealed bags.
> And 'tis the very riches of thyself
> That now I aim at. (III.4.15–18)

It is proper indeed, Anne's father would maintain, not to regard his daughter as property, be it Fenton's or be it as a part of her father's. Yet Anne does not appear to mind Fenton's shamelessly Petrarchizing commodification of her as "value" and "riches". Does her father mind? Mr. Page, though objecting to this suitor, sees no reason not to "sell" her as a business bargain to Fenton's "well landed" rival Slender—who, almost as if the qualities were exchangeable, is branded "an idiot" (IV 4.84). A gauche wooer who "buys" into the honesty of belying any keen desire, Slender declares to the girl: "Truly, for mine own part, I would little or nothing with you. Your father and my uncle hath made motions" (III.4.60–61). Indeed they have, in the opening scene, where the word "motions" was introduced (I.1.199) for the same situation—and bears the meaning not only of the legal moving of a matter but the *fabliau* implication of evacuating the bowels.[6] What seems good business can be heard as fecal, beyond control of one's desires. To appreciate the semic complexity unfolding in the play's presentation of business and property issues, it is worth listening closely to what this speaker unwittingly reveals. "For mine own part": according to the *Oxford English Dictionary*'s range of contemporary meanings, the body's privy part plays into Slender's words, as does the allotted portion which one possesses (the "own part"), along with a show in a box of puppets moving, by wires and the theatrical part which one feigns, each of them semanticizable in the context (or *con-texte?*). As in the innuendos of *Hamlet* (III.2), Slender involuntarily invokes a slacking of the male "thing", as overspread with ordure—inverting Mr. Page's reported assertion that Fenton's "thing" is "impossible". As Carol M. Rose has observed, the notion of property and its transaction is inseparable from a text with "ambiguous subtexts" that create a symbolic structure, and it involves a "story, told within a culture that shapes the story's content and meaning";[7] property claims may accordingly be unstable and open to interpretation, in defamiliarizing of what appears to be known. The semic interweaving may help to explain why "property" in Fenton's confession and elsewhere evokes the theatre's elastic signifying: during preparations for the final shaming of Falstaff, Anne's mother urges "Go get us properties / And tricking for our fairies" (IV.4.76–77). The "properties" are the theatre's, inseparable from the notions of dressing up and beguiling. As re-presentation energizes presentation beyond a scopic register, we should "hear" the erotic quest as well as an anxiety to protect the status of one's property, to maintain what a bourgeois household owns, as resonant with innuendo, fabliau, and pretence. This is more difficult for our age, which has inevitably lost much of the historical horizon of meanings conveyed to many in the early modern audience attending closely to a vocatory field.

There is another way in which metamorphic speech may threaten the solidity of a household such as the Pages'. One instance is the improvised Latin lesson already spoken of, an episode which, detached from any immediate plot progression, used to be treated as amusing but dispensable and which has only recently exercised the imagination of acute critics. Within the decorously sheltered Page household, young William (a stand-in for the author?) is being quizzed

EVANS. What is your genitive case plural, William?

WILLIAM. Genitive case?

EVANS. Ay.

WILLIAM. *Gen tivo horum, harum, horum.* (IV.1.50–53)

The "case" pluralizes the inflection of language forms which become "enclosed" for Will's taking—"your" case, an ethical dative used so insistently throughout the scene that the language is turning into the boy's possession, as part of the domestic capital that will ensure his social status. It is this association that sparks a protest:

QUICKLY. Vengeance of Jenny's case, fie on her! Never name her, child, if she be a whore.

EVANS. For shame, 'oman.

QUICKLY. You do ill to teach the child such words.—He teaches him to hick and to hack, which they'll do fast enough of themselves, and to call "whore 'em"!—Fie upon you! (IV.1.54–60)

As a guest, bumbling Quickly has been impatiently waiting and forced to listen. Her hearing makes the surface Latin transparent to expose underlying terms of desire as she veers indignantly from the schoolmaster to Will's mother. "Case" becomes a whore's vagina, just as it suggests its own etymological source (as "fall"); "Jenny" or "ginny" is "ensnaring, seductive". "Hick" (the *"hic"* Will had just rehearsed) has a lascivious meaning if it isn't the "hiccup" of excessive drinking, "hack" (just practiced as *"haec"*) is to go whoring. Quick-lie would have an ear for "lie" in both its major senses. Pluralizing the possessive relation may speak of multiple tokens of wealth, even as its inverse reference to a subject rather than an object veils a prospect of dispersion, disbandment. Latin itself is a paronomasic "latten", a mixed metal of unclear composition often used in making household items. And in any *case*, it is a *Latin* wielded by a Welsh speaker who, before long, makes fritters of any language, as of genders (the intralexically transformed *o-man*). As English housekeeper and dry-nurse, Quickly appears concerned to domesticize and curb linguistic promiscuity—actually, often enough, in the play, to mal-a-prop, against the "proper". Even as she does so, however, her expectation of the lad's adult conduct does not bode well for the economic future of his *domus*.

EVANS. Thou art as foolish Christian creatures as I would desires.
MISTRESS PAGE. *[to Quickly]* Prithee hold thy peace. (IV.1.63–65)

Evans's Welsh adds a comic complication in that not only are two ostensible languages (Latin and English) at stake, but a threefold and fluid circulation of semantic energies. In trying to curb Quickly, the Welsh *pedante* unwittingly strengthens the sexual "desires" he wishes to deny, and pluralizes them together with the syntactic object so as to fuse linguistic and sexual promiscuity. The enunciation veils and fans out a suppressed libidinal drive through the plural cases or coverings of language in a linguistic and cultural dislocation, enclosed in no single form—desires are always "elsewhere". In a variant of suture, the supposedly absent "I" as subject of desire, displaced onto Quickly, nonetheless recoils on the signifying chain. This is the pastor who in the previous Act has been singing the "Passionate Shepherd" sonnet: "There will we make our peds of roses / And a thousand fragrant posies" (III.1.18–19)—turning "fragrant" into "vagram" a few seconds later and thus suggesting "vagrant" (inconsistent, wayward). Vagram desires do not augur well for the future of hog-hanging affluence. The outbreak of bickering in her household and in her presence finally provokes Mistress Page's intervention to safeguard the propriety of her domestic space, its stability and wealth, against a "fall", the threat of dissipating good management in alcohol and erotic seduction—the kind of fear that drives her husband's spurning of Fenton and, for that matter, much of the play's action. The scene appears designed to stage a "vision of national community founded on the 'everyday' language of the home", in a "nationalistic terrain structured on proper speaking".[8] Yet there is some indeterminacy: the stage direction *("to Quickly")* is not included in any early printed version (the First Folio or the 1602 Quarto) and was not introduced before the twentieth century; it is not clear whether Mrs. Page is following Evans in chiding Quickly (for being so outspoken about Will's future will?) or whether she is disturbed by Evans's scolding as much as by Quickly's. In either case, her curt speech is like that of Evans—hardly a model of "proper speaking"—in yielding an unwanted implication: after all that has gone before, an audience may easily hear "peace" as "piece", woman as sexual object, so that "hold" opens an enticing range of contemporary registers from "to own" (your Jenny, that is) to "bear endure" (her). Mrs. Page has requested Evans to ask her son "some questions about his accidence" (IV.1.14), a term signifying both the grammar of inflections and, more ominously, "mishap". What has become of this household's moderate government?

## II

From different perspectives, critics have tended—for centuries in fact—to find an affirmation, even a celebration of middle-class norms and values in *Merry Wives,* with a reassuring stability or in some cases even absence of meanings. Recent discussions often employ a variety of research methods, some antithetical, to give a new voice to this overall assessment. One instance is David Crane's introduction in the New Cambridge edition of 1997: from a generalized sense of "human substance" and "the stuff of life"[9] derived from Falstaff's plea "Give me life" (*1 Henry IV* V.3.59),[10] Crane declares that the "world" of *Merry Wives* is "not significant",[11] whether in terms of the prose or the plot. The assessment is congruent with the view described by Wendy Wall that housework is "by definition a trivial and trivializing activity",[12] a definition that easily spreads to cover the play's whole action. For that matter, Arthur Kinney's view of this play as speaking to the "needs of a populace desperately paying only to be entertained" by analogy with "movies of romance and the good life" during the Great Depression is not too different.[13] As Crane goes on to describe it, with a rather strict distinction between the play's plot and its language, "everything in this play remains itself",[14] the "values and attitudes" of middle-class families "remain unchanged" as the play demonstrates "with how firm a hold they keep a grip on property"—while "the notion that possessions should be jealously guarded is not called into question". There is here no Morality tradition of "Indignant Virtue punishing Vice"; the play neither points nor calls into question a "system of morality". From a quite different angle, Natasha Korda, in an important study of *Shakespeare's Domestic Economies,* finds that "the 'disquietnesse' surrounding the housewife's supervisory role with respect to marital property" is "dispelled" by "the wives' consummate self-discipline"; their trustworthy domestic supervision is "carried on to the next generation of the play's women" by Anne's discreet marriage.[15] Building on this study, David Landreth examines the language and rhetoric of erotic desire in *Merry Wives* and finds that the wives as "arbiters of the mother tongue" demonstrate how "bawdiness can be contained in the surface of English as innocent merriment", they "guarantee the integrity of their bodies and that of the social body of Windsor" in completing a "domestic labor of chastening".[16] Whereas Crane had stressed some analogies between Falstaff and the burgher wives, Landreth highlights difference, with the wives appearing as the "definers of a working sexual, linguistic, and even national body through a consistent principle of grammatical decorum", guaranteeing their chastity and honesty by "defining the complex disciplinary systems of proper English" and its "decorous discipline".[17] When Fenton eventually wins Anne, it is because of his decorum and propriety. His language "indulges" in no "metamorphic fantasy": his "trope is conversion, the happy conclusion of the parable of the Prodigal"[18]—quite unlike Crane's argument of the absence of Morality. Fenton's trope is that of Prince Hal turning into the King, so that *Merry Wives* resembles *Henry V* in its "English Pedagogy", preparing and constructing "a disciplined, and reliably masculine speaking position in English" as "of great importance to the shaping of the modern English state" and "the English nation"—"thanks to the labor of the wives".[19] (Again, a considerable contrast to Crane's belief in the play's lack of significance.) Thus Henry V becomes at least temporarily able to appropriate "the female and domestic labor of Englishing" for "the foundations of empire"—while "domestic labor persists".[20] Landreth, that is, stresses the disciplinary character of the wives' speech mode which he sees exploited and appropriated by Fenton/Hal, an argument that (despite some rhetorical gestures) suggests a fairly smooth transition. It acknowledges but then almost glosses over Fenton's thwarting and shaming both Anne's parents—as well as Mrs. Page's insistent fancy for one of the play's most maladroit speakers, the French physician Dr. Caius, who plays next to no part in Landreth's argument. Shouldn't one consider the deeper truth of Leo Salingar's radically different proposition that "the foreigners serve to bring out the vanity of the native English speakers "?[21]

It is heartening at first blush to think of this popular play in terms of firm and healthy middle-class family attitudes nourishing the merry substance of life, with or without a morality overlay, or of women's discipline in linguistic and domestic labour duly taken over and perhaps even magnified by men. It would show Shakespeare celebrating the rise of a level-headed citizen class concerned to safeguard wealth and property in his era, even to the point (*pace* Crane) of making that class serve or advance the national monarchy's imperial interests. In a historical imaginary, witty mothers and housewives would be doing nothing less than piece together the cradle of a grandly English or British empire—a cat's cradle, of sorts, offering significance with a vengeance. The national community would be consolidated by having "English lore affirm citizens' values", with an Englishness that "nominates the values of the emergent middle class as the foundational world for which everyone supposedly yearns".[22] I will look more closely at the scholarly work that underpins this and similar views, then offer some supporting evidence (section 3), a rather different view of the evidence (section 4), and, finally, (section 5) further grounds for doubting the alleged consolidation.

We can learn something about the society Shakespeare is here depicting from research which is favoured by the process of singular History's giving way to a postmodern plurality of socially and culturally particularized histories. Discussion of the heuristic and civilizatory import of what Michel de Certeau has called *The Practice of Everyday Life* (the title of his 1984 monograph) has gained considerable esteem. Accordingly, research has focused on the material (shading into linguistic and symbolic) economies of early modern middle-class households. If such concerns are not significant in a traditional sense, there may nonetheless be more to the matter—the matter of which both household and theatre property is made, and that of speech whose physical sound can be metamorphic. In conjunction with women's social position, at any rate, this body of research enables a revalorization of the play in question as suggested by Lena Orlin in her discussion of "material life" in Shakespeare: "As a document in the history of gender relations in the early modern period, *The Merry Wives of Windsor* is arguably the most interesting of Shakespeare's comedies".[23] Scholarship has made generally available a body of discourse representing contemporary expectations concerning household management and married women's socioeconomic practice. As one can gather from treatises, diverse enough among themselves in scope and purpose, such as for instance *Fiue Hundreth Points of Good Husbandry* by Thomas Tusser (1573), *A Godlie Forme of Householde Government* by Robert Cleaver (1598), *The Treasurie of Hidden Secrets, Commonlie called, The Good hus-wives Closet of Provision* by John Partridge (1600), *Christian Oeconomie* by William Perkins (posthumously 1609), *The Whole Art and Trade of Husbandry* by Barnabe Googe (1614), *The English Huswife* by Gervase Markham (1615), or *Of Domesticall Duties* by William Gouge (1622), which account for both the ideological and sometimes the practical aspects of social roles, English married women or those expecting to marry were often the focus of instructive and prescriptive energies. In an early modern household a wife was responsible for her husband's material goods, as objects—like the hang-hog—have a share in configuring the mutual relations of domestic subjects. A side-glance at Plautus's *Casina*, for that matter, from which some of *Merry Wives* draws inspiration, reveals a somewhat similar notion: *"Nam peculi probam nihil habere addecet / Clam uirum et, quae habet, partum ei haud commode est"*.[24] She was also responsible for their children as well as for the domestic servants, and the literature available would instruct her in the knowledge she needed to organize the cooking, clothing, medical care and education of her charges.[25] The suitable "ordering" of the family as a unit of discipline, but also of production and consumption, is a means to ensure a like ordering "both of Church and Common-wealth", as Perkins (before 1609) declares;[26] society and the nation rest on the regulation of household affairs by a proper relationship between husbands and wives—the husband exercising domestic sovereignty—and by the wives' discreet and effective practices. These women are expected to be disciplined enough to monitor their own conduct for the sake of controlling their desires along with their bodies and of course the household property. A careful and thrifty management of financial and material resources ensures the stability and continuing prosperity of the unit to which the wife belongs. It is not quite clear from historical evidence whether treatises announcing their instruction in good or godly or Christian husbandry are describing an accepted and widespread domestic reality or rather an ideal that needs to be asserted because families (and women) do not always work that way; one may suspect that exploratory transgression or uncertainty may actually be as frequent as an observation of norms.[27]

### III

From any angle, in *Merry Wives* a straitened Sir John can only appear an invader in this kind of thrifty and well-ordered household unit, and a needy Fenton is not much different. What, then, is the evidence for reading the play in the light of a defence of thrift and order?

When Mrs. Page receives Falstaff's letter of courtship, her indignation is unmistakable:

> One that is well-nigh worn to pieces with age, to shew himself a young gallant? [ . . . ] Why, I'll exhibit a bill in the parliament for the putting down of men. How shall I be revenged on him? For revenged I will be, as sure as his guts are made of puddings. (II.1.17–18, 23–26)

She seems to suspect Falstaff of being *louche* ("gallant" language being specious), though the wives never actually penetrate his amatory mask. Samuel Johnson's *Dictionary* (1755) even defines "gallant" here as "whoremaster".[28] "Putting down" (with a *double entendre*) leads to "puddings", a domestic concoction not far from the hang-hog: her revenge plot like her style will defend domestic management. Her neighbour, Mrs. Ford, who has received a similar letter, becomes a gleeful ally: "O, that my husband saw this letter! It would give eternal food to his jealousy" (I.1.89–90). A twin revenge unfolds, with the wives acting against both Falstaff's intrusion and Mr. Ford's hornmadness, both of which threaten household peace and stability. (As we will

see, the implied bond between these men assumes a life of its own.) Act III
shows the wives making a first use of their domestic possessions in taking
revenge, when they lure Falstaff into a buck-basket—the play's most famous
incident since it is usually the most memorable in the theatre—and have him
borne out to be ditched in the Thames:

MISTRESS FORD. I am half afraid he will have a need of washing: so throwing
   him into the water will do him a benefit. (III.3.167–169)

A loss of muscular control from fright will put him in need of the kind
of cleansing that a domestic government is called on to ensure; the male
encroacher sees himself becoming one with "foul shirts and smocks, socks,
foul stockings, greasy napkins" (III.5.83–84). In a logical extension household utensils are appropriated and transgendered in the linen, muffler and
thrummed hat in which Falstaff gets enwrapped / entrapped the second
time he responds to an invitation (IV.2): Mr. Ford is right to suspect his
wife's handling of her linen, yet her managerial skills are exercised with
"consummate discretion" for the purpose of restoring confidence in her
jurisdiction.[29] The authority that burgher wives are privileged to exercise
in their realm (Gouge in 1622: it is the wife's place "to guide or governe
the house")[30] legitimizes their treatment of invaders, belittling them in the
process. The play's final scene translates the theme of successful domestic
conduct in a grandly public way into a masque of homage to royalty, especially in the Folio, as Pistol/Hobgoblin "makes the fairy oyez":

> Cricket, to Windsor chimneys shalt thou leap:
> Where fires thou find'st unraked and hearths [un-
>                                             swept,
> There pinch the maids as blue as bilberry—
> Our radiant queen hates sluts and sluttery.
> (V.5.43–46)

In such unassuming verse the merry common house-cricket is to punish
domestic equalling sexual filth, as the queen—England's Elizabeth as much
as the scene's pretended Fairy Queen—becomes an overly grand housekeeper
and dry-nurse doing, as it were, the merest chores. The play's domestic man-
agers give royal as well as religious sanction to their scorning of Falstaff's
seductive efforts, which are identical with a panoply of household goods:

MISTRESS PAGE. Why, Sir John, do you think, though we would have thrust
   virtue out of our hearts by the head and shoulders, and have given

ourselves without scruple to hell, that ever the devil could have made you our delight?

FORD. What, a hodge-pudding? A bag of flax?

MISTRESS PAGE. A puffed man? (V.5.145–151)

With the merest (and supremely dangerous) hint that the wives might not rule out entertaining a more persuasive gallant, a hint that becomes explicit only much later in Otto Nicolai's opera, *Die Lustigen Weiber von Windsor* (first performed in 1849), Mr. Ford and Mrs. Page actually sound as though they would revile the wives' being tied to domestic products, the cooking and spinning and costume-shaping commonly expected of the housewife;[31] they, it seems, would expect more. But at the end a contrite Falstaff is generously accepted into the reconfirmed community which now embraces Fenton, who with some sleight and right has succeeded in his quest for Anne. Composed of speakers of vernacular English, excluding or marginalizing the foreign, together with the homely cups and saucepans (and the latten) that it takes to prepare a posset by a country fire, Windsor gathers round to feast the triumph of "the 'good English' that Anne, Fenton and Mistresses Ford and Page represent", defeating "characters who embody the social and linguistic instabilities "[32]—of "diligent domestic supervision"[33]—of the "bonds of national culture built on shared speech, *oeconomia*, and the everyday"[34]—of male speech mastering "feminine systems of self-discipline".[35]

I've been retracing the recent scholarly narrative of *Merry Wives*' disciplinary and domestic foreclosing of mutable values. Before we make up our minds that this is the story also of *Merry Wives*, however, we should pause to consider that in both its Quarto (1602) and its Folio versions the play does not exactly depict an everyday or workaday or household situation, but—for all the money-minded marriage intrigue carried on in and around the local inn—an unnamed and uncommon occasion, perhaps a holiday: even Fenton, the winner, capers and "speaks holiday" (III.2.62). As in Plautus's *Casina*, the banks and shops are closed (*"Ludi sunt, ludus datus est argentariis"*, *Casina* 25) and the play calls the audience's attention explicitly away from the world of work. This gap may enable a certain detachment, to anatomize or dissect household activities, items and relations. If we are to regard Fenton as contributing decisively to "a disciplined, and reliably masculine speaking position in English" (Landreth), we should not forget that he is described above all in the context of festivity, dancing, writing verses, at the furthest possible remove from household or materialistic concerns—and perhaps from empire. An array of characters from outside the community—from Wales, Gloucestershire, France and Germany—have in fact descended on Windsor and its inn, in all likelihood, for some of them at least, to attend a special occasion, after which they will return to their respective homes. The Pages are not shown at work, nor are the Fords; we see them at various sports but learn nothing about their sources of income—unless we take Falstaff's scornful "salt-butter" (II.2.264) to be a hint, but that is slippery as Falstaff is no reliable reporter and may merely be double-entendring. We can be reasonably sure that the play capitalizes on knowledge concerning not only sports but also the contemporary household and its economy in the city and suburbs around the theatre, but does it replicate that knowledge with any rigid notion of verisimilitude? If conduct book discourse is not merely descriptive, it would be odd if the drama were to be, taking into account Paul Ricoeur's concept of the transfiguring dimension of mimesis. The wives are not busy at home caring for their charges—Will's Latin lesson comes about by chance—but have leisure to muse about exhibiting a bill in Parliament, about naval exploration and privateering, about the printing industry, about classical mythology—or about the legal niceties of leasing and inheriting land, the "fee-simple" which is "a propertie in the highest degree" (as Minsheu's *Ductor* informs us),[36] hardly the housewife's usual domain. The housekeeper Mrs. Quickly does not actually attend to the housekeeping chores she apostrophizes but is busy as "she-Mercury" to lure Falstaff to the wives' bait—and all of us to slippery terrains of domestic signification. We see the wives directing their servants, but not to carry real buck-washing to Datchet Mead. There is a playful mood in all this, and maybe we should not try to read too much early modern social history and domestic (economic, material, symbolic) discipline through *Merry Wives* but rather what the play does with it. Property claims always harbour an inner story, and what seems homely and familiar may be, as Wall well observes, subject to imaginative estrangement.[37]

## IV

What are we to make of the evidence in this light? When Mrs. Ford receives Falstaff's letter and bursts out "O, that my husband saw this letter! It would give eternal food to his jealousy" (II.1.89–90), her "that" is an optative subjunctive, leading George Steevens, already to ponder "Surely Mrs. Ford does not wish to excite the jealousy, of which she complains?".[38] When the wives' first ruse succeeds, Mrs. Ford declares "I know not which pleases me better, that my husband is deceived, or Sir John" (III.3.163–164), unstitching a little any discipline in the scheme's weaving. This is her reaction to her husband's hysterical ranting upon seeing the huge basket of washing about to be borne out, the plays biggest household item in a scopic register: "Buck? I wish I could wash myself of the buck! Buck, buck, buck! Ay, buck! I warrant you, buck—and of the season too, it shall appear" (III.3.144–146). His beastly fantasy identifies the property with the adulterer, the adulterer with himself, and both with a rutting animal, be it a goat or deer or even a rabbit. Here as in other instances (Mrs. Ford's description of the house's hollow spaces, the press, coffer, chest, trunk, well" at IV.2.57) the domestic region is no longer itself but figures or conceals a body, a beast's or a man's. As signifiants tied firmly to signifiés, the objects speak of burgher affluence, their material solidity undergirding its permanence. Yet a metamorphic turn unties them and then blocks any automatic restoration. It's true enough that in a decisive reversal of *Taming of the Shrew* the wives are in control of men's fantasizing, but do they retain their control? Dramatic speech goes beyond what Joel Fineman has called "linguistic idealization",[39] being more than a dialogue that *is* the things of which it speaks and that illustrates spectacle rather than performing and shaping. When Mr. Ford masked himself as the would-be cuckolder "Brook" in goading Falstaff to a vicarious seduction, he was indeed, as the knight suspects, prescribing to himself "very preposterously" (II.2.229–230) in preferring, even craving the adulterer's role before the husband's, seduction before married faith, "ouerthwarth" as in Huloet's *Abcedarivm* of 1552,[40] topsy-turvying accepted order. The point is that this affects more than Mr. Ford bargained for. Chastened at the play's end, when he has learned the true purpose of the wives' scheming, Mr. Ford seems constitutionally unable to imagine wedded loyalty as he taunts the Welshman: "I will never mistrust my wife again, till thou art able to woo her in good English" (V.5.132–133). Sexual and linguistic aberration work through each other as he thinks of the clock of proper conduct running down. The jest is harmless in the Quarto, where Evans retains his Welsh accent in at least parts of the final fairy masque, but less so in the Folio, where the pastor who has shown himself intimately familiar with erotic madrigals in Act III Scene 1 succeeds elastically in rising (as Welsh parson, as impersonated devil/satyr, as actor stepping out of his earlier role?) to impeccably standard speech forms. In other words, Evans *has* just shown himself, as Mr. Ford must have heard, capable of "good" English. Only about a hundred lines later, Mr. Ford confirms his view that sexual trading is good business: "Money buys lands, and wives are sold by fate" (V.5.227). A mysterious fate may, that is, sell his wife to another, just as it has surprisingly sold the Pages' daughter to Fenton. Mr. Ford generalizes by transforming proverbial wisdoms to highlight impersonal agency with the individual's powerlessness against wayward energies; the last time he says anything about his personal outlook is at V.5.132–133, quoted above. Not even in the play's very last words does Mr. Ford return to being an individual "self". Triumphantly and wittily, he displays unabated glee in unruly passion when he taunts Falstaff with the couplet

> To Master Brook you yet shall hold your word,
> For he tonight shall lie with Mistress Ford
> (V.5.238–239)

In these lines, their shape confirmed by the Quarto, the correct family man who had superseded the adulterer once again turns into Brook, the fluid signifier of a split self that speaks his hysteria for "buck"-ing into preposterity. Nominally in control, the husband not only revives but perpetuates his cozening bond with Sir John. As he does so, he maintains his carving of entrance points for the audience's lascivious fantasy, which maybe nourished further by an awareness of lusty associations surrounding the historical origins of the Garter ritual for which we may imagine the production of a version of *Merry Wives* to have been designed: one explanation of the play's "holiday". In the humdrum world of everyday a Ford, or a Mistress Ford (it could be both), would enable the crossing of a Brook. Here, the Brook engulfs the Ford, "overthwart", to make the crossing a "lie"—with a playful caesura before the speaking rhythm offers the relief of "with". And once we register that he means copulation (lexically split, *interruptus*, a *lie?*), the ear recalls how iambic stress falls heavily on the particular moment, "tonight", almost a plea for just this once, but without assurance that the nights to come will see the inundated husband rise—can Ford enjoy sex without fantasizing adultery? With a presence to evocalization, the theatre page figures words "nicking" one another, what George Puttenham calls "auricular" figures ravishing the ear and the mind,[41] of the kind that negotiate a sensorial semiosis on a listener's or reader's material body, a "weft of voicings" tucked under each other.[42] The same couplet harbours the marriage bed, a supreme domestic item that Mr. Ford had evoked with anxiety ("my bed shall be abused": II.2.276–277) and that is now turned over to the cuckolder. As with the buck-basket, its signification of social position is mobile. The wives' disciplinary washing and cleansing of Windsor has Brooked no unruly breach, but has led only to the community's flooding.

## V

The wives themselves, of course, take pleasure in breaching. For them being "merry" is to translate a married woman's variable situations into theatrical roles capable of being manipulated at will, turning the adulteress, or the indignant spouse, with a number of supporting parts to their advantage. They "do not act that often jest and laugh" (IV.2.101), hence have no interest in a social performance or simulation of what they impersonate since it is the roles that give meaning and fire their imagination:

MISTRESS FORD. [ . . . ] Mistress Page, remember you
                                                          [your cue.
MISTRESS PAGE. I warrant thee: if I do not act it, hiss
                                                          [me.

MISTRESS FORD. You use me well, Master Ford, do

                                    [you?

FORD. Ay, I do so.

MISTRESS FORD. Heaven make you better than your

                                    [thoughts.

(III.3.33–34, 187–190)


The first of these speaks of the adulteress's role, the second of the wronged spouse. The only role the wives refuse is the "still swine" (IV.2.102), plain social without imaginative performance with a single rhetorical and stylistic register, so that they pick up the previous scene's "hang-hog" (see above) to underscore the rightly performative Englishing of domestic experience. The moment the wives decide to reveal their plotting to their husbands and make the shaming of Falstaff a public event, their motivation is undiminished "jest": "Come, to the forge with it, then shape it: I would not have things cool" (IV.2.211–213). By adapting a proverb, they move out of the woman's domestic sphere, in which they would be tied forever to "shaping" hodge-puddings, and related chores, to assume a masculine role of blacksmith which, no longer femininely inferior to husbands, at once reveals its capacity for fraud and falsehood. The whole subsequent scene of disclosure and reinvestment in the husbands' primary role is indeed a forgery, as it ends with a short soliloquy by Mrs. Page which reveals her intention to use their new device for the sake of thwarting her goodman (IV.4.82–88, particularized in V.3). For Mrs. Page, the rest of the play is the wives' script, im-paging an action directed no longer so much against Falstaff as against her husband. The reason is the Page parents' antagonistic desires concerning their daughter's future: where Mr. Page, counter-paging a drama plot of his own (IV.4.71–73), vehemently favours Slender's suit, his wife is just as zealous in preferring Dr. Caius's, for similarly financial reasons coupled with an interest in courtly power (IV.4.86–88). Some of this material is influenced from afar by the *joie de vivre* of Plautus's titillating *Casina*. The *Merry Wives*' plot unconformities, for that matter, by accident or design advance a sceptical presentation of domestic discipline: resolving an initial dispute over the theft of a deer by a convivial invitation to a venison pasty plants the seeds of the Pages' split. The parents agree only in their mutual antagonism, bearing dubious witness to the wife's effective government of her family's business, or to that unit's stability. Young Anne has no say in the matter, even to the extent that her mother has no scruples about being brazenly *fausse* when she calms Fenton: "My daughter will I question how she loves you, / And as I find her, so am

I affected" (III.4.89–90). Her words would lead anyone to believe that Anne's taste matches her mother's, as against the same scene's other visual and vocatory registers. A zest for mutual cross-scheming actuates the Page parents' agreement to set up the final masque in which (as nominal purpose) Falstaff is to be publicly exposed, a zest that, by championing the play's absurdities, Dr. Caius or Slender, as the play's Fairy King has the potential to rupture the "bonds of national culture" along with the more homely bond. This breach is averted by Anne and Fenton who counterscheme against both parents, setting Anne free to elope with her lover. By his disrespect for her parents, responding as he does to her own defiance, Fenton is a threat to the family's authority in an alternative way—not only its authority and government, for that matter, but also its economic standing, since Anne's parents wanted her to marry money. Extremity rather than control and discipline reigns within the play's families. Mr. Page had chastised Mr. Ford's excessive repentance upon learning the truth about his wife's scheme: "'Tis well, 'tis well, no more. / Be not as extreme in submission as in offence" (IV.4.10–11). A proper wedded relation lies *in extremis* —in a clunky heptameter that, like Mr. Ford, goes to great lengths. But "extreme", as either one of two objects removed as far as possible from each other, meets "overthwart" as an apt description of the Pages as well.

These somewhat unsettled conditions last through the final scene, culminating in the disguised citizens' courtly masque which has been read as a populist consolidation of aristocratic power[43]—a highly erratic monarchizing, however, if one considers that it is apparently Mrs. Quickly who plays the royal role. When the masque with a further ambivalence dissolves into nothing (like the aristocratic power?), leaving not a rack behind, Fenton re-enters with his bride to announce their marriage. Yet not all is at it seems. Tongue-in-cheek, one might read the struggle for Anne since the play's opening quasi-allegorically as one for control of an aptly named and feminized *Page* as theatrical script, whether in print or manuscript, a property and medium that will form or transfigure material possessions along with the social community—as Anne will reveal the fallacy of possession in her own *persona* (to be shown in a moment). With a measure of social propriety a youth of aristocratic associations gains the prize, a fitting Fairy Queen beyond the spoofing masquerade. It was noted above that during the masque a split has become discernible between the assumed role and the actor, a split extending to the boys who are dressed as stand-in fairy queen girls and with whom Slender and Dr. Caius are fobbed off, each with *"un page"* (as it were, embracing a sexual pun) instead of Anne Page. In the midst of theatrical artifice, is Anne really a *person* or rather a "page"? And a singular entity, or rather one of three? Fenton seems assured of what he holds as he chides her parents:

> You would have married her most shamefully
> Where there was no proportion held in love.
> The truth is, she and I, long since contracted,
> Are now so sure that nothing can dissolve us.
> (V.5.215–218)

When he declares they are "sure" he indicates (of course) that they are safely married, yet the *OED* records, in this period, meanings that remain below objective security: "subjectively certain" or "persuaded" (8.b); to "be sure that" means "take care that" (14); "make sure" could even mean "to make away with" (3). Fenton foregrounds "she" after a telling caesura, with an effect lost in the last three centuries' theatres in which Anne is played by an actress. How easy is it to distinguish Anne's "true" self from that of "a great lubberly boy" (V.5.182), as Trevor Joscelyne asks?[44] In the Quarto Mr. Ford's final speech shows him relishing the notion that Slender and Dr. Caius each have "a boy / To waite vpon you, go God giue you ioy" (sig. G4ᵛ),[45] in verse that conveys unmistakably sexual connotations.[46] Would anyone thinking of Anne as quite different, or firmly possessed and not "dissolved", be traduced as a homophonic "âne"? On her phonotext, even as it bests the parental rift, performance inscribes a dispersal of parts and aphanistic role illusion. The original theatrical effect may be lost forever, as any effort to regain it in the study would be a "retrospective hallucination".[47] Repercussions may have been far-reaching, however: if Anne is not "really" a woman, can Fenton "really" be a man, his speaking position reliably masculine? How sure is possession, the "holding" of identity, persons, goods, or words, such as the "selling" of wives (with which Mr. Ford responds to Fenton's declaration) or the "word" that Sir John shall yet "hold" at the plays very end?[48]

Writing about the performativity of gender, Judith Butler has declared that "what is exteriorized or performed can only be understood by reference to what is barred from performance, what cannot or will not be performed".[49] When young Anne, even within her role, meekly begs her parents' pardon and leaves the speech arena to Fenton, is she duly empowering his patriarchal, "disciplined, and reliably masculine speaking position" (as Erickson and Landreth see it)? Or should we rather see her as exteriorizing, *staging* filial and wifely submission to her advantage? It is not in isolation that we should hear and see these subtle effects; they are in tune with the business of the masque and the gradual unstitching of firm roles. As Mrs. Page describes it, *Merry Wives* offers "sport" (V.5.236), a term that blends "amorous dalliance" with the artifice of "theatrical performance" and places the play in the province of Mercury, now a re-gendered "she-Mercury" (II.2.76), who according to Marsilio Ficino transports words, presides over merry songs, and is responsible for deception.[50] The social community whose core feasts its expectation

of merry days may not be as Englishly localized as it seems: throughout it is
vocally shaped to embrace the globe's exotic barbarisms, including "Vizier"
(I.3.9), "Phrygian Turk" (I.3.85), the inscrutable "An-heires" (Anne-heir, heirs
of Ann?) who for all we know may be "Ameers" or "myn-heers" (II.1.197),
"Dutch dish" (III.5.110), "anthropophaginian" (IV.5.8), even "Hungarian"
(I.3.19) or "nape" (the "ape" of I.4.100) or "Cathayan" (II.1.130). The simply
English "Bohemian-Tartar" (IV.5.18) seems eventually to be bounced, but
Mr. Ford has assured us he would rather trust a Fleming or an Irishman than
his wife (II.2.286–287). The native is the "babbling barbarian" who is "always
at the gate", a foreign body possessed—as in the early English Bibles—of
"a familiar spirit", inverting the meaning of possession.[51] And in any *case*,
English may be "out of honesty" (I.3.47). Ingle-ish, open to lewd advances.
The good people of Windsor then, whose men could consider themselves
representatives of a rising class (of benefit to their wives) concerned with both
social and financial mobility, like Will Shakespeare himself, have an outside
and an inside, their chief characteristic from the beginning being "as properties, as objects of possession and sites of investment and fortune" (as Arthur
Kinney perceived).[52] This is consistent throughout, from the opening scene's
effort to assuage the fury of worth-y Shallow, who is possessed "of" a dozen
white luces (or "louses", as "familiar"?) and has been robbed of his deer, by the
device of introducing Anne as "seven hundred pounds of moneys" (I.1.46), to
landing a wife at the close. Such moneys are not easy to distinguish from human bodies: the "purse" over which a wife is said to have "all the rule" conceals
the semiotic currency of her husband's scrotum (I.3.50), while unconfinable
desires may lurk at the heart of domestic control. To gain such moneys may
be to become possessed by a tautology of *making away with* or dissolving
dissolution while embracing something *faux,* as volatile as the actor's role.
Much of the popular theatre's audience would be invited to recognize itself
in the play's realism, whereas a courtly audience (if such a one did actually
come about) might be allowed the amusement of disdain accompanying their
enjoyment of the antics of Falstaff. Even if Crane might not agree, the propriety of a passion for holdings and possessions of all kinds, as in the "riches" of
Anne's "self", becomes subject to doubt in the theatre's domain of "tricking".
Later growing into something of a penny-pincher himself, the bard nonetheless appears to have been able to take note of flaws at least in others (and to
displace them accordingly)—an assessment which affects our understanding
of his position in relation to the realities of his own times. Perhaps we would
do well to think of *Merry Wives* as not having to be overly profound in order to revel in the empty spaces between firm significances, as its audience
becomes sutured into what the play's laughter joys in undoing: the illusion
that a community and its tradings, its very goods, can exist without being
"Englished rightly"—this time on a theatrical page.

NOTES

1. William Shakespeare, *The Merry Wives of Windsor*, ed. Giorgio Melchiori, The Arden Shakespeare (Walton-on-Thames: Thomas Nelson, 2000). Quotations from *Merry Wives* are taken from this edition throughout.
2. Melchiori, ed. *The Merry Wives...*, 5.
3. Patricia Parker, *Shakespeare from the Margins: Language, Culture, Context* (Chicago & London: Chicago University Press, 1996), 139.
4. H. C. Hart, *The Merry Wives of Windsor*, The Arden Shakespeare (London: Methuen, 1904), liv, lxxi.
5. Jeanne Addison Roberts, *Shakespeare's English Comedy: The Merry Wives of Windsor in Context* (Lincoln & London: University of Nebraska Press, 1979), 73.
6. Cf. Michel de Montaigne, *The Essayes*, trans. John Florio (London: Dent, 1897), vol. 1, 1.20, p. 127: "Those instruments that serve to discharge the belly, have their proper compressions and dilatations, besides our intent, and against our meaning."
7. Carol M. Rose, *Property and Persuasion: Essays on the History, Theory, and Rhetoric of Ownership*, (Boulder, Col.: Westview Press, 1994), 17, 25.
8. Wendy Wall, *Staging Domesticity: Household Work and English Identity in Early Modern Drama*. (Cambridge: Cambridge University Press, 2002), 113.
9. David Crane, *The Merry Wives of Windsor*, The New Cambridge Shakespeare (Cambridge: Cambridge. University Press, 1997), 8.
10. *The Riverside Shakespeare*, textual ed. G. Blakemore Evans, (Boston: Houghton Mifflin, 1974).
11. Crane, *The Merry Wives...*, 6.
12. Wall, *Staging...*, 9.
13. Arthur F. Kinney, "Textual Signs and Economic Signals in *The Merry Wives of Windsor*", *Shakespeare et l'argent*, ed. Marie-Thérèse Jones-Davies (Paris: Les Belles Lettres, 1993), 23–37, 34, 36.
14. Crane, *The Merry Wives...*, 7 and following.
15. Natasha Korda, *Shakespeare's Domestic Economies: Gender and Property in Early Modern England* (Philadelphia: Pennsylvania University Press, 2002), 83, 102.
16. David Landreth, "Once More into the Preech: *The Merry Wives'* English Pedagogy", *Shakespeare Quarterly* 55 (2004); 420–449, 421, 422.
17. Landreth, "Once More into...", 433, 437, 439.
18. Landreth, "Once More into...", 445.
19. Landreth, "Once More into...", 446. The argument should not be stretched too far: it does not account for the fact that the wives' only speeches that Fenton might have overheard and appropriated—just a few brief lines at III.4.87–92—are too slight to carry such a weight; he is not present at Mrs. Ford's speech at II.1.48–56.
20. Landreth, "Once More into...", 449.
21. Leo Salingar, "The Englishness of *The Merry Wives of Windsor*", *Cahiers Élisabéthains* 59 (2001), 9–25, here 24.
22. Wall, *Staging...*, 124, 125.
23. Lena Cowen Orlin, "Shakespearean Comedy and Material Life", *A Companion to Shakespeare's Works*, vol. 3, ed. Richard Dutton and Jean E. Howard (Oxford: Blackwell, 2003), 159–181, 175.

24. *Plaute Tome II: Bacchides— Captivi—Casina,* texte établi et traduit par Alfred Ernout (Paris: Les Belles Lettres, 1970), *Casina* 1. 199–200.

25. For a vivid description, see Wall, *Staging. . . ,* 19–21. See also Lorna Hutson, *The Usurer's Daughter: Male Friendship and Fictions of Women in Sixteenth-Century England* (London & New York: Routledge, 1994) 17–22.

26. William Perkins, *Christian Oeconomie: Or, A Short Survey of the Right Manner of Erecting and Ordering a Familie* (published posthumously, London: Felix Kyngston, 1609), sig. A3ʳ. Perkins goes onto declare: "The corruption or declination of this first gouernment, must of necessitie giue way to the ruinating of the rest" (A3ᵛ). Declining, of course, is practiced literally in *Merry Wives* IV.1.

27. See also Margaret Ezell, *The Patriarch's Wife* (Chapel Hill, N.C.: University of North Carolina Press, 1987), 36–61.

28. Samuel Johnson, *A Dictionary of the English Language,* 2 vols. (London: Knapton, 1755; 4ᵗʰ, rev. ed. 1773),

29. Korda, *Shakespeare's Domestic Economies. . . ,* 93, 95.

30. William Gouge, *Of Domesticall Duties* (London: William Bladen, 1622), 291.

31. For the flax, see also Henry N. Ellacombe, *The Plant-lore and Garden-craft of Shakespeare* (London: Satchell, 1878; 2ⁿᵈ ed. 1884, rpt. New York: AMS, 1973), 96.

32. Deanne Williams, "*The Merry Wives of Windsor* and the French-English Dictionary", *Actes de longue française et de linguistique* 10–11 (1997–1998), 233–242, 240.

33. Korda, *Shakespeare's Domestic Economies. . . ,* 110.

34. Wall, *Staging. . . ,* 126.

35. Landreth, "Once More into . . .", 446.

36. John Minsheu, *Ductor in Linguas, the gvide into tongves* (1617; rpt. Delmar, N.Y.: Scholars' Facsimiles & Rpts., 1978).

37. Wall, *Staging. . . ,* 2, 18.

38. Samuel Johnson and George Steevens, ed., *The Plays of William Shakespeare,* vol. 1 (1778; rpt. London: Routledge/Thoemmes, 1995).

39. Joel Fineman, *Shakespeare's Perjured Eye: The Invention of Poetic Subjectivity in the Sonnets* (Berkeley: University of California Press, 1986), 15.

40. Richard Huloet, *Abcedarivm anglicolatinvm* (1552; rpt. Menston, England: Scolar Press, 1970).

41. George Puttenham, *The Arte of English Poesie* (1589; rpt Menston, England: Scolar Press, 1968), 164, 169.

42 As theorized by Garrett Stewart, *Reading Voices: Literature and the Phonotext* (Berkeley: University of California Press,, 1990), e.g., 26.

43 See especially Peter Erickson, "The Order of the Garter, the Cult of Elizabeth, and Class-Gender Tension in *The Merry Wives of Windsor*", *Shakespeare Reproduced: The Text in History and Ideology,* ed. Jean E. Howard and Marion F. O'Connor (London: Methuen, 1987), 116–140; Richard Helgerson, "The Buck Basket, the Witch, and the Queen of Fairies: The Women's World of Shakespeare's Windsor", *Renaissance Culture and the Everyday,* ed. Patricia Furnerton and Simon Hunt (Philadelphia: University of Pennsylvania Press, 1999), 162–182, here 175–178.

44. Trevor Joscelyne, "'Money buys lands, and wives are sold by fate': Characterization by Culture and Gender in *The Merry Wives of Windsor*", *Discourse*

*and Character,* ed. Wojciech Kalaga and Tadeusz Slawek (Katowice: Uniwersytet Slaski, 1990), 56–75, here 72.

45. See facsimile in the Arden edition of 2000.

46. See also Wendy Wall, "*The Merry Wives of Windsor:* Unhusbanding Desires in Windsor", *A Companion to Shakespeare's Works,* vol. 3, ed. Richard Dutton and Jean E. Howard (Oxford: Blackwell, 2003), 376–392, here 386. Wall suggestively discusses the significance of expansive identity in the play.

47. Jean Baudrillard, *Simulations,* trans. Paul Foss, Pail Patton and Philip Beitchman (New York: Semiotext(e), 1983), 22.

48. In discussing *elenches* Francis Bacon, like Michel de Montaigne (e.g., *Essayes* 3.13 on endless substitution of words), attacks the notion that one can govern words as fallacious, the origin of the Idols of the Marketplace: "words, as a Tartar's bow, do shoot back upon the understanding of the wisest, and mightily entangle and pervert the judgment" (*The Advancement of Learning,* ed. G. W. Kitchin [London: Dent, 1915; 1973] 134). See also the later *Novum Organum,* trans. and ed. Peter Urbach and John Gibson (Chicago: Open Court, 1994), Book 1 Aphorism 59.

49. Judith Butler, *The Psychic Life of Power: Theories in Subjection* (Stanford, Ca.: Stanford University Aress, 1997), 144–145.

50. See Marsilio Ficino, *Three Books on Life,* ed. and trans. Carol V. Kaske and John R. Clark, Medieval & Renaissance Texts & Studies 57 (Binghamton, N.Y.: Renaissance Society of America, 1989), 208, 360.

51. Steven Connor, *Dumbstruck: A Cultural History of Ventriloquism* (Oxford: Oxford University Press, 2000), 417.

52. Kinney, "Textual Signs . . .", 25. It is not easy to reconcile Kinney's account of the Folio play as being about "merchants who prey on customers and the poor who must con their way for survival" (34), evoking an authentic Windsor "characterized by starvation, theft, and death", with his conclusion that, as against the apparently earlier Quarto version, it is a work of "good humour and mirth" as described by T. W. Craik (quoted by Kinney, "Textual Signs . . .", 36). From an overriding interest in production and theatre setting, Craik had declared (in his introduction to his ed. of *The Merry Wives of Windsor* [Oxford: Oxford University Press, 1990]) that, far from being thematically dominant, social and monetary issues are merely a plot condition, a "means of setting events in motion" (Craik, 42). Despite this difference from Kinney, Craik had likewise stressed the Play's "thoroughly happy ending" without ironies (Craik, 47). Neither scholar questions the stability and consistency of the play's dramatic roles.

CYNTHIA LEWIS

# "We know what we know":
# Reckoning in Love's Labor's Lost

Berowne they call him, but a merrier man,
Within the limit of becoming mirth,
I never spent an hour's talk withal.
His eye begets occasion for his wit,
For every object that the one doth catch
The other turns to a mirth-moving jest,
Which his fair tongue, conceit's expositor,
Delivers in such apt and gracious words
That aged ears play truant at his tales
And younger hearings are quite ravished,
So sweet and voluble is his discourse.

—Rosaline on Berowne[1]

Oft have I heard of you, my lord Berowne,
Before I saw you, and the world's large tongue
Proclaims you for a man replete with mocks,
Full of comparisons and wounding flouts,
Which you on all estates will execute
That lie within the mercy of your wit.
To weed this wormwood from your fruitful brain
And therewithal to win me, if you please—

*Studies in Philology*, Volume 105, Number 2 (Spring 2008): pp. 245–264. Copyright © 2007 The University of North Carolina Press.

> Without the which I am not to be won—
> You shall this twelvemonth term from day to day
> Visit the speechless sick and still converse
> With groaning wretches; and your task shall be
> With all the fierce endeavour of your wit
> To enforce the pained impotent to smile.
>                    —Rosaline to Berowne (5.2.829–842)

How does the audience of *Love's Labor's Lost* reconcile these two speeches, which are so specifically opposed as to create a contradiction? And how do the actors playing Rosaline and Berowne make sense of the gap? In the first speech, Rosaline praises Berowne's wit as "mirth-moving" and his mirth as "becoming." His "fair tongue," speaking as it does "apt and gracious words," delights both young and old—presumably moving all ages to the laughter that, in the second speech, from the play's last scene, Rosaline enjoins Berowne to evoke from the "speechless sick" as if he had never before delighted anyone. The very sense of humor that is said to "ravish" young people in the first speech becomes, in the second speech, "wounding" and toxic as "wormwood." The wit that is clearly described as salutary in the first passage has turned hurtful in the second.

This about-face is a particularly salient element of the play's larger shift from romantic comedy, seemingly headed for a quadruple wedding, to something more like satire or comedy manqué, in which the couples separate for a year before reassessing the prospect of marrying. What appears a failure of the play to cohere as a whole has been addressed by many critics. Kristian Smidt, for example, has argued that when Shakespeare began writing *Love's Labor's*, he intended to write a romantic comedy that he could neither abandon completely nor believe in wholeheartedly, so that, as the play progresses, it increasingly reflects his "two minds" about the project.[2] While I do not want to over apologize for what Smidt and others identify as the play's flaws, I also believe that its interest and involvement in the idea and action of reckoning bridges its opening and closing more logically than might at first appear. Such was my experience when working with students on a production of the play. Rosaline's revised judgment of Berowne is one of many examples of reckoning—ranging from simple counting to more complex formulations of value—that, taken together, shape the play both subtly and profoundly and thus reward close inspection.

Both the term *reckoning* and various concepts of reckoning permeate the play and, in fact, Shakespeare's canon. The term carries as many different meanings in the plays as it does today. When Don Armado confesses that he is "ill at reckoning" (1.2.40), he means that he cannot add and subtract.

Indeed, as the scene makes clear, he cannot so much as count to three (39–53). In a more sophisticated mathematical sense, *reckoning* refers to account keeping. So the Princess means when she tells the King that, at the point of "annual reckoning," she will review his success at his living without worldly pleasures for a year in an effort to win her hand (5.2.792). His accumulation of "deserts" will serve as penance for having failed to keep his original oath of austerity (5.2.799). The Princess's manner of tabulating good deeds and bad savors of the double entry bookkeeping that, historians have recently shown, was inaugurated in late sixteenth-century England and taught to students at John Mellis's "reckoning school" very near the site of the Globe Theater.[3] More abstractly, the broader notion of reckoning in *Love's Labor's* is that of judgment, preserved even today in quaint caricatures of Texans—"How much you reckon that truck's worth?"—and more soberly in the idea of the Last Judgment, a final reckoning that occurs at the point of death or of the Second Coming.[4]

All of these connotations appear in many of Shakespeare's plays, as when, in *Much Ado about Nothing*, Claudio refers to the entrance of his masked bride, the disguised Hero, as "other reck'nings" than that of settling the score with Benedick.[5] Claudio is alluding to marrying the woman he believes is Antonio's daughter both as a compensation for having injured Leonato (through Hero's presumed death) and as a matter to be reckoned with—dealt with—immediately. Earlier in the same scene, Benedick refers to his aborted duel with Claudio as a "reckoning," payment for having maligned Beatrice's cousin (5.4.9). In *Antony and Cleopatra*, Cleopatra's dismissal of "love that can be reckoned" as "beggary" refers to love that can be measured, counted, and computed (1.1.15). Myriad conceptions of reckoning also run throughout the *Henriad*, including those in *1 Henry IV* to tavern bills and to paying the price of one's life in battle (2.4.101 and 5.1.135). When Michael Williams says in *Henry V* that "if the cause [for going to war with France] be not good, the King himself hath a heavy reckoning to make," he means that Henry will be called to divine judgment "at the latter day" to answer for his soldiers' "legs and arms and heads, chopped off in a battle," bodily parts that will be reckoned—counted—as his responsibility (4.1.134–137). Henry, however, is long acquainted with such moral reckoning, since, as Prince Hal, he anticipates being put to the test when he becomes king and "redeeming" his lost "time" when people least expect him to (*1 Henry IV*, 1.2.217). Soon after his conversation with Williams in *Henry V*, the King prays to the "God of battles" to remove the "sense of reckoning" from his soldiers' hearts, lest their fear of defeat at Agincourt become a self-fulfilling prophecy (4.1.289–291). Reckoning here connotes the judgment that would accompany their deaths, but it also glances at the possibility that a loss at Agincourt could be a moral consequence of Henry's father's having usurped Richard II, a possibility that he prays fervently to avoid: "Not to-day, O Lord! / O not to-day, think not upon the fault / My father made in compassing the crown" (292–294).

As in many of these instances from other plays, in *Love's Labor's*, a single use of the term *reckoning* may prove multivalent, and the act of reckoning, whether or not called by that exact name, can involve such multiple tasks as, say, counting and making moral judgment. But in general, reckoning is a matter of assigning value, either quantitative, qualitative, or both, and the very word encourages the audience to consider such apparently disparate actions as mathematical figuring, which concerns fixed, objective value, and deriving moral judgment—the evaluation of which is more subjective and inclined to flux—in terms of one another. At points, what would appear to be the most straightforward of mathematical calculations is confusing, and, by the same token, what seems a more complex, difficult judgment becomes clarified and simplified. Rosaline's two judgments of Berowne, the one earlier and the other at the play's conclusion, focus attention on the problem of determining value—in this case, of evaluating Berowne as a suitor according to what she has seen of and heard about him.

One spare clue to Rosaline's transformed opinion of Berowne may lie in the suggestion that the second speech traces back to an earlier time than the first speech; the second appears to involve what Rosaline heard about Berowne before ever having met him, while the first refers to a time after she has had the direct experience of conversing with him and being herself enraptured by his speech.[6] That her attraction to his wit is already established becomes evident when, upon first seeing Berowne, she quickly engages him in the first of many verbal skirmishes between them, just lines after she has characterized his "discourse" as "sweet and voluble" (2.1.114–127). Possibly, then, she has been temporarily taken in by a smooth operator who, during the course of the play, she comes to see as the cad she heard criticized before she met him herself.

I believe a version of this explanation helps account for Rosaline's turn-around. It also applies to the other ladies' apparent change of heart in regard to the men. Katherine's praise of Dumaine in 2.1 is unadulterated (56–63), making her firm rejection of the same lord in 5.2 baffling in it own right (815–820). Only Maria's initial description of Longaville—the first in the series of girlish confessions to crushes—is at all mixed (2.1.40–51). Maria cites as Longaville's only flaw a wit that comes noticeably close to Rosaline's description of Berowne's wit in the second speech above: Longaville's "sharp wit," unmonitored by his reason and given free rein by his will, has power to hurt (2.1.49). When the Princess asks if Longaville is a "merry-mocking lord," Maria hedges, "They say so most that most his humours know" (2.1.52–53). Maria hesitates to subscribe to received opinion about Longaville, but the Princess unhesitatingly marks him as unsuitable for a long-term relationship:

"Such short-lived wits wither as they grow" (2.1.54). This skepticism toward the first of the lords to be described perhaps causes Katherine and Rosaline to censor their subsequent portrayals of Dumaine and Berowne, deleting any reason for the Princess to reject them as suitors. In any case, the Princess's objection to wit, like Longaville's, foreshadows all of the ladies' final refusals of the men's marriage proposals, including the King's to her, which Boyet predicts twice in this same scene, once by referring to Aquitaine as a "dowry for a queen" and later by speculating that Navarre is "infected" with love for the Princess (2.1.8 and 229). The Princess's reprimand to Boyet for his "pride" in this same scene looks forward both to her criticism of Longaville in the short term and to the ladies' refusals of the men's proposals in the long term (35–36).

This scene, in which Rosaline, Katherine, and Maria all speak so admiringly of Berowne, Dumaine, and Longaville, contains the seeds of a recurring tendency: the inclination of verbally adept people to talk themselves into a position they fancy. Such flair for rationalization is epitomized by Berowne's facility at defending the lords' abandonment of their original oath in 4.3 and urging them to court the women (285–360). It is also made light of by the Princess as she prepares to hunt the deer in 4.1:

> Thus will I save my credit in the shoot:
> Not wounding, pity would not let me do't;
> If wounding, then it was to show my skill,
> That more for praise than purpose meant to kill.
>
> (26–29)

Either way, the Princess saves face. She implies that reckoning, including that in love, is provisional and subject to rhetorical spin. The ladies' first speeches about the lords, noting that they are "garnished / With such bedecking ornaments of praise," as the Princess says, reflect what the women would like to think about men they barely know first-hand (2.1.78–79).

The proclivity to rationalize a position, a like, or a dislike, is linked in *Love's Labor's* with the difficulty of reckoning absolute value, whose slipperiness is indicated throughout the play. What, for example, is the value of Aquitaine? Is it, as Boyet says, a "dowry for a queen" (2.1.8)? Or is that assessment merely part of his pep talk to a royal woman who is about to try to sell the King of Navarre on accepting Aquitaine in lieu of one hundred thousand crowns? The King protests that "gelded" Aquitaine does not amount to that sum (2.1.136 and 148). Determining the worth of Aquitaine eludes royalty as surely as the sum of "one thrice told" escapes Don Armado in the preceding scene (1.2.39). In another instance, Costard seeks to fix the value of his payment. "How much carnation ribbon may a man buy for a remuneration?" he asks (3.1.141–142). "What is a remuneration?" responds a puzzled Berowne, suggesting that its value varies with each new set of circumstances (143). By the scene's end, Costard understands that, at least provisionally, "remuneration" pales next to "guerdon" (165–168). Costard's new vocabulary for identifying worth calls attention to the indeterminacy of worth.

Early on, Costard also demonstrates the flexibility of reckoning. The judgment on his wayward behavior, which predicts the lords' eventual departure from their initial oath, is the first such reckoning in *Love's Labor's*. It is a judgment vexed first by Don Armado's impossibly florid testimonial to having seen Costard with Jaquenetta (1.1.226–264) and second by Costard's efforts to dodge the language of the accusation against him:

*KING:* It was proclaimed a year's imprisonment to be taken with a wench.

*COSTARD:* I was taken with none, sir; I was taken with a damsel.

*KING:* Well, it was proclaimed a damsel.

*COSTARD:* This was no damsel neither, sir; she was a virgin.

*KING:* It is so varied too, for it was proclaimed a virgin.

(1.1.273–279)

And so forth. Costard's wriggling prefigures Berowne's defending the indefensible in 4.3. Moreover, his punishment, to "fast a week with bran and water," is not only a far cry from the "year's imprisonment" specified in the proclamation but is also sketchily enforced (1.1.284–285 and 273). Although Costard next appears after hearing the King's sentence in the custody of Constable Dull and on his way to being "shut up" in "prison" (1.2.147–151), he soon seems to have broken out of custody by having broken (or by feigning to have broken) a shin (3.1.67). Thereafter, he is free to roam the countryside delivering letters (e.g., 4.1.40), consorting again with Jaquenetta (e.g., 4.2.79), and performing in a court entertainment (5.2). That Don Armado is his jailer contributes to the absurdity of Costard's punishment, since Armado is chasing Jaquenetta himself and sets Costard loose to deliver a love letter to her (3.1.125–129). The hypocrisies and ironies, too obvious to belabor, satirize the process and prospects of rendering strict judgment and enforcing punishment.

Don Armado, who in his first appearance seeks "some mighty precedent" to justify ("example") his own defeat by love, can out-rationalize all other characters (1.2.111). In so doing, he comically exaggerates other characters' inclination to rationalize, posture, and believe what they want to believe, often imposing their wills in substitution for fact and proof, as the Princess and the King appropriate the words *shall* and *will* to gain the upper hand upon first meeting:

*KING:*  You shall be welcome, madam, to my court.
*PRINCESS:*  I will be welcome then. Conduct me thither.
                . . . . . . . . . . . . . . . . . . . . . . . . . . . .
*PRINCESS:*  Vouchsafe to read the purpose of my coming
                And suddenly resolve me in my suit.
*KING:*  Madam, I will, if suddenly I may.
*PRINCESS:*  You will the sooner that I were away,
                For you'll proved perjured if you make me stay.
                                    (2.1.95–96 and 109–113)

The Princess carefully marshals her own language as she undermines the King's, a tactic elaborated in 4.3 when the four lords enter individually, observe one another's broken oaths, then blame one another's perjury while denying their own.

In other, similar examples, characters manipulate value to please them-selves. When each lord bestows outlandish praise upon the lady of his fancy in 4.3 and the King, Dumaine, and Longaville conspire to criticize Rosaline's appearance (217–277), the men indulge in such self-delusion. As Berowne re-alistically observes in a soliloquy, a lover may "write, sigh, pray, sue and groan," but the object of his affection may remain a plain "Joan" (3.1.199–200). Fit-tingly, no sooner have the men stopped disparaging Rosaline's dark complex-ion in 4.3 than they petition Berowne to conjure "some flattery for this evil" of abandoning their oath and falling in love (282). Longaville, fully aware that he is embracing self-deception, begs Berowne for "some authority how to proceed. / Some tricks, some quillets how to cheat the devil" (283–284), much as Don Armado earlier demands "authority" from Moth for falling in love (1.2.65). With equal gusto, Holofernes, Nathaniel, and Don Armado convince themselves of their verbal and theatrical prowess; although Don Armado fleetingly suspects that their earnest portrayal of the Nine Worthies could dissolve into an "antic" (5.1.138), the performers, like their social su-periors, spare no effort to think well of themselves, Holofernes presuming to play three of the nine roles (134).

Despite all such conscious and unconscious evasions of reality, the claims of final reckoning are the most persistent and tenacious in the play. The players in the pageant of the Nine Worthies will be disabused of their high opinions of themselves, learning the hard way that, as the Princess predicts, they are entertaining because they are incompetent (5.2.514–518). Truth may be temporarily obscured, but the moon will eventually appear from behind the word *Dictynna* (4.2.36). Likewise, rules may be broken and toyed with for the time being, but ultimately the last accounting will have to be settled. That, of course, is Marcadé's message upon interrupting the entertainment to announce the death of the Princess's father (5.2.711ff.). There is no getting around death. News of the French king's demise precipitates the last reckoning between the lovers, which results in the foiled marriage proposals and the injunctions given by each lady to her lord. Marriage has turned from a "sport," a "mockery merriment," into a serious proposition, as every sign in the play suggests that it should be (5.2.153 and 139). Death affords a harsh, but needed, clarity.

The final negotiations about love between the men and the women, which lead toward such clarity, parallel the lords' and ladies' first meeting, in 2.1, just after the women have sung the men's praises. More particularly, those last negotiations underscore the contrasting lightheartedness of the couples' first meeting while mirroring the serious negotiation between the two kings in 2.1, mediated by the Princess. What exactly is the purpose of the document that the Princess delivers to the King of Navarre in their first encounter? Its terms are vague, referring as they do to an earlier contract whose origins are even vaguer. The dispute incited by the paper gets the King and the Princess off to a conventionally rocky comic start, with an obstacle to surmount; it puts the King immediately on the defensive with a woman he would woo. But it also subordinates the Princess to her father. She is the messenger, not the author, and she seems hardly interested in its contents. While the King reads, she is apparently happy to be distracted by the banter between Rosaline and Berowne (2.1.114–127), and, once the King has finished reading and sets about refuting the paper's position, the Princess barely engages in a discussion about it. She asserts that the King maligns her father, insists that France is in the right (153–156), then shuts down the conversation when the King attempts to defend himself. "We arrest your word," she says to him, dispatching Boyet to retrieve a mysterious "packet" that has not yet arrived but that will, she protests, prove her father's claim (159–165).

The packet, of course, never materializes. Nor does it need to, since the disagreement between Navarre and France is apparently settled privately, owing to the King's acquiescence (5.2.732–733). Here again, a reckoning has been circumvented, this time through generosity, but the political controversy is notable less for its specific details regarding ownership and property than for its distinction from the last scene, where reckoning cannot be avoided. Another contrast between the negotiations in 2.1 and those at the play's closing involves the Princess's changed position. Her father's death renders her the author, not just the messenger. Now she is responsible for her future; choosing wisely depends upon exercising her own powers of judgment, upon engaging with her prospects rather than observing from the sidelines. Although stricken with grief at the news of her father's death, she is also left in a position of considerable, indeed enviable, power: like England's queen at the time (notorious in her own right for using courtship as a means of political manipulation), she possesses a kingdom and is eminently marriageable.[7] She need not marry to survive or to resolve a political situation. She can afford to pause and take her time deliberating.

In the last acts of the play, the men give the women plenty to deliberate about. Gradually, they reveal sides to themselves that challenge the ladies' high opinions of them. Most important, the women justifiably question them for throwing over their initial oaths and have been implying all along how ill-advised they were in the first place. These broken oaths are the very crux of the ladies' decision to distrust the lords' vows of love for them. The Princess lightly mocks the King for his hypocrisy when, unaware, he has pledged his love to Rosaline, not to her: "Your oath once broke, you force not to forswear" (5.2.440). She returns to the same theme more seriously when rejecting the King's marriage proposal: "my lord, your grace is perjured much, / . . . Your oath I will not trust" (5.2.784 and 788). Her women echo her, Katherine most plainly to Dumaine: "Yet swear not, lest ye be forsworn again" (5.2.820). The ever perceptive Berowne understands that he and the men have a problem of credibility with the women, and he tries to repair it:

> Our love being yours, the error that love makes
> Is likewise yours. We to ourselves prove false
> By being once false, for ever to be true
> To those that make us both—fair ladies, you.
>
> (5.2.765–768)

But the time for such rationalization—holding the women responsible for the men's double-dealing because the men cannot resist them—has passed.

In addition, the men's protestations fail to convince because their affection for the women is repeatedly shown to be based on superficialities, especially looks and particularly "women's eyes" (4.3.324). Ironically, in a play replete with references to "light," the men's judgment proves dim, based as it is on outward signs, like the brooch and the glove that confuse them when the ladies switch their love tokens (5.2.134–309). The men, whose hackneyed love poems in 4.3 reveal that they are more in love with love than with individual women, cannot love the women because they do not know them. When the women approach the men to this effect in 5.2, prodding them to understand the trick of the switched tokens, only Berowne figures out, though none too quickly, that they have been duped (435–460). Instead of owning up to their combined silliness, however, Berowne berates Boyet for leaking the

Muscovite plot in advance to the women (460–481). From this point on, the lords' behavior tumbles downhill.

I would argue that, until the performance of the Nine Worthies, the men's good repute would, with some apology and honest effort to set things right, be salvageable and the play's conventional comic outcome, still possible. Rather than address their shortcomings, however, the men proceed on the course that Berowne has established already as a means of displacing his and his friends' embarrassment—attacking Boyet before the performance is underway. Although the King at first worries that the performance will "shame" them further, Berowne assures him that they are "shame proof" and can only rise in the women's esteem in contrast to the pitiful players (5.2.509–511). But Berowne and his companions are not content to let the Nine Worthies, admittedly one of the funniest bits in any Shakespeare play, embarrass themselves. Their browbeating of Nathaniel-Alexander, Holofernes-Judas Maccabeus, and Don Armado-Hector is a mean-spirited way to salve their humiliation, more pitiful than the poorest of the Worthies' bad acting (590–624 and 627–665). It is about proving themselves, feathering their pride, and refusing to make amends with the women that they protest they want to marry; it is not about the players' feelings. The King's men resemble others from Shakespeare's comedies who appear to cope with embarrassment by belittling different social groups—for example, when Lysander and Demetrius scoff at the mechanicals' play after losing face in the woods (*A Midsummer Night's Dream*, 3.2 and 5.1) and when Claudio and Don Pedro rudely taunt Leonato and Antonio in *Much Ado about Nothing* (5.1). As Louis A. Montrose writes of *Love's Labor's*: "The fear of being shamed . . . impels the lords to devise strategies for saving face," and "within the society of Navarre, the noblemen abuse hierarchy by exploiting the commons in order to obfuscate their own shortcomings."[8]

One by one, the wounded entertainers are dismissed by the lords to their "shame." Costard advises Nathaniel to "Run away for shame" for having "overthrown Alisander the conqueror" (5.2.574 and 569–570); Dumaine rubs in Judas's "shame" (596); Armado risks his "reputation" for shrinking from fighting in his shirt (696–706). In a last-ditch effort to escape their own humiliation by projecting it onto vulnerable surrogates, the lords shift in whatever direction necessary. Berowne's sudden embrace of Boyet—"Well said, old mocker. I must needs be friends with thee" (5.2.544–545)—would seem an incomprehensible turnabout on the order of other extreme shifts in the play were the reason for it not so painfully obvious: the unfair competition among the men has shifted from ganging up on Boyet for his effeminacy to ganging up on the players for their theatrical inadequacies.[9] Berowne now decides Boyet can be one of the gang for having just insulted Costard (5.2.544).

The lords, however, fail to recognize their own bloated sense of self-worth until the women confront them with it. And it is precisely Berowne's indiscriminate use of wit to hurt someone else for his own purposes that Rosaline isolates in her rejection of his marriage proposal:

> the world's large tongue
> Proclaims you for a man replete with mocks,
> Full of comparisons and wounding flouts,
> Which you on all estates will execute
> That lie within the mercy of your wit.
>
> (5.2.830–834)

By now, she has seen the truth of this proclamation and seizes the opportunity to avoid a hasty marriage that she may later regret.

*Love's Labor's* thus traces the learning curve that is courtship. As historians such as David Cressy, Laura Gowing, and Martin Ingram have recently demonstrated, many an actual English Renaissance attempt at wooing stopped short of wiving, often because women either deflected the potentially serious intent of love tokens, like those in the play, in order to avoid commitment or understood such tokens as mere flirtation, not symbols of desired matrimony.[10] Cressy writes, "Courtship gifts . . . are frequently mentioned in the course of disputes over frustrated, questionable, or clandestine marriages. They were taken to demonstrate the progress of courtship and to corroborate other evidence of matrimonial intent. . . . But it was no easy matter to determine whether the proffering and acceptance of a gift was in jest or in earnest, whether it should be understood as a token of goodwill or as a sign of matrimonial consent."[11] The perplexity that Cressy describes is mirrored in the ladies' assertions that, all along, they have been taking the lords' gifts and letters as mere play:

PRINCESS: We have received your letters full of love,
Your favours, the ambassadors of love,
And in our maiden counsel rated them
At courtship, pleasant jest and courtesy,
As bombast and as lining to the time.
But more devout than this in our respects
Have we not been; and therefore met your loves
In their own fashion, like a merriment.
DUMAINE: Our letters, madam, showed much more than jest.
LONGAVILLE: So did our looks.
ROSALINE: We did not quote them so.

(5.2.771–780)

That the women do not take the men's protestations seriously owes not only to their nearly comical extravagance (5.2.1–9 and 34–40), but also to the disjuncture between the men's trivial method of wooing and the high stakes of a courtly marriage, especially a royal marriage. In specific regard to *Love's Labor's*, Ann Jennalie Cook explains, "In these sophisticated circles an interlude of play—compliments, love poetry, hunting, masking, dancing, pageantry—offers acceptable diversion. But it would be unthinkable for casual amusement to substitute for the serious negotiations of a royal or noble marriage, especially with men who so lightly regard their oaths of commitment."[12] Under any circumstances, though, whether courtly or otherwise, Elizabethan women—even women under pressure to accept binding vows and gifts of betrothal—could decline a marriage proposal, as Gowing asserts, "When men made all the arrangements, settling their 'claims' to women, women still exercised the power of evasion and refusal."[13]

The Princess and her women, in other words, have ample grounds for rejecting the men's proposal. With clear cause to read the lords' amorous gestures as casual pastime, these ladies are justified in large part for handling that courtship as a mere game. But clear cause does not necessarily apologize for the elements in their responses to the lords that border on cruelty. When, for example, the Princess proposes that the women turn their backs on their suitors who are about to enter disguised as Muscovites, Boyet, who himself spares small derision in other situations, asks her if her proposed act will not make the men forget their love speeches (5.2.146–150). "Therefore I do it," retorts the Princess (151). Her intent, she reveals, is to foil the wooers' plans, which she takes to be "sport," and to humiliate them in the process: "So shall we stay, mocking intended game, / And they, well mocked, depart away with shame" (153 and 155–156). The Princess almost seems resentful that the men have not ascertained better how to woo in earnest. Her word *shame,* so prominent in the lords' mistreatment of the Nine Worthies, invites comparison between the two instances of embarrassment—the lords' of the Worthies and the ladies' of the lords. Although the lords may be thought to deserve the ladies' scorn for approaching the women disguised as Muscovites, rather than admitting their broken oaths, the women's judgment and behavior—the reckoning they visit upon the men—may nonetheless seem harsh.

Indeed, although the men prove shallow and unprepared for matrimony by the play's conclusion, the portrayal of how the sexes relate to one another and among themselves in *Love's Labor's* does not unequivocally champion the women but is instead nuanced, balanced, and fair. I do not see the "gap between men and women" that Peter B. Erickson describes in his provocative essay as both wide and incapable of being "bridged."[14]

Rather, the women and the men are not so far apart, even in their flaws: the women reveal many of the same distasteful tendencies that they eventually rebuke in the men. Nor do the men invariably escape the audience's sympathy.

The women's behavior toward the men, in fact, has sometimes been viewed as nastier than the men's behavior.[15] The Princess seems to feel entitled to pay back the lords' wooing as Muscovites with trickery, "mock for mock" (5.2.140). For the Princess's assurance that "We are wise girls to mock our lovers so," Rosaline offers the justification that the men have earned their ridicule: "They are worse fools to purchase mocking so" (5.2.58–59). Rosaline first plans to "torture" Berowne for his "jests" in wooing (5.2.59–66), then urges the Princess, who wonders what to do when the lords return without their Muscovite disguises, to "mock them still" (298–301). Boyet affirms that the ladies have skewered the lords with their words: "The tongues of mocking wenches are as keen / As is the razor's edge invisible" (256–257). In this context, Berowne's charge that Rosaline's "wits makes wise things foolish" has a ring of truth, his own gift for verbal maneuvering notwithstanding (5.2.374).

Whether the women should feel entitled to provide such shrewd comeuppance for the men is one question. Whether they have any justification at all for their infighting is another. Their keen insults to one another—most of them issuing from Rosaline—parallel the men's competitiveness. Both the men and the women show the capacity for working together, as when all the men masquerade as Muscovites or the women cooperate by switching their love tokens, but both groups, at their least attractive, can also turn against themselves. That Rosaline's promise to "torture" Berowne occurs just moments after she has insulted Katherine for her pockmarked and ruddy complexion is suggestive: the conflicts among women and those among men may sublimate to form conflicts between women and men (5.2.43–45 and 60). Indeed, the Princess tends to avert cattiness among the women by diverting their attention to men: "I beshrew all shrews. / But, Katherine, what was sent to you from fair Dumaine?" (5.2.46–47).

Whatever the origins of their tensions, both the men and the women would seem to have some maturation ahead of them before they are ready to be married. Richard Corum's view that the lords go out of their way to fail at courtship, lest it lead to a marriage that they in fact do not desire, mistakes, in my view, the characters' viewpoint for the playwright's.[16] That is, the characters seem drawn to the prospect of marriage that the play implies is a reach currently beyond their grasp. For all of the teasing, lampooning, and criticism that Berowne endures, he may finally reveal more maturity than the rest. His apology and promise to convert, for love's sake, from "spruce affectation" to "honest kersey noes" are, granted, only words and words to which affectation, ironically, still clings (5.2.394–415), as Rosaline's famous retort to Berowne's line incisively shows:

*BEROWNE:* My love to thee is sound, sans crack or flaw.
*ROSALINE: Sans sans,* I pray you.

                                                                    (415–416)

But, while critics have unanimously sided with Rosaline in this instance, noting her more mature judgment and even superior wit, her line is intolerant, even if comically delivered, and perhaps less appealing than Berowne's willingness to throw over his verbal pretension: "Bear with me, I am sick; / I'll leave it by degrees" (417–418). Significantly, Berowne later calls for "Honest plain words" when the Princess is dealing with "grief" at the news of her father and the King of Navarre cannot make sense of his feelings in language (5.2.734–747). Rosaline's final ultimatum to Berowne, to "Visit the speechless sick" and "To enforce the pained impotent to smile," does not seem to credit his progress toward speaking truthfully, but, rather, appears a stringent and even haughty imposition (5.2.838–842).

Much as the genders fare equally (and falter often) in their efforts at reckoning, so do the unlearned match the educated characters in their ability, or, rather, inability, to so much as count on one hand. References to and examples of threes spill over the edges of a play in which a braggart cannot count to three nor even a king to five (1.2.39–54 and 5.2.536–541).[17] Several references in the play to the practice of accurate counting consign it to the lower classes, as reflected in the absence of numerical accounting from the upper-class curriculum of grammar schools in Shakespeare's London.[18] Don Armado scorns such "reckoning" because "It fitteth the spirit of a tapster," and Costard tells Berowne, "it were pity you should get your living by reckoning, sir," as if multiplying three times three were beneath his social standing (1.2.40–41 and 5.2.495–496). Yet in truth, Costard is, for now, equally unable to tell the sum of three squared, deflecting the simple mathematical problem: "I can assure you, sir; we know what we know" (5.2.490). That all of the characters in *Love's Labor's* will in time become subject to account-keeping is signaled by Don Armado's accepting responsibility for Jacquenetta's pregnancy as surely as it is by the ladies' refusing of the lords. If the characters are not already being held accountable by the play's end, they will become accountable perforce. In time, they will know precisely what they know. To this eventuality, class is irrelevant.

Indeed, status has no special purchase in acquiring another means of knowledge requisite to judging wisely—knowledge gained through the senses. The play abounds in references to the senses, especially smell, and, as critics have noted, pits emotion, the knowledge of the heart, against intellect, the knowledge of the head.[19] Still, the limits of reason aside, the play insists repeatedly on the claims of absolute truth, ultimately governed by and mirrored in the fact of mortality.[20] Significantly, moreover, the sense of smell, by which characters figuratively discern such fakery as "false Latin" and such "odiferous flowers of fancy" as Ovid's, was, according to Danielle Nagler, associated in the Renaissance with mortality and thus with "truth."[21] Writes Nagler, referring to the Fool's line in *King Lear:* "While [the] stench of decaying fortunes leads gravewards, it smacks of integrity and permits accurate perception since 'there's not a nose among twenty but can smell him that's stinking.'"[22]

Another recurring sign of factual validity in *Love's Labor's* is the written word, sure testimony to Don Armado's ornamental prose (1.1.226–264 and 4.1.61–92), to the two kings' contract and subsequent monetary exchange (2.1.109–167), and to Berowne's confederacy in breaking the King's oath by writing a letter to Rosaline that, even torn to shreds, bears irrefutable witness to his perfidy (4.3.199). Written documents are subject to miscarrying, as Berowne's and Don Armado's letters are, and they can be read aloud by impersonators, playfully usurping authorship and substituting themselves for others' selves. Some of those substitutions, moreover, create suggestive parallels between characters; for example, the King's mockery of Armado's letter in 1.1 ironically foreshadows the failure of his own words in 5.2, and Boyet's performance of Armado's letter to Jacquenetta in 4.1 underscores the role of each as entertainer, Boyet to the ladies and Armado to the men. But authorship, authority, and authenticity are displaced, despite such confusion of identity, only temporarily. Likewise, for a time, numbers can be fudged and, as Feste says in *Twelfth Night,* "a sentence . . . [turned to] a chev'ril glove" (3.1.11–12), the meaning disassociated from the word or the word stretched beyond recognition by such acute wits as Costard, Moth, and even Dull.[23] In the end, however, words, like Marcadé's pronouncement of the French king's death, come to convey specific, clear, straightforward meaning.

As in the case of both the lords and the ladies, how a character reacts to and behaves under the duress of reckoning or being called to reckoning reveals much. That only Don Armado emerges unequivocally to meet the consequences of his actions with Jacquenetta is rich in implication. Costard interrupts Armado's grand fantasy of embodying Hector, a warrior he will never resemble, with the disillusioning news of Jacquenetta's condition and Armado's alleged paternity (5.2.666–669). Rather than retreat, rationalize, or reroute attention from what threatens him, as Costard has just done, Armado rises to the occasion, his words flavored with the urgency of paying a debt: "For mine own part, I breathe free breath. I have seen the day of wrong through the little hole of discretion and I will right myself like a soldier"

(5.2.717–719). Although some readers (including the editor of the Arden edition) understand Armado to be referring to righting himself in regard to taking revenge on Costard, I disagree.[24] He breathes free breath because he has awakened to reality and, instead of using his sword on Costard, means to put it down and own up to his duty to Jacquenetta. That, of course, is exactly what he proceeds to do.

Armado is, without doubt, a buffoon. All the more remarkable and telling, though, that a character who is humiliated at every turn by his betters (the King in 1.1), his inferiors (Moth), and those in between (Boyet) should willingly humble himself so dramatically. This turn of events is predicted long before, by his falling for a "base wench" to begin with, but also in 5.2, when he is forced to admit to the "naked truth" that he wears "no shirt" (1.2.57–58 and 5.2.705). Although Armado apparently misrepresents his motive for going shirtless as "penance," Moth divulges the real reason—Armado's poverty (707–708). The braggart is exposed, shown fully for who he is (and is not) and at risk of losing his "reputation," such as it is (5.2.698). Once called to reckoning, however, Armado answers with what is for him notable integrity: although his speech is still disconcertingly ornate, his choices peel away pretensions to courtliness and address crucial matters of domesticity. The bawdy overtones of his pledge to "hold the plough" for Jacquenetta point to the true meaning of *vulgar* (universal) in that they lower him to the level of humanity *(mortality)*, as do the sexual urges they represent (5.2.871). They join other racy, scatological, and base references that, Patricia Parker has shown, saturate the play, suggesting that distinctions like class and gender mask the common anatomical features, cravings, failings, and frailties of all human beings.[25]

Whether the fleeting mention of Katherine's unnamed sister's death by love or the far less threatening instances of keeping count, reminders abound in *Love's Labor's* that a mortal's days are numbered (5.2.13–15). But all such references target the same point: the ending, whether of a life, a courtship, or a play, gives meaning to the rest, stripping away the inessential and sorting out what matters and why. Learning to keep accounts and becoming accountable is the challenge posed at the end of a play that might be thought of as a comedy in process—on its way, but not quite there.[26] The full story, "too long for a play," has been launched. Don Armado has perhaps taken the first of many steps ahead by laying down his sword (and his pen), taking up the plough, and finally understanding the concept of three years (5.2.871–872).

## NOTES

1. William Shakespeare, *Love's Labour's Lost,* ed. H. R. Woudhuysen (Walton-on-Thames, Surrey: Thomas Nelson and Sons, 1998), 2.1.66–76. All

subsequent quotations from *Love's Labor's Lost* are taken from this edition and will be cited parenthetically within the text.

2. Smidt, "Shakespeare in Two Minds: Unconformities in *Love's Labour's Lost*," *English Studies* 65 (1984): 219.

3. Linda Woodbridge, *Money and the Age of Shakespeare: Essays in the New Economic Criticism* (New York: Palgrave, 2003), 1.

4. Woudhuysen, in the introduction to *Love's Labour's Lost,* comments on the prevalence of "telling" in the play, "as in telling a story or a lie and as in counting" (30).

5. Shakespeare, *Much Ado about Nothing,* in *The Riverside Shakespeare,* ed. G. Blakemore Evans, 2nd ed. (Boston: Houghton Mifflin, 1997), 5.4.52. All quotations from *Much Ado about Nothing, Antony and Cleopatra,* the *Henriad, A Midsummer Night's Dream,* and *Twelfth Night* are from this edition and will be cited parenthetically in the text.

6. Another possibly significant difference between the two speeches is that one is spoken out of Berowne's hearing and the other is directed to him.

7. Many critics have remarked on the similarities between Shakespeare's fictional Princess and his real queen. See, for example, Mark Thornton Burnett, "Giving and Receiving: *Love's Labour's Lost* and the Politics of Exchange," *English Literary Renaissance* 23 (1993): 310; Richard Corum, "'The Catastrophe is a Nuptial': *Love's Labor's Lost,* Tactics, Everyday Life," in *Renaissance Culture and the Everyday,* ed. Patricia Fumerton and Simon Hunt (Philadelphia: University of Pennsylvania Press, 1999), 283; and Suzanne Gossett, "'I'll Look to Like': Arranged Marriages in Shakespeare's Plays," in *Sexuality and Politics in Renaissance Drama,* ed. Carole Levin and Karen Robertson (Lewiston, NY: Edward Mellen, 1991), 62–63.

8. Monstrose, "'Sport by sport o'erthrown': *Love's Labour's Lost* and the Politics of Play," *Texas Studies in Literature and Language* 18 (1977): 535 and 541.

9. Many commentators see Boyet as objectively effeminate, but, though he may be supercilious and courtly, he is also an obvious ladies' man. He speaks salaciously to the women on several occasions (e.g., 4.1.126–138). Berowne describes him twice as effeminate, but in both instances, it is because he is so eager to please the Princess; abusing his manliness, then, may be an unfair way to insult him (5.2.315–334, 460–481).

10. Cressy, *Birth, Marriage, and Death: Ritual, Religion, and the Life-Cycle in Tudor and Stuart England* (Oxford: Oxford University Press, 1997); Gowing, *Domestic Dangers: Women, Words, and Sex in Early Modern London* (Oxford: Clarendon Press, 1996); Ingram, "The Reform of Popular Culture?: Sex and Marriage in Early Modern England," in *Popular Culture in Seventeenth-Century England,* ed. Barry Reay (New York: St. Martin's Press, 1997).

11. Cressy, *Birth, Marriage, and Death,* 263–264.

12. Cook, *Making a Match: Courtship in Shakespeare and His Society* (Princeton, NJ: Princeton University Press, 1991), 257. That the relationship between Shakespeare's King and Princess parallels the historical courtship of Marguerite de Valois by Henri of Navarre, who were married in 1572, is widely observed. See, for example, Corum, "'The Catastrophe is a Nuptial,'" 283–284.

13. Gowing, *Domestic Dangers,* 148. For additional information on women's agency in practical Elizabethan courtship, see Eric Carlson, "Courtship in Tudor England," *History Today* 43 (1993): 23–29; Cressy, *Birth, Marriage, and Death;* and Ingram, "The Reform of Popular Culture."

14. Erickson, "The Failure of Relationship between Men and Women in *Love's Labor's Lost*," in *"Love's Labour's Lost": Critical Essays*, ed. Felicia Hardison Londré (New York: Garland, 1997). Erickson understands the power differential between men and women to be fixed and incapable of being changed: "For all its comic charm, *Love's Labor's Lost* presents an extraordinary exhibition of masculine insecurity and helplessness . . . female power is virtually absolute" (243). As I shall continue to explain, I see these boundaries as more fluid.

15. See, for example, Smidt, who explains, "The women are far unkinder than the men, and their cruelty is not just that of the conventional coy mistress of the Petrarchan tradition. There is too much malice in some of their speeches" ("Shakespeare in Two Minds," 212). Compare her comments with those of Montrose, who writes that although the lords "are trapped in a position of consistently inferior awareness relative to the ladies," "the Princess and her ladies . . . are engaged in a winning game of glittering but nonetheless quite ruthless one-upmanship. . . . There has been a consistent [critical] attempt to endow the Princess with a normative function in the world of the play or to associate her with some ideal that is presumed to be Shakespeare's. The roles that the Princess does enact in the play are both more complex and more ambivalent than the play's critics usually perceive" (537, 539, and 543).

16. Corum, "'The Catastrophe is a Nuptial,'" 276 et passim. Corum develops his argument to suggest that the action of *Love's Labor's* parallels the every day lives of Elizabethans who sought to thwart unwanted marriage (271–282). At the same time, Corum asserts, the failed courtship in the play applauds the capacity of Queen Elizabeth I to dodge political marriage altogether and alludes to what ought to have occurred between Marguerite de Valois and Henri of Navarre, whose ill-advised union, he observes, led to the St. Bartholomew's Day Massacre (283–285).

17. See Jörg Hasler on recurring references to and instances of three in the play, many of which are rhetorical, in "Enumeration in *Love's Labour's Lost*," *English Studies* 50 (1969): 176–185. Examples of nouns, adjectives, and verbs that come in three's appear on nearly every page of the script. Dorothea Kehler intriguingly links such numerical reckoning with determining that Costard, not Don Armado, is the father of Jaquenetta's baby, in "Jacquenetta's Baby's Father: Recovering Paternity in *Love's Labour's Lost*," in *"Love's Labour's Lost*," ed. Londré, 306–307.

18. Quoting historian Foster Watson, Woodbridge notes that "[a]nother curricular stream was created to teach poor students 'to write, read, and cast accompts, and so to put them forth to prentice.' This was a common class distinction—Latin and Greek and university for young gents, bookkeeping and apprenticeship for common folk" (*Money and the Age of Shakespeare*, 3).

19. See, for example, Ronald Berman, "Shakespearean Comedy and the Uses of Reason," *The South Atlantic Quarterly* 63 (1964): 1–9. Judith Dundas writes about the unreliability of the senses, particularly in *King Lear*, drawing the more general conclusion that, in Shakespeare, the "senses . . . prove inadequate either to comprehend or express the heart" ("'To See Feelingly': The Language of the Senses and the Language of the Heart," *Comparative Drama* 19 [1985]: 56).

20. A comment by Montrose is relevant here: "The world of history, conflict, obligation, anxiety, and suffering that the characters' playworld is designed to evade is precisely the context in which Shakespeare's play becomes meaningful for his audience, who are themselves Time's subjects" ("'Sport by sport o'erthrown,'" 546).

That the most reliable way of obtaining knowledge is obscure in this play reflects the historical reality that thinking about epistemology was in transition at the turn of the century. At this time, just before the scientific revolution, the scholastics were universally seen as antiquated. But who would replace them? The question had not been decided. Shakespeare's appreciation of this transition comes up repeatedly in his plays, perhaps nowhere more poignantly than in *Othello*, where so-called "ocular proof," in the form of the handkerchief, turns out to be anything but "proof." On the relationship in Shakespeare's time between physical object and knowledge, see especially Ellen Spolsky, *Satisfying Skepticism: Embodied Knowledge in the Early Modern World* (Aldershot, England: Ashgate, 2003), which includes a chapter on *Coriolanus* and another on *Othello*.

Other recent studies have explored both early modern faith in reason and anxiety toward its limits in Shakespeare's plays. A few that may be relevant here include Eric Brown, "Shakespeare's Anxious Epistemology: *Love's Labor's Lost* and Marlowe's *Doctor Faustus*," *Texas Studies in Literature and Language* 45 (2003): 20–41; and B. J. Sokol, *A Brave New World of Knowledge: Shakespeare's "The Tempest" and Early Modern Epistemology* (Madison, NJ: Fairleigh Dickinson University Press, 2003), the former because it addresses epistemology specifically in *Love's Labor's Lost* and the latter because, although it deals centrally with *The Tempest*, it delves into late sixteenth- and early seventeenth-century views of reason and science.

21. Nagler, "Towards the Smell of Mortality: Shakespeare and Ideas of Smell, 1558–1625," *The Cambridge Quarterly* 54 (1993): 455.

22. (*King Lear*, 2.4.70–71), qtd. in ibid., 56. Patricia Parker associates the prevalent references to smelling with a "whole series of scatological double entendres" ("Preposterous Reversals: *Love's Labor's Lost*," *Modern Language Quarterly* 54 [1993]: 465).

23. Repeated references in the play to words as food suggest their malleability and the ephemerality of their meaning (e.g., 4.1.56–57, 4.2.24–26, and 5.1.35–41). Although Costard and, more often, Dull in *Love's Labor's Lost* both seem less verbally adept than the lords and ladies, each has his moments of verbal triumph, as when Dull plays with the words *collusion* and *pollution* more astutely and purposefully than Holofernes and Nathaniel can appreciate (4.2.43–47) and when Costard ridicules Don Armado's verbal pretentiousness as Costard enters in 3.1.66–71. Aware of Costard's craftiness, Berowne refers to him at one point as "pure wit" (5.2.484). Costard's bombastic put-down of Boyet, Armado, and even Moth parodies each character's infatuation with his own verbal facility and implicates Costard as well (4.1.139–147).

24. Woudhuysen paraphrases the speech thus in his edition of the play: "I've had a narrow escape. I've been given just enough prudence or circumspection to know what it is to be utterly humiliated." "Right" is glossed as "revenge" (*Love's Labor's Lost*, 5.2.717–719n).

25. Parker, "Preposterous Reversals," especially 441, 455, and 475. Some critics view Don Armado's pledge to Jacquenetta as an ill-advised rush into matrimony befitting a fool. Cook, for example, writes, "Don Armado concludes his hapless pursuit of Jaquenetta . . . by declaring 'The catastrophe is a nuptial'" (*Making a Match,* 167). Cook's statement, however, is inaccurate in two ways. First, the line she cites is from 4.1 and does not conclude the pursuit; nor does it pertain directly to Armado and Jaquenetta, but to King Cophetua and the beggar Zenelophon (75–76), to whom Armado's letter compares himself and his love. Second, to read

the word *catastrophe* as implying disaster is anachronistic. In Shakespeare's time, as the *Oxford English Dictionary* reveals, it meant "dénouement" (from Spenser in 1579) or "final event, conclusion" (from *All's Well That Ends Well*, 1601); not until the mid-eighteenth century did it come to mean "sudden disaster" (*Oxford English Dictionary*, 2nd ed., s.v. "catastrophe"). Thus the title of Corum's article, which is meant to suggest the painful mistake of marrying too soon, without maturity, is not reflected as such in Armado's line. My ultimate point is that dismissing Don Armado's union as a joke is simplistic.

26. In a discussion from June 2004, one of my students, Kathryn Wyle, noted a repeated narrative pattern in *Love's Labor's:* a beginning and a conclusion are collapsed without a middle to connect them. The negotiation between the kings is one salient example, as is the production of the Nine Worthies, which, while not performed in its entirety, is begun and then, at the last, finished with the song of Ver and Hiems. The larger play, in a sense, mimics this pattern: the conclusion a year hence is posited, but the process is invisible and only implied.

AARON KITCH

# Shylock's Sacred Nation

Thomas Middleton's *Triumphs of Honour and Industry* (1617) features a "Pageant of Several nations" celebrating George Bowles's election as Lord Mayor of London. The printed quarto includes the following list of "nations" who show Bowles "a kind of affectionate joy . . . which by the virtue of Traffic, is likely ever to continue" on his inaugural procession to and from Whitehall:

An Englishman.
A Frenchman.
An Irishman.
A Spaniard.
A Turk.
A Jew.
A Dane.
A Polander.
A Barbarian.
A Russian or Moscovian.[1]

Like other Jacobean civic pageants, *The Triumphs of Honour and Industry* defends the civilizing power of commerce. A key function of the civic

*Shakespeare Quarterly,* Volume 59, Number 2 (Summer 2008): pp. 131–155. Copyright © 2008 The Johns Hopkins University Press.

pageant was to prepare Bowles for his official duty as overseer of a commerce that was increasingly dependent on foreign trade. The Irish were active importers of Flemish spices, silks, and groceries in the sixteenth century, and they expanded their export of hides, yarn, skin, and cloth to England and the Continent in the seventeenth century.[2] The "Barbarian" was probably a Native American or tribal African with whom English merchants and explorers might trade. Both would have been categorized by English viewers as infidels who, like the Jews, were potential candidates for religious conversion. Unlike the other nations of Middleton's pageant, however, the Jews had no homeland to call their own. Why, then, is a Jewish "nation" on this list?

Middleton's pageant registers a new meaning of such a nation as defined by trade. Following the Jews' expulsion from the Iberian peninsula in the late fifteenth century, European trading capitals such as Rome, Venice, Prague, and Amsterdam extended denizenship rights of limited residency and restricted trade privileges to Jews in exchange for their mercantile services. These cities hoped that Jewish trading connections would boost import and export duties and help maintain peace between nations. Such Jewish trading "nations" were modeled on Christian European mercantile "nations" of merchants from cities like Genoa and Venice, and they sparked intellectual debate among Christians who were in the process of redefining their own political and economic identities. Christian scholars such as Carlo Sigonio in Bologna and Bonaventure Corneille Bertram in Geneva took new interest in Jewish religious and intellectual traditions.[3] In England, theologian Richard Hooker and legal scholar John Selden could both write of the Jewish nation in their exploration of such diverse topics as divorce, observation of the Sabbath, and the authority of the church.[4] These and other authors approached the topic of Jewish identity primarily from an international perspective, since there were so few Jews living openly in England. This fact may also help to explain why only one of the dozen or so extant plays with major Jewish characters is set in England.[5] This essay traces the influence of new Jewish trading nations on two of the most prominent representations of Jews in sixteenth-century England: Marlowe's *Jew of Malta* and Shakespeare's *Merchant of Venice*. Our historical understanding of Jews in this period tends to focus on negative stereotypes, but there are other, more positive accounts of Jewish integration that have been overlooked. Where some new historicist and postcolonial accounts of these plays read the early modern Jew as a universal "other," I show how both plays situate Jews within discourses and practices of early modern political economy.[6]

Between 1492, when Spain began to exile Jews who refused to convert to Christianity, and the late seventeenth century, when Jews achieved new prominence in trade and as members of European courts, displaced Jews gained residency under temporary contracts that granted shelter from religious persecution in exchange for their contribution to what in 1598 Daniel Rodriga referred to as the "public good" of well-ordered commerce.[7] From Italy to Poland to the Low Countries, Jews negotiated these rights in numerous commonwealths and under diverse political conditions.[8] By the seventeenth century, Jewish lawyer Martin Gonzales de Celorico defended the *Gente de la Nacion Hebrea* (1619) in explicitly mercantilist terms, and Duarte Gomes Solis argued in his *Discorso sobre los Commercios de las Indias* (1621) that Jews sustained the "'life blood'" of the Portuguese empire, which he defined as "'commerce.'"[9] As the *Oxford English Dictionary* suggests, the emergence of a Jewish "nation" based on trade in sixteenth-century Europe did not supplant earlier definitions of the "nation" as a biblically ordained category of ethnic identity, but rather drew on older models of the biblical nation even as it designated new mercantile structures of early modern Europe.[10]

A Jewish nation based on trade challenged foundational beliefs of some Christians about Jewish identity. Gentiles defined themselves as a nation distinguished specifically from that of the Jews.[11] Authors from Martin Luther to Samuel Purchas associated Jews with homelessness and failed assimilation. Henry Blount, for example, regarded the Jews he encountered during his travels to the Levant as "a race from all others so averse both in nature and institution."[12] Andrew Willet likewise determined that Jews were unique in their tendency to remain aliens in Christian nations where they lived: "a Jew ... whether he journeys into Spain, or France, or into whatever other place he goes to, declares himself to be not a Spaniard or a Frenchman, but a Jew."[13] Several sixteenth-century Jewish merchants challenged such stereotypes in their petitions for civic charters, which highlighted the potential of Jews to enhance trade as an engine of political power. These claims offer one type of evidence for the strengthening of links between trade and political hegemony in Europe during the sixteenth and seventeenth centuries.

Although they petitioned many European capitals for denizenship rights and trading privileges between 1490 and 1570, Jews found little sanctuary anywhere in Europe, with the minor exception of Charles V's toleration of those Jews who participated in his anti-Protestant campaigns during the 1540s. Rome also offered a temporary safe haven for exiled Jews before Pope Paul IV adopted strict Counter-Reformation policies in the 1550s and 1560s.[14] Largely rejected by Christian Europe, many exiled Jews emigrated to the Ottoman Empire, where they became actively involved in trading networks with both the East and West. Several Italian cities, including Florence, Savoy, and Ancona, admitted Jewish "nations" in the sixteenth century.[15] The commercial empire of Venice was home to at least five legally designated alien communities: German merchants, many from Nuremberg, Ratisbon (Regensburg), or Augsberg; Greek Orthodox immigrants from eastern colonies

of the Venetian empire; and three separate populations of Jews—Tedeschi,
Sephardic, and Levantine.[16] Venice was also celebrated for its population of
aliens: French envoy Philippe de Commynes noted that "most of their people
are foreignners."[17] Tedeschi Jews of Germanic origin who acted primarily as
moneylenders lived in Venice as early as the fourteenth century, but following
the 1502 discovery by Portuguese merchants of a new trade route to the East
around the Cape of Good Hope, Venice increased its Jewish population in
defense of its established trading monopoly.[18] Levantine Jews came from the
East (their name is derived from the Latin verb *levare*, referring to the rising
sun), while Ponentine Jews came from the West (their name comes from the
verb *ponere*, alluding to the setting sun). In the sixteenth century, both sects
were largely composed of New Christians who were allowed to engage in
trade with the East or West and were given restricted citizenship rights. Both
groups of Jews were originally permitted to reside in Venice for only fifteen
days a year, but in 1516 the Great Council established the first European
"ghetto" for permanent residence by all Sephardic Jews who fled persecution
in Spain and Portugal.[19] Venice gave sanctuary to Jewish moneylenders of the
Venetian mainland who fled the armies of the League of Cambrai in 1509.
Levantine Jews earned admittance to the city after they had adopted Ottoman citizenship and then migrated to Venice, where they were given official
status as Ottoman merchants.[20]

Celebrated for its justice, equality, and independence from centralized
monarchies like the Hapsburgs, the Venetian Senate nevertheless struggled
to accommodate its diverse populations.[21] The Senate officially recognized
Levantine Jews in 1541 and suggested that Jews with trading and citizenship rights would have "better reason to bring their merchandise here, to
Venice's advantage."[22] Thereafter, Venice allowed Jewish merchants to live in
the city for up to two years, although some in the Senate periodically tried
to exile Jewish *Marranos*.[23] Occasional persecution and heavy taxes led Jews
to demand official charters, or *condotte*, that would codify their rights. Venetian authors in the first half of the sixteenth century defined trade as what
Manfredo Tafuri called a "foundation of internal harmony" that could restore
peace to the Venetian empire.[24] Later, the Jewish merchant Daniel Rodriga
petitioned the Venetian senate directly for extended privileges for Jewish
merchants, including the right for immediate family members to join their
merchant spouses and fathers. Rodriga's 1589 charter proposed that Jews be
given rights equivalent to those of Venetian citizens in order to trade with
the Levant.[25] Rejected a number of times, a modified bill was approved by
the College of the Senate in 1589 that guaranteed safe conduct to all "Levantine or Ponentine Jewish merchants," along with their families, and offered
them freedom from molestation so long as they remained in the increasingly

crowded ghetto.[26] All Jews were required to pay a hundred ducats to the state in exchange for this privilege.

Over the course of the sixteenth century, Jews were forced by law and circumstances to renew their charters of denizenship approximately once a decade, sometimes in the face of vocal objections from Venetian citizens and rival merchants. Efforts by Venetian Christians to expel Jews climaxed in 1638, following a number of robberies falsely attributed to Jewish denizens. One of the most important defenses of the Jewish nation in Europe emerged from this conflict—Rabbi Simone Luzzatto's *Discourse on the State of the Jews, Particularly Those Dwelling in the Illustrious City of Venice.* The treatise argues explicitly that the "particular devotion" of Jews "to the mercantile profession" increases import and export duties to Venice, since Jews 1) pay over 70,000 ducats to the state annually, 2) bring goods from remote places to "serve men's needs as well as to ornament civil life," 3) supply "the workers and artisans with" the "wool, silk, cotton," and other goods that they need, 4) export Venetian goods, and 5) promote "commerce and mutual negotiation between neighboring peoples" to counter the natural human inclination for warfare.[27] Echoing previous charters that define the Jews as a trading nation, Luzzatto identifies placelessness as an essential component of Jewish mercantilism:

> It seems that having the trade handled by the Jews is a perfect help . . . since they do not have their own homeland to which they aspire to transport the possessions they amassed in the City, nor in any place do they have permission and right to acquire real estate; nor, if they had it, would it be in their interest to do so and tie up and commit their possessions while their persons are subject to many changes, since they abide in every place with safe-conducts and permissions of the rulers.[28]

Scattered throughout the world, Jews, according to Luzzatto, were naturally suited to assist in the global circulation of goods and money. Deprived of land, vessels, and schools, Jews had to seek permission from Christian rulers to engage in commerce. Luzzatto defends Jews' continuing presence in Venice on mercantilist principles, emphasizing both a balance of trade and the enhancement of customs revenues through trade.[29] He suggests that a state based on commerce offers greater stability than one based on war and notes that the "greatest attractor of business is freedom to live and security in one's possessions, which is what Venice exactly and punctually provides for its inhabitants and its merchants." These economic privileges provide a "real stimulus to the Jewish nation, naturally diffident due to its weakness."[30] Luzzatto measures peace not just as an absence of warfare, but also in terms of the vitality of civic trade. The *Discorso* emphasizes that Jewish merchants pay duties on exports that are lost when foreigners conduct trade and suggests that Jews are more eager to supply artisans and provide tradesmen for naval service than are representatives of other religions.[31]

The language of Luzzatto's discourse—religious toleration, freedom of trade, security of possessions—anticipates the arguments of Bruno Bauer in the nineteenth century, which Marx critiques in his essay "On the Jewish Question."[32] To the extent that a "Jewish question" existed in early modern Europe, it was focused on mercantile issues. Authors such as Jean Bodin, Barthélémy de Laffemas, Gomes Solis, Lopes Pereira, and Antoine de Montchrétien urged religious toleration of Jews based on their potential mercantile service to the state.[33] Following their example, Luzzatto and others emphasized economic pragmatism over abstract ideals of statesmanship. Bodin's influential theory of sovereignty, for example, suggests that sound fiscal policy contributed to political stability by helping to temper abuses of royal power. He substitutes a bureaucratic structure for the legal checks on royal power as a means of elevating the ideology of monarchy and implementing practical solutions to theoretical problems. Bodin invokes the Jewish nation in his essay on sovereignty, as well as in his early mercantilist tract on inflation rejecting the "paradoxes" of Malestroit. Bodin also wrote a 1593 essay on religious toleration *(Colloquium Heptaplomeres de Rerum Sublimium Arcanis Abditis),* which argued for the universal harmony of diverse religions in the service of the state.[34] The *Colloquium* stages a respectful debate among representatives of Catholicism, Judaism, natural philosophy, Lutheranism, Calvinism, skepticism, and Islam. The dialogue attempts to imagine toleration of belief and suggests that the state should not concern itself with the establishment of a single true religion. Bodin naturally sets his dialogue in Venice:

> Whereas other cities and districts are threatened by civil wars or fear of tyrants or harsh exactions of taxes or the most annoying inquiries into one's activities, this seemed to me to be nearly the only city that offers immunity and freedom from all these kinds of servitude. This is the reason why people come here from everywhere, wishing to spend their lives in the greatest freedom and tranquillity of spirit, whether they are interested in commerce or crafts or leisure pursuits as befit free man.[35]

Drawing on this Venetian example, Bodin regards both religious toleration and economic policy, including the maintenance of a stable currency, as essential for the success of the state.

Sixteenth-century studies of comparative religion such as Bodin's *Colloquium* raised new questions about the place of Jews, pagans, and Native Americans in the Japhetan lineage outlined in the Old Testament.[36] From the genealogical perspective of Mosaic history, Jews played a fundamental role in establishing Christianity's authority: they witnessed the historical validity of Christ, as marked in the opening passages of Matthew tracing the generations of Jesus back to Abraham, and they embodied the elect nation that was prophetically replaced by Christianity.[37] Like pagan mythology that could be assimilated to Christian truth through the application of allegorical interpretation, Jewish "error" in rejecting the Christian messiah could be redeemed through conversion. Yet, so long as they failed to convert to Christianity, Jews remained obstacles to the universal church. Martin Luther first displayed tolerance for the continued presence of the Jews in Europe but later composed the notoriously anti-Semitic tract *On the Jews and Their Lies* in 1544, which advocated violence against Jews who refused to convert.[38] At the same time, Protestants in England such as John Bale could look forward to the time when the conversion of the Jews would usher in the Second Coming, and John Knox regarded biblical Israel as a precursor for a new English Protestant nation of the elect.[39] In *Actes and Monuments,* however, John Foxe rejects the model of the Jewish nation by denying Jewish election in the first place, equating Judaism and Catholicism as forms of false Christianity that must be overcome. But, as Sharon Achinstein argues, Foxe mixes this position with a more sympathetic account of Jews, exemplified by his portrait of the Jewish martyr Gonzales Baez.[40]

Foxe's *Actes and Monuments* reflects an ambivalence characteristic of English Protestants who studied Hebrew and Jewish *kabbalah* in the name of purifying the Catholic church. Many such Protestants employed traditional stereotypes of Jews as social and religious pariahs. Foxe, for instance, invokes the myth of the *foetor judaicus* or "Jewish odor" in a story about a Jew who falls into a privy, a tale he links to violence against Jewish rebels in 1189.[41] Foxe's anti-Semitism follows in the tradition of Luther and Erasmus, who feared that the study of Hebrew by reformers would also lead them away from Christ. Erasmus went so far as to assure Hochstraten, the representative of the Inquisition in Cologne, that he secretly supported antisemitic pogroms, saying, "If it is Christian to hate the Jews, here we are all Christians in profusion."[42] James Shapiro describes numerous ways that Christians feared Jewish "contamination" and recognized in Judaism the origins of their own religion.[43] As Saint Paul remarks in his epistle to the Romans, the Jews have the "profite" of receiving "the oracles of God" (Rom. 3:1–2).[44] Early modern Jews could represent, paradoxically, both an intransigent particularism, symbolized by the covenant of circumcision, and a potential universalism, realized in part through trading and other financial activities. Following Paul, Christians revised the literal and exclusionary act of circumcision into a spiritual covenant with God that depends on the heart rather than the external mark of the flesh. But Jewish circumcision contains the seed of Christian universalism, a notion of brotherhood from which civic rights could be derived.[45]

Christian commonwealths emphasized Jewish capacity for maintaining trade and banking services as necessary elements of civic life and political stability. Such is the schizophrenia of a process of state building that, as Walter Benjamin suggests, finds barbarism at the heart of its civilizing principles.[46] And yet, by dividing trading Jews from moneylending Jews and by isolating both groups in ghettos, European cities preserved Jewish otherness in religious and cultural terms; the emergent "state" (newly defined as a political entity in the sixteenth century) secretly coveted what it publicly despised.[47] In many European cities, Jews could be punished for identifying themselves in public. In Amsterdam, for example, Jews were forced to refrain from observing religious rites and other practices—a rabbi noted in 1616 that "each [Jew] may follow his own belief but may not openly show that he is of a different faith from the inhabitants of the city."[48] By contrast, the Venetian senate required Jews to express their religious differences, forcing them to enact the very rituals of faith that would have marked them as targets of the Inquisition elsewhere in Europe.[49] This policy directly violated the Pope's counter-Reformation policies.[50] Fra Paolo Sarpi, a chief apologist for the Venetian senate, draws specifically on Rodriga's 1589 charter (shown here in italics) in explaining this Venetian practice:

> The Marranos cannot be subjected to the office of the Inquisition, having received a safe-conduct enabling them to come and live with their families in the Dominion and leave at their pleasure, *with their possessions,* living in the ghetto and wearing the yellow hat, and *to exercise their rites and ceremonies without hindrance* and this permission was granted to them for the public benefit of Christianity, so that they should not carry so much wealth and needed industriousness to the lands of the Turks.[51]

This forced publicity of the Jews—the requirement that they display the external "rites and ceremonies" of their faith—confirmed their status as resident aliens within the commercial state and as emblems of the origins of Christianity. Justifying Venetian policies in mercantilist terms, Sarpi acknowledges that commercial competition necessitates the extension of trading privileges to Jews because they might otherwise aid the Turks, chief military and commercial competitors to the Venetian empire. In offering protection from the Inquisition, Venice also emphasized Jewish identity as an externalized set of practices and actions, perhaps to distract Christians from Venetian dependence on the Jews as economic agents. In the same spirit, Venetian *condotte* defined Jews as culturally other, even as they acknowledged their economic utility. Sarpi alludes to the "public benefit" that Jews provided to Christians, defined specifically as the "wealth and needed industriousness" that Jews offered Venice.

***

The historic emergence of a Jewish trading nation in early modern Europe helps explain key elements of Jewish figures in *The Jew of Malta* and *The Merchant of Venice*. Marlowe's Barabas is a Levantine Jew engaged in overseas mercantile trade, while Shakespeare's Shylock is a Tedeschi Jew who practices moneylending and other small-scale banking services. But both plays represent their Jewish protagonists as central to the commercial and political life of their host states in the face of religious and political prejudice. As *The Jew of Malta* opens, Barabas proclaims his membership in a pan-European community of merchants:

> They say we are a scatter'd Nation:
> I cannot tell, but we have scambled up
> More wealth by farre then those that brag of faith.
> There's *Kirriah Jairim*, the great Jew of *Greece*,
> *Obed* in *Bairseth, Nones* in *Portugall*,
> My selfe in *Malta*, some in *Italy*,
> Many in *France*, and wealthy every one.
>
> (1.1.118–124)[52]

Barabas includes at least one actual merchant in his list of fellow Jews, since "Nones" probably refers to the Nunes family of Portuguese *Marranos* that had connections with the government of Elizabeth I.[53] The word "scamble"—to scavenge for money—carries with it the connotations of a disgraceful act, but Marlowe uses the term to signify the improvisatory nature of Jewish mercantilism. Barabas goes on to celebrate the ways in which commerce provides him and his fellow Jews with new types of power, the kind that traders use to "[rip] the bowels of the earth" in search for gold, "making the Seas their servants" (ll. 106, 107). Such power elevates Jewish mercantilism over a Christian poverty that masks "malice, falshood, and excessive pride" (l. 114).

In claiming that his substantial wealth derives from the "Blessings promis'd to the Jewes" (l. 102), Barabas links commercial activity to the biblical covenant between God and Abraham, the "father of manie nacions" (Gen. 17:5). Like several authors of Jewish charters for denizenship in early modern Europe, Barabas regards his successful commerce as biblically ordained. As God says to Abraham: "Knowe this of a suretie, that thy sede shal be a stranger in a land, that is not theirs, foure hundreth yeres, and shal serue them: and thei shal entreate them euil. Notwithstanding the nacion, whome thei shal serue, wil I iudge: and afterward shal thei come out with great substance" (Gen. 15:13–14). God tells Abraham that his "sede" will inherit the land of Canaan in which he is presently a "stranger"(Gen. 17:8). But in the intervening centuries, to the great profit of the rulers of the nation that they inhabit, the Jews will serve as strangers. Paul and other Christians separate Christian "gentiles" from the Jewish "nation." For instance, Paul explains how Christ has liberated Christians from the "curse of the Law" so that "the blessing of Abraham might come on the Gentiles through Christ Iesus" (Gal. 3:13, 14). In the process, he isolates Jews from the universality implied in the phrase "many nations"of Genesis, substituting instead a Christian version of abstract universalism.[54] For Barabas, the "blessings" promised to the Jews arrive in the potentially sacrilegious form of money. If Genesis promises the Jews land, Barabas suggests that Jews must reap wealth, since his people are not destined for "principality" (1.1.132). Such a revision of the original biblical injunction demonstrates one way that Marlowe remakes Barabas into a villain, but it also invokes the logic of the sixteenth-century Jewish nation.

As a crossroads of trade famed for its immigrant population, Malta offered Marlowe an appropriate setting for staging conflicts between trading wealth, religious identity, and political power. The island was also historically important for the emergence of Jewish trading nations. A Spanish dominion overseen by Sicily, the island had a community of Jews dating at least as far back as the Roman Empire. Following the expulsion of the Jews from Spain in 1492, this community was offered the choice of exile or conversion.[55] Charles V gave the island to the Order of the Knights Hospitaller of St. John in 1530, after the Order was exiled from Rhodes by the Turks eight years earlier. It was only after the arrival of the Knights that Maltese Jews lost their status as citizens, becoming slave-like captives of the newly governing Christians.[56] Christian Knights from Auvergne, Provence, France, Aragon, Castile, England, and Italy managed the defense of the island against attack, including the Great Siege of Suleiman I in 1565.[57] This four-month assault, in which 250 Knights and 7,000 soldiers from Malta and Spain defended the island against a Turkish force of more than 30,000 men, was identified as part of an apocalyptic struggle between East and West. As Queen Elizabeth conceded on the eve of the battle, "If the Turks shall prevail against the Isle of Malta, it is uncertain what further peril might follow to the rest of Christendom."[58]

European Catholics and Protestants alike greeted the failure of the Turkish assault on Malta with relief. Anti-Turkish sentiment increased in England, which regarded the defeat of the Ottoman Empire as essential to its own imperial ambitions.[59] Rather than focus on this recent military victory against alien incursion, however, Marlowe depicts the Governor and Senate of Malta as weak and conniving victims of Spanish and Ottoman power. Instead of framing Malta as a site of heroic defense against Ottoman incursion, Marlowe explores the relationship between Jewish trading wealth and the management of the state. *The Jew of Malta* displays the religious and political hypocrisy of Malta's Governor, first in his seizure of the wealth of the Jews and then in his willingness to submit to Spain, represented by Martin del Bosco, in order to avoid paying tribute money to the Turks. This emphasis on the Catholicism of the Knights of Malta allows Barabas, like Faustus, to operate as a crowd-pleasing agent of anti-Catholic farce. Yet the conflict between Christian and heathen gives way to a conflict between the management of the state and the mercantile wealth amassed by Barabas as part of a Jewish nation. Barabas's praise of his "infinite riches" in the opening soliloquy invokes the idolatrous worship of money familiar from morality plays, but Marlowe shows how this wealth actually maintains political and national stability in *The Jew of Malta*.

Like other Marlovian heroes, including Faustus and Tamburlaine, Barabas is a radical individualist; he only wants the freedom to accumulate his private wealth and refuses to be lumped together with the "Tribe" from which he is "descended" (1.2.114). His international trading connections offer him a surrogate community, at once cosmopolitan and dispersed. It is not surprising that he strives throughout the play to isolate his wealth from political actions, remaining indifferent about who will "conquer, and kill all" (1.1.149) in Malta "So they spare me, my daughter, and my wealth" (l. 150). But Ferneze and the Christian leaders of Malta refuse to let Barabas enjoy his wealth in private, citing the "common good" (1.2.99) in seizing Jewish wealth in order to pay the neglected tribute money to the Turks. As Ferneze explains in response to Barabas's question ("Is theft the ground of your Religion?" [l. 96]):

> No, Jew, we take particularly thine
> To save the ruine of a multitude:
> And better one want for a common good,
> Than many perish for a private man:
> Yet *Barrabas* we will not banish thee,
> But here in *Malta*, where thou gotst thy wealth,
> Live still; and, if thou canst, get more.
>
> (ll. 97–103)

The name "Barabas," of course, is also the name of the murderer set free by Pilate at the request of the crowds, who condemn Christ instead, an event recorded in Mark 15:7 and John 18:40. Marked as both a Jew and a scapegoat who allows Jesus to be crucified, Barabas exemplifies both individualism and nationalism. Echoing the words of Pilate to Christ, Ferneze isolates Barabas as a necessary sacrifice for the good of the commonwealth. Ferneze's commonwealth ideology rings hollow, shadowed as it is by his executive order against a particular minority. Wealth turns out to be a sign of power for Barabas, but it is not directed toward the state's stability. Instead of banishing Barabas to a foreign land, Ferneze insists that he remain in Malta as a resident alien, where he can gain more private wealth useful to the state.

*The Jew of Malta* exposes the inadequacies of the ancient system of tribute money, as well as the futility of Ferneze's attempt to replace the tribute system with Spanish hegemony, represented by the Spanish slave trader Martin del Bosco (2.2.36–56).[60] Ferneze and his fellow Knights compound their incoherent fiscal policy by relying on del Bosco—whom English audiences would have associated with the Spanish Inquisition and with rapacious colonialism—to prop up the kingdom of Malta. Despite the Governor of Malta's victory over the Calymath and his destruction of Barabas, the play shows trade to be an essential component of political stability: the peace in Malta with which *The Jew of Malta* begins, in which "all the merchants with all ther merchandize / are safe arriv'd" (1.1.50–51), dissolves into a violent farce of religious conflict. Barabas begins the play as a merchant whose "credit" is based on his personal reputation, one strong enough to serve as if he himself "were present" (ll. 56, 57) in the custom house. Trade enables his reputation: as he asks, "Tush, who amongst 'em knowes not *Barrabas?*" (l. 66). It is only after the Governor of Malta makes unjust demands on the Jews that Barabas assumes the stereotypical role of Jewish villain—"We Jewes can fawne like Spaniels when we please" (2.3.20)—against the Christians.

In the same sense that Venice required Jews to wear the signs of their faith externally, Marlowe depicts religious identity as a series of behaviors that can be put on and off in reaction to changing political and economic conditions. Christian hypocrisy breeds Jewish vengefulness and subversion, as Barabas engages in increasingly outrageous plots of murder and deceit. But his character is not merely an expression of Machiavellian policy, and the conventional argument that Marlowe frames religion as a cover for economic exploitation overlooks religion's importance in the administration of the Maltese state.[61] Professions of religious sincerity mask a desire for gold, as suggested by the cross marking the location of hidden gold in Barabas's house, which is turned into a convent after Barabas refuses to pay tribute money. Yet the play ironizes Martin del Bosco's famous argument that the "Desire of gold" (3.5.4) rules the world. As G. K. Hunter notes, Barabas's materialist philosophy also contains specific theological propositions: the language with which Barabas urges his daughter to help him reclaim his wealth is enriched by a second layer of biblical allusions to spiritual profit, and Barabas later tries to claim an individual covenant with God. In addition, the governor's arguments justifying the seizure of Jewish assets to pay the Turks resemble those used by Peter the Venerable to force the Jews to pay for the Second Crusade.[62] Barabas's increasingly violent schemes—setting the two suitors to his daughter against one another, poisoning the nuns, conspiring with the Turks, murdering the friar and framing his companion—challenge the political and economic stability of the island.

Religious violence thus emerges out of the failed commercial relations in the play. The seizure of Jewish wealth by the Knights of Malta compensates for the immoderate wealth of the individual merchant but compromises the political stability derived from peaceful trade. The short-lived friendship between Barabas and Ithamore, Jew and Muslim, invokes the possibility of what Lupton calls the *"universitas circumcisorum"* as a means of linking disparate peoples in bonds of civic affiliation.[63] Ultimately, wealth and the flow of capital rather than religious friendship determine both status and personal relationships in the play, suggesting that only economic bonds can overcome national and religious differences. Malta falls into chaotic violence because it fails to recognize the importance of Jewish mercantilism.

*The Jew of Malta* refuses to make stereotypical connections between Jews and usury. Instead, it stages the centrality of mercantile wealth to political economy. To this end, Marlowe echoes contemporary treatises on the uses of money that identify new connections between commerce and national productivity. Elizabethan authors such as Thomas Gresham, John Dee, and John Wheeler tied trade and national defense to the prestige of the British monarchy, focusing less on the church's rejection of usury than on how commerce could serve God and nation. Although authors continued to attack usury as a violation of natural law and a crime against Christian unity, Elizabethan tracts also defined usury in terms of English nationhood. The anonymous author of *The Lawfull Use of Riches*, for example, argues that wealth is primarily to be used to glorify God, and then to sustain the commonwealth.[64] Thomas Lodge's *Alarum against Vsurers* praises the "publyke commoditie" that merchants "bring in store of wealth from forein Nations" while condemning their "domesticall practices, that not only they inrich themselves mightelye by others misfortunes, but also eate our English Gentrie out of house and home."[65] The Preacher in Thomas Wilson's *Discovrse vpon Vsury* maintains that usurers deserve death for destroying "not only whole families, but also whole countreys . . . theire offence hurteth more universallye and toucheth a greater nomber" than do thieves and murderers.[66] In his preface, Wilson targets greed as a crime against the commonwealth, singling out Rome as a place where "private gaine thrust oute common profite," while in the text itself, the Lawyer acknowledges the centrality of mercantile activity to the state when he says that "treasure is the welfare of the realme and countreye where you dwel, and where merchants are not cheryshed, that countreye or realme wyl soone

perish."[67] The Lawyer understands usury in relation to commercial relations
with France, Portugal, and Spain and argues that the courts rather than the
church should have jurisdiction over cases of usury.

Elizabethan architects of commercial policy, especially Thomas Gresham and Gerrard de Malynes, also approach usury from the perspective of
national interest, maintaining a mercantilist insistence on the balance of trade
between England and other countries. Such an approach shifts the question
of usury from individual ethics to national politics.[68] Marlowe registers this
historical shift to the extent that *The Jew of Malta* invites us to reconceptual-
ize the state in terms of the "publyke commoditie" of commerce. By using the
figure of the Levantine Jew to explore the relationship between trade, religion, and the state, Marlowe's play registers the historical dynamic of Jewish
assimilation and the scattered trading nations of sixteenth-century Europe.[69]

*  *  *

In *The Merchant of Venice*, Shakespeare demonstrates his own interest in the
historical Jewish nation while revising the specific portrait of the Jewish
villain he found in Marlowe. Shylock's vengeance, unlike that of Barabas,
stems from a failed monetary contract. But in both cases the Jewish protagonist connects the play with larger issues of trade, religion, and political economy.

*The Merchant of Venice* includes Jews among the necessary "strangers" in
Venice and explores the relation between the Jewish community and political
stability.[70] Invoking the special status of foreign merchants, Antonio explains
to Solanio why

> The duke cannot deny the course of law;
> For the commodity that strangers have
> With us in Venice, if it be denied,
> Will much impeach the justice of the state,
> Since that the trade and profit of the city
> Consisteth of all nations.
>
> (3.3.26–31)[71]

Antonio here defines the trade of "all nations" as fundamental to the city's
survival. It is Shylock who complains that Antonio "hates our sacred nation"
(1.3.45; see also 3.1.53) and later feels the "curse . . . upon our nation" (3.1.81)
in contemplating the loss of his daughter, Jessica, along with the money and
jewels she has taken. Antonio labels Shylock a "stranger," just as Portia will
at the end of the trial scene, where she invokes a law that protects citizens
against an "alien" (4.1.347) like Shylock. In the short exchange between

Antonio and Solanio quoted above, Shakespeare prepares the audience to regard the trial scene as a test of the Jewish nation.

Shakespeare emphasizes the degree to which economic relationships embroil characters in legal, national, and intrapersonal relations: the opening scene presents Bassanio's "venture" for Portia as a parallel to his friend Antonio's risky overseas trade; the suitors who vie for Portia's hand imagine their prize in terms of the "golden fleece" (1.1.170) of mercantile enterprise; even Shylock ostensibly enters into his bond with Antonio in the name of "love" (1.3.136) and friendship. Shakespeare exposes the networks of financial exchange that prop up aristocratic marriage negotiations. Shylock must procure tangible assets from the wealthy Jew, Tubal, just as Antonio, short of money to lend to Bassanio, finds himself compelled to ask Shylock for a loan. But the play is also interested in defining forms of religious and commercial affiliation on which national identity might be constructed.[72]

Shakespeare's Venice, like that of Rodriga and Luzzatto, depends in many ways on Jewish commerce, although the play refuses the utopian idea that commerce smoothes over religious and national differences.[73] Like the pound of flesh at stake in the bond, Shylock cannot be extracted without risking the lifeblood of the Venetian republic. The defeat of Shylock and the conversion of Jessica through marriage to Lorenzo might likewise appear to be a victory of provincialism over cosmopolitanism, but Shylock's character cannot be expelled from the play so easily.

The trial scene of act 4 confirms what Shylock has already acknowledged about his status in Venice—he is a "stranger cur" (1.3.116), valued in moments of necessity but subject to scorn most of the time. As much as Shylock works to humanize himself as a Jew, especially in the notorious speech in which he asks, rhetorically, "Hath not a Jew eyes?" (3.1.55–56), he more often invokes the right to purchase and own property as a foundation for his legal and political claims. In response to Antonio's insulting description of him as a "stranger cur," Shylock responds, "'Hath a dog money? Is it possible / A cur can lend three thousand ducats?'" (1.3.116, 119–120). The same logic appears in his comments to the court in Act 4, where he invokes the legal right of a purchaser of slaves in defending his bond with Antonio:

> You have among you many a purchased slave,
> Which, like your asses and your dogs and mules,
> You use in abject and in slavish parts,
> Because you bought them. Shall I say to you,
> "Let them be free, marry them to your heirs!"
>
> (4.1.90–94)

Shylock suggests that legal rights in Venice depend on the power of the purse. Rather than appeal to the essential humanity of slaves as an argument for their liberation, Shylock shows how economic exchange underwrites state law.[74] We know that, beginning in the fifteenth century, Venetian citizens purchased African prisoners from Portuguese slave traders and forced them to row as galley slaves up and down the Adriatic Sea.[75] The Duke's threat to dissolve the court at this moment suggests that Shylock has articulated a difficult truth. The "freedom of the state" of Venice, supposedly at stake in the trial itself, denies subject positions based on economic practice to one group of people while justifying citizenship on economic grounds for another.

Portia frames Shylock's economic investments as signs of Jewish worldliness, portraying him as a symbol of the Old Law of Jewish vengeance as someone who is blind to the New Law of Christian mercy.[76] She goes on to assimilate the freedom of state to the theology of Christian universalism in her famous "quality of mercy" speech:

> It blesseth him that gives and him that takes.
> 'Tis mightiest in the mightiest; it becomes
> The thronèd monarch better than his crown. . . .
> But mercy is above this sceptered sway;
> It is enthronèd in the hearts of kings;
> It is an attribute to God himself.
>
> (ll. 185–187, 191–193)

Portia hopes to assimilate Shylock within a model of universal Christian brotherhood, signified by the Pauline circumcision of the heart, on the condition that he will show mercy. She imagines Venetian law as derived from a "mercy" that is itself above the "sceptered sway" of kings. By this logic, Shylock's insistence on his bond and the pound of flesh due to him by his contract with Antonio enacts the logic of the Old Law that rejects mercy in the name of vengeance. But the civil law of the state for which Portia stands returns Shylock to the status of "alien" or stranger by virtue of his supposed threat to Antonio's life. Some readers may regard this legalistic turn of events as a narrative contrivance, but Shylock rejects its logic.

Portia's speech on mercy also affirms the connection between goods and citizenship. Her own extraordinary wealth allows her to adopt an attitude of aristocratic scorn toward tangible sums of money, offering to pay twelve times the amount of the original debt to Shylock (3.2.299–300). It is the symbolic rather than economic value of objects (such as the ring she gives her husband) that matter to her, just as the pound of flesh finds its ultimate expression in its relation to the "freedom of the state" (l. 278) in the courtroom scene. Like the decisions of the English Chancery court, which was coming into new prominence in the 1590s, Portia's ruling frames Shylock's rejection of mercy as a form of idolatry, since his statement that he "crave[s]" (4.1.204) the law would register with Christian audiences as covetousness.[77] Although Portia's language recalls the debate between Mercy and Justice as represented in the medieval *Processus Belial,* her speech also addresses the relationship between commercial, religious, and political affiliations in the construction of the early modern nation.[78]

The Duke shows "mercy" to Shylock by offering to spare his life—even as he confiscates his property—but Shylock understands that his life is defined in terms of his house and goods rather than his biological or religious identity:

> Nay, take my life and all! Pardon not that!
> You take my house when you do take the prop
> That doth sustain my house. You take my life
> When you do take the means whereby I liue.
>
> (ll. 372–375)

By insisting on property rights rather than rights to engage in commercial activity, Shylock goes a step beyond the Jewish *condotte* examined above. Indeed, with his pun on "prop" and "property," Shylock anticipates the equation of property ownership, the marketplace, and political franchise that the Putney debates of the 1640s elevated to the center of English political economy.[79] Shylock rejects the assumptions behind the court's expression of mercy—that he possesses a "life" independent of the "means whereby" he makes a living. This passage alludes to Deuteronomy 24:6: "No man shal take the nether nor ye vpper milstone to pledge: for this gage is *his* liuing." But Shylock's defense of ownership and commerce does not signify Jewish materialism so much as his rejection of Christian mercy defined by Portia and the Duke.

By invoking such mercy as a component of universal brotherhood, Portia and the court frame the defeat of Shylock's bond, the seizure of half of his estate, and his forced conversion as a triumph of community over the destructive literalism of the law. But the law that Portia invokes to seize half of Shylock's goods is one reserved for an "alien" who has sought the life of any "citizen" (4.1.347, 349), so the verdict reaffirms Shylock's status as a resident alien in Christian communities at the moment that it tries to make him a member of that community. The Duke spares Shylock's life, but only on the condition that he convert to Christianity and forfeit half of his estate to Antonio and the other half to the state as a "fine" (l. 370). Antonio modifies the terms of Shylock's punishment at Portia's request in order to allow Shylock to keep half his goods, provided that he give the other half to Antonio "in use" (l. 381), to administer until Shylock's death, at which time it will be given to

Lorenzo and Jessica. This arrangement contrasts Antonio's "mercy" (1. 376) with Shylock's lack thereof, but it also gives Shylock what he asks for in returning a portion of his goods.

Antonio's revision of the Duke's sentence restores Shylock's possessions that would have gone to the state. Antonio, a native merchant, earns the right to administer justice by seeking to raise funds for the Jew's daughter, aligning the universalism of Christian mercy with the conversion of the Jew through Jessica's conversion and that of her father. The private citizen becomes the ultimate conduit of mercy, as the play shifts from the public venue of the courtroom to the private world of Belmont, where romance attempts to smooth over the rough edges of the trial scene. Here, in the final scenes, the economic elements of "credit" (5.1.245), "surety" (1. 253), and mercantile venture (ll. 276–277) are replaced by the romance harmonies of the three married couples—Jessica and Lorenzo, Portia and Bassanio, and Nerissa and Gratiano. In contrast to Marlowe, Shakespeare criticizes a mercantile state that reserves the right of private ownership to an elite class that benefits from the mercantile activities of a politically oppressed group.

Ironically, the economics of Venice undermines Shylock's efforts to retain his core private and religious identity. Shylock does not shun all kin and society in the way that Barabas does, but he does reject potential associations with the Christians with whom he does business. In response to Bassanio's invitation to dine with him, Shylock says "I will buy with you, sell with you, talk with you, walk with you, and so following, but I will not eat with you, drink with you, nor pray with you" (1.3.33–35). However, like Barabas, Shylock cannot avoid the company of Christians. The victory of the Venetian court over Shylock ensures that, as in *The Jew of Malta,* the private sphere remains within the province of Christians. The court turns Shylock's claim that his power to purchase guarantees his rights against him, emptying him of his political and religious rights but leaving him with half of his estate. The containment of Shylock allows the Venetian state to continue to separate its ideals of legal justice and independence from the economic realities of slaveholding and the Jewish ghetto. Shylock's lust for flesh raises the specter of the Jewish blood libel (the belief that Jews sacrificed Christians and used their blood for ritual purposes), reinforced by many allusions to eating in the play (e.g., Shylock's reluctant feast with Christians on the night that Jessica elopes with Lorenzo). But the play specifically aligns appetites with economics in Lorenzo's joke about Launcelot and Jessica. As Jessica reports of Lorenzo: "He tells me flatly there's no mercy for me in heaven because I am a Jew's daughter; and he says you are no good member of the commonwealth, for in converting Jews to Christians you raise the price of pork" (3.5.30–34). Lorenzo's joke reveals how economic laws of supply and demand trump religious identity in a mercantile nation.[80] At the same time, the Venetian state refuses

Shylock a concept of the sacred beyond his material attachments. Where *The Jew of Malta* justifies Barabas's trading nation as an inherently Jewish enterprise, *The Merchant of Venice* subjects Shylock's legal and economic materialism to the corrective of Matthew 6:19–21: "Lay not vp treasures for your selues vpon the earth, where the mothe & canker corrupt, & where theues digge through, and steale. But lay vp treasures for your selues in heauen. . . . For where your treasure is, there wil your heart be also."

Shakespeare attempts to overcome the trial scene's spectacle of political and religious terror against Shylock in Act 4 by highlighting Jessica's marriage to Lorenzo and her admission to the upper class of aristocratic Venice in Act 5. Returning to Belmont, the play invokes the power of romantic love to transcend religious difference, as well as the possibility of religious conversion. But from Lorenzo's opening allusion to Troilus and Cressida to his references to Dido and Jessica's invocation of Medea in the first fifteen lines of Act 5, Shakespeare also invokes specific obstacles to romantic closure. The reigning trope is a musical one, culminating in Lorenzo's defense of the Orphic power of music to pacify "savage" nature (5.1.78):

> The man that hath no music in himself,
> Nor is not moved with concord of sweet sounds,
> Is fit for treasons, stratagems, and spoils;
> The motions of his spirit are dull as night
> And his affections dark as Erebus.
>
> (ll. 83–87)

Lorenzo's language suggests that Jessica herself is like the "savages" who should be ruled by the "concord of sweet sounds." He implies that either music is inherently within a person or it is not, but those who lack music in their souls are threats to society at large: "treasons, stratagems, and spoils" indicate crimes against the state. The passage invokes the thrifty killjoy, Shylock, even as it tries to move beyond the trial scene and to the realm of cosmic harmony.[81] Shakespeare registers his doubts that the theater can create a form of national unity that would transcend the concrete religious, political, and economic conflicts around which the Elizabethan state formed itself. Such doubt lingers in Jessica's response to her beloved in her final words of the play: "I am never merry when I hear sweet music" (l. 69).

Shylock invokes his "sacred nation" as a principle of economic rights on which citizenship might be founded, but Portia denies such rights under the banner of Christian universalism. On the surface, the defeated Jew joins the defeated suitors Aragon and Morocco, whose choice of the gold and silver caskets, respectively, symbolizes their materialistic lust. But Shylock's

materialism is of a different sort, grounded as it is on the principles of justice
and economic vitality that hold up the Venetian state.

NOTES

1. Thomas Middleton, *The Triumphs of Honour and Industry*, in *The Works
of Thomas Middleton*, ed. A. H. Bullen, 8 vols. (London: John C. Nimmo, 1885),
7:291–307, esp. 299.
2. See Susan M. Lough, "Trade and Industry in Ireland in the Sixteenth
Century," *Journal of Political Economy* 24 (1916): 713–730.
3. See Carlo Sigonio, *De Republica Hebraeorum* (Bologna, 1583), and
Bonaventure Corneille Bertram, *De Politia Judaica* (Geneva, 1574). James Shapiro
describes unprecedented interest in the Jewish nation as a theological and political
category by sixteenth-century English authors, but he overlooks the commercial
elements; see *Shakespeare and the Jews* (New York: Columbia University Press, 1996),
esp. 13–17, 167–180.
4. Shapiro, 174.
5. Robert Wilson's *Pleasant and Stately Morall, of the Three Lordes and Three
Ladies of London* (London, 1590) is the exception. For a comprehensive list, see
Edgar Rosenberg, "The Jew in Western Drama," *Bulletin of the New York Public
Library* 72 (1968): 442–491; see also *The Jew in English Drama: An Annotated
Bibliography*, comp. Edward D. Coleman, pref. Joshua Bloch (New York: New York
Public Library, 1968), 242–244.
6. For an influential reading of the colonial context of *The Jew of Malta*, see
Emily C. Bartels, "Malta, the Jew, and Fictions of Difference: Colonialist Discourse
in Marlowe's *The Jew of Malta*," *ELR* 20 (1990): 1–16. For an account of Shylock as
a symbol of Jewish "fiscalism" as opposed to Christian "mercantilism," see Stephen
Greenblatt, "Marlowe, Marx, and Anti Semitism," *Critical Inquiry* 5 (1978): 291–
307, esp. 294. For a defense of the idea of "political economy" in sixteenth-century
England, see Neal Wood, *Foundations of Political Economy: Some Early Tudor Views
on State and Society* (Berkeley: University of California Press, 1994).
7. Quoted in Benjamin C. I. Ravid, *Economics and Toleration in Seventeenth-
Century Venice: The Background and Context of the "Discorso" of Simone Luzzatto* (New
York: H. Kraus, 1978), 34.
8. For an overview of the charters or *condotte* governing Jewish trading
privileges, see Robert Bonfil, *Jewish Life in Renaissance Italy*, trans. Anthony
Oldcorn (Berkeley: University of California Press, 1994), 85–90.
9. Solis is quoted in Edgar Samuel, *At the End of the Earth: Essays on the
History of the Jews in England and Portugal* (London: Jewish Historical Society of
England, 2004), 89.
10. The *Oxford English Dictionary*, 2d ed. (Oxford: Oxford University
Press, 1989), s.v. "nation, *n.*$^1$," 1c. *OED Online*, http://dictionary.oed.com/cgi/
entry/00181778 (accessed 29 February 2008).
11. *OED Online*, s.v. "gentile, *a.* and *n.*," 1.
12. Henry Blount, *A Voyage into the Levant*, 2d ed. (London, 1636), 2 (sig.
A2$^r$).
13. Andrew Willet, *De Vniversali et Novissima Ivdæorum Vocatione* (Cambridge,
1590), sig. 25$^v$; translated and quoted in Shapiro, 168.

14. Jews in Frankfurt and Regensburg, for instance, received protection from Charles V during the War of the Schmalkaldic League (1546–1547) in exchange for contributions of food and money to his soldiers. See Jonathan I. Israel, *European Jewry in the Age of Mercantilism, 1550–1750* (Oxford: Clarendon Press, 1985), 16, 17–20.

15. See Benjamin C. I. Ravid, "First Charter of the Jewish Merchants of Venice, 1589," *AJS Review* 1 (1976): 187–122, esp. 193–194. Census figures estimate that 1,694 Jews lived in Venice; roughly 200 lived in Padua and about 225 lived in Verona; see Brian Pullan, *Rich and Poor in Renaissance Venice: The Social Institutions of a Catholic State, to 1620* (Oxford: Basil Blackwell, 1971), 546–547n28–29.

16. David Chambers and Brian Pullan, eds., *Venice: A Documentary History, 1450–1630* (Oxford: Blackwell, 1992), 325–327.

17. *The Memoirs of Philippe de Commynes*, ed. Samuel Kinser, trans. Isabelle Cazeaux, 2 vols. (Columbia: University of South Carolina Press, 1969–1973), 2:493 (book 7, chapter 18).

18. See Frederic C. Lane, "Venetian Shipping during the Commercial Revolution," in *Crisis and Change in the Venetian Economy in the Sixteenth and Seventeenth Centuries*, ed. Brian Pullan (London: Methuen, 1968), 22–46, esp. 31–32.

19. The word "ghetto" refers to the foundry around which the original settlement was arranged. A Jewish district existed in Prague as early as 1262, and many cities of the Holy Roman Empire had Jewish quarters between this period and the sixteenth century. But following the establishment of the Venetian ghetto in 1516, other Italian cities gave the same name to their enclosed, regulated Jewish communities. See Robert C. Davis's introduction to *The Jews of Early Modern Venice*, ed. Robert C. Davis and Benjamin Ravid (Baltimore: Johns Hopkins University Press, 2001), vii–xix, esp. ix–x.

20. Ravid, "First Charter," 188.

21. Pullan, *Rich and Poor*, 3.

22. Quoted from and translated in Chambers and Pullan, eds., 344. The Jewish ghetto expanded in 1541 to include the Ghetto Vecchio, the only expansion allowed by the city until the formation of the Ghetto Nuovissimo in 1633. See Brian Pullan, *The Jews of Europe and the Inquisition of Venice, 1550–1670* (Totowa, NJ: Barnes and Noble, 1983), 157.

23. Ravid, "First Charter," 190.

24. Manfredo Tafuri, *Venice and the Renaissance*, trans. Jessica Levine (Cambridge: MIT Press, 1989), 1.

25. Ravid suggests that Jews had the same rights as Venetian citizens; see "The Legal Status of the Jewish Merchants of Venice, 1541–1638," *Journal of Economic History* 35 (1975): 274–279, esp. 274. Benjamin Arbel argues that a "closer examination of the charter and the developments related to it indicates that in matters of international trade the republic was not quite ready to put these Jewish merchants on an equal footing with Venetian full-rights citizens." See "Jews in International Trade: The Emergence of the Levantines and Ponentines," in Davis and Ravid, eds., 73–96, esp. 88.

26. A translation of the 1589 charter appears in Chambers and Pullan, eds., 346–349.

27. Simone Luzzatto, "Discourse on the Condition of the Jews, Especially in Venice," in *Italy in the Baroque: Selected Readings,* trans. and ed. Brendan Dooley (New York: Garland, 1995), 385–398, esp. 386–387.

28. Trans. in Ravid, *Economics and Toleration,* 62.

29. This distinguishes early modern English mercantilism from the kind of protectionist policies later associated with mercantilism by economists like Adam Smith. For a general introduction, see Eli F. Heckscher, *Mercantilism,* trans. Mendel Shapiro, 2 vols. (London: George Allen & Unwin, 1962), 2:13–22.

30. Trans. in Dooley, ed., 392.

31. Trans. in Dooley, ed., 393–394.

32. Bruno Bauer first coined the phrase "Jewish Question" or *Judenfrage* in a pamphlet by that title in 1842. Marx responded with his 1843 essay "On the Jewish Question," which argued that the political emancipation of the Jews actually demotes religion and property rights to an alienated "civil society" that is also in need of emancipation. See *Writings of the Young Marx on Philosophy and Society,* trans. and ed. Loyd D. Easton and Kurt H. Guddat (Indianapolis: Hackett, 1997), 216–248. Greenblatt (see n. 6 above) reads Barabas in *The Jew of Malta* as the alienated essence of capitalism, as opposed to Christianity (291–292).

33. See Israel (n. 14 above), 56–57.

34. Israel, 37.

35. Jean Bodin, *Colloquium of the Seven about Secrets of the Sublime: Colloquium Heptaplomeres de Rerum Sublimium Arcanis Abditis,* trans. and intro. Marion Leathers Daniels Kuntz (Princeton: Princeton University Press, 1975), 3.

36. See the discussion in Colin Kidd, *British Identities before Nationalism: Ethnicity and Nationhood in the Atlantic World, 1600–1800* (Cambridge: Cambridge University Press, 1999), 9–33.

37. On the relation between Protestantism and philo-Semitism in England, see David S. Katz, *Philo-Semitism and the Readmission of the Jews to England, 1603–1655* (Oxford: Clarendon Press, 1982).

38. Martin Luther, "On the Jews and their Lies" *(De Judaeis et Eorum Mendaciis),* trans. Martin H. Bertram, in *Luther's Works,* ed. Jaroslav Pelikan and Helmut T. Lehmann, 55 vols. (Philadelphia: Concordia, 1958), 47:121–306. See also Salo Wittmayer Baron, *A Social and Religious History of the Jews,* 2d rev. ed., 18 vols. (New York: Columbia University Press, and Philadelphia: Jewish Publication Society, 1969), 13:216–229; Mark U. Edwards Jr., *Luther's Last Battles: Politics and Polemics, 1531–1546* (Leiden: E. J. Brill, 1983), 115–142; and Steven Rowan, "Luther, Bucer and Eck on the Jews," *Sixteenth-Century Journal* 16 (1985): 79–90.

39. See Arthur H. Williamson, "British Israel and Roman Britain: The Jews and Scottish Models of Polity from George Buchanan to Samuel Rutherford," in *Jewish Christians and Christian Jews: From the Renaissance to the Enlightenment,* ed. Richard H. Popkin and Gordon M. Weiner (Dordrecht: Kluwer, 1994), 97–118. Bale could also dismiss the Jewish church as Satanic, as in *Image of Both Churches* (1550), 484.

40. Sharon Achinstein, "John Foxe and the Jews," *Renaissance Quarterly* 54 (2001): 86–120, esp. 101.

41. Achinstein, 86, 96.

42. See "The Journal of Rabbi Josel of Rosheim," ed. and trans. J. Kracauer, *Revue des études juives* 26 (1888): 84–105, esp. 101.

43. Shapiro, 44–51, esp. 50.

44. All biblical citations are from the Geneva Bible and made parenthetically in the text. See *The Geneva Bible: A Facsimile of the 1560 Edition,* intro. Lloyd E. Berry (Madison: University of Wisconsin Press, 1969).

45. Julia Reinhard Lupton, *Citizen-Saints: Shakespeare and Political Theology* (Chicago: University of Chicago Press, 2005), 31–48.

46. Walter Benjamin, *Illuminations,* ed. Hannah Arendt, trans. Harry Zohn (New York: Schocken Books, 1986), 258–259.

47. The first author to use the English word "state" in its modern sense as a political entity was Thomas Starkey in his *Dialogue between Pole and Lupset,* ed. T. F. Mayer, Camden Royal Historical Society 37 (London: Royal Historical Society, 1989), 40.

48. See Simon Schama, *The Embarrassment of Riches: An Interpretation of Dutch Culture in the Golden Age* (New York: Random House, 1987), 587.

49. As Benjamin Arbel argues, the protection of Jewish merchants by the Ottoman Empire spurred the extension of similar privileges in Christian countries of the Mediterranean, especially in Italy. See *Trading Nations: Jews and Venetians in the Early Modern Eastern Mediterranean* (Leiden: E. J. Brill, 1995), esp. 2–4, 29–54.

50. On to the effects of the Inquisition on Venetian Jews, see Pullan (n. 22 above), *Jews of Europe,* 3–71; and Pier Cesare Ioly Zorattini, "Jews, Crypto-Jews, and the Inquisition," in Davis and Ravid, eds. (n. 19 above), 97–116.

51. Quoted and trans. Ravid, "First Charter," 210.

52. *The Complete Works of Christopher Marlowe,* ed. Roma Gill, 5 vols. (Oxford: Clarendon Press, 1987–1998), vol. 4. All quotations from *The Jew of Malta* are from this edition, cited by act, scene, and line.

53. See Gill, ed., 99 (1.1.122n); and Lucien Wolf, "Jews in Elizabethan England," *Transactions of the Jewish Historical Society in England* 11 (1924–1927): 1–91, esp. 8–9.

54. I thank Jason Rosenblatt for pointing this out to me.

55. Julia Reinhard Lupton, *"The Jew of Malta,"* in *The Cambridge Companion to Christopher Marlowe,* ed. Patrick Cheney (Cambridge: Cambridge University Press, 2004), 144–157, esp. 145.

56. See Godfrey Wettinger, *The Jews of Malta in the Late Middle Ages* (Malta: Midsea Books, 1985), 15.

57. See Ernle Dusgate Selby Bradford, *The Great Siege: Malta, 1565* (London: Hodder and Stoughton, 1901).

58. *Elizabeth I: Her Life in Letters,* ed. Felix Pryor (Berkeley: University of California Press, 2003), 39.

59. Simon Shepherd, *Marlowe and the Politics of Elizabethan Theatre* (Brighton, UK: Harvester Press, 1986), 170. See also Bartels (n. 6 above), 5.

60. Luc Borot, by contrast, sees competing political economies in the play: "The Knights are an aristocratic commonwealth, the Turk a tyrant, the Spaniard a traditional monarch, Barabas . . . a short-time tyrant." See "Machiavellian Diplomacy and Dramatic Developments in Marlowe's *Jew of Malta,*" *Cahiers élisabéthains* 33 (1988): 1–11, esp. 2.

61. An example of such a conventional reading is that of Howard S. Babb, "Policy in Marlowe's *The Jew of Malta,*" *ELH* 24 (1957): 85–94.

62. G. K. Hunter, "The Theology of Marlowe's *The Jew of Malta,*" *Journal of the Warburg and Courtauld Institutes* 27 (1964): 211–240, esp. 225, 237, 235–236.

63. Lupton, *Citizen-Saints*, 66.

64. *The Lawfull Use of Riches* (London, 1578), 4.

65. Thomas Lodge, *An Alarum against Vsurers* (London, 1584), sig. B$^r$.

66. Thomas Wilson, *A Discovrse vpon Vsury . . . [1572]*, ed. R. H. Tawney (New York: Harcourt Brace & Co., 1925), 186.

67. Wilson, *Discovrse vpon Vsury*, 180, 203.

68. See, e.g., Thomas Gresham, *Memorandum for the Understanding of the Exchange*, in Raymond de Roover, *Gresham on Foreign Exchange: An Essay on Early English Mercantilism* (Cambridge: Harvard University Press, 1949).

69. Scholars have been too quick to read the historical setting of most plays about Jews in the Mediterranean as a means for English authors to project their own national anxieties about sexuality, commerce, and social order onto a generalized Other. Phyllis Rackin, for instance, argues that in *The Jew of Malta* as "in *The Merchant of Venice*, the figure of the Jew signals the dangers, both moral and physical, to which the Europeans become vulnerable as they move to the East in pursuit of increasingly remote trading partners." See "The Impact of Global Trade in *The Merchant of Venice*," *Shakespeare Jahrbuch* 138 (2002): 73–88, esp. 76.

70. Lupton identifies "three circles of citizenship in the play: the *civility* of the ruling class; the *civil society* of economic exchange; and the *Jewish community* created and maintained by external mandate and internal laws" (*Citizen-Saints*, 82). Drawing on Pauline discourse of universalism, she primarily defines the Jewish nation as an "*ethnos,* a stranger-people defined by both a religious code and a genealogical imperative that sets them apart from the 'nations' united in Christ" (81).

71. *The Complete Works of Shakespeare*, 5th ed., ed. David Bevington (New York: Longman, 2004), 203. All quotations from Shakespeare's *Merchant of Venice* are taken from this edition, cited parenthetically by act, scene, and line.

72. Walter Cohen and Lars Engle give comprehensive accounts of the economics of the play, but they apply anachronistic categories of economic thought in their analyses and misrepresent the historical situation of the Jews in early modern Europe. Cohen suggests that the government of Venice banned Jewish moneylenders from the city and made them give low-interest loans to the poor; see "*The Merchant of Venice* and the Possibilities of Historical Criticism," *ELH* 49 (1982): 765–789, esp. 770. Engle reads Shylock's story of Jacob and Laban "as a model for the relationship between usury and venture capitalism" in "'Thrift is Blessing': Exchange and Explanation in *The Merchant of Venice*," *Shakespeare Quarterly* 37 (1986): 20–37, esp. 31.

73. A representative example of this view of commerce is found in Russian Emperor John Vasilivich's comments on the establishment of the English Muscovy Company in 1555: "God hath planted all realms and dominions in the whole world with sundry commodities, so as the one hath need of the amity and commodities of the other, and by means thereof traffic is used from one to another, and amity thereby increased. . . . planted to continue, and the enjoyers thereof be as men living in a golden world." See Richard Hakluyt, *Principal Navigations*, ed. R. H. Evans, 5 vols. (London, 1809), 2:295–296.

74. This definition would have been familiar to English mercantilists such as Gresham who aligned citizenship with the right to engage in mercantile practices like private trading. For an overview, see de Roover.

75. Venice imported slaves of Tartar and Russian descent from Tana before the fall of Constantinople in 1453, creating new slave markets. See Frederick Chapin

Lane, *Venice: A Maritime Republic* (Baltimore: Johns Hopkins University Press, 1973), 133. In the sixteenth century, both "slaves" and "offenders sentenced to the galleys" were employed by Venice mostly for rowing when manpower was scarce, as during war. See Martin Garrett, *Venice: A Cultural and Literary Companion* (New York: Interlink Books, 2001), 26.

76. See Barbara K. Lewalski, "Biblical Allusion and Allegory in *The Merchant of Venice*," *SQ* 13 (1962): 327–343, esp. 338-339.

77. Charles Spinosa argues that Shylock represents the early modern common-law court, while Portia stands for the principles of the more "broad-minded" and "equitable" Court of Chancery; see "Shylock and Debt and Contract in 'The Merchant of Venice,'" *Cardozo Studies in Law and Literature* 5 (1993): 65–85.

78. John D. Rea, "Shylock and the *Processus Belial*," *Philological Quarterly* 8 (1929): 311–313.

79. See, e.g., J.G.A. Pocock, "Authority and Property: The Question of Liberal Origins," in *Virtue, Commerce, and History: Essays on Political Thought and History, Chiefly in the Eighteenth Century* (Cambridge: Cambridge University Press, 1985), 51–71.

80. Kim F. Hall reads the joke as part of the play's anxiety about miscegenation in "'Guess Who's Coming to Dinner?' Colonization and Miscegenation in *The Merchant of Venice*," *Renaissance Drama* n.s. 23 (1992): 87–111, esp. 89.

81. Contemporary readings tend to be split between scholars who emphasize the power of the aesthetic "harmonies" of the play to overcome its discordant notes and those who point to the tensions that disrupt such resolutions. Of the former, the most prominent is Lawrence Danson's *The Harmonies of "The Merchant of Venice"* (New Haven: Yale University Press, 1978). Of the latter, see Cohen (n. 72 above); and René Girard, *A Theater of Envy: William Shakespeare* (New York: Oxford University Press, 1991), 245–246.

ACKNOWLEDGMENT

I thank Julia Reinhard Lupton and Graham Hammill for organizing the "Sovereigns, Citizens, and Saints" seminar at the 2004 meeting of the Shakespeare Association of America, for which this essay was originally written. I appreciate the assistance of Gail Kern Paster, David Bevington, Julia Reinhard Lupton, Jason Rosenblatt, Ann Kibbie, and *SQ's* anonymous readers, who offered valuable suggestions for revision. I am also grateful to Allison Cooper for her help with Italian source texts.

HUGH GRADY

# Shakespeare and Impure Aesthetics: *The Case of* A Midsummer Night's Dream

To speak of the aesthetic in the early twenty-first century in Shakespeare studies is to risk multiple misunderstandings. The word has been in bad odor for the last twenty years or so, serving as the subordinated member of key binary opposites of contemporary critical practice. In an era dominated by French poststructuralist theory, the aesthetic has been the opposite of the political. It identified the *passé* critical practice of Northrop Frye and the New Critics before him; it meant discussing literature decontextual-ized from its larger social milieu, purposes, and intertextuality.[1] As John J. Joughin wrote, "For most radical critics, aesthetics still tends to be discarded as part of the 'problem' rather than the 'solution.'"[2]

There have been, however, a number of critics—Fredric Jameson, Terry Eagleton, and Stephen Greenblatt among them—who have resisted this reductive thinking.[3] All of these critics know that many radical political traditions, including more than one version of Marxism—not to mention German post-Kantian philosophy generally—contained an extensive, ap-preciative archive of writings on the aesthetic, which valued art as a highly significant human practice in itself and, in the case of Marxist aesthetics, specifically refused to reduce art to ideology.[4] This is especially true of the Frankfurt School theorists Walter Benjamin and Theodor Adorno, whose work draws on Kant, Hegel, Nietzsche, and Freud, as well as Marx. They are

*Shakespeare Quarterly*, Volume 59, Number 3 (Fall 2008): pp. 274–302. Copyright © 2008 Hugh Grady.

at once both developers and critics of Marxism and major sources for what I am calling "impure aesthetics"—aesthetics conceived as creative of an imagined realm separate from empirical reality, but one that draws its materials from that reality.

Where aesthetics has not been marginalized in Shakespeare studies, it has instead been removed from the work of art and applied to cultures as a whole, effacing the distance between art itself and the society which produced it and thus threatening to rob the artwork of its critical stance. The new historicism set the terms for this trend, but perhaps Patricia Fumerton's *Cultural Aesthetics*,[5] which developed from Greenblatt's writing and in turn helped to give birth to "the new materialism," is the pioneering work. Replacing "cultural poetics" with "cultural aesthetics"—traditionally, the distinction has differentiated a theory of artistic production called "poetics" and a theory of artistic reception called "aesthetics"—Fumerton used "aesthetics" to refer to the semiology of aristocratic ornamentation displayed in clothing, food, jewelry, household furnishings, and other articles of daily life, investigating their kinship with and reproduction within literary works, particularly allegorical ones. Although brilliantly argued and suggestive, *Cultural Aesthetics* never fully theorized itself or the category of the aesthetic. At several points, Fumerton comes close to Walter Benjamin's theory of allegory as an aesthetic space of disunified fragments in which any object can mean anything else because the world is assumed to be valueless and emptied.[6] But the anthropological lure of turning society into an aesthetic space leads Fumerton to abandon aesthetic form as what separates art from society proper and to see commodities and commodity trade paradoxically as empty and dehumanizing, yet at the same time meaningful and intimately tied to selfhood and identity. While premodern societies always look "aesthetic" to participants in disenchanted modern and/or postmodern cultures, there is a crucial case for maintaining the distinction between the artwork and the society which produced it.

In what follows, the term "aesthetic" will be a polysemous one, but its main meanings devolve from an expansion beyond its traditional attributes, the purely beautiful and the organically unified. In fact, one way to think about impure aesthetics is to understand it to be possible only in our postmodernist present, when new critical methodologies have permitted us to think of the artwork as disunified, constituted by internal clashes and by the insubordination of repressed materials. Thus, the aesthetic can and does have political effects and intentions; indeed, a major line of aesthetic practice from the Romantics to contemporary writers and artists takes many of its central concepts and much of its justification from political ideals of several, often revolutionary, socialist ones. Adorno's argument for detached rather than committed art is a variation within this larger political tradition, inasmuch as it affirms a broad, socially critical role for all art worthy of the name while warning against artists' falling into oversimplifying ideologies based on short-sighted commitments.[7]

## Impure Aesthetics in Today's Critical Context

Despite criticism's nearly three-decades-long experiment in nonaesthetic interpretation of texts, aesthetics has not simply disappeared. Rather, many aesthetic themes have entered into contemporary cultural and literary theory obliquely and invisibly. Discussed through other concepts (ideology, cultural poetics, artifact, or theatricality, for example), aesthetic themes have inhabited the margins of discourses that declared the aesthetic either a retrograde conception or a construct of bourgeois ideology. One result has been that art's utopian potential—its ability to create visions of the nonexisting, to embody desire and not just received ideas—has become virtually unthinkable.

Precisely because the previous aesthetic criticism of the New Critics and Northrop Frye made political and ideological issues taboo subjects within mainstream English studies, the assumptions and practices of the critical revolution of the 1980s filled a gaping hole and defined the agenda for a generation. Three decades later, however, this kind of political criticism is in danger of becoming domesticated and academicized. Speaking generally, the outcome of new historicism and cultural materialism has been the gradual evolution of a new, nontheoretical "materialism" harder and harder to distinguish from old-fashioned positivist historical criticism. In the current period of "post-theory," there has occurred a blunting of the theoretical and political edges of these approaches. New materialism seems to have abandoned both the political and the aesthetic simultaneously, in favor of "fact" fetishism.[8] We have seen studies solely concerned with uncovering lost historical contexts and material practices in the absence of any larger political or aesthetic purposes. We have learned about mirrors, beards, codpieces, writing tablets, fruits, condiments, clothing, stage props, and other commodities and artifacts in early modern daily life—sometimes in the vain belief that such detail will deliver us reality sandwiches, more often because such studies have become fashionable and therefore publishable.[9] There is often a hidden aesthetic dimension in many of these studies—the fascination with objects embodying meaning evidences a pleasurable, aesthetic experience—and many of these works provide useful information about the social contexts of early modern texts. But for most such critics, the aesthetic has simply not been thought through.

In one of those Hegelian ironies so common in intellectual history, it is of course possible that the hegemony of an absolutizing, aesthetics-blind criticism will give birth to a politics-blind "new aestheticism." Jameson, who sees precisely such a process in France and Germany, fears that a new aestheticism will amount to a return of the most scholastic and socially isolated components of the philosophical aesthetic tradition.[10] Rather, I believe that a reinvigoration of impure aesthetics is a step toward a new appreciation of the specifically aesthetic content of Shakespearean drama and a deeper understanding of the imbrication of Shakespearean aesthetics with the social, the political, and the historical, in its original context and in our own.

It is possible, then, to bring the aesthetic to the fore again, but with a different content from that of Kant, the New Critics, and Northrop Frye. In the United States and the United Kingdom, interest in aesthetics has arisen within the last decade, often by critics determined not to lose criticism's engagement with the political since the 1980s. And this new engagement with the aesthetic comes in part through a perception that nonaesthetic criticism has largely exhausted itself or led to disconcerting dead ends. There are many theoretical sources for this developing movement—the late works of Derrida and Levinas, for example—but the great theorists of impure aesthetics are Walter Benjamin and Theodor Adorno.[11] Benjamin was most notable for charting the intricate choreography enacted by the work of art and the commodity, while Adorno explored issues of art's utopian and truth-asserting functions in an increasingly bleak world of almost-complete domination by commodities. Both of these philosopher-critics were influenced by the utopian theory of Marxist theorist Ernst Bloch, whose utopia is generated from desire and has a certain affinity with Northrop Frye's myth criticism—except that Frye's method lacked a historicizing dimension.[12] Bloch situates utopias in sociomaterial situations, reading utopias as responses to the inabilities of societies to meet human needs, both innate and historically generated. The fairy realm of *A Midsummer Night's Dream*—momentarily disturbed by Oberon and Titania's quarrel, but otherwise a domain of nature's harmony with human society—is an excellent example, structured for a rapidly urbanizing society haunted by the memory of a rural, feudalistic past and by the actual power of a female monarch.

I will focus here on the utopian aspects of the aesthetic, on art's ability to create a vision of a world which does not exist but which we find desirable and beautiful, so that it defines what is lacking in our experience. Contrary to Kant but in agreement with Adorno, I believe it is an aesthetic suffused with, rather than unsullied by, eros, even when it is remembered that eros is by no means an entirely beneficent force.

## The Meta-Aesthetics of *A Midsummer Night's Dream*

*A Midsummer Night's Dream* is one of Shakespeare's fullest explorations of aesthetic ideas. It is thus a meta-aesthetic drama, as well as a development of the comic genre to new levels of complexity and self-reflection. For any post-Enlightenment reader or viewer, it has much to say about the aesthetic *avant la lettre*. Such modern interpretations raise the question, always, as to whether original audiences could have had similar interpretations, even without benefit of the term *aesthetic*. As I have argued elsewhere, all our perceptions of the past are presentist, in the sense that we are always immersed in our own ideologies and aesthetics as we work to reconstruct the past; the past reveals new facets to us as our own understanding of it changes and develops.[13] In this case, presentism is inevitable in my use of a concept that was not named and crystallized until 1750.[14] But the hindsight involved in this renegotiation with the past allows us to interpret texts like *A Midsummer Night's Dream* in ways that bring new focus, but not necessarily completely anachronistic perception, into our reading. An interpretation of *Dream* as a play about the aesthetic is both presentist and historicist because the play implies such a concept. The first critics to appreciate *Dream* as something more than a hodgepodge were specifically influenced by late Enlightenment, early Romantic ideas of the aesthetic, first in German thought and then in other international philosophy and literature. Schlegel, whose writings provided Coleridge with his basic ideas, first defined an overarching structural unity for the play,[15] unity being a privileged category in classical aesthetics. The aesthetic idea of organic unity in turn influenced innumerable mid-twentieth-century critics who attempted to find a harmony in the play's myriad materials and styles.[16]

This classical emphasis on unity tends to create an Apollonian aesthetic, one that imposes order by suppressing or marginalizing the Dionysian, "dangerous" content of art.[17] A distressing number of such Apollonian critics have found that an Elizabethan ideology of male chauvinism provides the aesthetic linchpin of the play,[18] and most of their New Critical readings achieved unity in a hierarchical arrangement of the play's elements that almost inevitably supported aristocratic and male privilege.[19] Jonathan Dollimore has argued that it is precisely the relatively recent development of a hermeneutics which celebrates disunity that has revealed the text's fissures, its fault lines, its Other—a change that amounts to a shift from one kind of aesthetic to another.[20] In that sense, the new critical approaches of the last thirty years have been based on a shift in aesthetic perception.

Recent criticism has tended instead to deconstruct the play's hierarchies of domination and to become overwhelmingly political and/or historicist. Dehierarchization and a subsequent awareness of political subtexts are both essential to impure aesthetics, precisely by bringing out what has been an occulted aesthetic dimension within the newer criticism. "Art is related to its other as is a magnet to a field of iron filings," wrote Theodor Adorno.[21] By respecting the separation of the artwork from society (while also seeing that what is "in" the artwork comes "from" that society), it becomes possible to analyze aesthetic qualities of Shakespeare's plays while retaining a suspicion of hierarchical unity and the imprint of ideology. Indeed, it becomes possible to see the suspension of hierarchy and the resistance to ideology as integral to the work's aesthetics. Interestingly, an "aesthetic" reading of the play is often assumed and alluded to, but not actually performed, in much recent criticism. In her brilliant study of the words and puns in *Midsummer Night's Dream*, which extends into surrounding cultural and social contexts, for example, Patricia Parker wrote, "Apprehension of this play's famous metadramatic aspect would lead in this regard not to the purely formalist or self-reflexive, but rather to its linkages with the partitions and joints of other early modern structures, social and political as well as rhetorical, logical, and grammatical."[22] Thus, the "formalist or self-reflexive" reading remains a road not taken in a work which describes itself as self-consciously historicist.

But it is precisely the interplay between the enclosed work of art and the larger world from which it draws its material that constitutes the aesthetic situation conceptualized in what I am calling impure aesthetics, where it is still perfectly possible to pursue ideology critique and aesthetic analysis simultaneously. Within the complex fictive space of *A Midsummer Night's Dream*, we can see antagonistic discourses at work—most centrally for my purposes here, an antagonism between two different representations of nature and the relation of humanity to nature, creating a dialogue of differing "visions" or perceptions of reality.[23] In part, it is a matter of the dynamic described in Northrop Frye's concept of green-world comedies. *A Midsummer Night's Dream* is a canonical example of the form, beginning in a recognizable setting, undertaking a withdrawal into the green wood to a kind of freedom from many of the oppressive social norms that had created the play's comic dilemma, and concluding with a return to the normal world after a resolution to the conflict in the green world.[24] The idea of the aesthetic as a separate, idealizing, and self-reflecting space of imagination works itself out within this interaction in a paradoxical, mirrors-within-mirrors fashion.

Of course, *A Midsummer Night's Dream* is an aesthetic object from beginning to end; it is a shaped semblance of reality in a complex relation of similarity to and difference from the world from which it draws its materials—but clearly distanced from that world through its defining forms and idealizations. But some parts of it, as George Orwell might say, are more aesthetic than others. The play recreates in its fictionality the very relationship of the artwork to the world in which it participates. In this way, the play shares a self-reflective "baroque" nature with such plays as Calderón's 1635 *La vida es sueño (Life is a Dream)* or Corneille's 1636 *L'Illusion*—and has an affinity to the complex metadramatic and meta-aesthetic effects of the inset plays within *Hamlet* and *The Tempest*. Not only does the play's own inset play "Pyramus and Thisbe" produce this effect; so too do the highly charged lyric language and the charming images of the harmony between humankind and the natural world in the fairy segments of the play.

In relation to the privileged or heightened material of the fairy plot in *Midsummer Night's Dream,* the young-lovers plot represents the familiar world of human experience in an idealized form and language, but clearly in a more realist mode than the fairy realm. The play models in its own aesthetic space an implied theory about the relation of the aesthetic to the larger social world. That it is a mirror within a mirror is the key to its meta-aesthetic quality. And although the difference between these two realms is clear, the barrier between them, like Wall in the inset play, has chinks in it, and within each separate domain there are traces of its excluded Other. This interrelationship is the main enabling frame in which the play produces an implicit theory of the aesthetic within itself.

That the world of Oberon and Titania is disrupted by a lovers' quarrel of course links the fairy world with the human world—desire is disruptive in both realms, and an ideology of patriarchy rules in both as well. At the same time, however, the humanized Oberon and Titania control the forces of nature and live in a fairy paradise of rare beauty distinct from the human world and with its own poetic stylization. They are personifications of the natural world even as they display human foibles. This is not an unfamiliar combination. Shakespeare (and all educated Elizabethans) had seen something very similar in Ovid and other sources of Greco-Roman mythology. The Greek and Roman gods had exactly this combination of qualities—embodying and controlling powerful natural forces but still subject to human emotions and weaknesses, desire and jealousy prominent among them. At one level, the fairy realm is thus a mirror of human society, but at another level it is far superior to it. It is neither heaven nor Eden; it is more like Olympus. Shakespeare puts this mythological-poetic frame to work especially through the allegorical figures of Titania and Oberon, aestheticizing them as emblems of a potentially harmonious relation between the human and the natural, but at the same time displaying them as at odds with this potentiality.

In short, while much recent criticism has seen the fairy realm as mirroring the human world, it has neglected to show how that realm is also utopian and aesthetic.[25] Despite the fairies' quarreling, we find here an "as-if" structure in which the human and the natural are permeable to each other—a harmony expressed allegorically by the humanized spirits themselves. This quality is not really ideological, because it does not imply belief.[26] Rather, it is utopian in Ernst Bloch's sense: it defines an ideal space, clearly designated as such, in which it is possible to represent and contemplate determinate human wants and desires in various stages of satisfaction, to reflect on human needs and their impediments, and to imagine alternatives to the world as it currently exists.[27] "In art," Adorno wrote, "ideology and truth cannot be neatly distinguished from one another. Art cannot have one without the other."[28] Thus, here as elsewhere in Shakespeare, the utopian space is itself open to interrogation and qualification within the play's dialogic structure. But it is an important locus within a more complex framework. This utopian aspect of the play expresses one of the crucial components of the idea of the aesthetic that informs it.

In one of its most important functions, the aesthetic models a relation of humanity to the cosmos, exploring human meaning and in its utopian mode figuring an immediate meaningfulness unavailable in societies dominated by commodity exchange and capital accumulation. In postreligious sectors of modernity, aesthetics thus takes on many of the functions that religion once fulfilled, especially in providing patterns of ideality against which to measure empirical experience. Even where religion is a continuing force, art has established enough prestige to act as a supplement to religion proper and share in its idealizing tasks. Precisely because the idea of the aesthetic developed in relation to the increasing instrumentalization of nature implicit in capitalism, the aesthetic becomes both the means for enacting noninstrumental orientations to the natural and the enclave in which they are preserved. This was an idea, as Andrew Bowie has shown, central to the concerns of post-Kantian German aesthetic theory,[29] and it has been preserved and reinserted by Theodore Adorno and his followers within a more sober estimate of the potentials for disaster, as well as liberation, inherent within modernity. In this, art always coquettes perilously with ideology, and the attempt to separate the aesthetic from the ideological is always a major issue for critical interpretation.

The artwork's construction of a specific relation of the human to the natural is a quality connected to Kant's idea that in aesthetic experience it is as if there were a perfect epistemological fit between subject and object, one that the author of *Critique of Pure Reason* knows contradicts his central doctrine of the inaccessibility to human perception of the thing-in-itself.[30] Nevertheless, for Kant, this aesthetic intuition of the porous boundary between subject and object is not the least part of aesthetic pleasure, forever uncertain as it is. Benjamin and Adorno both emphasized art's depiction of the nonexistent, including what never was, what has ceased to be, and what perhaps will be. There is a larger context for what can sometimes seem trivial—that the aesthetic is a site for fantasies of all kinds, social as well as sexual. Adorno put it this way: "The iridescence that emanates from artworks . . . is the appearance of the affirmative *ineffable,* the emergence of the nonexisting as if it did exist. Its claim to existence flickers out in aesthetic semblance; yet what does not exist, by appearing, is promised. The constellation of the existing and nonexisting is the utopic figure of art. Although it is compelled toward absolute negativity, it is precisely by virtue of this negativity that it is not absolutely negative."[31] In *A Midsummer Night's Dream,* we see this quality of the artwork in one of its consummate forms.

## Utopian Vision and the Fairy Realm

Oberon and Titania live in an enchanted, aestheticized world that occupies the same space as the one mere mortals inhabit but that operates according to a different kind of reality. Or we could say that they possess a different form of perception[32]—one that is utopian and aestheticizing. This is an ability which the play presents as lacking in humans—and lacking as well in common fairies. Oberon tells Robin Goodfellow of the origin of the magic flower whose drops induce a state of amorous madness.

> My gentle puck, come hither. Thou rememb'rest
> Since once I sat upon a promontory
> And heard a mermaid on a dolphin's back
> Uttering such dulcet and harmonious breath
> That the rude sea grew civil at her song
> And certain stars shot madly from their spheres
> To hear the sea-maid's music? . . .
> That very time I saw, but thou couldst not,
> Flying between the cold moon and the earth
> Cupid, all armed.
>
> (2.1.148–157)[33]

These are lines which historicist critics since the eighteenth century have identified as performing local and power-accommodating work in deference to Queen Elizabeth,[34] said to be the western vestal (1.158) or "imperial vot'ress" (1.163) who is Cupid's target—but who is untouched by the love-inducing dart. Such a reference would help immunize the play from an undesired infernal interpretation of Titania—the Fairy Queen of this play—who might easily be seen, thanks to Spenser, as an allusion to Elizabeth.[35]

A reader in our own day, however, is likely not to notice this brief local moment because of the lush lyric intensity of the verses. If Titania and Oberon constitute Shakespeare's homage to Spenser, the story of Cupid's shaft attests his homage to Ovid.[36] As in the *Metamorphoses*, nature is populated by humanized gods serving as intermediaries between natural objects and human society. Dympna Callaghan has argued that of the many Elizabethan poets who made use of Ovidian motifs and allusions, it was Shakespeare who best reproduced Ovid's subversive eroticism. "Totally unlike his predecessors in eschewing didacticism," she writes of *Venus and Adonis*, "this new, more aesthetic and pagan conception of Ovid represents a breach with orthodox allegorical Christian interpretation of classical authors."[37]

The same is true of *A Midsummer Night's Dream*. Mermaids, nymphs, fairies—all, at one level, personifications of natural places—inhabit an intermediate zone in harmony and intimate connection with the nonhuman.

The mermaid on a dolphin's back might serve as a reference to Mary Stuart, but far more to the point here is that this "sea-maid" (l.154) is said to be singing in so lovely a manner that nature is moved at her song and responds sympathetically. The aesthetic act of singing allows mutual communication between the natural and the human, and this mythical figure personifies that harmony and links it to the art of music. Lines 148 to 157 are a microcosm of the aesthetic ambitions of the play as a whole, which represents to us an idealized aesthetic realm in complex relations to a realistic, human one. Even more unambiguously in Shakespeare than in Ovid, the gods and goddesses are figural, imaginary, aesthetic images evoking and standing for a certain privileged, desired, but nonexistent harmony between the human and natural worlds.[38]

The very essence of the play's aestheticizing strategy can be seen in its treatment of these mythological figures. In a classic move of the dialectic of enlightenment, supernatural beings are reconfigured as aesthetic, fictional ones, "emancipat[ing] themselves from mythical images," Adorno writes, "by subordinating themselves to their own unreality."[39] The aesthetic arises in this process of enlightenment precisely in a refusal to annihilate objects of the pagan past; instead, the aesthetic attempts to recuperate their truth value by refunctioning them as art, preserving something that had lurked in the mythology in mystified form. In *A Midsummer Night's Dream,* the something involves the connection of the human and the natural as it might be and perhaps one time was. This connection is the very essence of the Kantian moment when aesthetic perception gives us a world attuned to human sensibility in order to produce the mysterious power of a noncognitive aesthetic pleasure—although of course Kant would have insisted that any erotic component of the charm is simply incidental.

The charm of both Ovid and Shakespeare is so delicately balanced and evocative that one is tempted to acquiesce to this Kantian claim. We would be mistaken to do so, however, not only because of the poetry's pronounced erotic aura, but also because of a clear intellectual component to this aesthetic experience: the presentation for our delight of a world of our desires, a world of reconciliation and harmony between the sexes, between humanity and nature, between imagination and reality. And as we will see shortly, it is a conception that the play itself reflects on and holds up for our scrutiny, especially in Theseus's triple comparison between love, madness, and poetry—and in the inset play that concludes the action after all the other dramatic conflicts have apparently been resolved.

## The Aesthetic and the Ideological

Part of Shakespeare's *hommage* to Spenser is his use of an allegorical method—a poetic strategy unusual for him—in his treatment of Oberon and especially of Titania.[40] To be sure, Louis Montrose and others have shown us in great detail how patriarchal anxiety in the face of female power permeates the play.[41] But Titania is much more than an object of displacement for anxieties aroused by the real Queen Elizabeth; she exists in *A Midsummer Night's Dream* as more than a marker in a power struggle. She is a personification of natural fertility and its associated properties of sexuality and maternity; she is a kind of fertility and love goddess,[42] and these qualities constitute a profound, and not merely ideological, connection of humanity and the natural. These significations become apparent in her famous speech to Oberon explaining why she refuses to give up the human boy to be Oberon's "henchman" (2.1.121):

> Her mother was a vot'ress of my order,
> And in the spicèd Indian air by night
> Full often hath she gossiped by my side,
> And sat with me on Neptune's yellow sands,
> Marking th'embarkèd traders on the flood,
> When we have laughed to see the sails conceive
> And grow big-bellied with the wanton wind.
>
> (ll. 123–129)

The fertility attributes here are not all focused on Titania herself; they are distributed, some to her votaress, some to the big-bellied sails, some to the boy himself, but they all create a poetic interconnectedness that colors the theme of sexual reproduction with a surface beauty not unlike what Spenser gives us in his erotic landscapes, but more concentrated, more enabled by the imagery's affect and less by one-to-one correspondences between the details of the poetic surface and the abstract signified. Indeed, one is tempted to say that there is no allegory at all here, that all is poetic aura. Nevertheless, taking into consideration the larger context, the parallel with Spenser is clear, and the allegorical effect created for Titania not hard to see. She "stands for" and focuses the dispersed erotic aura which surrounds her in this passage, not unlike Spenser's Amoret, who grows up and learns "true feminitee"[43] in the Garden of Adonis, absorbing the dispersed qualities of the eroticized and ideologized landscape. The references to India constitute a subtext connecting to the era's colonializing mentality,[44] and the charged affect surrounding the boy is also suggestive of homoerotic components of the poetic aura. But these allusions are translated into the play's aesthetic space and made to serve atmospheric, erotic, and aesthetic functions, as well as ideological ones.

Oberon is less well developed as an allegorical figure, but he shares some of Titania's functions. When Titania identifies their quarrel as the cause of the disordered seasons, she thus clearly links Oberon to her own signification of nature and eros, designating both of them as personifications of a natural world grown out of kilter:

> The ox hath therefore stretched his yoke in vain,
> The ploughman lost his sweat, and the green corn
> Hath rotted ere his youth attained a beard.
> The fold stands empty in the drownèd field,
> And crows are fatted with the murrain flock.
> The nine men's morris is filled up with mud,
> And the quaint maze in the wanton green
> For lack of tread are undistinguishable.
>
> (ll. 93–100)

Their reconciliation is allegorized as the restoration of natural order to the seasons. And their disunion takes a specifically sexual form. Titania says of Oberon, "I have forsworn his bed and company" (l. 62). Natural harmony, it seems, is a matter of frequent conjugal relations between the fairy King and Queen. And this sexual symbolism is clearly connected to the agricultural human world in Titania's speech.

The emphasis is on reestablishing boundaries and distinctions and reimposing order so that the land's fertility can be renewed—although it should be noted that order, in this case, conspicuously includes May games and country dancing. The connection between the human and the natural is virtually seamless, and we are invited to imagine ourselves within it. Read from a distance of four hundred years, in our own dehumanized and denaturalized world, the poignancy is deep and the poetry compelling. We could call such a reading green criticism, but to the extent that the idea of the aesthetic is centrally concerned with the relation between human perception and the natural world, it is a crucial aesthetic notion as well. But it seems clear, as recent feminist criticism has underlined, that "natural" sexuality in this play involves female submission.[45] "Do you amend it, then," Oberon tells Titania, "It lies in you" (l. 118). Nor, of course, is the motif of female submission confined to this plot. Hippolyta was an Amazon queen conquered and wooed with Theseus's sword. Hermia is made to undergo comic humiliation in the woods, and her humiliation continues even when she is the object of her beloved's ardent desire rather than his scorn. Lysander, Demetrius, and especially Bottom have their moments of abasement, so that domination is not always a case of male over female. But male superiority is the only form coded as being natural. From a twenty-first-century point of view, then, the aesthetic harmony achieved in such satisfyingly comedic knitting together of the plots at the end of Act 4 is tinged with the ideology of male supremacy.

## Sexuality and Hierarchy

The play's sexual politics have been discussed many times, but its aesthetic properties and thematics are understudied while older aesthetic treatments are badly in need of updating. One of the central political-aesthetic issues of the play, as I have suggested, involves the complicated linkage of the fairies, the natural world, sexuality, and human attempts to govern sex. As mentioned, Titania is a key link in this chain, as is her consort Oberon—he is never called her husband, although he claims to be her lord and she his lady. And these offhand references give us insight into the family life of the fairy world which creates a dissonant subtext beneath the ideological affirmations of male supremacy. A marriage between Titania and Oberon is almost taken for granted, but never explicitly confirmed. And this uncertainty, I would argue, creates an ambiguous place for marriage in the ideal natural order conceived by this play, and this is a difference that marks the distance of the play's utopian fairyland from the human world under the aegis of the law. In the fairy realm, those figures of a fecund nature and natural sexuality are not monogamous:

TITANIA    Why art thou here

Come from the farthest step of India,

But that, forsooth, the bouncing Amazon,

Your buskined mistress and your warrior love,

To Theseus must be wedded, and you come

To give their bed joy and prosperity?

OBERON    How canst thou thus for shame, Titania,

Glance at my credit with Hippolyta,

Knowing I know thy love to Theseus?

(2.1.68–76)

Although there is a level of accusation in such assertions, these amorous indiscretions are not the source of the discord: the disposition of the boy is. What occurs to Oberon as a punishment for his estranged beloved is to set her up in a sexual liaison with a plebeian mortal. We are meant to understand that in the fairy realm, there is no give and take in marriage. As nonhumans, the fairies are as exempt from traditional moral injunctions to marital fidelity as the animals of the woods—or, for that matter, the Greco-Roman gods. Or we could see fairyland as an Olympian world where the gods marry but are not bound to marital fidelity. In either case, the fairy realm remains a sexually open, preternatural place—a quality which undermines that institutional keystone of the Elizabethan ideology of gender relations, marriage. The four lovers, in contrast, live in an all-too-human place where marriage is a necessity. Thus, where Spenser attempts to distinguish the wanton, alluring, but shameful lust of the Bower of Bliss from the allowed joys of sex with reproduction (presumably in marriage) of the Garden of Adonis, Shakespeare makes a distinction between a utopian or aesthetic sexuality unrestrained by marriage and a social, "human" world where marriage is the only solution to desire in unconstrained circulation. The result is one of the fundamental possibilities of aesthetic representation: to distantiate us from the familiar human world, to lead us into imagining other modes of living and loving, to look critically into received ideologies of love and marriage.

The implied allegorization of Oberon and Titania, then, works in two related domains. Both of them evoke the forces of nature, especially the rhythms and order of the growing seasons, with their impact on the land's fertility and hence on the human world. And they evoke human sexuality—its power of attraction, its fertility, its pleasures, its involvement in sexual difference displaced to the love drops released by Oberon's orders on the unsuspecting young lovers. And these two levels, of course, function as mutually mirroring metaphors through a figure with an ancient lineage: the fertility of the land, the fertility of human sexuality. Oberon and Titania are a sexual couple—but also allegorical figures whose (familiar, "human") quarreling and mutual estrangement tropically constitute and cause a violation of the natural order.

In older, Apollonian aesthetics, male domination is part of the idealized natural world represented allegorically in this play—and a previous generation of critics reflected this tendency in many variations. In light of the new aesthetics of disunity and fragmentation, however, we are able to see this idea contested by the various forms of resistance to male domination throughout the play—the formidable, autonomous figure of Titania especially, as well as the independent Helena and Hermia. In reconstituting the play for our own era, we can and should critique the ideology of male domination connected to the play's idea of the natural. With that done, the aesthetic implication of the Titania and Oberon allegory of the play is still clear: the force that through the green fuse drives the flower also drives the human heart and genitalia. This is the same force of nature, the play is at pains to show us, that can generate sexual violence, domination, and subordination. But it is also the force that makes possible sexual generation, in a more harmonious linking of the human and the natural worlds.[46] In this play, sexuality is a kind of "nature within"; a utopian vision of such a connection constitutes one of the chief aesthetic characteristics of the play, one that starkly contrasts an aestheticized, utopian vision of potential harmony with a familiar world of law and ideology.

The allegorization of Titania and Oberon thus constitutes the presentation of an aesthetic, harmonious continuity between the natural and the human worlds—one subject to (comic) disruptions and unruliness, one with a continually visible subtext of potential violence, and one with a possibly disturbing linkage of the human and animal. But for all that, the play continually alludes to an Ovidian harmony between the human and the natural—a possibility, of course, that is an artifact of desire rather than the real. Lacanians would ground this harmony in Lacan's prelinguistic Imaginary, labeling with which I have no argument, so long as such a diagnosis does not reduce the richness of this motif to mere psychologism. A key point of this continuity, we will see, is the production of children—a fundamental part of human life at once natural and ideological. The play ends with the fairies' blessing of the newlyweds' beds specifically against birth defects or abnormalities.

This play is clearly implicated in Elizabethan ideologies of love as a prelude to patriarchal marriage, but its aesthetic richness surpasses these ideological investments—without, however, erasing them. In the intensely imagined fairy world, in the rich, lyric language of the play, in its complex dramatic interactions, *A Midsummer Night's Dream* discloses that *promesse de bonheur*—an image of a life beyond our present constraints—that is a crucial function of the aesthetic. And it embodies an Adornoan mimesis of sexuality and desire that is far from being merely ideological.

## Nature as Other

There is, as I have tried to emphasize, another nature in the play, one not so idealized, aesthetic, or harmonious: the nature perceived by the four lovers and by Robin Goodfellow. A rustic, plebeian fairy, Robin is unable to see Cupid between earth and the cold moon, as Oberon did (2.1.155–157). Robin both perceives and is a figure for a nature in which sexual desire is troublesome and disruptive and where sexual violence is never very far away.[47] For this mode of perception, the woods outside Athens constitute a wilderness, not an enchanted forest. Demetrius warns Helena against this wilderness:

> You do impeach your modesty too much,
> To leave the city and commit yourself
> Into the hands of one that loves you not;
> To trust the opportunity of night,
> And the ill counsel of a desert place,
> With the rich worth of your virginity.

> (ll. 214–219)

As the argument builds, Demetrius threatens to leave Helena "to the mercy of wild beasts" (l. 228). If we missed the contrast, Oberon soon appears to remind us of his quite different view of the green woods, with the celebrated, lyrical set piece that begins, "I know a bank where the wild thyme blows" (ll. 249–256). This is a vision of the forest as a haven of beauty and as a safe refuge for sleeping and dreams, where, in contrast to Hermia's disturbing dream, snakes—those traditional signifiers of sexuality—are aestheticized as supplying "enamelled skin" (l. 255) to make fairy garments and where everything is tranquil. But it is the human, fear-inducing nature (a nature of the Other, in the Lacanian sense of the Other as the unconscious, the repository for repressed psychic materials) that is the site for the play's depiction of sexual desire among the four young lovers. When we think about how desire is represented in this segment of *A Midsummer Night's Dream*, we have to say that it is shown to be an urgent problem in need of solution, a menace unleashed into the world. We see it at work first in a purely realistic world, in the confines of the familiar space of Latin comedy when Egeus appears before Theseus demanding enforcement of the law against Hermia.

Desire, instead of representing a glue for human sociality, is here portrayed as a potentially deadly disruption of the social order. As in so many Elizabethan works, this one seems to be preparing for what recent critics have described as the play's chief ideological work: the mobilization of heterosexual desire and its eventual containment in marriage. This ideological formation was complexly linked to Reformation redefinitions of marriage and family life and to Queen Elizabeth's specific preoccupations and her court's cultural response to them. But as Fredric Jameson argued long ago, any ideology has utopian dimensions, and aesthetic productions both incorporate and distance themselves from the (merely) ideological.[48] Sexuality is a problem for ideology precisely because it is potentially transgressive and disruptive of the social order and its property relations. And since Freud, it is clear as well that desire is a component of all aesthetic forms, including the narrative and the lyric—both memorably mobilized in this play. To see the danger of love/ desire clearly, however, we have to get beyond its power of enchantment. We are led outside the charmed circle by Robin Goodfellow, the main articulator of this distanced, dispassionate view of erotic desire, as shown in his comments on the irrational absolutizing of the lovers' perceptions:

ROBIN     Shall we their fond pageant see?
          Lord, what fools these mortals be!
OBERON    Stand aside. The noise they make
          Will cause Demetrius to awake.
ROBIN     Then will two at once woo one.
          That must needs by sport alone;

And these things do best please me
That befall prepost'rously.

(3.2.114–121)

Robin is constructed from different cultural materials than those drawn on for Oberon and Titania, coming directly from English folklore, although considerably sanitized in the idealizing logic of this comedy. The term "puck" with which Robin is associated was commonly applied to an evil spirit and sometimes identified as a devil. However, we are warned away from that interpretation when Oberon tells the audience, "But we are spirits of a different sort" (l. 389). Robin is a "merry wanderer of the night" (2.1.43), with "merry" implying fun-loving and mischievous. We soon get a list of his antics, including frightening maidens, misleading night wanderers and laughing at them, and spilling ale on an elderly drinker (ll. 32–57). He is more plebeian than aristocratic, a country spirit, a "lob" (l. 16), and he speaks in favor of the masculine world and Oberon's desire to remove the changeling boy from the maternal world (where, from this point of view, the boy is being feminized with crowns of flowers and too much doting) to a male sphere of training for knighthood. We don't see Robin doing anything very harmful or frightening. Instead he is a bungler, although he means to carry out his assignments. In terms of his affect, what most distinguishes him from Oberon and Titania is his apparent immunity from sexual desire. He is the anthropologist from Mars who observes the absurdities of desire and its radical impact on perception with a distanced, unempathetic, merry scorn. Although he has libidinal aspects, they are aggressive rather than oriented to sexual pleasure. Like all the fairies of the play, he seems an allegorical figure for the natural world and its powers, but he is on the "all-too-real" rather than the idealized side of the natural world. Like Titania, he personifies libido, but as an alien and aggressive force from the Other, not, as in the case of Titania, as one who shows it to us from the inside.

As the fairies observe the shifting allegiances of the four young lovers, they clearly see (as the audience does) how dangerous desire can be: breaking hearts, destroying friendships, promoting jealousy and violence, undermining family stability. but by the end of the play we see as well that, with a bit of guidance from without, it can produce harmony, beauty, reconciliation, and a stable base for raising the next generation. Just how this is managed is the matter of discussion between Theseus and Hippolyta that provides the play's most startling and illuminating reflection on its own action and seems to reopen commerce between the two realms of the play's green world closed before—in an aesthetic harmony that is, however, an unstable one.

In effect, the play's structure poses the question: how do we get from a nature of the Other to a harmonized nature, from the discord of unruly desire to the concord of a naturalized human world and a humanized natural world? The relation of the artwork to nature has been a fundamental one for aesthetics since Aristotle defined poetry as a mimesis or imitation of nature. But the problem has been reformulated by aesthetic theorists of the modern era dissatisfied with Aristotle's relatively simple epistemology. In particular, the Romantics revolted against the notion that art was a copy of anything else, rather than a vision in its own right. But Adorno attempts a complex dialectical weaving among several of these theories, affirming that every artwork attempts and fails to enact a reconciliation with nature, that every kind of art involves a rationality of form and a mimesis of nature in a special sense of the word—as "the nonconceptual affinity of the subjectively produced with its unposited other."[49] That is, mimesis is the artwork's ability to reproduce within itself aspects of nature to which conceptual thought and certainly ideology are blind. *A Midsummer Night's Dream*, with its mixture of ideology and something that escapes ideology, would seem to be a prime example; the play uses the motif of the dream as its surrogate for the unnamed concept of the aesthetic.

Thus, in *A Midsummer Night's Dream* (and later, in *As You Like It*), the answer to the question of how to achieve harmony seems to be: in our dreams—that is, in a counterfactual and comic realm that can help clarify our unmet needs by conceptualizing their fulfillment in an artifactual, unreal form. This is the realm of the aesthetic, figured here in the restored world of Titania and Oberon.

## The Aesthetic Space of Dreams

When Titania awakens after Oberon administers the antidote to the love drops, she exclaims, "My Oberon, what visions have I seen! / Methought I was enamoured of an ass" (4.1.73–74). Earlier, Oberon had foretold that all Bottom would remember of his experience would be "the fierce vexation of a dream" (l. 66). And on cue, Bottom gives us his account of "Bottom's Dream." Clearly, one of the devices that helps unify the disparate materials of this play is the motif of the dream or its synonym, vision. "Dream" is one of the many shifting placeholders for the absent term "aesthetic." The four lovers are soon talking about dreams as well. After the early rising hunters Theseus and Hippolyta find them in the woods sleeping near each other, the lovers puzzle over their clouded memories, so oddly conjoint. Demetrius seems to speak for all when he states, "It seems to me / that yet we sleep, we dream" (ll. 189–190).

Just after this, Bottom tells the audience of his "most rare vision," his "dream past the wit of man to say what dream it was" (ll. 199–201). Because he cannot explain it, he will transfer it to (what we would call) an aesthetic realm, involving both song and drama to be inserted at the play's climactic moment. And his vision, it should be noted, involves the kind of "systematic deregulation of all the senses"[50] that Rimbaud advocated as the necessary means for achieving poetic vision: "The eye of man hath not heard, the ear of man hath not seen, man's hand is not able to taste, his tongue to conceive, nor his heart to report what my dream was. I will get Peter Quince to write a ballad of this dream. It shall be called 'Bottom's Dream', because it hath no bottom, and I will sing it in the latter end of a play, before the Duke" (ll. 204–210). Significantly, then, Bottom's vision cannot be classified under any of the received categories of his own experience, and so it is "translated" (3.1.105)—a word applied to Bottom himself—to the aesthetic realm. A number of critics have noticed that Bottom's speech echoes the language of Paul's first epistle to the Corinthians, on the indescribability of Paradise: "The things which eye hathe not sene, nether eare hathe not heard, nether came into ma[n']s heart, *are*, which God hathe prepared for them that loue him."[51] But Bottom's parodic allusions by no means suggest a literal claim for divine insight. It is the nature of the aesthetic, Adorno argued, that "its object is determined negatively, as indeterminable. It is for this reason that art requires philosophy, which interprets it in order to say what it is unable to say, whereas art is only able to say it by not saying it."[52] In that sense, Bottom is being secular and true to aesthetics, rather than being theological.[53] If anything, Bottom's inability to speak in determinate, rational concepts links his experience to the "divine frenzy" of the poet (a notion dear to Neoplatonism), which Theseus will address as well. The veiled allusions to the divine serve as metaphors for an experience that is otherwise coded secular and natural, if marvelous: the concept-without-a-name, the aesthetic. And Bottom is the privileged vessel of this experience.

The quasi-theological negations of Bottom's description of his dream, in fact, implicitly invite the audience that has just witnessed his experience to try to get to the bottom of this dream in the very proclamation of the impossibility of doing so. We have seen a foolish, plebeian artisan, accidentally inducted into a fantasy-as-reality and happily succumbing to it. He is brought into the enchanted, erotic, aestheticizing vision-world of Titania, with its dainty, fairy artifices made from objects of sensuousness and natural beauty (with a slight undertone of violence). As Titania puts it:

> Feed him with apricots and dewberries,
> With purple grapes, green figs, and mulberries;
> The honeybags steal from the humble-bees,
> And for night tapers crop their waxen thighs
> And light them at the fiery glow-worms' eyes
> To have my love to bed, and to arise;

And pluck the wings from painted butterflies
To fan the moonbeams from his sleeping eyes.

(ll. 148–155)


This moment of aesthetic concord with nature is followed by Bottom's attempt to befriend his servants in this new realm and make himself at home within it. And of course there is an undercurrent of sexual tension through-out this scene—carried here through references to going to bed—giving the whole experience a distinctly erotic aura. Bottom is a prisoner of love, as Ti-tania makes clear: "Out of this wood do not desire to go. / Thou shalt remain here, whether thou wilt or no" (ll. 134–135). For his part, Bottom, relaxing into his gilded cage, creates his own version of the fairyland aesthetic mode in workmanlike prose and soon calls for rustic music as well.

The running gag in all this comes from the audience's ability, seconded by Robin and Oberon, to see the ordinary, disenchanted, "material" Bottom in utter disjunction from Titania's doting vision. Bottom's name itself is one important signifier of this materializing strand. When Robin Goodfellow said that he loved to see things "That befall prepost'rously" (3.2.121), Latin-savvy members of the audience could note the reference to "bottoms" in the word "preposterous" (etymologically, posterior-first). The closeness of the word "ass" to "arse" (the word in American English remains "ass") is another of these associations.[54] Bottom's corporality is underlined when Titania, in her attempt to lure Bottom to stay with her voluntarily (after her announce-ment that he could not leave in any case), promises him, "And I will purge thy mortal grossness so / That thou shalt like an airy spirit go" (3.1.139–143). The comic, preposterous concord of Bottom's corporality with airy spirits is among several versions of *concordia discors* in the play; like most of those other versions, it is related to an implied concept of the aesthetic. Like Bottom, the aesthetic is sensuous, dependent on materiality for its very form and ex-pression, and yet perceived as spiritual, signifying, and revelatory of human experiences without a definite name. The aesthetic is the "rare vision" "that hath no bottom to it" (4.1.209)—no bottom because it lacks a determinate concept, because it suggests access to an unlimited world of new experiences, because it somehow transcends its own materiality—perhaps no Bottom be-cause, as Rimbaud's famous and enigmatic dictum puts it, *"Je' est un autre"* ("'I' is another").[55] With Bottom and in the rude mechanicals more generally, Shakespeare pays homage to the aesthetic usefulness of the ugly, as a moment of discord which, Adorno claimed, both violates and confirms aesthetic unity, creating a dynamic tension.[56] Bottom in this way completes the aesthetic, even as he is transformed by it.

The play-within-the-play that takes up most of Act 5 is the long and hilarious gloss on Bottom's dream. Bottom himself expressed a desire to incorporate the dream into the play as a song to be sung at Thisbe's death (4.1.210–211). The song never in fact appears, but the connection has been made: the play itself embodies the same concept of the aesthetic that the dream does.[57] There is, of course, a strong element of parody at work, and Hippolyta and the three bridegrooms keep up witty patter to drive the point home. The rustic players have had recourse to their own kind of allegory or personification in the production—just as this play personifies concepts in the allegories associated with the fairies. In the parody version, concrete objects are signified by Wall and Moonshine; the method is self-parodying, another call of attention to the techniques of the larger play it both represents and is a part of. The impersonators of Pyramus and Thisbe (Bottom and Flute) distance us from the convention of using men to play women and to the craft of acting itself. Bottom is an obvious ham, and we see parodied precisely the kind of scenes of death and grief, which in plays like *Romeo and Juliet* are prime examples of the theater's power to move audiences. The result of the parodic elements is precisely the meta-aesthetic one of creating self-consciousness of the aesthetic space of illusion within the audience—the fictionality in which it has been immersed—and to show us the materiality of the signifiers used to create the illusion. This reminder of materiality was, as we saw previously, the function of Bottom throughout his erotic captivity by Titania, and thus we have within the action the same parallel between love / desire and poetry that Theseus develops in his famous speech on imagination. This insistence on the materiality of the aesthetic—one of Shakespeare's recurrent themes throughout the play—is skeptical in that it anchors the potentially extravagant claims of Neoplatonist poetics (to which the play indirectly alludes twice) to the poet's mystical power of insight. Nowhere in the play are we outside the natural world; that world has been poeticized and idealized through imagination, but never transcended. It is a world permeated with a quite human aura of eros, not the supernatural celestial heights of a Dante.

However, there is another point of view in dialogue with the skeptical materializing thread embodied in the parody, a dialogic strand that insists that the material signifiers of aesthetic experience may not transport us to heaven, but they do transport us—in the sense of the word "transported" used by Starveling (4.2.3–4) to refer to Bottom's metamorphosis—to the region where Bottom experienced his visions. During the inset play we also hear evidence that Bottom (as Pyramus) is still involved in his posttransport synesthesia: "I see a voice. Now will I to the chink / To spy an I can hear my Thisbe's face" (5.1.190–191). The confused sensory references clearly allude to Bottom's dream and imply that Bottom has brought back something with him from the aesthetic realm. The poet, Rimbaud had claimed, must be a *voleur de feu*—Prometheus—a seer who mediates to the rest of mankind the harmonious realm of aesthetic imagination.[58] But it is not a proposition

communicable in utilitarian language, as we discover in Bottom's words to his
fellows upon his return:

BOTTOM  Masters, I am to discourse wonders; but ask me not what. For if
        I tell you, I am no true Athenian. I will tell you everything right as it
        fell out.
QUINCE  Let us hear, sweet Bottom.
BOTTOM  Not a word of me.

(4.2.25–29)

Bottom's transgressive experience of pleasure for pleasure's sake—a humiliation
for Titania, but an ennoblement of Bottom the weaver—is a version of the eros-
suffused aesthetic celebrated in this play. Bottom is, as Rimbaud recognized,
the aestheticizing Symbolist poet of *A Midsummer Night's Dream*.

### Love, Madness, and the Aesthetic

The play's aesthetic theorist, on the other hand, is clearly Theseus, in the
often-quoted lines I alluded to above:

> Lovers and madmen have such seething brains,
> Such shaping fantasies, that apprehend
> More than cool reason ever comprehends.
> The lunatic, the lover, and the poet
> Are of imagination all compact.

(5.1.4–8)

Although some critics have seen these words as choral,[59] the consensus for
many years has been that there is a strong element of irony here, that his
rationalism too strongly contradicts the main themes of the play to merit
acceptance at face value. My own view is that Theseus's rationalism is
dialogically related to the claims that the other characters make about experiences which seem to them transcendent. While his rationalism is reductive, it serves to question the kind of transcendent claims about aesthetic
visions that Renaissance Neoplatonists (and later Romantics) made about
aesthetic vision.

Certainly the comparison that he makes between lovers and madmen
does not really strain the audience's credulity after it has witnessed the tur-
moil created by mobile desire, with its attendant jealousy, rage, fighting, and
murderous threats. It is when he makes it a triple comparison, by bringing in
the poet, that he raises our suspicions. We have been engrossed in a poetic
feast so rich that Theseus's confidence that the poetic is merely a form of

madness must give us pause. Hippolyta's counterargument is an assertion that a shared dream, recounted consistently by four different dreamers, is surely something to be wondered at and perhaps beyond the ken of Theseus's narrow rationalism. A shared vision, we can surmise, has a reality of its own. If, as I argued above, the dream space is one of this play's chief signifiers of the aesthetic, then Hippolyta's last words affirm a positive role for the aesthetic against Theseus's debunking.

And if we are spirits of another sort, we will be discontented with Theseus's Platonic reduction of poetry to the status of mere illusion.[60] To the extent we have allowed ourselves to share in the magic of *A Midsummer Night's Dream*, we have implicitly found a value in imagination, in an aesthetic experience. And yet there is little warrant in this play to elevate the imagination to Romantic levels, to make it the privileged portal to the deepest reality of creation. The play's fifth act is mostly taken up with a farcical anatomizing of drama at its degree zero in the version of "Pyramus and Thisbe" given by the workmen. In this inset play, we see all the artifice of the theater, its rehearsals, its props and costumes, its calculations of audience reaction, on display before us. Just as the character Bottom never allows us to forget the flesh, materiality, and irrationality of love and desire, just as he shows us how the aesthetic, for all its spiritualizing effects, remains rooted in materiality, the inset play in which he performs meta-theatrically reinforces this message. The aesthetic magic we have witnessed is based on nothing less material than can be supplied by "hard-handed men . . . / Which never laboured in their minds till now" (5.2.72–73). The poet's eye, after all, as Theseus tells us, "Doth glance from heaven to earth, from earth to heaven" (5.1.13) in its fine frenzy. Its vision is not of the real, but of what the real lacks, what is desired, what we dream of. Desire, in short, is one of the crucial links between the poet and the lover; it is the engine of the imagination. Rooted in a material world represented by the civic life of Athens and by the play of destructive desire among the four lovers, desire has recourse to imagination in order to body forth from the airy nothing of lack the needs and wants that could potentially humanize the world, if the world would wake up to them.

For now, this play tells us, all the magic is theatricality, stage illusion, aesthetics, wrought in a material world from a motley collection of resources. It is a play that presciently constructs a modern concept of the aesthetic and at the same time shows us the constructedness of this concept, its relation not only to imagination and the artistic past, but to desire and labor as well. In *A Midsummer Night's Dream*, we see Shakespeare engaged in precisely this double task. In the travesty that is the rude mechanicals' play, he presents us with the final truth of his own masterpiece—its made-ness, its materiality, its resistance to the artist's shaping fantasies. In case we missed it, Shakespeare ends the play with the plebeian voice of Robin Goodfellow, who speaks the epilogue—quite against the wisdom of the imperious rationalist Theseus, who had told the artisans, "No epilogue, I pray you; for your play needs no excuse" (5.2.340). Robin reinforces Theseus in one sense, but in a mode which he expects will lead rather to applause than to skepticism:

> If we shadows have offended,
> Think but this, and all is mended:
> That you have but slumbered here,
> While these visions did appear;
> And this weak and idle theme,
> No more yielding but a dream,
> Gentles, do not reprehend. . . .
> Give me your hands, if we be friends,
> And Robin shall restore amends.
>
> (Epilogue, ll. 1–7, 15–16)

Thus, it is a misleadingly self-deprecatory assertion of the purpose-less purposiveness of aesthetic production, creative of a specialized "place," a sphere where materials of the social text are refunctioned into an autono-mously structured aesthetic realm made from, and imprinted with, all the cultural materials that inform the autonomous artifact. *A Midsummer Night's Dream* is Shakespeare's paean to, and anatomy of, impure aesthetics.

## Notes

1. Indeed, one can still find approving usage of the term in this sense in contemporary works. See Harold Bloom, *Shakespeare: The Invention of the Human* (New York: Riverhead, 1998), 9; and Jonathan Bate, *The Genius of Shakespeare* (London: Picador, 1997), 320–321.

2. John J. Joughin, "Shakespeare, Modernity and the Aesthetic: Art, Truth and Judgement in *The Winter's Tale*," in *Shakespeare and Modernity: Early Modern to Millennium,* ed. Hugh Grady (London: Routledge, 2000), 61–84, esp. 61.

3. Fredric Jameson is one example, especially in his work on postmodernist aesthetics. See Fredric Jameson, *Postmodernism, Or, The Cultural Logic of Late Capitalism* (Durham, NC: Duke University Press, 1991). Terry Eagleton, while never as friendly to aesthetic theory as his American Marxist counterpart Jameson, wrote the appreciative if cautious *Ideology of the Aesthetic* (Oxford: Blackwell, 1990) and more recently the less cautious *Sweet Violence: The Idea of the Tragic* (Oxford: Blackwell, 2003). Stephen Greenblatt has consistently kept the aesthetic as an important and autonomous category for critical analysis and for understanding the interactions of the work of art and its larger social and cultural context; see, in particular, *Shakespearean Negotiations: The Circulation of Social Energy in Renaissance England* (Berkeley: University of California Press, 1988), 1–20.

4. See Mikhail Lifshitz, *The Philosophy of Art of Karl Marx,* trans. Ralph B. Winn (1938; repr., London: Pluto, 1973); Theodor Adorno, *Notes to Literature,* ed.

Rolf Tiedemann, trans. Shierry Weber Nicholsen, 2 vols. (New York: Columbia University Press, 1991–1992); Maynard Solomon, ed., *Marxism and Art: Essays Classic and Contemporary* (New York: Knopf, 1973; Terry Eagleton, *Ideology: An Introduction* (London: Verso, 1991); Herbert Marcuse, *The Aesthetic Dimension: Toward a Critique of Marxist Aesthetics,* trans. and rev. Herbert Marcuse and Erica Sherover (Boston: Beacon, 1978); Fredric Jameson, *Marxism and Form: Twentieth-Century Dialectical Theories of Literature* (Princeton: Princeton University Press, 1971); and Louis Althusser, "A Letter on Art in Reply to André Daspre," in *Lenin and Philosophy and Other Essays,* trans. Ben Brewster (New York: Monthly Review Press, 1978), 221–227.

5. Patricia Fumerton, *Cultural Aesthetics: Renaissance Literature and the Practice of Social Ornament* (Chicago: University of Chicago Press, 1991).

6. Walter Benjamin, *The Origin of German Tragic Drama,* intro. George Steiner, trans. John Osborne (London: Verso, 1998).

7. See, for example, Theodor W. Adorno, *Aesthetic Theory,* ed. Gretel Adorno and Rolf Tiedemann, trans. Robert Hullot-Kentor (Minneapolis: University of Minnesota Press, 1997), 103–105, 123, 246–248.

8. For more details, see Hugh Grady, "Shakespeare Studies, 2005: A Situated Overview," *Shakespeare* 1:1 (2005): 102–120.

9. See Jonathan Gil Harris, "The New New Historicism's *Wunderkammer* of Objects," *European Journal of English Studies* 4 (2000): 11–23; and Douglas Bruster, *Shakespeare and the Question of Culture: Early Modern Literature and the Cultural Turn* (New York: Palgrave Macmillan, 2003), 191–205.

10. On recent European works by Karl-Heinz Bohrer and Antoine Compagnon, see Fredric Jameson, *The Cultural Turn: Selected Writings on the Postmodern, 1983–1998* (London: Verso, 1998), 113–123.

11. For the United States, see, for example, George Levine, ed., *Aesthetics and Ideology* (New Brunswick, NJ: Rutgers University Press, 1994); Alan Singer, *Aesthetic Reason: Artworks and the Deliberative Ethos* (University Park: Pennsylvania State University Press, 2003); Stephen Regan, ed., *The Politics of Pleasure: Aesthetics and Cultural Theory* (Philadelphia: Open University Press, 1992); James Soderholm, ed., *Beauty and the Critic: Aesthetics in an Age of Cultural Studies* (Tuscaloosa: University of Alabama Press, 1997); and Michael Clark, ed., *Revenge of the Aesthetic: The Place of Literature in Theory Today* (Berkeley: University of California Press, 2000). For the United Kingdom, see Jay Bernstein, *The Fate of Art: Aesthetic Alienation from Kant to Derrida and Adorno* (Oxford: Polity Press, 1992); Andrew Bowie, *Aesthetics and Subjectivity: From Kant to Nietzsche,* 2d ed. (Manchester: Manchester University Press, 2003), and *From Romanticism to Critical Theory* (London: Routledge, 1997); Isobel Armstrong, *The Radical Aesthetic* (Oxford: Blackwell, 2000); and John J. Joughin and Simon Malpas, ed., *The New Aestheticism* (Manchester: Manchester University Press, 2003).

12. Fredric Jameson, *The Political Unconscious: Narrative as a Socially Symbolic Act* (Ithaca, NY: Cornell University Press, 1981), 110–113.

13. See Hugh Grady, *Shakespeare's Universal Wolf: Studies in Early Modern Reification* (Oxford: Clarendon Press, 1996), 15–25, and *Shakespeare, Machiavelli, and Montaigne: Power and Subjectivity from "Richard II" to "Hamlet"* (Oxford: Oxford University Press, 2002), 1–25. See also the closely related work of Terence Hawkes, *Shakespeare in the Present* (London: Routledge, 2002); and the recent critical

anthology edited by Hugh Grady and Terence Hawkes, *Presentist Shakespeares* (London: Routledge, 2007).

14. The word *aesthetic* was coined by German Enlightenment philosopher Alexander Baumgarten in his 1750 work *Aesthetica*.

15. August Wilhelm Schlegel, *A Course of Lectures on Dramatic Art and Literature*, rev. ed., ed. A. J. W. Morrison, trans. John Black (London: Henry G. Bohn, 1846), 379–399, esp. 393–394.

16. See Dorothea Kehler, "*A Midsummer Night's Dream*: A Bibliographic Survey of the Criticism," in Dorothea Kehler, ed., "*A Midsummer Night's Dream*": *Critical Essays* (New York: Garland Publishing, 1998), 3–76, for a very usefully organized history of criticism, to which I am indebted in what follows.

17. This point is argued eloquently by Jonathan Dollimore, "Art in Time of War: Towards a Contemporary Aesthetic," in *New Aestheticism*, 36–50, esp. 42–49.

18. Examples include George A. Bonnard, "Shakespeare's Purpose in *Midsummer-Night's Dream*," *Shakespeare Jahrbuch* 92 (1956): 268–279; Paul A. Olson, "*A Midsummer Night's Dream* and the Meaning of Court Marriage," *ELH* 24 (1957): 95–119, esp. 95–110; and Rose A. Zimbardo, "Regeneration and Reconciliation in *A Midsummer Night's Dream*," *Shakespeare Studies* 6 (1970): 35–50.

19. See Barbara Freedman, "Dis/Figuring Power: Censorship and Representation in *A Midsummer Night's Dream*," in "*A Midsummer Night's Dream*": *Critical Essays*, 179–215, esp.188–189.

20. Dollimore, in *New Aestheticism*, 43–49.

21. Adorno, *Aesthetic Theory*, 7.

22. Patricia Parker, *Shakespeare from the Margins: Language, Culture, Context* (Chicago: University of Chicago Press, 1996), 113.

23. Freedman provides a lucid and insightful analysis of contrasting viewpoints and slippery textuality in the play; see 195–198, 202–208.

24. Northrop Frye, *Anatomy of Criticism: Four Essays* (Princeton: Princeton University Press, 1957), 182.

25. A notable exception from a previous critical generation is C. L. Barber, *Shakespeare's Festive Comedy: A Study of Dramatic Form and its Relation to Social Custom* (1959; repr., Cleveland, OH: Meridian, 1963). Barber states, "Part of the delight of this poetry is that we can enjoy without agitation imaginative action of the highest order. It is like gazing in a crystal: what you see is clear and vivid, but on the other side of the glass" (147). More recently, Kathleen McLuskie, "'Your Imagination and not Theirs': Reception and Artistic Form in *A Midsummer Night's Dream*," in *Autour du "Songe d'une nuit d'été" de William Shakespeare*, ed. Claire Gheeraert-Graffeuille and Nathalie Vienne-Guerrin (Rouen: Publications de l'Université de Rouen, 2003), 31–43, has argued for more attention to the aesthetic and utopian in the play.

26. The groundbreaking work defining the play's ideological investments was that of Louis Adrian Montrose, "'Shaping Fantasies': Figurations of Gender and Power in Elizabethan Culture," *Representations* 1 (1983): 61–94, considerably expanded and revised in Louis Montrose, *The Purpose of Playing: Shakespeare and the Cultural Politics of the Elizabethan Theatre* (Chicago: University of Chicago Press, 1996), 109–205.

27. See Ernst Bloch, *The Principle of Hope*, trans. Neville Plaice, Stephen Plaice, and Paul Knight (Cambridge, MA: MIT Press, 1986). See also Ernst Bloch, *The Utopian Function of Art and Literature: Selected Essays* (Cambridge, MA: MIT

Press, 1988). I summarized and applied the concept of the utopian to *As You Like It* in Grady, *Shakespeare's Universal Wolf,* 191–212.

28. Adorno, *Aesthetic Theory,* 234.

29. Bowie, *Aesthetics and Subjectivity,* 102–113.

30. Immanuel Kant, *Critique of Judgment,* trans. Werner S. Pluhar (Indianapolis: Hackett, 1987), 98–99, famously noted, "(Independent) natural beauty carries with it a purposiveness in its form, by which the object *seems as it were* pre-determined for our power of judgment, so that this beauty constitutes in itself an object of our liking" (emphasis added). That is, the beautiful creates a premonition that reason cannot confirm, of the permeability of nature to human perception, as if the world had achieved its end in being apprehended as beautiful by us.

31. Adorno, *Aesthetic Theory,* 233.

32. The interaction of vision and imagination as conceptualized by Renaissance writers, who generally thought that imagination, because it was influenced by desire, tended to corrupt vision, is the subject of the classic essay by R. W. Dent, "Imagination in *A Midsummer Night's Dream,*" *Shakespeare Quarterly* 15 (1964): 115–129; reprinted in *"A Midsummer Night's Dream": Critical Essays,* 85–106.

33. This and subsequent quotations from *A Midsummer Night's Dream* are from Stephen Greenblatt, gen. ed., *The Norton Shakespeare: Based on the Oxford Edition* (New York: W. W. Norton, 1997).

34. Stephen Greenblatt, with *Will in the World: How Shakespeare Became Shakespeare* (New York: W. W. Norton, 2004), 47–53, is another in a long line of historicist critics discussing these connections. Unlike many of them, however, he also discusses the considerable aesthetic qualities of these lines as well. My thanks to Terence Hawkes for pointing out this passage from Greenblatt's work to me.

35. Montrose, *Purpose of Playing,* finds Elizabeth's *cultural* presence as a female authority central to the play, but he adds that the play, for all its anxiety about female power, is not directly about Elizabeth and depends for its complex effects on her exclusion (160, 176). Lisa Hopkins, *Writing Renaissance Queens: Texts by and about Elizabeth I and Mary, Queen of Scots* (Newark: University of Delaware Press, 2002), 104–107, suggests that Shakespeare, here and elsewhere in his work, is employing a "strategy of avoidance" *vis-à-vis* the queen. Maurice Hunt, "A Speculative Political Allegory in *A Midsummer Night's Dream,*" *Comparative Drama* 34 (2000–2001): 423–453, suggests that a reading of Titania as Elizabeth may exist in the play for a small coterie (probably from the Essex faction) who may even have asked for such an episode. But Hunt emphasizes that if this were the case, Shakespeare disguised this level of meaning to give it "deniability."

36. Barber, 122–123, influentially linked Ovid to the play's depiction of the fairies. See also Leonard Barkan, *The Gods Made Flesh: Metamorphosis and the Pursuit of Paganism* (New Haven: Yale University Press, 1986), 251–270; Terence Hawkes, *Meaning by Shakespeare* (London: Routledge, 1992), 20–23; Leah Scragg, "Shakespeare, Lyly and Ovid: The Influence of 'Gallathea' on 'A Midsummer Night's Dream,'" *Shakespeare Survey* 30 (1977): 125–134; and Dympna Callaghan, "Comedy and Epyllion in Post-Reformation England," *Shakespeare Survey* 56 (2003): 27–38.

37. Callaghan, "Comedy and Epyllion," 28.

38. Cf. Greenblatt, *Will in the World,* 48.

39. Adorno, *Aesthetic Theory,* 86.

40. Barber thinks the method is more indebted to Ovid and that the fairies generally are "embodiments of the May-game experience of eros in men and women and trees and flowers, while any superstitious tendency to believe in their literal reality is blocked" (122–124, esp. 124).

41. Montrose, *Purpose of Playing*, 144–150, 151–178; esp. 160.

42. Barber, 137–139; Shirley Nelson Garner, *"A Midsummer Night's Dream"*: 'Jack Shall Have Jill; / Naught Shall Go Ill,'" in *"A Midsummer Night's Dream"*: *Critical Essays*, 127–143, agrees with Barber on this diagnosis and rightly emphasizes the way in which Titania is also implicated in an ideology of male supremacy; however, Garner largely ignores the aesthetic implications.

43. Edmund Spenser, *The Faerie Queene*, ed. Thomas P. Roche and C. Patrick O'Donnell (London: Penguin, 1979), 3.6.51.5.

44. See Margo Hendricks, "'Obscured by dreams': Race, Empire, and Shakespeare's *A Midsummer Night's Dream*," *SQ* 47 (1996): 37–60; and Shankar Raman, *Framing "India": The Colonial Imaginary in Early Modern Culture* (Stanford: Stanford University Press, 2001), esp. 244–247, 274–275.

45. Notable examples would include Madelon Gohlke, "'I wooed thee with my sword': Shakespeare's Tragic Paradigms," in *Representing Shakespeare: New Psychoanalytic Essays*, ed. Murray M. Schwartz and Coppélia Kahn (Baltimore: Johns Hopkins University Press, 1980), 170–187; Christy Desmet, "Disfiguring Women with Masculine Tropes: A Rhetorical Reading of *A Midsummer Night's Dream*," in *"A Midsummer Night's Dream"*: *Critical Essays*, 299–329; Garner; Valerie Traub, "The (In)Significance of 'Lesbian' Desire in Early Modern England," in *Erotic Politics: Desire on the Renaissance Stage*, ed. Susan Zimmerman (New York: Routledge, 1991), 150–169; and Dympna Callaghan, "What Is an Audience?" in *Shakespeare without Women: Representing Gender and Race on the Renaissance Stage*, ed. Dympna Callaghan (London: Routledge, 2000), 139–165, esp. 146–160.

46. Two critics from an earlier generation strongly emphasized the insight that the play celebrates human sexuality as an impersonal power of nature. See Jan Kott, *Shakespeare Our Contemporary*, trans. Boleslaw Taborski (Garden City, NY: Doubleday, 1964), 207–228; and Barber, 132–139. Barber argues that this aspect of the play is influenced by the surviving pagan associations of the rites of May and midsummer's night, which are evoked several times in the play.

47. A number of studies have emphasized the play's subtext of sexual violence coexisting with comic lightness—Theseus's conquest of Hippolyta, Demetrius's veiled threat of rape against Helena, Titania's coercion of Bottom, and the story of Pyramus and Thisbe, as well as several details in the sources used. See Kott, 212–222; Laura Levine, "Rape, Repetition, and the Politics of Closure in *A Midsummer Night's Dream*," in *Feminist Readings of Early Modern Culture: Emerging Subjects*, ed. Valerie Traub, M. Lindsay Kaplan, and Dympna Callaghan (Cambridge: Cambridge University Press, 1996), 210–228; Callaghan, "What Is an Audience?" 146–160; and Orgel, 87–97.

48. Jameson, *Political Unconscious*, 281–299, esp. 286.

49. Adorno, *Aesthetic Theory*, 54.

50. Arthur Rimbaud, letter to Georges Izambard, 13 May 1871; reprinted in Arthur Rimbaud, *Oeuvres*, ed. Suzanne Bernard (Paris: Garnier Frères, 1960), 344. All English translations of Rimbaud's correspondence quoted here and below are my own.

51. *The Geneva Bible: A Facsimile of the 1560 Edition* (Madison: University of Wisconsin Press, 1969), 1 Cor. 2:9.

52. Adorno, *Aesthetic Theory*, 72.

53. See John J. Joughin, "Bottom's Secret . . . ," in *Spiritual Shakespeares*, ed. Ewan Fernie (London: Routledge, 2005), 130–156, for a similar analysis, which treats the unnamed category of Bottom's confused attempts at defining the indefinable as "an epistemological and ontological transformation" based on an "'aesthetic attitude' . . . [which] refuses to be prescribed by predetermined categories" (134, 136). Joughin's analysis, however, is much more oriented to unearthing religious attitudes in the play than is my own.

54. On this point, see Annabel Patterson, Shakespeare and the Popular Voice (Cambridge: Basil Blackwell, 1989), 66–68; and Parker, 20–55. Lars Engle argues that with these allusions, Shakespeare was creating a distanced, symbolic version of the close encounter with Alison's lower bodily stratum by the fastidious, love-sick clerk Absalom in Chaucer's "Miller's Tale"; see his *Shakespearean Pragmatism: Market of his Time* (Chicago: University of Chicago Press, 1993), 141.

55. Rimbaud, letter to Georges Izambard, 13 May 1871; reprinted in *Oeuvres*, 344.

56. Adorno, *Aesthetic Theory*, 46, 48–49.

57. Cf. Joughin, "Bottom's Secret . . . ," 148.

58. Rimbaud, letter to Paul Demeny, 15 May 1871; reprinted in *Oeuvres*, 347.

59. See John Vyvyan, *Shakespeare and Platonic Beauty* (London: Chatto & Windus, 1961), 77–91, esp. 79–80. The literature on this topic is summarized and critiqued in Claire Gheeraert-Graffeuille, "'Call you me fair? That "fair" again unsay': La beauté et ses monstres dans *Le songe d'une nuit d'été*," in *Autour du "Songe d'une nuit d'été" de William Shakespeare* (see n. 25 above), 257–274, esp. 273–274.

60. Cf. Gheeraert-Graffeuille, "'Call you me fair?'" 273–274.

ACKNOWLEDGMENT

I acknowledge the support of a summer grant from the National Endowment for the Humanities in the research and writing of this essay.

# Chronology

| | |
|---|---|
| 1564 | William Shakespeare born at Stratford-on-Avon to John Shakespeare, a butcher, and Mary Arden. He is baptized on April 26. |
| 1582 | Marries Anne Hathaway in November. |
| 1583 | Daughter Susanna born, baptized on May 26. |
| 1585 | Twins Hamnet and Judith born, baptized on February 2. |
| 1588–1590 | Sometime during these years, Shakespeare goes to London, without family. |
| 1590 | *The Comedy of Errors.* |
| 1593–1594 | *The Taming of the Shrew, The Two Gentlemen of Verona.* Shakespeare becomes a sharer in the Lord Chamberlain's company of actors. |
| 1595–1596 | *A Midsummer Night's Dream, Love's Labour's Lost.* Son Hamnet dies. Grant of arms to father. |
| 1597 | *The Merchant of Venice.* Purchases New Place in Stratford. |
| 1598–1600 | *As You Like It, Much Ado About Nothing, Twelfth Night,* and *The Merry Wives of Windsor.* Moves his company to the new Globe Theatre. |
| 1601 | Shakespeare's father dies, buried on September 8. |

| 1603–1604 | *All's Well that Ends Well, Measure for Measure.* Shakespeare's company becomes the King's Men. |
| 1607–1608 | *Pericles.* Marriage of daughter Susanna on June 5. Mother dies, buried on September 9. |
| 1609 | *Cymbeline.* The King's Men move to Blackfriars Playhouse. |
| 1610–1611 | *The Winter's Tale, The Tempest.* Shakespeare retires to Stratford. |
| 1616 | Marriage of daughter Judith on February 10. William Shakespeare dies at Stratford on April 23. |
| 1623 | Publication of the First Folio edition of Shakespeare's plays. |

# Contributors

HAROLD BLOOM is Sterling Professor of the Humanities at Yale University. He is the author of 30 books, including *Shelley's Mythmaking* (1959), *The Visionary Company* (1961), *Blake's Apocalypse* (1963), *Yeats* (1970), *A Map of Misreading* (1975), *Kabbalah and Criticism* (1975), *Agon: Toward a Theory of Revisionism* (1982), *The American Religion* (1992), *The Western Canon* (1994), and *Omens of Millennium: The Gnosis of Angels, Dreams, and Resurrection* (1996). *The Anxiety of Influence* (1973) sets forth Professor Bloom's provocative theory of the literary relationships between the great writers and their predecessors. His most recent books include *Shakespeare: The Invention of the Human* (1998), a 1998 National Book Award finalist; *How to Read and Why* (2000); *Genius: A Mosaic of One Hundred Exemplary Creative Minds* (2002); *Hamlet: Poem Unlimited* (2003); *Where Shall Wisdom Be Found?* (2004); and *Jesus and Yahweh: The Names Divine* (2005). In 1999, Professor Bloom received the prestigious American Academy of Arts and Letters Gold Medal for Criticism. He has also received the International Prize of Catalonia, the Alfonso Reyes Prize of Mexico, and the Hans Christian Andersen Bicentennial Prize of Denmark.

LISA MARCIANO is associate professor of English at Christendom College in Front Royal, Virginia. Her 1998 dissertation at the University of Dallas was "'Love's Labor's Lost,' 'Twelfth Night,' 'The Winter's Tale,' and 'The Tempest': The Awareness of Death as a Catalyst to Wisdom in Shakespeare's Comedies."

LINDA WOODBRIDGE is Josephine Berry Weiss Professor of Humanities at Pennsylvania State University. Her books include *Women and the English Renaissance: Literature and the Nature of Womankind, 1540 to 1620* (1984), *Shakespeare, A Selective Bibliography of Modern Criticism* (1988), *True Rites and Maimed Rites, Ritual and Anti-Ritual in Shakespeare and His Age* (1992), *The Scythe of Saturn: Shakespeare and Magical Thinking* (1994), *Vagrancy, Homelessness, and English Renaissance Literature* (University of Illinois Press, 2001), and two volumes of essays, which she edited, *Money and the Age of Shakespeare: Essays in New Economic Criticism* (2003) and, with Sharon Beehler. *Women, Violence, and the English Renaissance: Essays Honoring Paul Jorgensen* (2003).

EMILY DETMER-GOEBEL is associate professor of English at Northern Kentucky University. She has written articles on Thomas Heywood and Thomas Middleton and on *Titus Andronicus*.

ELIZABETH RIVLIN is assistant professor of English at Clemson University. Her 2005 dissertation at the University of Wisconsin was "Service, Imitation, and Social Identity in Renaissance Drama and Prose Fiction."

ROY ERIKSEN is professor of English Renaissance Literature and Culture, University of Agder at Kristiansand, Norway. His books include *"The Forme of Faustus Fortunes": A Study of the Tragedie of Doctor Faustus (1616)* (1987), and *The Building in the Text: Alberti to Shakespeare and Milton* (2001), as well as several edited volumes published in Europe.

PHILIP D. COLLINGTON is assistant professor of English at Niagara University. He has written several articles on Elizabethan drama, particularly Shakespeare's comedies.

KENT CARTWRIGHT is professor of English at the University of Maryland. He wrote *Shakespearean Tragedy and Its Double: The Rhythms of Audience Response* (1991) and *Theatre and Humanism: English Drama in the Sixteenth Century* (1999). He edited *Othello: New Perspectives* (1991).

MICHAEL STEPPAT is professor of English at the University of Bayreuth. He has published many articles on Renaissance drama over nearly thirty years. In 1990 he edited the New Variorum Edition of *Antony and Cleopatra* with Marvin Spevack, and he is presently preparing the New Variorum Edition of *The Merry Wives of Windsor*.

CYNTHIA LEWIS is professor of English at Davidson College. She wrote *Particular Saints: Shakespeare's Four Antonios, Their Contexts, and Their*

*Plays* (1997), and she has published many articles on Shakespeare in her twenty-five-year career.

AARON KITCH is assistant professor of English at Bowdoin College. His 2002 dissertation at the University of Chicago was "Paper Stages: The Intersection of Printing and Drama as Cultural Institutions in Tudor and Stuart England," and he has written articles on Renaissance drama.

HUGH GRADY is professor of English at Arcadia University. He wrote *The Modernist Shakespeare: Critical Texts in a Material World* (1994), *Shakespeare's Universal Wolf: Studies in Early Modern Reification* (1996), and *Shakespeare, Machiavelli, and Montaigne: Power and Subjectivity from Richard II to Hamlet* (2002). He edited *Shakespeare and Modernity: Early Modern to Millennium* (2000) and, with Terence Hawkes, *Presentist Shakespeares* (2006).

# Bibliography

Adamczyk, Magdalena. "The Formal Composition of Puns in Shakespeare's *Love's Labour's Lost:* A Corpus-Based Study." *Studia Anglica Posnaniensia: An International Review of English Studies* 42 (2006): 301–321.

Ardolino, Frank. "The Induction of Sly: The Influence of the Spanish Tragedy on the Two Shrews." *Explorations in Renaissance Culture* 31:2 (Winter 2005): 165–187.

Arthos, John. *The Art of Shakespeare.* New York: Barnes & Noble, 1964.

Aspinall, Dana E., ed. *The Taming of the Shrew: Critical Essays.* New York: Routledge, 2002.

Barber, C. L. *Shakespeare's Festive Comedy.* Princeton: University Press, 1959.

Barton, Anne (Anne Righter). *Shakespeare and the Idea of a Play.* London: Chatto & Windus, 1962. Reprint. Harmondsworth & Baltimore: Penguin Books, 1967.

Benson, Sean. "'If I Do Prove Her Haggard': Shakespeare's Application of Hawking Tropes to Marriage." *Studies in Philology* 103:2 (Spring 2006): 186–207.

Blake, Ann. "*The Taming of the Shrew:* Making Fun of Katherine." *Cambridge Quarterly* 31:3 (2002): 237–252.

Boehrer, Bruce. "Economies of Desire in *A Midsummer Night's Dream*." *Shakespeare Studies* 32 (2004): 99–117.

Bowden, Betsy. "Latin Pedagogical Plays and the Rape Scene in *The Two Gentlemen of Verona*." *English Language Notes* 41:2 (December 2003): 18–32.

Bradbrook, M. C. "Authority, Truth and Justice in *Measure for Measure*." *Review of English Studies* 17 (1941): 385–399.

———. "Dramatic Role as Social Image: A Study of *The Taming of the Shrew*." *Shakespeare Jahrbuch* 94 (1958): 132–150.

———. *The Growth and Structure of Elizabethan Comedy*. London: Chatto & Windus, 1962.

Brower, Reuben A. *The Fields of Light: An Experiment in Critical Reading*. New York: Oxford University Press, 1951.

Brown, Eric C. "Shakespeare's Anxious Epistemology: *Love's Labor's Lost* and Marlowe's *Doctor Faustus*." *Texas Studies in Literature and Language* 45:1 (Spring 2003): 20–41.

Brown, John Russell. *Shakespeare and His Comedies*. 2nd ed. London: Methuen & Co., Ltd., 1962.

———, and Harris, Bernard, eds. *Later Shakespeare*. London: Edward Arnold, 1966, and New York: St. Martin's Press, 1967.

Bryant, Joseph Allen. *Hippolyta's View: Some Christian Aspects of Shakespeare's Plays*. Lexington: University of Kentucky Press, 1961.

Burke, Kenneth. "Why *A Midsummer Night's Dream*?" *Shakespeare Quarterly* 57:3 (Fall 2006): 297–308.

Campbell, Oscar J. *Shakespeare's Satire*. 1943. Reprint. New York: Gordian Press, Inc., 1971.

Cartwright, Kent. "Language, Magic, the Dromios, and *The Comedy of Errors*." *SEL: Studies in English Literature, 1500–1900* 47:2 (Spring 2007): 331–354.

Chambers, E. K. *Shakespeare: A Survey*. New York: Hill & Wang, 1958.

Champion, Larry S. *Evolution of Shakespeare's Comedy: A Study in Dramatic Perspective*. Cambridge, Mass.: Harvard University Press, 1970.

Christensen, Jerome. "The Mind at Ocean: The Impropriety of Coleridge's Literary Life." In *Romanticism and Language,* edited by Arden Reed. Ithaca: Cornell University Press, 1984: 146–152.

Clayton, Frederick W., and Tudeau-Clayton, Margaret. "Mercury, Boy Yet and the 'Harsh' Words of *Love's Labour's Lost*." *Shakespeare Survey: An Annual Survey of Shakespeare Studies and Production* 57 (2004): 209–224.

Clemen, Wolfgang. *The Development of Shakespeare's Imagery*. London: Methuen & Co., Ltd., & Cambridge, Mass.: Harvard University Press, 1951.

Coghill, Nevill. "The Basis of Shakespearian Comedy." *Essays and Studies of the English Association* (1950): 1–28.

Collington, Philip D. "'Stuffed with all honourable virtues': *Much Ado about Nothing* and *The Book of the Courtier*." *Studies in Philology* 103:3 (Summer 2006): 281–312.

Conlan, J. P. "The Fey Beauty of *A Midsummer Night's Dream*: A Shakespearean Comedy in Its Courtly Context." *Shakespeare Studies* 32 (2004): 118–172.

Craig, Hardin. *The Enchanted Glass: The Elizabethan Mind in Literature.* Oxford: Basil Blackwell, 1950.

Danby, John F. *Poets on Fortune's Hill: Studies in Sidney, Shakespeare, Beaumont and Fletcher.* London: Faber & Faber, 1952.

———. "Shakespeare Criticism and *Two Gentlemen of Verona.*" *Critical Quarterly* 2 (1960): 309–321.

Dusinberre, Juliet. "Pancakes and a Date for *As You Like It.*" *Shakespeare Quarterly* 54:4 (Winter 2003): 371–405.

Edwards, Philip. *Shakespeare and the Confines of Art.* London: Methuen & Co., Ltd., 1968.

———. "Shakespeare's Romances: 1900–1957." *Shakespeare Survey* 2 (1958): 1–18.

Ellis-Fermor, Una. *The Jacobean Drama: An Interpretation.* London: Methuen Co., Ltd., 1936.

Empson, William. *Some Versions of Pastoral.* Norfolk, Ct.: New Directions, 1950,

Eriksen, Roy. "*The Taming of a Shrew:* Composition as Induction to Authorship." *NJES: Nordic Journal of English Studies* 4:2 (2005): 41–63.

Evans, Bertrand. *Shakespeare's Comedies.* Oxford: At the Clarendon Press, 1960,

Felperin, Howard. *Shakespearean Romance.* Princeton: Princeton University Press, 1972.

Fergusson, Francis. *Shakespeare: The Pattern in His Carpet.* New York: Delacorte, 1958.

Foakes, F. A. *Shakespeare: The Dark Comedies to the Last Plays—From Satire to Celebration.* Charlottesville: University Press of Virginia, 1971.

Ford, John R. "Estimable Wonders and Hard Constructions: Recognizing *Twelfth Night* at the Globe." *Shakespeare Bulletin: A Journal of Performance Criticism and Scholarship* 21:3 (Fall 2003): 47–60.

Freeman, Jane. "'Fair Terms and a Villain's Mind': Rhetorical Patterns in *The Merchant of Venice.*" *Rhetorica: A Journal of the History of Rhetoric* 20:2 (Spring 2002): 149–172.

Frye, Northrop. *Anatomy of Criticism.* Princeton: Princeton University Press, 1957.

———. "The Argument of Comedy." In *English Institute Essays* (1948), edited by D. A. Robertson. New York: Columbia University Press, 1949: 58–73.

———. *A Natural Perspective: The Development of Shakespearean Comedy and Romance.* New York: Columbia University Press, 1955. Reprint. New York: Harcourt, Brace & World, 1965.

———. *The Secular Scripture: A Study of the Structure of Romance.* Cambridge, Mass. & London: Harvard University Press, 1976.

Garber, Marjorie B. *Dream in Shakespeare: From Metaphor to Metamorphosis.* New Haven & London: Yale University Press, 1974.

Gesner, Carol. *Shakespeare and the Greek Romance*. Lexington: University Press of Kentucky, 1970.

Goddard, Harold C. *The Meaning of Shakespeare*. Chicago: The University of Chicago Press, 1951.

Granville-Barker, Harley. *Prefaces to Shakespeare*. 2 vols. Princeton: Princeton University Press, 1946–1947.

Halio, Jay L. *A Midsummer Night's Dream*. Manchester, England: Manchester University Press, 2003.

Hanley, R. "*Much Ado about Nothing:* Critical Realism Examined." *Philosophical Studies: An International Journal for Philosophy in the Analytic Tradition* 115:2 (August 2003): 123–147.

Hartwig, Joan. *Shakespeare's Tragicomic Vision*. Baton Rouge: Louisiana State University Press, 1972.

Hobgood, Allison P. "*Twelfth Night*'s 'Notorious Abuse' of Malvolio: Shame, Humorality, and Early Modern Spectatorship." *Shakespeare Bulletin: A Journal of Performance Criticism and Scholarship* 24:3 (Fall 2006): 1–22.

Hunt, Maurice. "The Reclamation of Language in *Much Ado about Nothing*." *Studies in Philology* 97:2 (Spring 2000): 165–191.

———. "Shakespeare's Venetian Paradigm: Stereotyping and Sadism in *The Merchant of Venice* and *Othello*." *Papers on Language and Literature: A Journal for Scholars and Critics of Language and Literature* 39:2 (Spring 2003): 162–184.

Hunter, Robert G. *Shakespeare and the Comedy of Forgiveness*. New York: Columbia University Press, 1965.

Kelsey, Lin. "'Many Sorts of Music': Musical Genre in *Twelfth Night* and *The Tempest*." *John Donne Journal: Studies in the Age of Donne* 25 (2006): 129–181.

Kermode, Frank. *English Pastoral Poetry: From the Beginning to Marvell*. London: Harrap, 1952.

———. *William Shakespeare: The Final Plays*. London: Longmans, Green, 1963.

Kirschbaum, Leo. *Character and Characterization in Shakespeare*. Detroit: Wayne State University Press, 1962.

Kitch, Aaron. "Shylock's Sacred Nation." *Shakespeare Quarterly* 59:2 (Summer 2008): 131–155.

Klause, John. "Catholic and Protestant, Jesuit and Jew: Historical Religion in *The Merchant of Venice*." *Religion and the Arts* 7:1–2 (2003): 65–102.

Knight, G. Wilson. *The Shakespearean Tempest*. London: Oxford University Press, 1932. Reprint. London: Methuen & Co., Ltd., 1971.

———. *The Wheel of Fire: Interpretations of Shakespearean Tragedy*. 4th ed. London: Methuen & Co., Ltd., 1949.

Laird, David. "'If We Offend, It Is with Our Good Will': Staging Dissent in *A Midsummer Night's Dream.*" *Connotations: A Journal for Critical Debate* 12:1 (2002–2003): 35–51.

Landau, Aaron. "'Past Thought of Human Reason': Confounding Reason in *The Comedy of Errors.*" *English Studies: A Journal of English Language and Literature* 85:3 (June 2004): 189–205.

Lawrence, W. W. *Shakespeare's Problem Comedies.* London: Macmillan, 1917, Reprint. Harmondsworth & Baltimore: Penguin Books, 1969.

Leech, Clifford. "The 'Meaning' of *Measure for Measure.*" *Shakespeare Survey* 3 (1950): 66–73.

———. *Twelfth Night and Shakespearean Comedy.* Toronto: University of Toronto Press, 1965.

Levin, Harry. *The Myth of the Golden Age in the Renaissance.* Bloomington: Indiana University Press, 1969.

Levin, Richard. *The Multiple Plot in English Renaissance Drama.* Chicago: The University of Chicago Press, 1971.

Lewis, Alan. "Reading Shakespeare's Cupid." *Criticism: A Quarterly for Literature and the Arts* 47:2 (Spring 2005): 177–213.

Lewis, Cynthia. "'We know what we know': Reckoning in *Love's Labor's Lost.*" *Studies in Philology* 105:2 (Spring 2008): 245–264.

Londré, Felicia Hardison, ed. *Love's Labour's Lost: Critical Essays.* New York: Routledge, 2001.

Luxon, Thomas H. "Humanist Marriage and *The Comedy of Errors.*" *Renaissance and Reformation/Renaissance et Réforme* 25:4 (Autumn 2001): 45–65.

Maurer, Margaret. "Constering Bianca: *The Taming of the Shrew* and The Woman's Prize, or The Tamer Tamed." *Medieval and Renaissance Drama in England: An Annual Gathering of Research, Criticism and Reviews* 14 (2001): 186–206.

Mazer, Cary M. "Solanio's Coin: Excerpts from a Dramaturg's Journal." *Shakespeare Bulletin: A Journal of Performance Criticism and Scholarship* 21:3 (Fall 2003): 7–46.

McCary, W. Thomas. *Friends and Lovers: The Phenomenology of Desire in Shakespearean Comedy.* New York: Columbia University Press, 1985.

McFarland, Thomas. *Shakespeare's Pastoral Comedy.* Chapel Hill: University of North Carolina Press, 1972.

Muir, Kenneth. *Last Periods of Shakespeare, Racine, and Ibsen.* Detroit: Wayne State University Press, 1961.

———, ed. *Shakespeare: The Comedies: A Collection of Critical Essays.* Englewood Cliffs, N.J.: Prentice-Hall, Inc. 1965.

Nelson, Thomas Allen. *Shakespeare's Comic Theory: A Study of Art and Artifice in the Last Plays.* The Hague & Paris: Mouton, 1972.

Nevo, Ruth. *Comic Transformations in Shakespeare.* London: Methuen & Co., Ltd., 1980.

Palmer, D. J. *Shakespeare's Later Comedies: An Anthology of Modern Criticism.* Harmondsworth & Baltimore: Penguin Books, 1971.

Parrott, Thomas Marc. *Shakespearean Comedy.* New York: Oxford University Press, 1949.

Penuel, Suzanne. "Castrating the Creditor in *The Merchant of Venice.*" *SEL: Studies in English Literature, 1500–1900* 44:2 (Spring 2004): 255–275.

Peterson, Douglas L. *Time, Tide, and Tempest.* San Marino, Ca.: Huntington Library, 1973.

Pettet, E. C. *Shakespeare and the Romance Tradition.* London & New York: Staples Press, 1949. Reprint. London: Methuen & Co., Ltd., 1970.

Phialas, Peter. *Shakespeare's Romantic Comedies: The Development of their Form and Meaning.* Chapel Hill: University of North Carolina Press, 1966.

Quinones, Ricardo J. *The Renaissance Discovery of Time.* Cambridge, Mass.: Harvard University Press, 1972.

Raman, Shankar. "Marking Time: Memory and Market in *The Comedy of Errors.*" *Shakespeare Quarterly* 56:2 (Summer 2005): 176–205.

Ramsey-Kurz, Helga. "Rising above the Bait: Kate's Transformation from Bear to Falcon." *English Studies: A Journal of English Language and Literature* 88:3 (June 2007): 262–281.

Rivlin, Elizabeth. "Mimetic Service in *The Two Gentlemen of Verona.*" *ELH* 72:1 (Spring 2005): 105–128

Ronk, Martha. "Locating the Visual in *As You Like It.*" *Shakespeare Quarterly* 52:2 (Summer 2001): 255–276.

Rossiter, A. P. *Angel with Horns.* London: Longman Group, Ltd., 1961.

Schafer, Carol. "David Auburn's Proof: Taming Cinderella." *American Drama* 15:1 (Winter 2006): 1–16.

Schalkwyk, David. "Love and Service in *Twelfth Night* and the Sonnets." *Shakespeare Quarterly* 56:1 (Spring 2005): 76–100.

Schanzer, Ernest. *The Problem Plays of Shakespeare.* New York: Schocken Books, 1963.

Schuler, Robert M. "Bewitching The Shrew." *Texas Studies in Literature and Language* 46:4 (Winter 2004): 387–431.

Shell, Marc. *Money, Language and Thought.* Berkeley: University of California Press, 1982.

Sherman, Anita Gilman. "Disowning Knowledge of Jessica, or Shylock's Skepticism." *SEL: Studies in English Literature, 1500–1900* 44:2 (Spring 2004): 277–295.

Smith, Amy L. "Performing Marriage with a Difference: Wooing, Wedding and Bedding in *The Taming of the Shrew*." *Comparative Drama* 36:3–4 (Fall–Winter 2002): 289–320.

Smith, Haller. *Shakespeare's Romances: A Study of Some Ways of the Imagination.* San Marino, Ca.: The Huntington Library, 1972.

Spencer, Theodore. "Appearance and Reality in Shakespeare's Last Plays." *Modern Philology* 39 (1942): 265–274.

Stoll, Elmer Edgar. *Art and Artifice in Shakespeare.* New York: Barnes & Noble, 1951.

———. *Shakespeare and Other Masters.* Cambridge, Mass.: Harvard University Press, 1940.

Teti, Dennis. "The Unbloody Sacrifice: The Catholic Theology of Shakespeare's *Merchant of Venice*." *Interpretation: A Journal of Political Philosophy* 33:1 (Fall–Winter 2005): 45–91.

Tiffany, Grace. "Law and Self-Interest in *The Merchant of Venice*." *Papers on Language and Literature: A Journal for Scholars and Critics of Language and Literature* 42:4 (Fall 2006): 384–400.

Tillyard, E. M. W. *Shakespeare's Early Comedies.* Atlantic Highlands, N.J.: Humanities Press, Inc., 1983.

———. *Shakespeare's Last Plays.* London: Chatto & Windus, 1938. Reprint. 1964.

Toliver, Harold E. *Pastoral Forms and Attitudes.* Berkeley: University of California Press, 1971.

Traversi, Derek. *Shakespeare: The Last Phase.* London: Hollis & Carter, 1954.

———. "*Troilus and Cressida*." *Scrutiny* 8 (1938): 301–319.

Turner, Henry S. "The Problem of the More-than-One: Friendship, Calculation, and Political Association in *The Merchant of Venice*." *Shakespeare Quarterly* 57:4 (Winter 2006): 413–442.

Wall, Wendy. "Why Does Puck Sweep? Fairylore, Merry Wives, and Social Struggle." *Shakespeare Quarterly* 52:1 (Spring 2001): 67–106.

Wehrs, Donald R. "Touching Words: Embodying Ethics in Erasmus, Shakespearean Comedy, and Contemporary Theory." *Modern Philology: Critical and Historical Studies in Literature, Medieval Through Contemporary* 104:1 (August 2006): 1–33.

Welsford, Enid. *The Court Masque: A Study in the Relationship Between Poetry and Revels.* Cambridge: Cambridge University Press, 1927.

Wilson, John Dover. *Shakespeare's Happy Comedies.* Evanston, Ill.: Western University Press, 1962.

Wynne-Davies, Marion. ed. *Much Ado about Nothing and The Taming of the Shrew.* Basingstoke, England: Palgrave, 2001.

Yates, Francis A. *Shakespeare's Last Plays: A New Approach*. London: Routledge & Kegan Paul, 1975.

Young, David. *The Heart's Forest: A Study of Shakespeare's Pastoral Plays*. New Haven: Yale University Press, 1972

# *Acknowledgments*

Lisa Marciano. "The Serious Comedy of *Twelfth Night:* Dark Didacticism in Illyria," *Renascence: Essays on Values in Literature,* Volume 56, Number 1 (Fall 2003): pp. 3–19. Copyright © 2003 Lisa Marciano. Reprinted by permission of the author.

Linda Woodbridge. "Country Matters: *As You Like It* and the Pastoral-Bashing Impulse," In *Re-Visions of Shakespeare: Essays in Honor of Robert Ornstein.* Gajowski, Evelyn (ed. and introd.) (Newark, Del.: University of Delaware Press, 2004): pp. 189–214. Copyright © 2004 Associated University Presses and Linda Woodbridge. Reprinted by permission of the author.

Emily Detmer-Goebel. "Agency and the Threat of Cuckoldry in *As You Like It* and *Merchant of Venice,*" *Kentucky Philological Review,* Volume 20, Numbers 4–5 (March 2005): pp. 14–19. Copyright © 2005 Emily Detmer-Goebel. Reprinted by permission of the author.

Elizabeth Rivlin. "Mimetic Service in *The Two Gentlemen of Verona,*" *ELH,* Volume 72, Number 1 (Spring 2005): pp. 105–128. Copyright © 2005 The Johns Hopkins University Press. Reprinted by permission of the author.

Roy Eriksen. "*The Taming of a Shrew:* Composition as Induction to Authorship," *NJES: Nordic Journal of English Studies,* Volume 4, Number 2 (2005): pp. 41–63. Copyright © University of Gothenburg, Sweden and Roy Eriksen. Reprinted by permission of the publisher and author.

261

Philip D. Collington. "'Stuffed with all honourable virtues': *Much Ado about Nothing* and *The Book of the Courtier*," *Studies in Philology*, Volume 103, Number 3 (Summer 2006): pp. 281–312. Copyright © 2006 The University of North Carolina Press. Reprinted by permission of the publisher.

Kent Cartwright. "Language, Magic, the Dromios, and *The Comedy of Errors*," *SEL: Studies in English Literature, 1500–1900*, Volume 47, Number 2 (Spring 2007): pp. 331–354. Copyright © 2007 The Johns Hopkins University Press.

Michael Steppat. "In Mercury's Household: *The Merry Wives of Windsor*," *Cahiers Élizabéthains: A Biannual Journal of English Renaissance Studies*, Volume 72 (Autumn 2007): pp. x, 9–19. Copyright © 2007 Michael Steppat. Reprinted by permission of the author.

Cynthia Lewis. "'We know what we know': Reckoning in *Love's Labor's Lost*," *Studies in Philology*, Volume 105, Number 2 (Spring 2008): pp. 245–264. Copyright © 2007 The University of North Carolina Press. Reprinted by permission of the publisher.

Aaron Kitch. "Shylock's Sacred Nation," *Shakespeare Quarterly*, Volume 59, Number 2 (Summer 2008): pp. 131–155. Copyright © 2008 The Johns Hopkins University Press. Reprinted by permission of the publisher.

Hugh Grady. "Shakespeare and Impure Aesthetics: The Case of *A Midsummer Night's' Dream*," *Shakespeare Quarterly*, Volume 59, Number 3 (Fall 2008): pp. 274–302. Copyright © 2008 Hugh Grady. Reprinted by permission of the author.

# Index